minicomputer research and applications

minicomputer research and applications

Proceedings of the First Conference of the HP/1000 International Users Group

Edited by

Helen K. Brown

Pergamon Press
New York Oxford Toronto Sydney Paris Frankfurt

Pergamon Press Offices:

U.S.A.	Pergamon Press Inc., Maxwell House, Fairview Park, Elmsford, New York 10523, U.S.A.
U.K.	Pergamon Press Ltd., Headington Hill Hall, Oxford OX3 0BW, England
CANADA	Pergamon Press Canada Ltd., Suite 104, 150 Consumers Road, Willowdale, Ontario M2J 1P9, Canada
AUSTRALIA	Pergamon Press (Aust.) Pty. Ltd., P.O. Box 544, Potts Point, NSW 2011, Australia
FRANCE	Pergamon Press SARL, 24 rue des Ecoles, 75240 Paris, Cedex 05, France
FEDERAL REPUBLIC OF GERMANY	Pergamon Press GmbH, Hammerweg 6, Postfach 1305, 6242 Kronberg/Taunus, Federal Republic of Germany

Library of Congress Cataloging in Publication Data
Main entry under title:

Minicomputer research and applications.

Includes index.
1. HP/1000 (Computer)--Congresses. I. Brown, Helen K.
II. H/P1000 International User's Group. III. Title.
QA76.8.H1M56 1981 001.64 81-5134
ISBN 0-08-027567-2 AACR2

Printed in the United States of America

contents

RTE PANEL
Moderator - Marvin McInnis
(McInnis-Skinner & Associates)

OPERATING SYSTEMS
Chairman - Ted Varga
(PDM Steel Co.)

OPERATIONS MANAGEMENT - 1
Chairman - Phil Hardin
(Consultant)

INSTRUMENTATION PANEL
Moderator - Dave Hall
(FMC Corp.)

INSTRUMENTATION
Chairman - William F. Browne
(Hughes Aircraft Co.)

COMPUTATIONAL APPLICATIONS - 2
Chairwoman - Judy Skinner
(McInnis-Skinner & Associates)

DATA COMMUNICATIONS
Chairman - Phil Hardin
(Consultant)

preface

This volume contains the invited and contributed papers presented at the HP/1000 International User's Group conference, held August 25-27, 1980, in San Jose, California. This was the first conference of the International User's Group, which was formed one year earlier, on August 23-24, 1979, in Cupertino, California. The meeting was attended by more than 300 members, including participants from many foreign countries.

The technical program included sessions on Computational Applications, Data Communications, Instrumentation, Operating Systems, Operations Management as well as seminars on HP/1000 products and subsystems. In addition there was an exhibit area in which over 15 companies exhibited products that are related to the HP/1000 computer.

The luncheon speaker was the Manager of the Data Systems Division of Hewlett-Packard, Mr. Dick Anderson. Mr. Anderson shared with us his feelings about the trends in the computer industry. He believes that computer technology, agriculture and energy are the three most important industries for the rest of this century and that these three industries will basically drive everything else. They will be the swing factors in the economic strength of nations and trading blocks. A copy of his keynote address is included in this publication.

The banquet speaker was Dr. James Blinn from the Jet Propulsion Laboratory. Dr. Blinn gave a fascinating presentation on animated computer graphics. He presented a series of slides and movies that simulated the flyby of the Voyager spacecraft past the planets of Jupiter and Saturn and their numerous moons. One of his simulations of the Jupiter flyby is on the cover of this volume. Other simulations of Dr. Blinn's can be seen on the PBS TV series, "COSMOS", produced by Professor Carl Sagan.

There are many elements which contribute to the overall success of first-of-a-kind meetings like this one. Companies dedicate large amounts of employee time in the planning and execution phases, many events are sponsored, and last but not least, attendees, speakers and seminar leaders from across the globe come together to share experiences and to learn. For the Conference Committee, the work began 8 months before the meeting and continued until about 3 months after the meeting. I would like to take this opportunity to show my appreciation to the committee members for a job well done and to thank the companies that provided the support of their activities. Many of the committee members had dual roles on the committee, in that they all assisted in the preparation of the technical program as well as performing the other duties for which they volunteered.

Conference Committee

Chairman	Glen A. Mortensen Intermountain Technologies, Inc.
Registration	Judy Skinner McInnis-Skinner & Associates
Finance	Ronald Kelley General Electric Co.
Exhibits	Ted Varga PDM Steel
Arrangements	Larry Thompson Fairchild Test Systems Group
Technical Program	William F. Browne Hughes Aircraft Co.
	Barry A. Goss Gerber Systems Technology, Inc.
	Dave R. Hall FMC Corporation
	Phil A. Hardin Resource Control Corporation
	Bob Kerr Rockwell International
	Don Leavitt TRW Electrical Systems Division
Conference Secretary	Helen Brown Intermountain Technologies, Inc.
HP Liaison	Gary Lim Hewlett-Packard

I am also grateful to the companies that generously contributed to the sponsorship of the various events and functions at the meeting:

Almaden Vineyards
Hewlett-Packard Co.
San Jose Hyatt Hotel

Two members of HP/1000 International User's Group Board of Directors, Norbert Todtenkopf and Marvin McInnis, gave invaluable assistance during the meeting. Mr. Todtenkopf assisted during the very busy registration period Sunday evening and Monday morning. Mr. McInnis assisted with the registration and also helped keep track of the income and expenses from the meeting.

It may not be obvious, but one individual spent a significant amount of time preparing the manuscripts for the trip to the publisher. In our case, a very high degree of journalistic and organizational skill was demonstrated by Helen Brown in preparing these manuscripts that you see in this volume. The conference committee is very grateful for her able assistance.

I want to personally thank Intermountain Technologies Inc. and my family for enabling me to dedicate the necessary time to the conference. I am hopeful that this volume will be a valuable reference document for you, and I look forward to seeing you at the next HP/1000 International User's Group Conference.

Glen A. Mortensen
Conference Chairman

an interactive color display station for IC layout

David M. Hoffman and William J. McCalla

Corporate Design Aids
Hewlett Packard Company
Cupertino, California

Abstract

A color display station is described which is used in the Hewlett Packard Interactive Graphics System (hp-IGS), an IC design system. The basic organization of the display station is described together with a summary of its capabilities. The display station is based upon an HP1000 running in an RTE environment. An intelligent display controller is employed to handle most low level graphic output functions. Communication is performed to a host HP3000 which performs all application dependent command interpretation and database management functions. Functional capabilities of the system include peripheral I/O control, coordinate transformation, a user programmable menu, and figure generation.

Introduction

This paper describes the display station for the Hewlett-Packard Interactive Graphics System (hp-IGS), a color based system for integrated circuit layout and design[1]. The system is being developed by Hewlett-Packard to supply many of the company's future LSI and VLSI design needs. An hp-IGS system consists of a central HP3000 tied to a maximum of four HP1000 based Advanced Interactive Display Stations (AIDS/1000). The HP3000 performs all command interpretation and database management functions. Details of hp-IGS operation and the HP3000 implementation will be discussed in this paper only as they relate to the operation of the HP1000 based display station.

AIDS/1000 is the primary interface between the designer and hp-IGS. The display station performs several basic functions: First, it provides an I/O interface between the HP3000 and associated graphics peripherals (e.g. color display, tablet, plotter). Second, AIDS/1000 is responsible for highly interactive operations such as cursor control and menu selection. Third, the station is an intelligent display processor performing all necessary graphics transformations including scaling, translation, mirroring, rotation, and clipping. Use of this separate, high speed processor operating concurrently with the host HP3000 off-loads I/O intensive operations and complex graphics calculations from the host and frees it for data retrieval and update.

Hardware Configuration

The hardware configuration of the display station is shown in figure 1. The system consists of the following primary components:

HP1000 F series Computer. The computer has 64Kb of memory, and interfaces to the station peripherals. It is running a memory based, unmapped version of RTE, RTE-M(II).

Color Monitor. A high resolution raster scan RGB monitor is employed for the display. The monitor screen is partitioned by software into a menu area, containing a list of names and parameters, and a graphic data display area.

Display Controller. An Intermedia Systems Model 4601 Graphic Display System (Frame Buffer) is employed by the HP1000 to interface with the color monitor. The Graphic Display System stores the video image separately from the main processor memory and provides continuous video refresh interlaced at 72 frames per second to provide a 36 frame/second refresh rate. It consists of a microprocessor-based controller board and two graphic memory boards which plug into I/O slots in the HP1000 computer. The controller board performs all vector-to-raster scan transformations and also generates the separate RGB video signals to drive the raster scan monitor. The memory boards are divided into four separate 768 x 512 bit graphics memory planes. Three memory planes, corresponding to red, green, and blue, are used for data display (for a total of six distinct colors in addition to black and white.) The fourth memory plane, always displayed in white, is used for cursor data, component highlighting, and graphic scratchpad. The Graphics Data System can respond to commands to draw vectors, generate text, clear/fill/blank specific memory planes, and send the contents of the display memory back to the HP1000.

2645 Terminal. The 2645 is used to display hp-IGS information and error messages to the user; functions as an auxillary command input device; and is used to enter local, station related commands (e.g. plotter control, RTE commands, etc.).

Tablet. The tablet is connected to the computer via the HPIB link. The tablet stylus has a pressure actuated switch which provides x,y coordinates and a two position "z-location" (on or off) for digitizing. A cross-hair cursor is shown on the display to track the position of the pen stylus on the tablet.

Hardcopy Output. Both four-color pen plotters (e.g. HP9872) and dot matrix raster printer/plotters (e.g. HP9876) are supported by the station as hardcopy devices. These are not intended as the primary hardcopy output devices of hp-IGS but rather are intended for "quick and dirty" plots of portions of devices as they are being edited. hp-IGS contains much more powerful plotting facilities when a large production plot is required.

HP3000 Link. The HP1000/HP3000 Real-Time Programmable Controller Interface[2] is used for communication between AIDS and the host HP3000. The link communicates via a 16 bit parallel format and is capable of data transfer rates in excess of 100K Baud. Within the link protocol, the HP3000 serves as master and the HP1000 serves as slave.

Software Configuration

AIDS/1000 software is composed of a main program (AIDS) and a 2645 terminal console input processor (KYBRD) which function in the RTE-M(II) environment. The software has been developed on a disc based RTE-IV system using a variety of programming languages. The input processor and about a third of the main program have been implemented in RAT-4 (a superset of FORTRAN employing many of the control structures found in structured languages like Pascal and C.) The remainder of the code is primarily FORTRAN with a sprinkling of HP1000 assembly language and SPL/2100.

The console input processor, KYBRD, is responsible for all input from this 2645 terminal. A separate program was necessary here for several reasons:

a. Input from the user may be asynchronous to the systems operation.
b. Output to the console can be sent by the host at any time; The console can not be tied up on a pending read operation unless the user actually has something to enter.
c. Local station commands (e.g. to interrupt the host during a display) must be processed when entered.

To satisfy the above requirements, the RTE-M(II) system has been configured to schedule KYBRD upon unsolicited interrupts from the terminal keyboard. Once scheduled, KYBRD issues a read request to obtain the remainder of the input (the driver is directed to use the struck character as the first character input). It then parses the input to see whether it is local or destined for the host (this is accomplished easily since local commands must be prefixed with a special character). If local, it is interpreted and executed by KYBRD (RTE commands may also be entered here, in which case KYBRD calls the RTE system message processor). For all other input, KYBRD routes the input to the main AIDS program via Class I/O.

The main program, AIDS, is responsible for all other station functions. As mentioned previously, this includes peripheral control, interactive input support, and display processing. The following sections describe these functions in more detail.

Peripheral Control

In its role as I/O controller, AIDS is used to route status information transmitted from the host to the console, and to merge tablet and keyboard inputs into a continuous stream for input to the host. AIDS will buffer up to 512 bytes of input until queried by the host for input. All input is sent back in ASCII form and data points, whether digitized on the tablet or entered from the terminal, are in user coordinates (usually microns). Whether input comes from the terminal or tablet is transparent to the host. Therefore, conversion from tablet coordinates to user coordinates must be done locally by AIDS (details of this conversion process will be described in the next section)

The AIDS user has several options when requesting hardcopy output. The user can obtain a raster dump of the screen (black and white, of course) at any time by entering a local station command of the form: 'PL,xxxx'; where xxxx may be either 2631,7310, or 9876. This command will cause the HP1000 to read the display image frame buffer, format the data appropriately, and send it to the plotter. If the user desires a four color pen plot instead, 'PL,9872' (HPIB I/F), or 'PL,7221' (RS232 I/F), may be entered. These commands enable a mode whereby graphic components sent to the station display will be duplicated on the plotter. This mode is disabled by entering 'PL'. The last local hardcopy operation supported by the station is the ability to echo host status messages sent to the console on the printer/plotter. Echoing is enabled by entering the local command 'EC,xxxx', where xxxx may be either 2631, 7310, or 9876; echoing is disabled by entering 'EC'.

Interactive Input Support

Several input related functions, though possible by the host, are performed by AIDS for reasons of performance and system integrity. The reader will recall that the display is divided into two regions: a menu area for command input, and a data area for graphic input. A sample display (produced by an HP9876 raster plotter) is shown in figure 2.

As shown, the menu region actually consists of two subregions. One of these is used as a number line. The number line is used for command parameters (e.g. counts) and to identify IC mask layers; it is not used to enter coordinate values. As the user moves the cursor up and down the number line, AIDS generates the number in green corresponding to the position of the cursor. Once the desired number is found, it is selected by pressing down on the stylus momentarily. When selected, numbers will be briefly highlighted in white, and the tablet will produce an audible tone. The second subregion is a menu for ASCII commands. Menu items are selected in a fashion similar to number line items. Users may either enter commands from the menu or enter them on the system console; AIDS sends them back to the host the same way (i.e. the particular input method is transparent to the host.) The menu is programmable in the sense that its initial contents are downloaded by the host and may be changed by the host at any time; The maximum number and size of menu items, however, is fixed. Currently, the menu is downloaded by hp-IGS when users begin their design session. It can subsequently be modified via a local AIDS command. This allows users to interactively configure the menu in a manner best suited to their design methodology and application.

One of the characteristics of all input from the graphics data region is that it is snapped to a grid. The grid is user definable and is specified in terms of a grid size (i.e. spacing in user units between grid points); a grid multiple, indicating which points should actually be displayed; and an offset, used to offset the grid from (0.0,0.0). These parameters are controlled via hp-IGS commands. In addition, grid display can be easily toggled on and off during the design session; this does not affect the snapping of tablet graphic input data to the grid. As an example of grid snapping, suppose a user defined his grid points 5.0 microns apart and centered on integral micron locations (e.g. 0.0, 5.0, 10.0, ,etc.). Inputing a point at (3.5,9.0) will cause the input to be snapped to (5.0,10.0), which is the nearest grid point. When input from the tablet, AIDS always sends the host snapped grid point. To reduce input errors, the user can specify a region between grid points in which tablet input (i.e. digitizing, not cursor tracking) is ignored. This region, known as a deadband, is specified as a percentage of the center region between grid points. For example, a deadband of 50% will cause input to be accepted from the tablet as long as it is no farther than 25% of the grid spacing from the nearest grid point. All grid related commands (including setting the deadband) are processed by the host. If acceptable, the grid parameters are then transmitted back to AIDS for their implementation.

As mentioned previously, input from the graphics data region of the display is converted by AIDS into the user's coordinate system before transmission to the host. This is made possible because AIDS can convert raw tablet data to display coordinates, using a tablet to display scaling factor (derived from device parameters); and convert display coordinates to user coordinates (using information supplied by the host).

Occasionally, the user will wish to calibrate a region on the tablet to a set of predefined user coordinates. This function is especially necessary when digitizing from drawings. Here, the drawing may be rotated and may not be perfectly square. In order to make digitizing useful in this case, the computer must compensate for the drawing as the data are being entered. AIDS performs this function by entering a calibration mode. The user enters the corner points of his drawing and the user coordinate values corresponding to each corner point.

Actually up to twenty-five subregions may be entered in this fashion. From this point on, when tracking the cursor in the graphic region of the display and processing input points, AIDS will implement a tansfer function to convert tablet coordinates (entered in four sided calibrated regions) to user coordinates (in their equivalent orthogonal regions); see figure 3. Given Xt and Yt tablet coordinates, we want to derive Xu and Yu user coordinates. If an imaginary line is constructed that contains point Tx,Ty and intersects both lines T1T2 and T3T4 by the same relative amount, r (expressed as a fraction between 0 and 1), then the corresponding user units for Ty can be given by: Uy = r(Uy2-Uy1)+Uy1. Similar arguments apply to the computation of Ux.

Display Processing

AIDS performs a variety of graphics related functions for the host; however, most of these functions are implemented in five basic steps:

1. Host Command Analysis.
2. Transformation To Display Coordinates.
3. Display Vector Generation.
4. Display Vector Clipping.
5. Formation and Output of Frame Buffer Commands.

The following paragraphs describe these steps in greater detail.

Host Command Analysis. AIDS commands are normally buffered in 1024 word blocks by the HP3000 before being sent over the Programmable Controller Link. All commands have basically the same format; particular fields may go unused or have specialized meanings depending on the nature of the command. Figure 4 illustrates the basic command format. The 'CODE' field is the basic command opcode; currently AIDS interprets fifteen distinct commands. The 'M' field normally controls the display mode: draw off, draw on (i.e. merge with current), complement, and jam (i.e. replace current). The 'T' field controls the type of display: outline with solid lines, outline with dotted lines, filled with solid lines, filled with dotted lines. The 'W','B','G','R' fields control output to the white, blue, green, and red display memories, respectively. The 'PARM1' and 'PARM2' fields contain additional parameters relevant to the specific function requested. 'XZERO' and 'YZERO' values are double integer coordinates which indicate the origin (in a multiple of user units) of the component to be drawn. The 'LENGTH' parameter determines the number of 'XY-COORDINATE' offsets supplied in the command buffer. A positive length indicates integers, a negative length indicates double integers. The 'XY-COORDINATE' array contains a list of vertice points for the component, or in some cases, an ASCII string. Vertice values in this array are relative to the 'XZERO' and 'YZERO' origins. This array is converted to reals before being passed to the functional processors.

Transformation to Display Coordinates. Within hp-IGS, geometric components (i.e. lines, rectangles, etc.) may be grouped together to form logical units like transistors, shift registers, etc. These groupings, called 'instances', may be included many times throughout the chip. Furthermore, instances may be nested (i.e. included in other instances) many levels deep. When an instance is included in a device, the user must specify an XY origin which serves as the location of the instance in the device. At this time, he may optionally change its orientation by rotating the instance or mirroring it along the X or Y axis.

In order to save space and to increase flexibility with respect to redefinition, hp-IGS stores the primary definition of each instance only once in the database. Each instance reference will contain a pointer to the primary definition, the origin of the instance in its parent device, and optionally, mirroring and rotation information. Component definitions inside the instance however, are stored relative to a local origin. These definitions must be transformed according to the reference origin, mirroring and rotation parameters before they will appear in their correct position and orientation in the display. The transformed coordinates are in terms of pixels (i.e. graphic display memory units). Rather than burdening the host with these geometric transformations, this function has been placed in the graphics station. Therefore, AIDS performs all necessary graphic transformations including scaling, translation, mirroring, and rotation. These operations are performed by operating on primitive coordinates with a transformation matrix which acts like a stack[3]. New transformations are pushed onto the current transformation matrix as nested instances are processed and popped off the current transformation matrix when processing of the instance is completed.

Display Vector Generation. Vectors for rectangle, polygon, circle, and line primitives are generated by AIDS for the host. For rectangles, hp-IGS supplies the lower left and upper right corners of the rectangle. Polygons are sent as a list of vertices and, therefore, require generation of the connecting edge segments. Circles are sent by the host in the form of an origin location, a point on the circumference, and a resolution factor.

Lines in hp-IGS are treated as centerlines with a width. AIDS will "fatten" this centerline before display. Centerlines are expanded as follows:

a. Construct line edge segments that are parallel to the centerline but separated from it by half a width in both left and right directions.
b. Extend the length of the constructed line segments by half a width in both directions. To prevent the expanded line from

becoming longer than the centerline, constructed segments are not extended beyond the endpoints of the centerline.

c. Generate the vertice points of the expanded line by using segment intersection points (where constructed line segments intersect) or segment end points (where no intersection exists).

d. Construct the expanded line's display vectors by connecting the vertices generated in the previous step.

Figure 5 illustrates a sample centerline and the steps taken to generate the expanded line. In addition to the primitives mentioned above, AIDS supports a stick font character set in the form of "notes" and "text". The software maintains a character set stroke table which is used to generate lines. The size of the characters is predetermined by the user. For text, this size is also used to control the width of the generated lines (notes generate zero width lines). Notes are used by the designer to identify parts of his design. Text is used to identify the integrated circuit and, as such, is intended to appear on the actual chip. An example note and text appear in figure 6.

In addition to the components mentioned above, which are saved in the database, AIDS is capable of generating display vectors for several 'scratchpad' components. These objects are used to facilitate data entry and verification. Included in this list are a data point identifier, which identifies point locations in the graphic data display area; a distance measurement, which displays actual and orthogonal distances between two points; and a ruler, which displays orthogonal distances between two points using tick marks to indicate grid points. In all three cases, the host causes the component to be drawn by supplying AIDS with one or two data points and the appropriate function code. These objects are always drawn in the white graphic memory plane so that they may be removed easily without affecting actual graphic data in the other three planes. Figure 7 illustrates each of the point, distance, and ruler scratchpad components.

<u>Display Vector Clipping</u>. After component display vectors have been generated, they must be clipped to the graphic display data region (i.e., vectors, or portions of vectors, not falling within this region are eliminated). Display coordinates are rounded to integral pixel addresses after clipping.

If requested by the user, database components can be displayed so that the areas inside the components are filled in with the color of the component. In this mode, AIDS performs vector-to-raster conversion of the components outline (given by the unclipped display vectors) and outputs display vectors for inside regions of the component. These vectors are then clipped and rounded as described above. (For reasons of space and clarity, the area fill algorithm employed by AIDS will not be described here. The reader is referred to [4].) Fill mode display is quite a bit slower than outline mode; consequently, it is used less frequently.

Formation and Output of Frame Buffer Commands. All frame buffer commands are in the form of a control word followed by zero or more data words. The format of the data words is dependent on the control word. To output display vectors, commands must be output to: selectively enable output to affected memory planes; set up the output image for each enabled plane; and set the output mode (either normal or complement). The frame buffer system is capable of accepting multiple output vectors in one command. Vector to raster conversion is performed automatically.

In addition to vector to raster conversion, several other functions of the Graphic Data System are employed by the HP1000. A fast screen 'wash' capabiltiy is used to set/clear selective memory planes; this has proven particularly useful when erasing the white memory plane to effect quick erasure of scratchpad components. A slower rectangular fill capability is used to clear the data region of the display. Finally, horizontal text and text backround commands are used to display menu items and status information.

Performance

Total hp-IGS system performance will vary considerably, depending both on the type of function the system is performing and on the particular structure of the user's chip in the host. However, under ideal conditions, AIDS has been observed to display a picture of 2500 rectangles (i.e. 10,000 vectors) in 5 seconds.

Conclusion

One desirable aspect of using separate processors for database management, graphic processing, and graphic output is the separate and concurrent processing of potentially time consuming tasks. That is, vector-to-raster translation is performed in the frame buffer while the clipping, scaling, mirroring, rotation, and translation is performed in the HP1000, and data sorting and searching is done in the host HP3000.

Another desirable aspect of this approach is cost: The use of a separate processor for each design station has allowed us to leverage the cost of the more expensive host HP3000 over several stations while still providing reasonable display speeds.

Currently, there are more than a dozen hp-IGS stations installed and in use throughout Hewlett-Packard. The system will also be used on an ongoing basis for VLSI Design courses taught within the company.

Acknowledgements

The authors would like to thank Fred Basham for supplying the calibration algorithms; Stu Bell and Tom Baker in HP Loveland, and Bill Sisson in HP Corvallis, used initial prototypes of the system and provided valuable feedback. Finally, we would like to thank the entire hp-IGS team for their constructive criticism and support.

References

1. B. Infante, D. Bracken, B. McCalla, S. Yamakoshi, and E. Cohen, "An Interactive Graphics System For The Design Of Integrated Circuits", Proceeding of the Design Automation Conference, 1978.

2. Hewlett-Packard Company, Real-Time Programmable Controller Reference and Application Manual, Part No. 30000-90067.

3. W. Newman, R. Sproull, Principles of Interactive Computer Graphics, McGraw-Hill, New York, 1973.

4. M. Newell, C. Sequin, "The Inside Story On Self-Intersecting Polygons", Lambda, Volume I, No. 2, 1980.

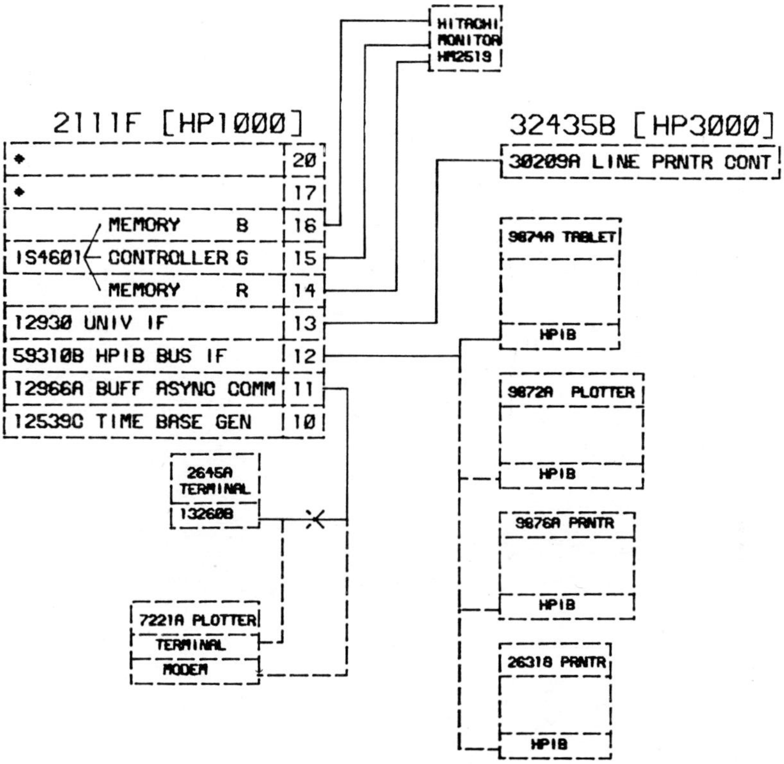

Figure 1. Station Hardware Configuration

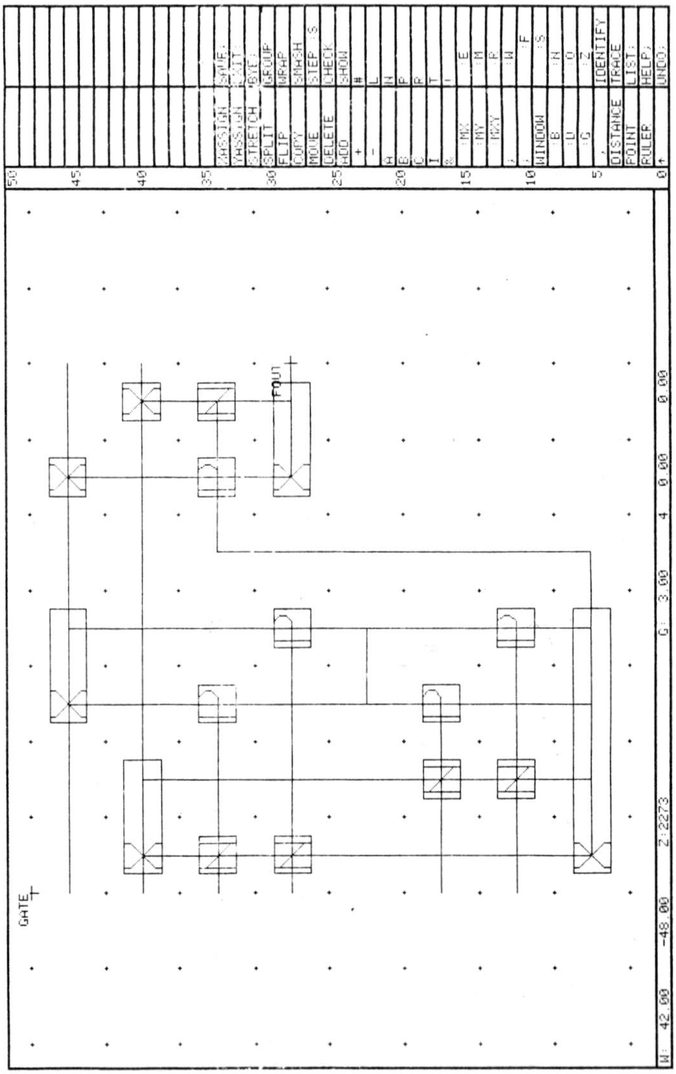

Figure 2. Sample display showing menu and graphic data regions

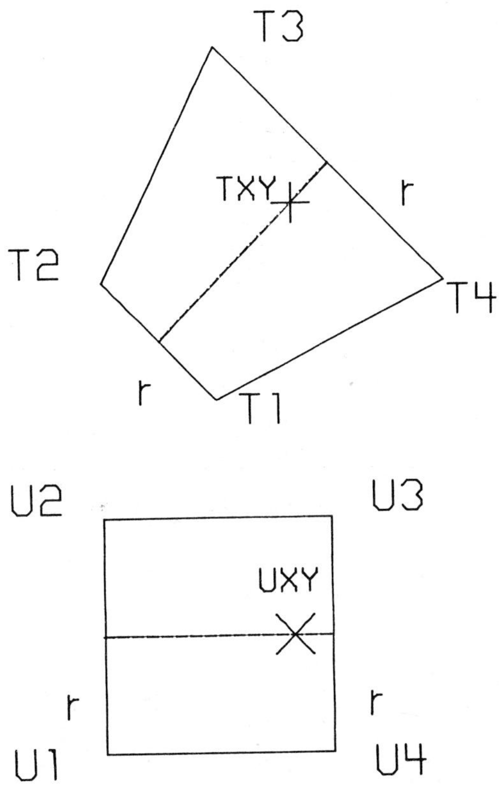

Figure 3. Transformation of digitized point in tablet coordinate system, Txy, to user coordinate system, Uxy.

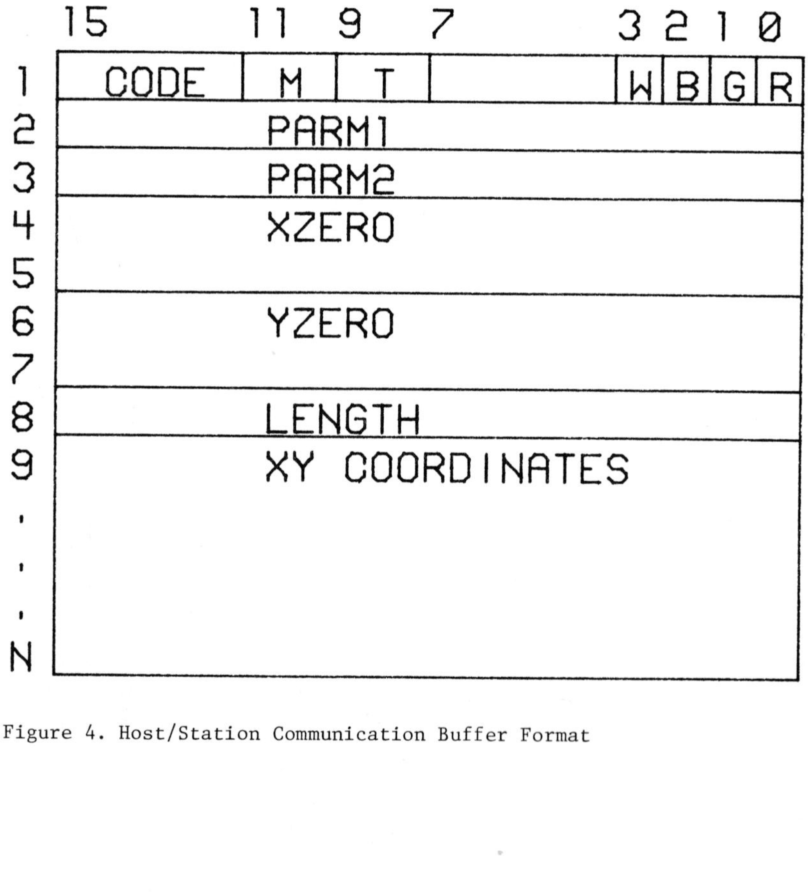

Figure 4. Host/Station Communication Buffer Format

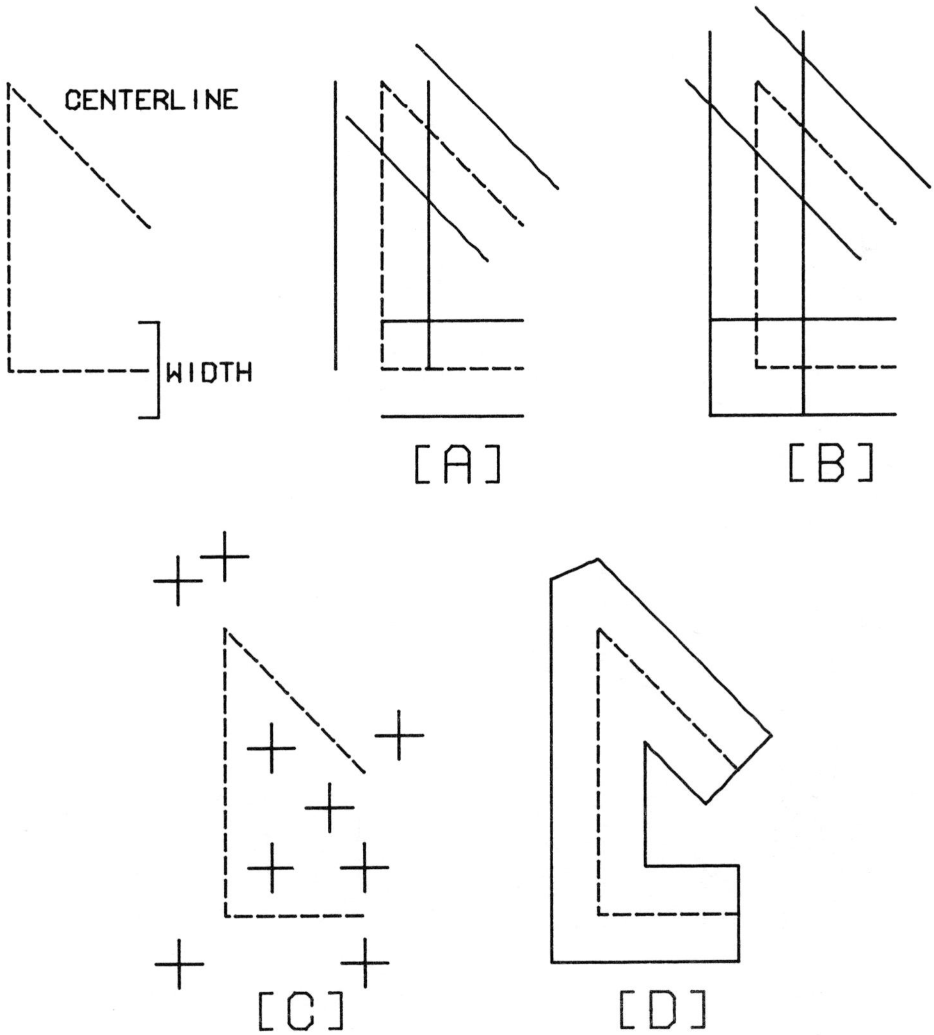

Figure 5. Example showing generation of an expanded centerline from a supplied centerline and width

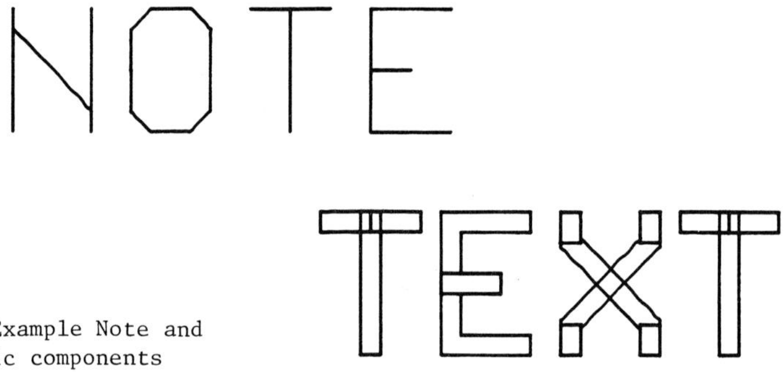

Figure 6. Example Note and Text graphic components

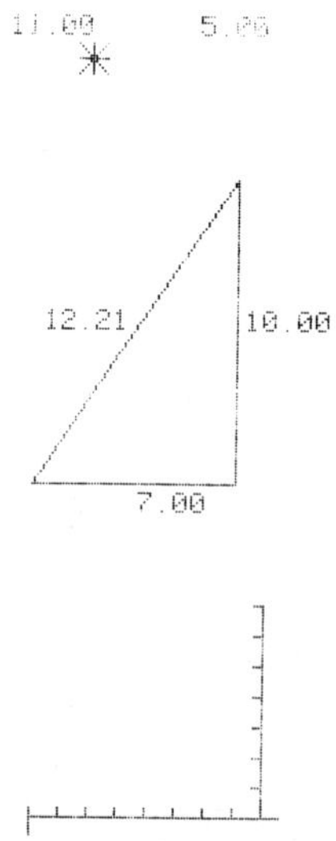

Figure 7. Example of Point, Distance, and Ruler graphic components

computer aided design in automatic control and logical automata

P. Bournai, C. Brie, J. P. LeBaron, C. Menendez

Laboratoire d'Automatique
Institut National des Sciences Appliquées
35043 RENNES Cédex - FRANCE

ABSTRACT

This work is concerned with an interactive multi-users system labelled SIRENA implemented on a minicomputer Hewlett-Packard 2113-E under the operating system RTE IV. This system allows to describe and study automatic control systems (linear and nonlinear in the transform plane s or z and in the state plane t or kT) and logical automata (Petri net).

The organisation of SIRENA is based on four major characteristics :

- an interactive high level language.
- a data structure which memorizes the semantic relations of the user's problem.
- interactive application programs which operate on the data structure.
- a graphical visualisation of the results in the user's desired way.

INTRODUCTION

Interactive systems for Education and Research are undergoing a rapid change and are bound to a promising future. During the last ten years, an increasing interest in interactive computer programs may be noticed at almost all institutes. Mostly these programs are developed by the institutes themselves for educational purposes or as a tool for researchers. All these considerations induce us to offer the possibility of integrating the computer in a system for Education and Research : it has indeed now become necessary for the treatment of practical problems.

In this paper, we describe an interactive multi-users system labelled SIRENA implemented on a minicomputer Hewlett-Packard 2113-E with 256 Kbytes under the operating system RTE IV. The central memory is divided into five background partitions of 36 K bytes. Five copies of SIRENA can be in memory at the same time and for each copy a small program with the data structure is always in the partition. The interpreter and all application programs corresponding to the various directives are organized as program segments.

A segment is loaded from any disc logical unit into the segment overlay area of an executing copy of SIRENA. This procedure allows SIRENA to run with a disc of small capacity (for example 7900). The data structure manipulation programs are written in assembly language to obtain an efficient use of the memory and computer time, whereas the application programs are written in Fortran IV. Figure 1 shows the hardware used for SIRENA.

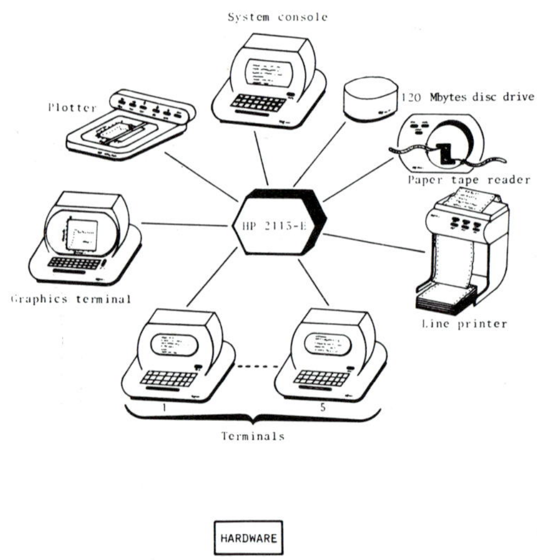

- Figure 1 -

The system SIRENA allows to describe and study automatic control systems (linear, nonlinear and sampled data systems) and logical automata (Petri net).

AUTOMATIC CONTROL

In automatic control SIRENA may be used to analyse the properties of a system, to solve the problem of identification and process-parameter estimation and to design control strategies for a particular system.

The dynamical linear or nonlinear systems are described by parametric models in terms of transfer functions (s or z) or state equations (t or kT). The data structure organisation easily allows structure modification (for example, feedback or insertion of compensator) and formal calculation between two particular variablesfor linear systems. This formal relation may be used for numerical computation to analyse the system (frequency response in Bode, Black or Nyquist plane, time response, root locus, etc...) for different values of system parameters.

Off-line or on-line identification algorithms allow the determination of real process models. Parameters variation, associated with classical nonlinear programming, may be used in interactive mode to obtain control parameters or models of industrial plants after identification.

For nonlinear and sampled data systems a simulation program based on a step by step path method in the data structure has been developed. This application program may support different numerical algorithms to calculate all system variables. As each variable of the system is computed (for several inputs), the user can visualise any of the variables either as a function of time, or as a function of another variable (which allows a phase plane representation).

An interactive package for study and implementation of real-time adaptive control algorithms is also included. The approach consists in determining a self-adaptive system based on the association of an on-line identification method and of a control method. The controller parameters are adjusted directly from the real-time estimates of the process parameters in order to stabilize the whole system with improved control. Within this structure, there are, of course, many different possibilities, depending on the control and identification algorithms used and the process to be controlled.

LOGICAL AUTOMATA

SIRENA allows to study complex digital systems with Petri nets representation. The properties, concepts and techniques of Petri nets are being developed in a search for natural, simple, and powerful methods for describing and analysing the flow of information and control in systems, particularly systems that may exhibit asynchronous and concurrent activities. The major use of Petri nets has been the modeling of logical automatisms in which events occur concurrently.

The data structure of SIRENA is very well adapted for net elaboration, modification, analysis and simulation. The Petri net analysis detects the bad workings of the system (for example partial or complete dead-locking, impossibility to return to a given state, etc...). The simulation allows to study the system evolution under fixed conditions, but it requires the definition of external environment, namely physical inputs or outputs of the system. The simulation may detect some design errors, like conflicts, loops, etc... The logical automata may be connected with linear or nonlinear systems to build complex systems which are simulated by a step path algorithm.

ORGANISATION OF SIRENA

A high level interactive language allows the user to describe and study complex systems with no specific knowledge of computer science and programming language. The procedure used is of a "question-answer" type. The language is modular and any new directives can be added without any important modification of the interpreter. Four types of directives have been developed and are shown in table I.

An internal representation (data structure) is associated with the external description of the system studied by the user. The data structure built along an orientated binary tree memorizes the semantic relations existing between variables. Each data has, besides its name and associated numeric file, its meaning and connections with the other terms of the structure. It is thus possible at any time to find the formal equations of the system and to remind the user of the description of the considered problem. The various nodes of the binary tree are represented in central memory by blocks of a constant size. During the description and treatment of a given problem, new nodes may appear and old ones disappear, which requires a memory dynamic allocation.

TYPE OF DIRECTIVE	FUNCTION	DIRECTIVE	TYPE OF SYSTEMS: TRANSFER FUNCTIONS (S or Z)	STATE EQUATIONS (t or KT)	LOGICAL	HYBRID
DECLARATION DIRECTIVES	. SYSTEMS DECLARATION	DEC(,NAME(,TYPE))	YES	YES	YES	NO
	. SYSTEMS ASSOCIATION	ASS(,NAME(,TYPE))	YES	NO	YES	YES
	. SYSTEMS MODIFICATION	MOD(,NAME(,TYPE))	YES	NO	YES	NO
	. SYSTEMS DESTRUCTION	DSY(,NAME(,TYPE))	YES	YES	YES	YES
DEFINITION DIRECTIVES	. SYSTEMS DEFINITION (ENTERING DATA TO DEFINE PARAMETERS OF THE SYSTEM: SIGNALS, MATRIX, TRANSFER FUNCTIONS, NONLINEAR FUNCTIONS, ACTIONS, EVENTS, ETC...)	DEF(,NAME(,TYPE))	YES	YES	YES	YES
FORMAL CALCULATION DIRECTIVES	. OVERALL TRANSFER FUNCTION BY MASON RULES (RELATIONSHIP BETWEEN TWO VARIABLES OF ANY NETWORK FOR LINEAR SYSTEMS)	MAS(,NAME(,TYPE))	YES	NO	NO	NO
	. RECALL SYSTEMS EQUATIONS (REMINDING THE USER OF THE DESCRIPTION OF THE CONSIDERED PROBLEM)	EQU(,NAME(,TYPE))	YES	YES	YES	YES
	. PETRI NET ANALYSIS (DETECTING THE BAD WORKINGS OF LOGICAL AUTOMATISM)	VER(,NAME(,TYPE))	NO	NO	YES	NO
NUMERICAL COMPUTATION DIRECTIVES	. FREQUENCY RESPONSE	RFR(,NAME(,TYPE))	YES	NO	NO	NO
	. TIME RESPONSE	RTE(,NAME(,TYPE))	YES	YES	NO	YES
	. ROOT LOCUS	EVA(,NAME(,TYPE))	YES	NO	NO	NO
	. MODELISATION	AJU(,NAME(,TYPE))	YES	NO	NO	NO
	. IDENTIFICATION	IDE(,NAME(,TYPE))	YES	NO	NO	NO
	. CONTROL	COM(,NAME(,TYPE))	YES	NO	NO	NO

- TABLE I - SIRENA DIRECTIVES -

The heart of the application programs are classical routines which run through computer on batch processing in Laboratories. But in order to connect these programs to the data structure, software interface modules are necessary. These programs must be interactive and also satisfy the numerical stability and robustness. Their initialisation and stop test must be transparent to the user.

In all computer aided design systems, the graphical results are of great interest to users and therefore SIRENA contains a powerful graphical display package. The numerical results are memorized in files connected to the data structure and visualized in a range of specified formats with alphanumeric labelling and automatic scaling. This plotting software has been designed to be device independent (CRT display or X-Y plotter). The display can be divided into four parts and in each part nine curves may be visualized. Here too, some high level directives have been developed (cf. table II) to select one part and/or one curve, to magnify a window, to copy the display on a plotter, to get the coordinates of a point, to write comments on the plotting, etc...

FUNCTION	DIRECTIVES
. THE DISPLAY CAN BE CUT INTO FOUR PARTS. THE DIRECTIVE CAD ALLOWS TO CHOOSE ONE OF THESE PARTS.	CAD, N $1 \leqslant N \leqslant 4$
. NINE CURVES CAN BE VISUALIZED IN EACH PART. THE DIRECTIVE COU ALLOWS TO CHOOSE ONE OF THESE CURVES.	COU, N $1 \leqslant N \leqslant 9$
. THE DIRECTIVE LOU MAGNIFIES A CURVE WINDOW.	LOU
. THE DIRECTIVE COP ALLOWS TO COPY THE DISPLAY ON A PLOTTER.	COP
. IT IS POSSIBLE WITH THE DIRECTIVE COM TO WRITE COMMENTS ON THE PLOTTING.	COM, "COMMENTS"
. END OF GRAPHICAL EDITION.	FIN

- TABLE II - GRAPHIC DIRECTIVES -

APPLICATION EXAMPLE

The SIRENA application example is about the simulation of the goods transfer by two waggons using a common track. The device is represented on Figure 2 and it works in the following way :

- at rest, the two waggons are empty and wait each on a separate track near their respective loading up stations YAC and YBC.

- at the starting signal M, the loading up of the two waggons is made simultaneously. It is finished after 45 seconds for waggon A and 30 seconds for waggon B.

- as soon as a waggon is loaded up, it leaves for the unloading station (YDA or YDB) placed on the common track.

  If one of the two waggons is already on the common track, the other waggon stops at the waiting station YAT or YBT until the track is free. It then starts again and selects the correct switching.

  On the contrary, if the common track is free, the waggon does not stop at the waiting station and goes straight to the unloading station. The unloading lasts 60 seconds whatever the waggon is.

- once it is empty, the waggon comes back to the starting point to be loaded up again.

  The process stops when the starting order M is cancelled or when 5 waggons have been unloaded. In any case, the waggons come back to the starting point.

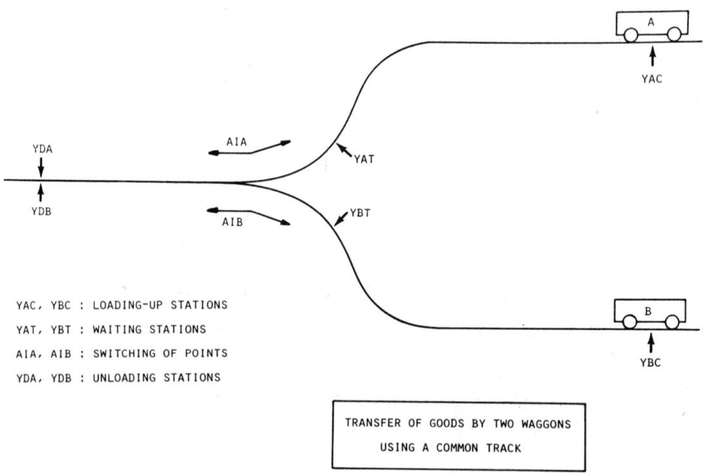

- Figure 2 -

The displacement of each waggon is realised by a velocity control system with a DC motor controlled by an amplifier with saturation. Figures 3 and 4 show the block-diagrams describing the physical working of each waggon. The EGA (or EGB) and EDA (or EDB) inputs are logical variables allowing to control the displacement of waggons towards the unloading station or the loading-up station. The STA and STB blocks represent the amplifiers, HAA and HAB the elements (motor, gear box and waggon). The HBA and HBB blocks allow to obtain the YA and YB positions of the waggons from their speeds WA and WB. The HGA, HGB, HDA, HDB, KEA, KEB blocks allow to give different values to the loading up and unloading speeds and tachometers.

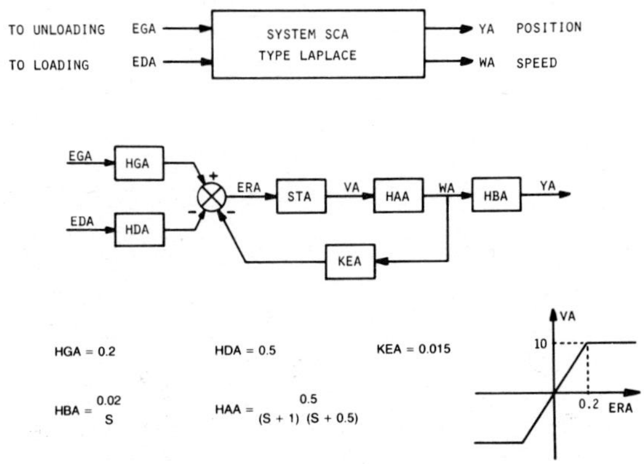

SCHEMATIC REPRESENTATION OF THE WAGGON A

- Figure 3 -

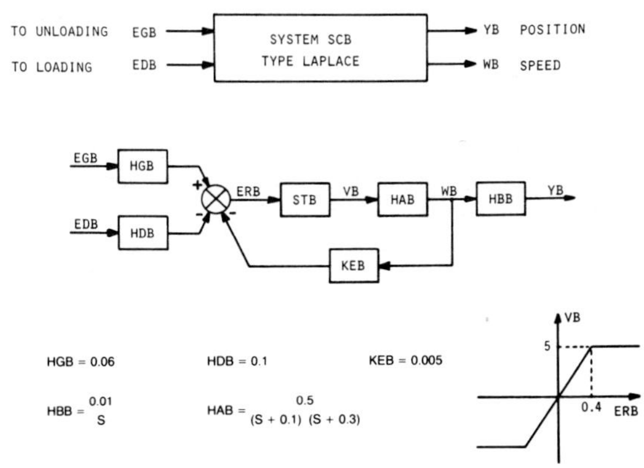

SCHEMATIC REPRESENTATION OF THE WAGGON B

- Figure 4 -

Figure 5 shows the description of the system SCA (model of waggon A) which has two inputs (EGA, EDA) and two outputs (YA, WA).

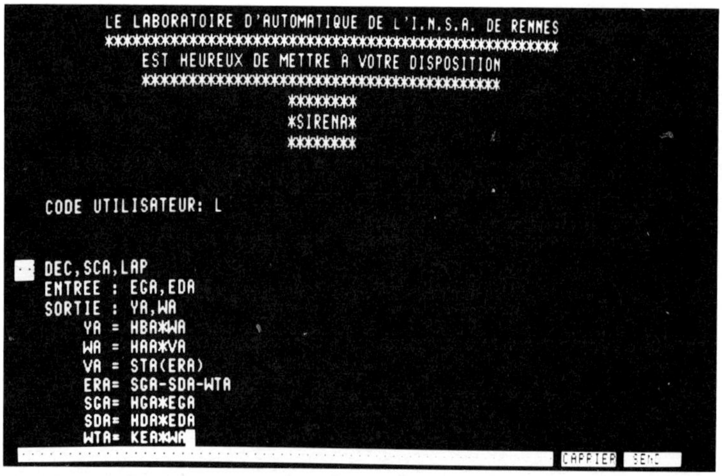

- Figure 5 - Declaration of the system SCA

The system SIRENA asks the user the inputs and the outputs of the system SCA as well as all relations which exist between these variables.

After the formal declaration of the system SCA, figure 6 shows the numerical definition of the transfer functions, the saturation and the two inputs (rectangular pulse with delay on each). The time response of the system SCA is given on figure 7. For the simulation, the user must answer different questions like, time domain, integration step, variables to be visualized, etc.... The graphical result of this application program (position YA and speed WA) is copied on a plotter with comments (figure 8)

```
DEF
PARAMETRE SYSTEME: HBA
NATURE : TRAN
GAIN   : 0.02
NUMERATEUR(POLYNOME/RACINES): POL
       : 1.
DENOMINATEUR(POLYNOME/RACINES): POL
       : 1.;0.
PARAMETRE SYSTEME: HAA
NATURE : TRAN
GAIN   : 0.5
NUMERATEUR(POLYNOME/RACINES): POL
       : 1.
DENOMINATEUR(POLYNOME/RACINES): RAC
       : (-1);(-0.5)
PARAMETRE SYSTEME: STA(ERA)
    X  = 0.2
    Y  = 10.
PARAMETRE SYSTEME: HGA
NATURE : GAIN
GAIN   : 0.2
PARAMETRE SYSTEME: HDA
NATURE : GAIN
GAIN   : 0.5
PARAMETRE SYSTEME: KEA
NATURE : GAIN
GAIN   : 0.015
PARAMETRE SYSTEME: EGA
NATURE : CREN
AMPLITUDE: 1.
DUREE  : 50
DELAI  : 20
PARAMETRE SYSTEME: EDA
NATURE : CREN
AMPLITUDE: 1.
DUREE  : 25
DELAI  : 100
PARAMETRE SYSTEME: *
```

- Figure 6 - Definition of the system SCA

```
RTE
DOMAINE TEMPOREL: 0.:200.
NOMBRE DE POINTS VISUALISES: 500
PAS D'INTEGRATION: 0.1
VARIABLES A VISUALISER: YA,WA
?CONDITIONS INITIALES: NON

COM,WAGGON A POSITION

COM,WAGGON A SPEED

COP
?FEUILLE PRETE SUR LA TABLE:OUI

FIN

?ITERATION SUR LES PARAMETRES APPLICATIONS: *

CARRIER  SEND
```

- Figure 7 - Time response of the system SCA

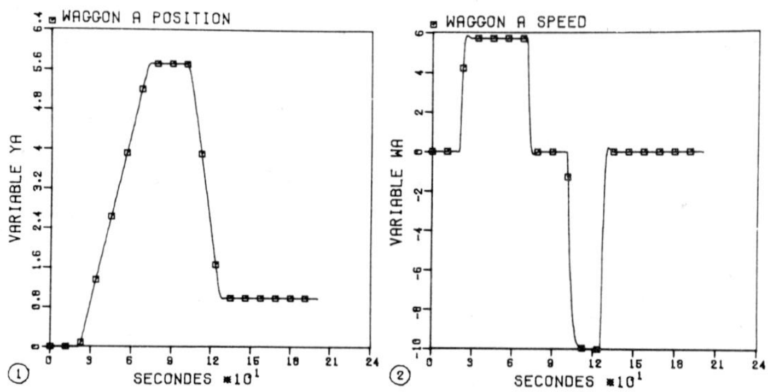

- Figure 8 - Position and speed of waggon A

For waggon B, it is the same dialogue to describe the system SCB, to define its parameters and to obtain the time response.

The automaton which controls the goods transfer by two waggons using a common track is represented by the Petri net on figure 9. The description of the system PET (logical type) is on figure 10. To the question "place de départ" the user must type the name of any place in the net. Then for any place or transition, the computer asks for the successor nodes (it is possible to give for each successor node, its particular successor nodes in parenthesis). When all the nodes of the graph have been defined, the user gives the initial marking.

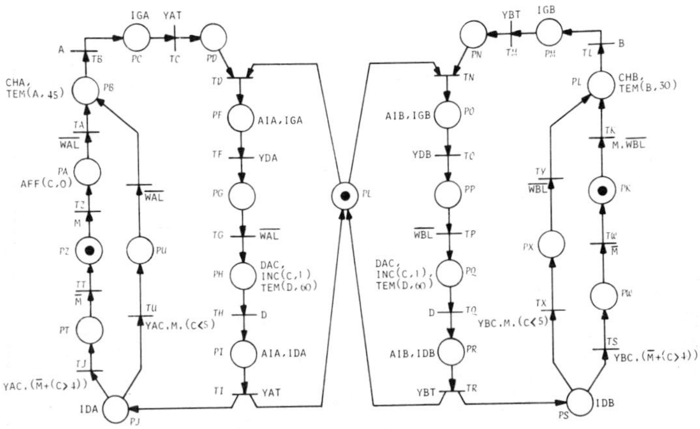

GOODS TRANSFER BY TWO WAGGONS
PETRI NET OF CONTROL AUTOMATON

- Figure 9 -

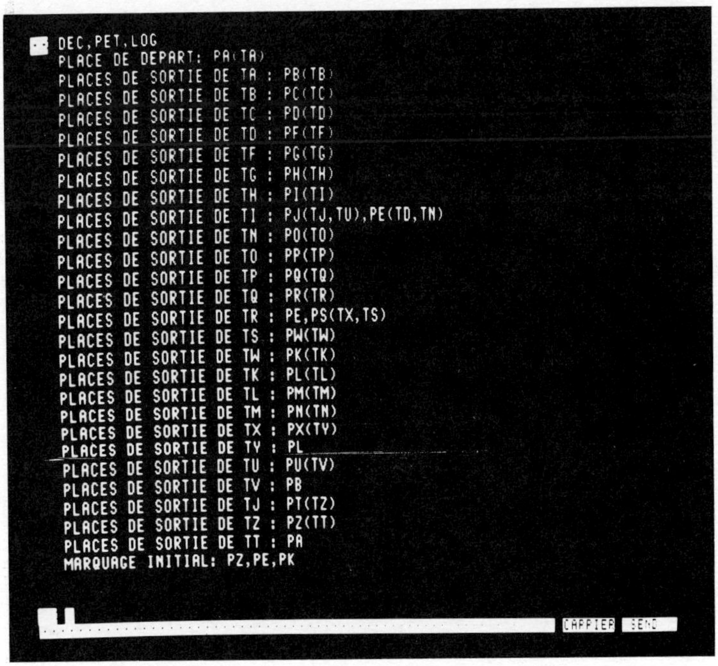

```
DEC,PET,LOG
PLACE DE DEPART: PA(TA)
PLACES DE SORTIE DE TA : PB(TB)
PLACES DE SORTIE DE TB : PC(TC)
PLACES DE SORTIE DE TC : PD(TD)
PLACES DE SORTIE DE TD : PF(TF)
PLACES DE SORTIE DE TF : PG(TG)
PLACES DE SORTIE DE TG : PH(TH)
PLACES DE SORTIE DE TH : PI(TI)
PLACES DE SORTIE DE TI : PJ(TJ,TU),PE(TD,TN)
PLACES DE SORTIE DE TN : PO(TO)
PLACES DE SORTIE DE TO : PP(TP)
PLACES DE SORTIE DE TP : PQ(TQ)
PLACES DE SORTIE DE TQ : PR(TR)
PLACES DE SORTIE DE TR : PE,PS(TX,TS)
PLACES DE SORTIE DE TS : PW(TW)
PLACES DE SORTIE DE TW : PK(TK)
PLACES DE SORTIE DE TK : PL(TL)
PLACES DE SORTIE DE TL : PM(TM)
PLACES DE SORTIE DE TM : PN(TN)
PLACES DE SORTIE DE TX : PX(TY)
PLACES DE SORTIE DE TY : PL
PLACES DE SORTIE DE TU : PU(TV)
PLACES DE SORTIE DE TV : PB
PLACES DE SORTIE DE TJ : PT(TZ)
PLACES DE SORTIE DE TZ : PZ(TT)
PLACES DE SORTIE DE TT : PA
MARQUAGE INITIAL: PZ,PE,PK
```

- Figure 10 - Declaration of system PET

The directive VER allows to analyse an uninterpreted Petri net (figure 11). The Petri net analysis detects the bad working of the automaton, for example, partial or complete dead lockings, impossibility to return to a given state, etc... If the Petri net is not correct, a message is given to the user.

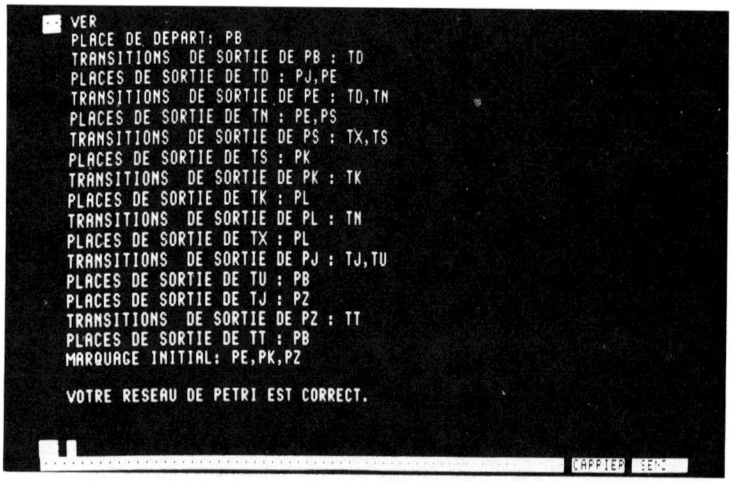

- Figure 11 - Analysis of the uninterpreted Petri net

A logical automaton is in constant relationship with the external environment. This dependency is modelised by interpreting the Petri net which represents the control automaton. So, with the places are associated the actions or commands made by Petri net, and with transitions are associated the events tested by Petri net.

The interpretation of the Petri net is given on figure 12.

```
DEF
NOEUD  : PA
ACTIONS: AFF(C,0)
NOEUD  : TA
EVENEMENTS: /WAL
NOEUD  : PB
ACTIONS: CHA,TEM(A,45)
NOEUD  : TB
EVENEMENTS: A
NOEUD  : PC
ACTIONS: IGA
NOEUD  : TC
EVENEMENTS: YAT
NOEUD  : PF
ACTIONS: AIA,IGA
NOEUD  : TF
EVENEMENTS: YDA
NOEUD  : TG
EVENEMENTS: /WAL
NOEUD  : PH
ACTIONS: DAC,TEM(D,60),INC(C,1)
NOEUD  : TH
EVENEMENTS: D
NOEUD  : PI
ACTIONS: IDA,AIA
NOEUD  : TI
EVENEMENTS: YAT
NOEUD  : PJ
ACTIONS: IDA
NOEUD  : TJ
EVENEMENTS: YAC*((C>4)+/M)
NOEUD  : TZ
EVENEMENTS: /M
NOEUD  : TT
EVENEMENTS: M
NOEUD  : TU
EVENEMENTS: (C<5)*YAC*M
NOEUD  : TV
EVENEMENTS: /WAL
NOEUD  : PO
ACTIONS: AIB,IGB
NOEUD  : TO
EVENEMENTS: YDB
NOEUD  : TP
EVENEMENTS: /WBL
NOEUD  : PQ
ACTIONS: DAC,TEM(D,60),INC(C,1)
NOEUD  : PR
ACTIONS: IDB,AIB
NOEUD  : TQ
EVENEMENTS: D
NOEUD  : TR
EVENEMENTS: YBT
NOEUD  : PS
ACTIONS: IDB
NOEUD  : TS
EVENEMENTS: YBC*((C>4)+/M)
NOEUD  : TW
EVENEMENTS: /M
NOEUD  : TK
EVENEMENTS: M*/WBL
NOEUD  : PL
ACTIONS: CHB,TEM(B,30)
NOEUD  : TL
EVENEMENTS: B
NOEUD  : PM
ACTIONS: IGB
NOEUD  : TM
EVENEMENTS: YBT
NOEUD  : TX
EVENEMENTS: (C<5)*YBC*M
```

- Figure 12 -

Interpretation of the Petri net

When the Petri net is interpreted, it is possible to connect it with analogous systems SCA and SCB. Figure 13 represents the association between the two waggons A and B and the control automaton.

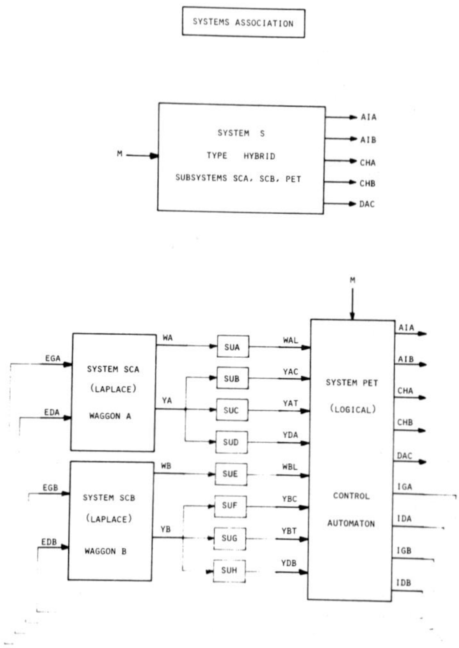

- Figure 13 -

After the association, we have a new system S (hybrid type) with one input (M) and five outputs (AIA, AIB, CHA, CHB, DAC). The dialogue is shown on figure 14.

Figure 15 shows the definition of interfaces between processes and control automaton and figure 16 the dialogue.

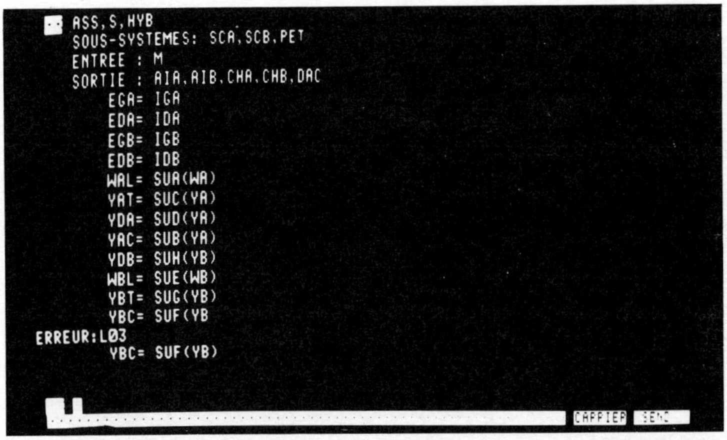

- Figure 14 - Association of systems SCA , SCB and PET

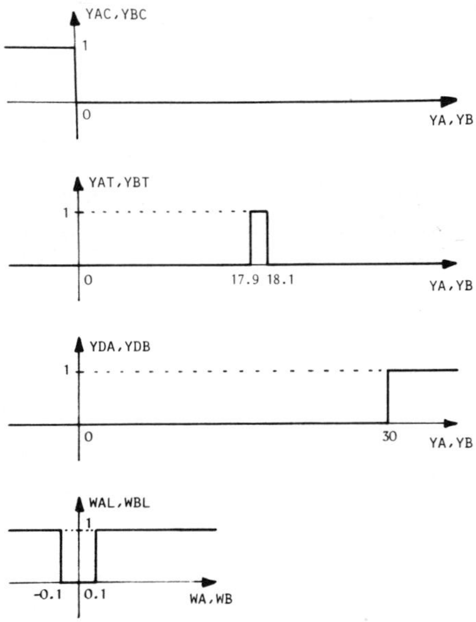

DEFINITION OF INTERFACES BETWEEN PROCESSES AND CONTROL AUTOMATON

- Figure 15 -

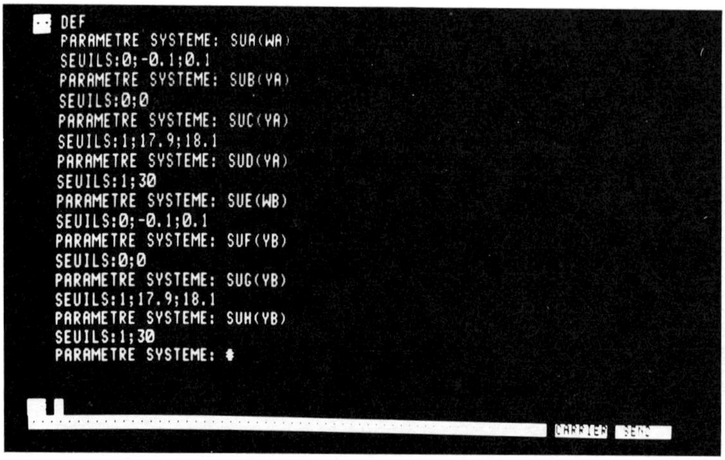

- Figure 16 - Numerical definition of interfaces

Now, it is possible to simulate this complex system by a step by step patch algorithm. This algorithm works on the data structure and calculates all the variables of the system. If the application program detects a loop in the Petri net, an error is mentioned and the simulation is stopped. If it detects a conflict between two places, it mentioned it to the user, makes a choice and goes on. To illustrate the association and simulation, let us consider the two following examples. For the first example (figures 17 and 18), the process stops when the starting order M is cancelled and for the second (figures 19 and 20) the process stops when 5 waggons have been unloaded.

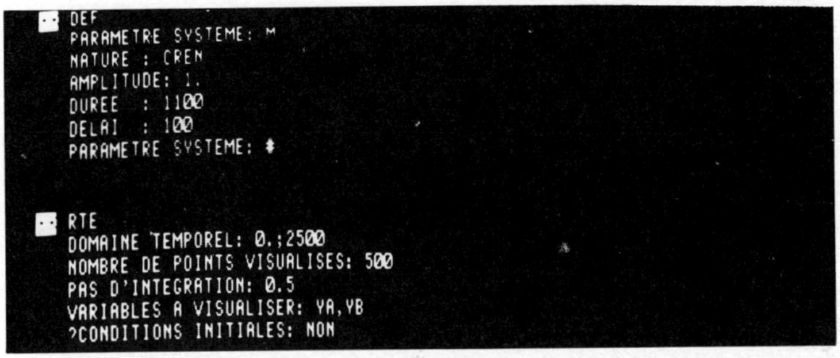

- Figure 17 - Definition of signal M and time response

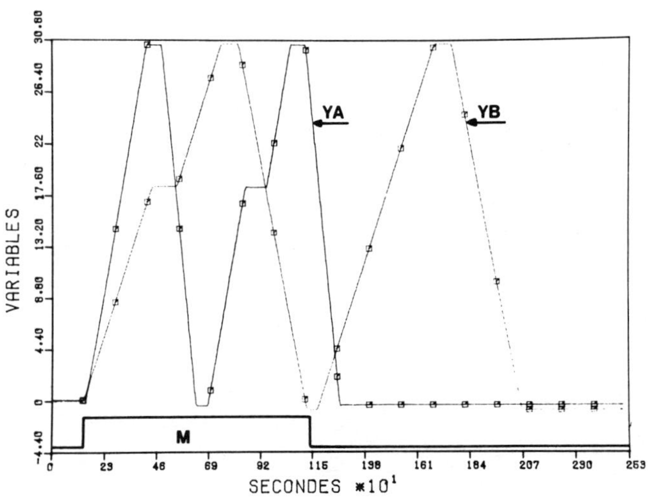

- Figure 18 - Positions of waggons A and B

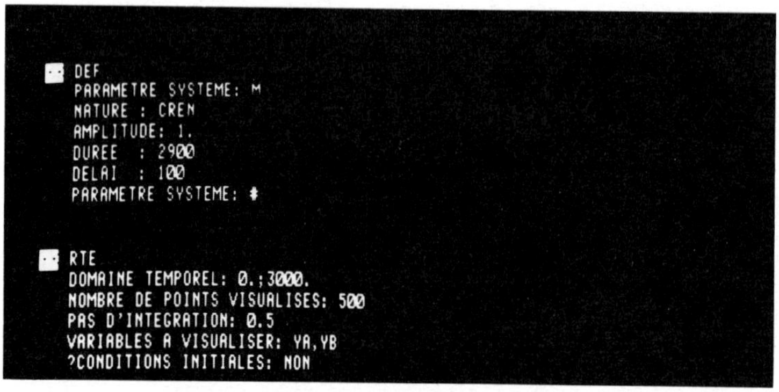

- Figure 19 - Definition of signal M and time response

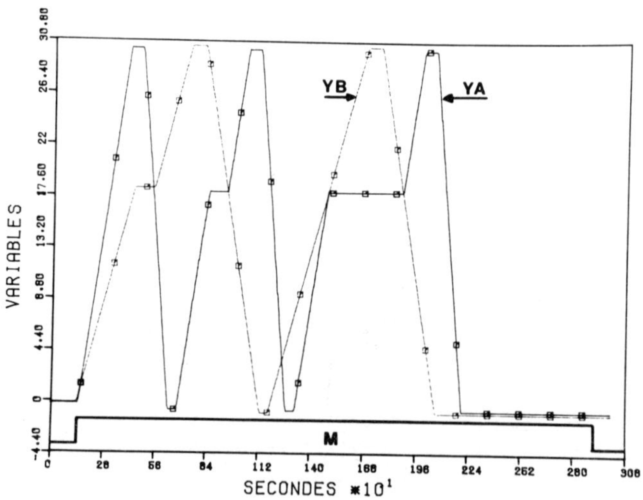

- Figure 20 - Positions of waggons A and B

CONCLUSION

SIRENA has been used for one year in Education and Research in our engineering school and laboratory. All students and searchers are very satisfied with the system performances. The time response of the system for the input/output language is quick even when all CRT terminals are used. The "question-answer" procedure is useful in educational environment and requires a minimal assistance from the teacher. All the responses of the user are checked and an error message is printed when a mistake is made. A "help" procedure should be provided when the user doesn't know to proceed or when he wishes to have any explanation about messages of SIRENA.

In conclusion, the characteristics of SIRENA (high level language, data structure, application programs, graphical display) make it a powerful tool in computer aided design in automatic control and logical automata.

ACKNOWLEGMENTS

This work has been supported by the french DGRST, the french "Ministère de l'Industrie" and the french "Ministère des Universités". The authors are greatly indebted to all persons who collaborated to this work.

REFERENCES

- Rapport D.G.R.S.T. n° 74-7-1250/1251/1252 Mars 1977

- GERBER R., QUENEC'HDU Y., THOMAS Y. Interactive systems as aids to teaching Automatic Control.IFAC Symposium on Trends in Automatic Control Education. Barcelona, March 30 and April 1, 1977.

- LE BARON J.P. Conception assistée en Automatique. Thèse de Docteur-Ingénieur, Université de RENNES (FRANCE) Juin 1979.

- BOURNAI P., LE BARON J.P., BUISSON J. Study and simulation of complex systems in Automatic Control. IFAC Symposium in Computer Aided Design of Control systems . Zurich, 29-31 August 1979.

a mini-based sculptured surface system

Michael P. Carroll, Ph.D.
David H. Hoitsma, Jr.

Gerber Systems Technology, Inc.
40 Gerber Road East
South Windsor, Connecticut 06074

ABSTRACT: In the last decade, mini-based turnkey graphic systems, such as Gerber Systems Technology's IDS, have provided a useful tool in engineering, design, and manufacturing. The increase in size and capability of minicomputer systems has permitted their use in increasingly complex tasks which were once reserved for large mainframe computers only. One area will be examined in this paper--sculptured surfaces.

INTRODUCTION

Computer Aided Geometric Design and Manufacturing is concerned with the creation and analysis of a computer model that will adequately describe two and three-dimensional shapes. Interactive computer graphic systems have provided a powerful method which not only gives us interactive design capabilities and output drawings, but analytic results and manufacturing data [1]. Many complex tasks, however, remained on batch systems (such as APT) which created a significant gap between them and mini-based graphic systems.

Now given minicomputers with high speed and accurate vector and mathematical firmware, these systems can compete favorably with the large mainframe systems. Further, the ability to view and modify parts and tool paths in an interactive mode is boosting CAD/CAM productivity and pushing mini-based systems beyond environments in several areas.

One area that will be examined in this paper is GST's sculptured surface package. Computer representations of surfaces are highly developed and have been used successfully for Computer Aided Design in the automotive, aircraft, and shipbuilding industries where multi-curved surfaces are essential [1,2].

COMPUTER SYSTEM ENVIRONMENT

The basic GST turnkey system (FIGURE 1) is a distributed processing system which consists of one or more graphics workstations connected to a processor subsystem (HP-1000F central processing unit, disk drive and controller, mag tape unit, system console, and line printer). The heart of the graphics workstation is a HP-1000E processor which controls the graphic display output to a Tektronix storage/refresh CRT.

The GST software includes the operating and data management systems, the graphics support routines, and application programs. These application routines bring together the interrelated tasks of design, analysis, and manufacturing, and are partitioned into the areas of detail drafting, printed circuit board design, geometric modeling, and numerical control.

The speed of the HP-1000F control processing unit (CPU) was the most important property required by the sculptured surface package. The features of this CPU include a minimum of 384K byte memory, floating point hardware for single and double precision calculations, and scientific instruction set firmware. The floating point hardware is very important for surface display and calculations, and represented a significant increase in the speed and performance of the surface package.

The display of complicated surfaces and general surface application routines require a significant amount of calculations. Many of the surface functions described in the following sections are implemented by using iterative algorithms which may require thousands of surface evaluations. These evaluations can involve millions of floating point operations. Timing tests have indicated that the HP-1000F processor is twice as fast as the E processor for these surface operations. This increase in speed provides the user with improved response time and makes the sculptured surface package a powerful design tool.

SCULPTURED SURFACES

The geometric modeling routine contains a sculptured surface package to represent three-dimensional shapes. A full range of surface types are supported which include ruled surfaces, surfaces of revolution, offset and mesh surfaces. In this section, we will discuss the structure and application of GST's mesh surface.

Mathematically, the mesh surface uses a bicubic Coon's patch as the basic element of its mesh. The entire surface consists of many patches which interpolate specified points such that second degree continuity is maintained between patches. GST's data structure allows non-standard features such as local mesh modification and three-corner patches. Furthermore, the geometric modeler supports many graphic functions for the mesh which include surface/surface intersection, section cuts, and machining.

The mesh can be defined through selection of splines created interactively or through batch input of points or points and cross-tangent vectors (FIGURE 2&3). The user has the option to vary the display gridding which will increase the number of u and v parameter curves displayed (FIGURE 4). Another option provided for the user is respecification of patch node points with the choice of local modification of the spline through that node. In local modification, only the four (4) adjacent patches on the changed spline (FIGURE 6) are modified.

Under normal construction, the mesh surface maintains second degree continuity at patch boundaries; however, it is possible to relax this constraint and retain only continuity of the tangents or just continuity across patch boundaries. This feature expands the mesh's ability to capture a wide variety of shapes such as box-like entities (see FIGURE 7).

SCULPTURED SURFACE MANIPULATION

There are many surface operations that the geometric modeling package supplies which are useful for design and manufacturing. If a user specifies an arbitrary plane, a section cut of the mesh will be obtained. The section cut is stored as a curve entity and can be used for analysis or machining (see FIGURE 8). For example, the GST analysis package can use these curves to compute cross-sectional areas or to define check and drive surfaces for machining.

Besides section cuts, intersections of meshes with lines or other meshes are provided. The mesh/mesh intersection routine will rapidly produce an intersection curve to within a specified tolerance. Options are given which permit the user to specify starting points for the algorithm and provide the capability to capture all the intersection curves (see FIGURE 9). These curves can be used to define part boundaries for surface trimming or for machining.

Other surfaces can be constructed from mesh surfaces such as offsets and mesh blends. The blending function smoothly joins together two (2) distinct meshes (see FIGURE 10), and can be used as a generalized fillet surface. The offset surface produced is a true offset at every point of the surface and is very useful for CAM applications (see FIGURE 11).

Finally, the mesh surface can be used as a part surface in GST's package. Since the GST application routines share a common database, the CAM program can be applied to the mesh to generate manufacturing information, such as tool path generation on the surface which is a useful process in mold work (see FIGURE 12).

FUTURE SURFACE DEVELOPMENT

This section describes some of the current and future development work on surface modeling at GST. The surface capabilities will be extended over a wide range of areas which include surface design, representation, and applications. Some of the developments are offset and fillet surfaces, rational bicubic surfaces, least squares fitting, and the capability for trimming and local mesh modification.

Surface representation will be based upon a parametric rational cubic formulation for edge curves and surfaces. Surface patch edge curves will be defined by rational cubic curves, which are extensions of cubic splines. The rational curves are an improvement over splines because they represent conic segments exactly and reduce to splines for all cubic type data. Thus, general composite edge curves can be introduced for the generation of complicated surfaces while retaining accuracy and efficiency for all computations.

The design of surfaces will be enhanced by the ability to modify portions of a surface model. The user will be able to locally introduce a new geometry by redefining existing patch boundaries or by defining new edge curves. This process will increase the number of patches but will leave unchanged all patch boundaries exterior to the modification. This local design process creates the need for a generalization of the surface database to a multi-level tree structure which will retain the association between the global model and the local refinements. This structure also permits the user to join two surfaces into one, or to create surfaces patch by patch.

Surface design will also include a trimming function to permit a user to restrict a surface to new boundaries which are defined by intersecting the surface with planes or other surfaces. The restriction of the surface will be accomplished by reducing the domain of the parameter values and generalizing the current surface evaluation algorithm.

The surface package will contain two new surface entities: offsets and fillets. The offset function will enable a user to specify a constant or variable distance from a specified surface which will produce a corresponding surface entity. This offset image will be defined such that the corresponding surface points lie on the same normal vector or the generating surface at a distance equal to the offset value.

Finally, a fillet surface for constant and variable radii will be provided. Given the radius function and specified surfaces, this routine will produce a smooth region joining the two surfaces and lying between two containment curves (see FIGURE 13).

SUMMARY

Sculptured surfaces represented an application that up until recently was useful within batch mainframe systems. With the increased performance of minicomputers, GST has implemented a sculptured surface package which is not only parallel to a system like APT, but includes the following graphic features:

- variable display gridding
- local node modification
- section cuts
- surface/surface intersection
- interactive machine processing

In fact, within an interactive graphics system, which includes such graphics features and user-oriented machine processing, certain applications of these surfaces can leap past the capability of batch systems.

REFERENCES

1. Barnhill, R.E. & Risenfeld, R.F., Eds.; Computer Aided Geometric Design; Academic Press (1974).

2. Baer, A., Eastman, C. & Henrion, M.; Geometric Modeling: A Survey; CAD, Vol. 11 (1979), pp. 253-272.

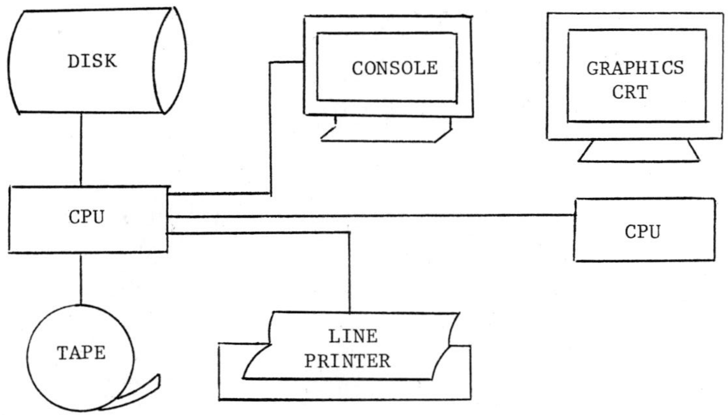

FIGURE 1 - GST DISTRIBUTED PROCESSING SYSTEM

(M.P. Carroll, D. Hoitsma; *A Mini-Based Sculptured Surface System*)

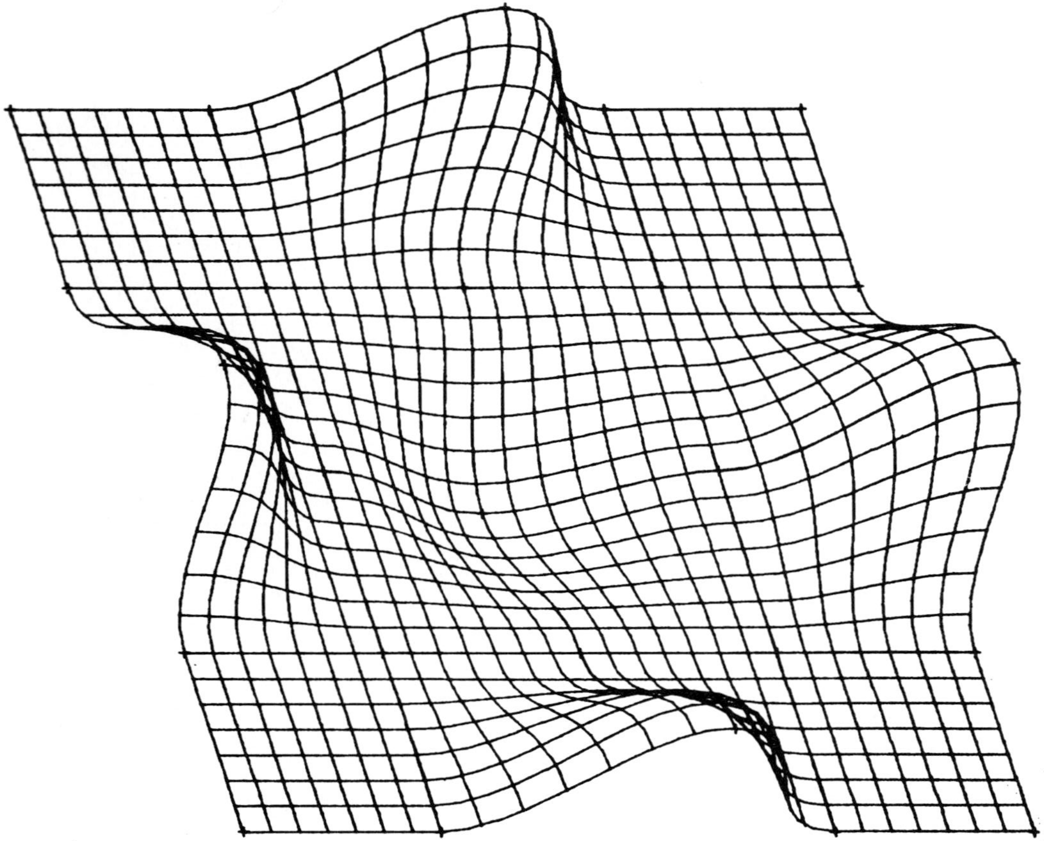

<u>FIGURE 2 - INPUT SURFACE</u> (M.P. Carroll, D. Hoitsma; <u>A Mini-Based Sculptured Surface System</u>)

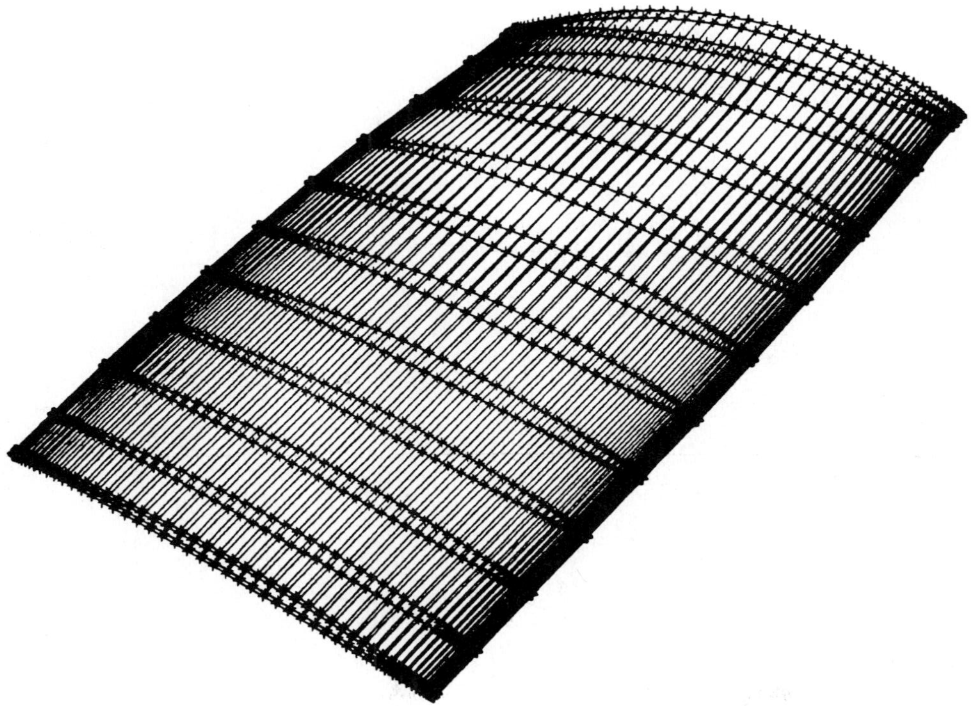

FIGURE 3 - TAPE INPUT SURFACE

(M.P. Carroll, D. Hoitsma; A Mini-Based Sculptured Surface System)

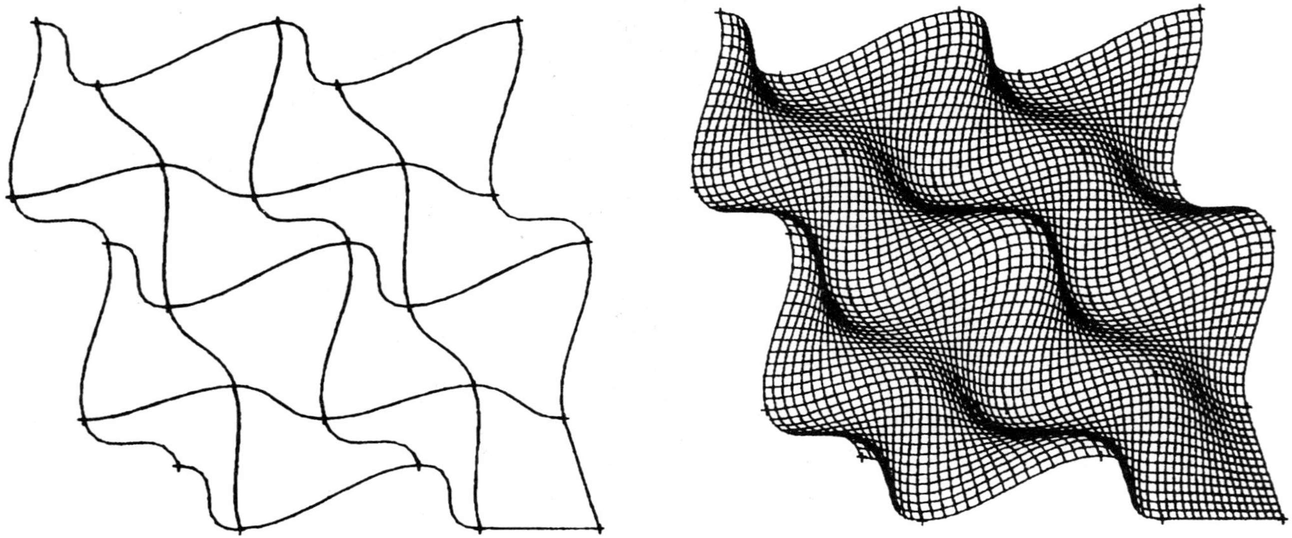

FIGURE 4 - VARIABLE GRIDDING

(M.P. Carroll, D. Hoitsma; A Mini-Based Sculptured Surface System)

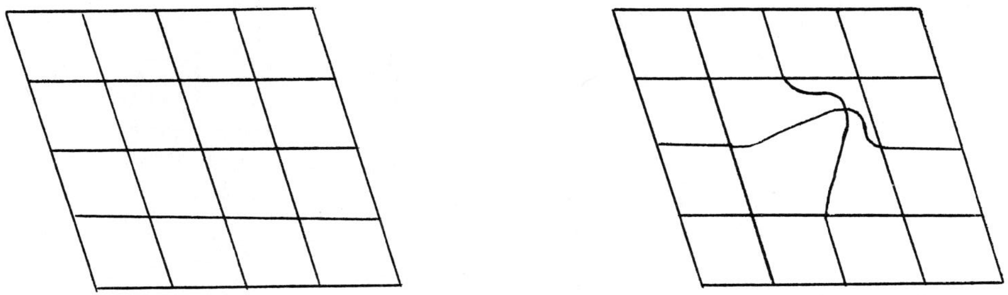

FIGURE 5 - LOCAL NODE MODIFICATION

(M.P. Carroll, D. Hoitsma; A Mini-Based Sculptured Surface System)

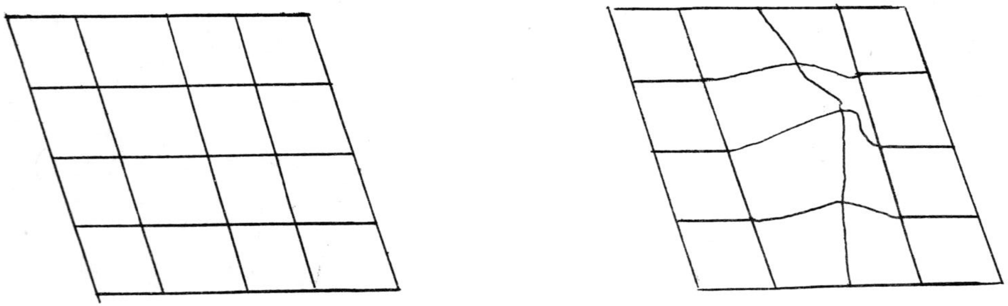

FIGURE 6 - RESPLINE NODE MODIFICATION

(M.P. Carroll, D. Hoitsma; A Mini-Based Sculptured Surface System)

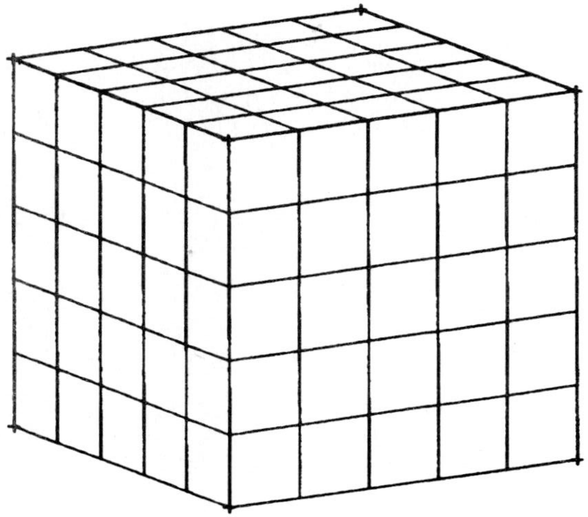

FIGURE 7 - BOX-LIKE SURFACE

(M.P. Carroll, D. Hoitsma; A Mini-Based Sculptured Surface System)

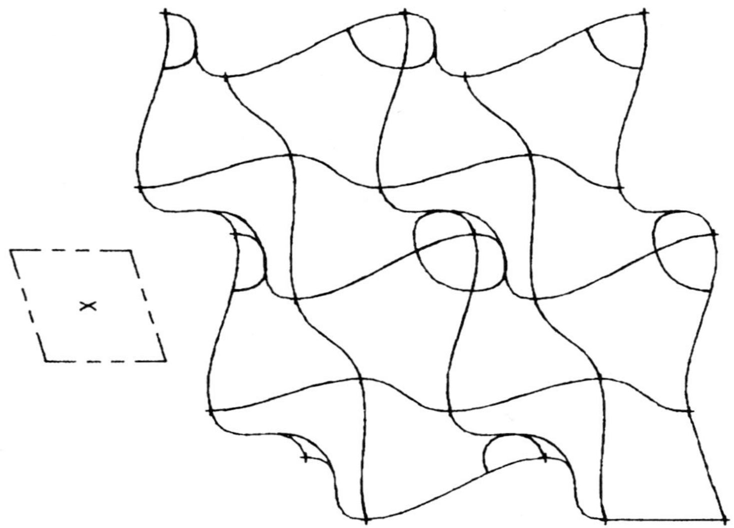

<u>FIGURE 8 - SECTION CUT</u>

(M.P. Carroll, D. Hoitsma; <u>A Mini-Based Sculptured Surface System</u>)

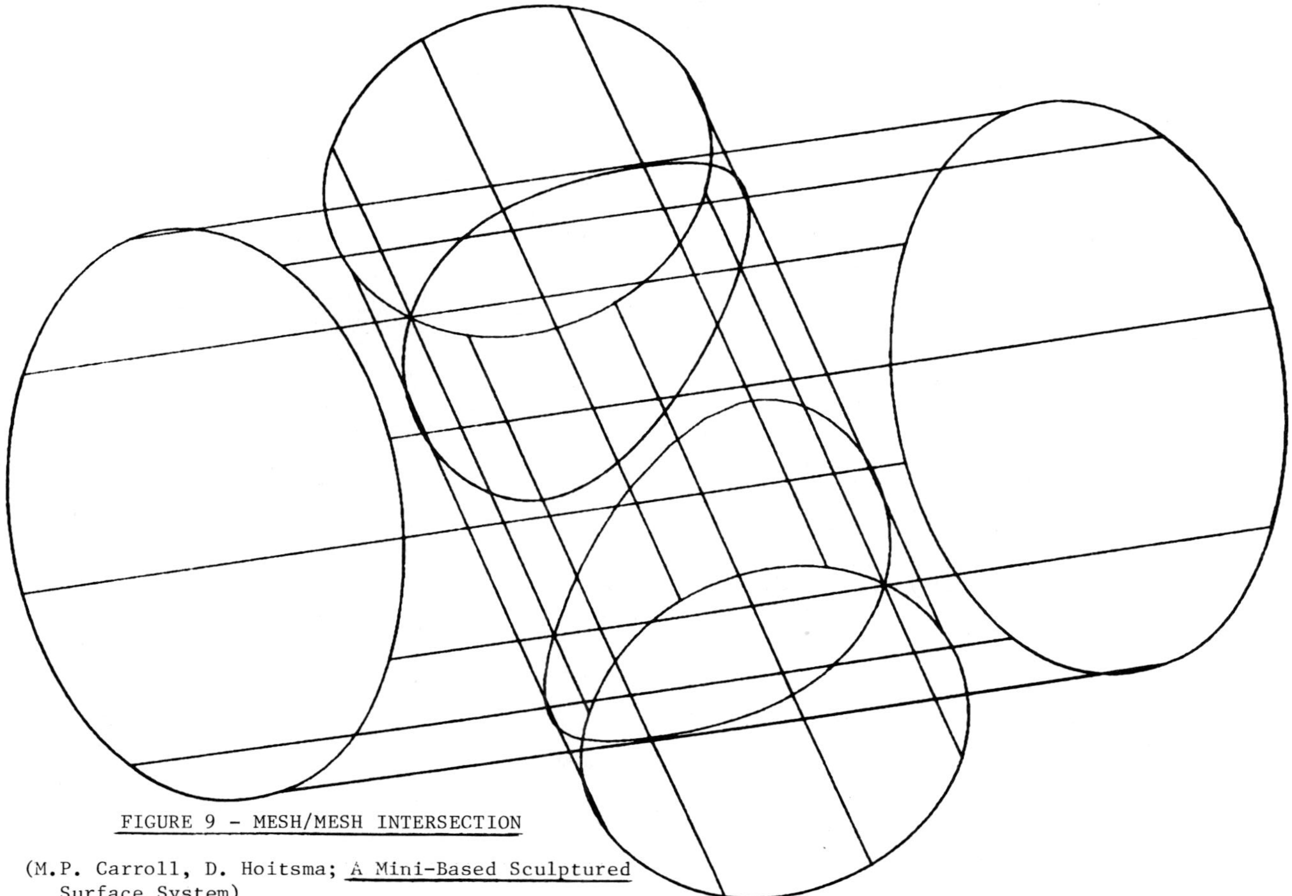

FIGURE 9 - MESH/MESH INTERSECTION

(M.P. Carroll, D. Hoitsma; *A Mini-Based Sculptured Surface System*)

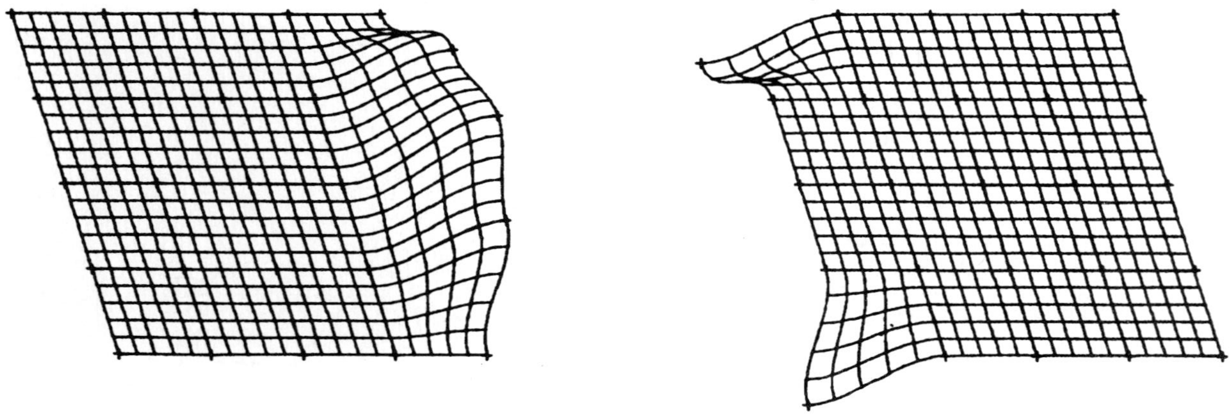

FIGURE 10A- MESH-BLENDING

(M.P. Carroll, D. Hoitsma; A Mini-Based Sculptured Surface System)

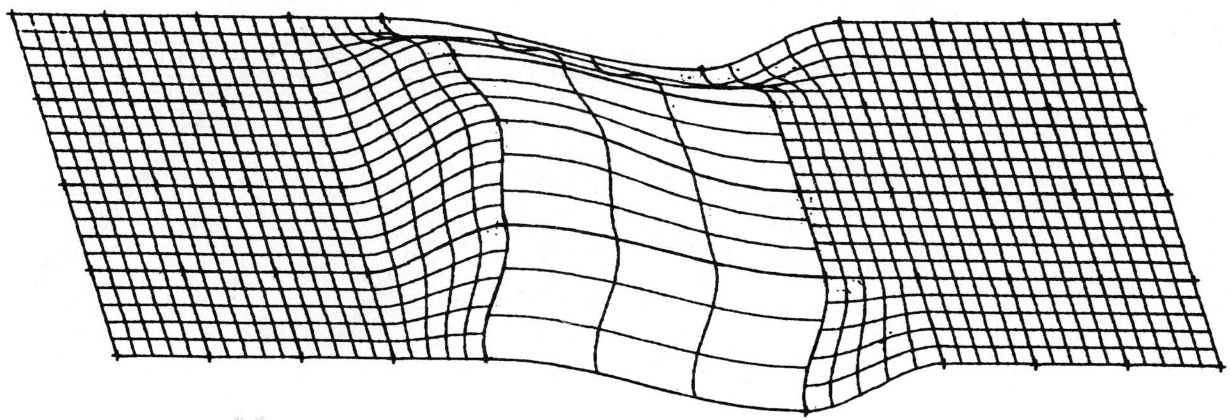

FIGURE 10B- MESH-BLENDING

(M.P. Carroll, D. Hoitsma; A Mini-Based Sculptured Surface System)

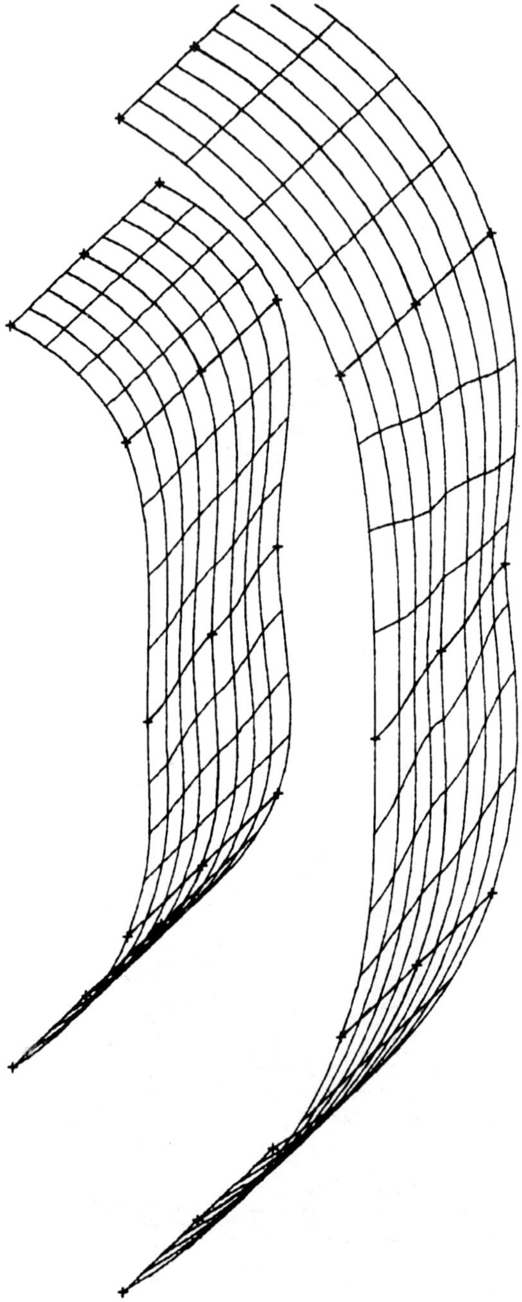

FIGURE 11 - OFFSET SURFACE

(M.P. Carroll, D. Hoitsma; A Mini-Based Sculptured Surface System)

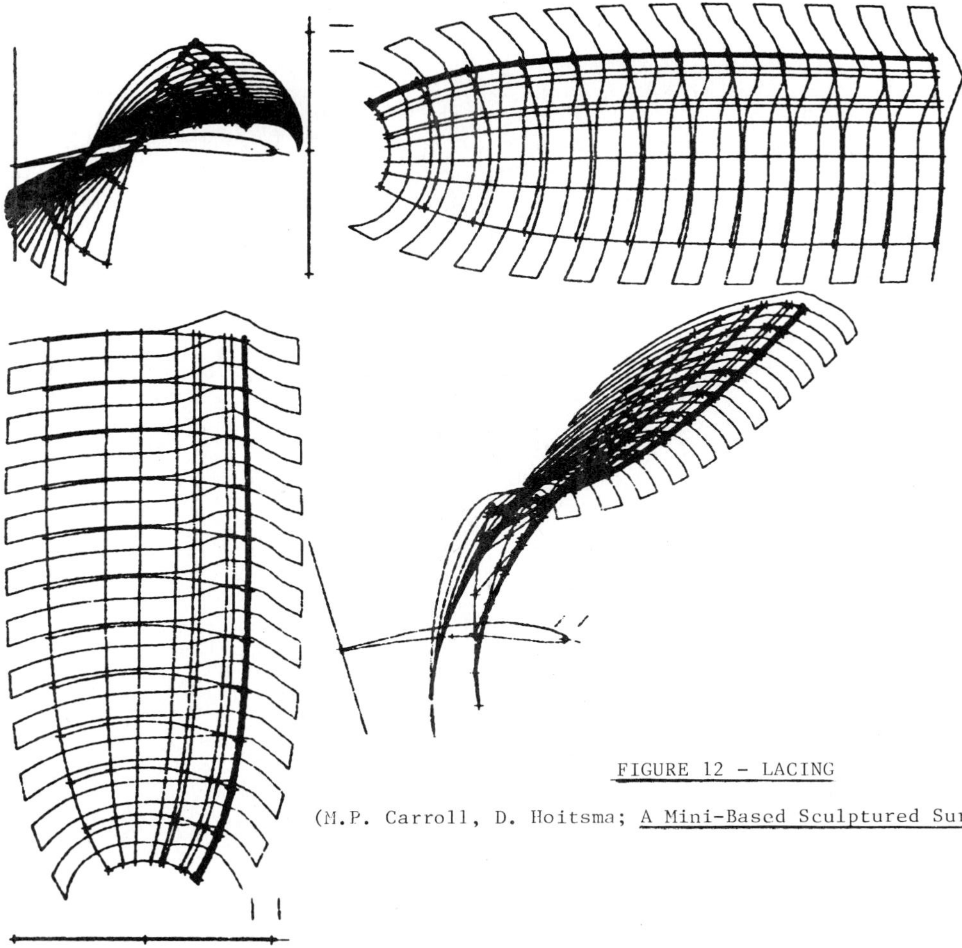

FIGURE 12 - LACING

(M.P. Carroll, D. Hoitsma; A Mini-Based Sculptured Surface System)

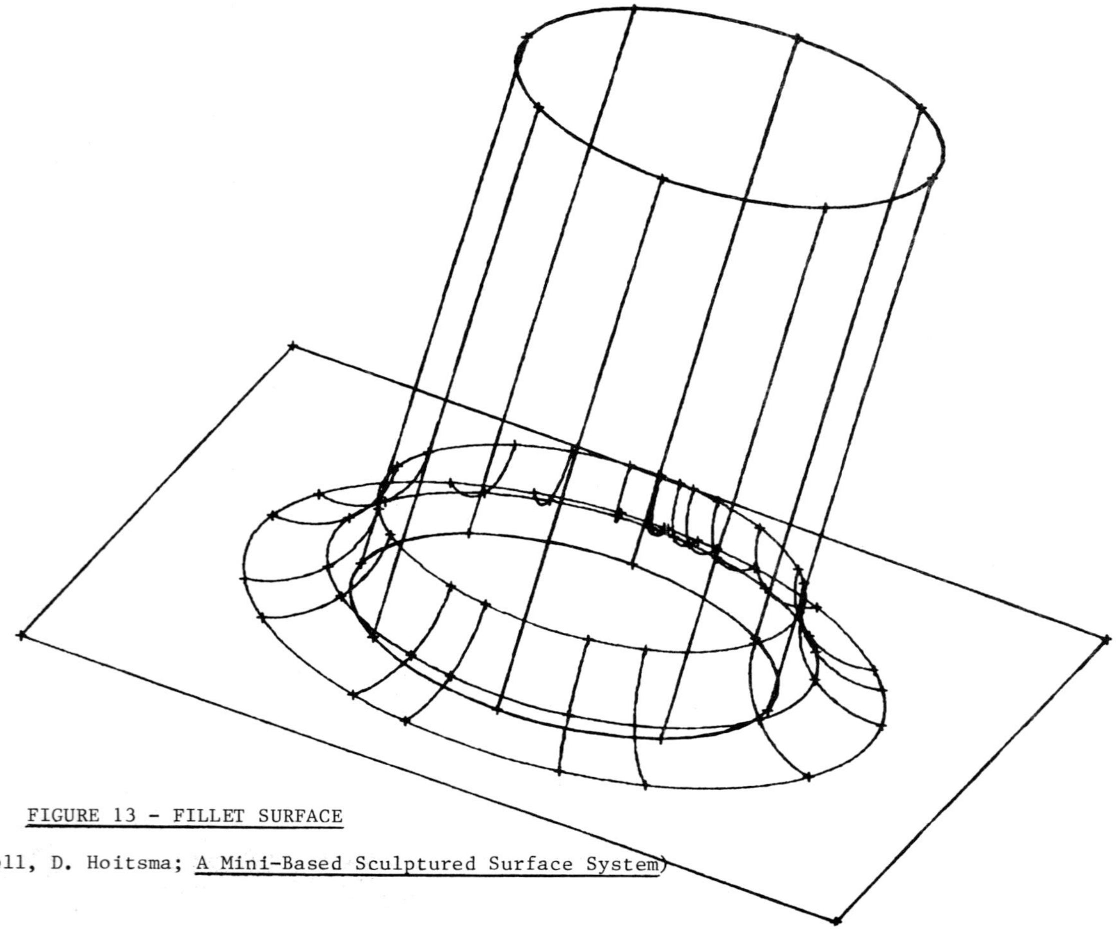

FIGURE 13 - FILLET SURFACE

(M.P. Carroll, D. Hoitsma; A Mini-Based Sculptured Surface System)

the finite element program NISA; the interactive graphics program DISPLAY/DIGIT and the modal synthesis program SAMS for HP/1000

Dr. Kant S. Kothawala

President
Engineering Mechanics Research Corporation
P. O. Box 696
Troy, Michigan 48099

NISA is a general purpose finite element program for analyzing actual problems encountered in civil, mechanical and offshore engineering enviornments and in the automotive and aerospace industries. Analysis capabilities include very diverse and exhausive features in Static, Dynamic, Steady State and Transient Heat Transfer and Field problems. Element types available include isoparametric linear and parabolic, for plane stress, plane strain, axisymmetric (with symmetric or unsymmetric loading), general shells, laminated composite or sandwich shells, thick shells, solids, beams, spars, springs, mass elements, and rigid elements. The extensive library of elements and post-processing capabilities (displacement & stress contours, mode shapes etc.) in NISA allows one to solve a wide variety of structures.

DISPLAY/DIGIT is an interactive software that uses the latest state-of-the-art graphics techniques to create finite element 2–D or 3–D models from drawings, generate mesh automatically and modify errors by viewing and listing element and node point data. The structure may be sectioned, windowed, rotated, scaled and sorted by element or material type before plotting. Multiple views may be displayed on the screen, and hidden lines may be eliminated.

The program SAMS predicts the dynamic performance of large complex structures. Each component of the total system is modelled independently by either finite element or experimental method. The dynamic characteristics of each component is then assembled and solved in the total system equation to obtain the frequency responses at the desired stations. Design modifications can be easily and quickly analyzed by this method to achieve the optimum dynamic performance of the structure.

NISA:

Numerically Integrated Elements for Systems Analysis (NISA) is a general purpose program for analyzing actual problems encountered in civil, mechanical and offshore engineering environments and in the automotive and aerospace industries. Analysis capabilities include very diverse and exhaustive features in Static, Dynamic, Steady State and Transient Heat Transfer and Field problems. Element types available include isoparametric linear, and higher order elements for plane stress, plane strain, axisymmetric (with symmetric or unsymmetric loading), general shells, laminated composite or sandwich shells, thick shells, solids, beams, spars, springs, mass elements, and rigid elements. The extensive library of elements in NISA allows one to solve any size or shape of the structure. NISA offers the advantages of simplified data preparation in free format, comprehensive graphics capabilities for creation, automatic generation and verification of finite element models, and numerous output options. NISA has been designed to be machine independent and is available on most other computers.

NISA is perhaps the first large general purpose program implemented on HP 1000. The largest NISA job that can run at present on HP 1000 is with maximum wavefront of 400. For larger jobs having a wavefront of more than 400, many organization who has availability of mainframe computer system (IBM, CDC, Univac, Honeywell, Amdahl etc.) can process the NISA pre- processing on HP 1000 conveniently and submit the NISA job to the mainframe computer available for final execution. NISA post-processing can again be done easily on HP 1000.

In the text that follows all capabilities marked with ** are under process of being converted on HP1000 and will be made available in near future for usage on HP1000. However since these capabilities are available on most other computers, pre- and post - processing can be conveniently done on HP 1000. Thus the present restriction of NISA on HP1000 of problem size or capability can be overcome whenever mainframe computers are available.

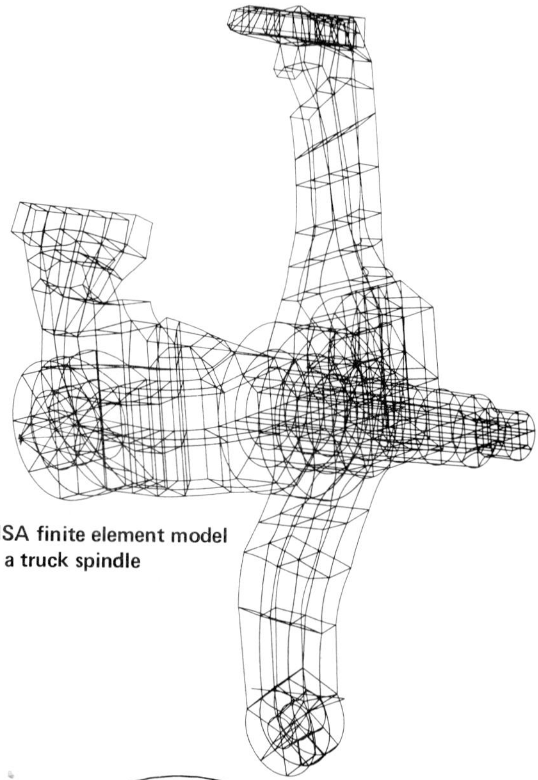

NISA finite element model of a truck spindle

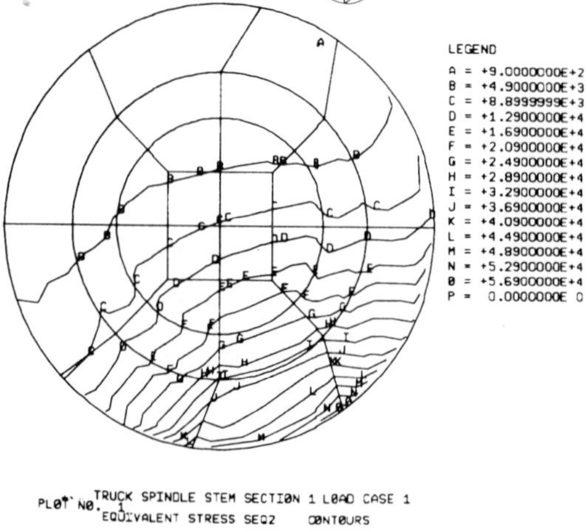

- *Wavefront check*

NISA uses the wavefront method of solution which allows arbitrary assignment of node numbering. However,for computational efficiency, elements have to be arranged for the optimum wavefront. The pre-processing program NISAWFR automatically minimize and/or checks the wavefront. It also minimizes the wavefront using a user specified sequence. The NISA program itself also checks the wavefront and/or executes the job after checking the wavefront.

- *Simple Nodal Location*

Only three coordinate components are required for any node point (X,Y,Z or R,θ,Z or R,θ,Φ) including curved shells.

- *Automatic Generation*

NISA's input structure lends itself to generation of input data through commands designed to duplicate already entered elements or sets of elements. At the first level, element node numbers are incremented by a fixed number to generate a string of elements. The resulting element group can then be used to generate, by command, any number of additional element groups to complete the model. The generation capabilities of the program are further extended for boundary conditions, external forces and face pressures. Repetitive data can be specified in a very neat and compact form.

- *Choice of Coordinate System*

Nodal coordinates can be described in the cartesian, cylindrical or spherical system. Also accomodated is the user-specified local orthogonal system. Ultimately, NISA transforms all coordinate data to the global cartesian system. Rotated coordinate system can also be established whenever it is desirable to input displacements and forces in directions other than the global coordinate directions.

TYPES OF LOADING

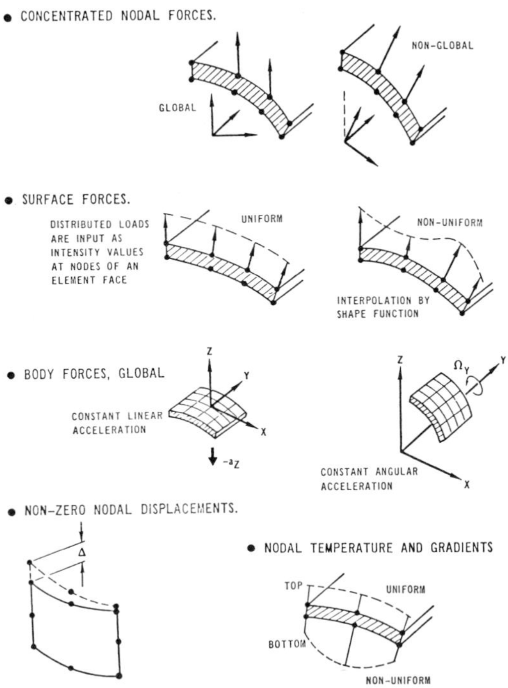

GENERATION OF NODES AND ELEMENTS

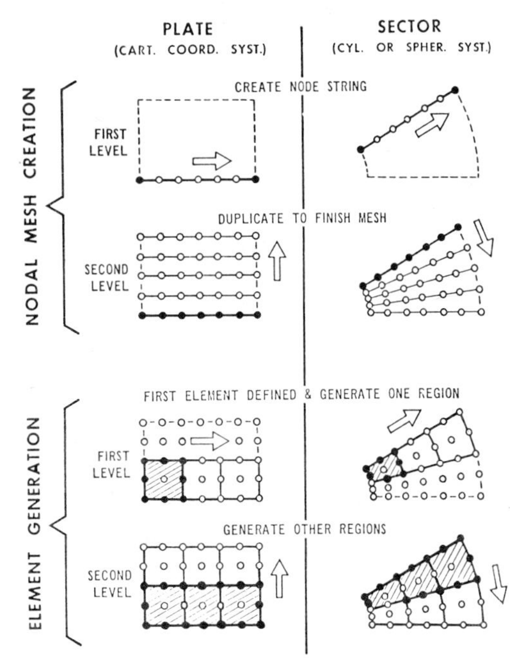

• *Shell to solid conversion*

Finite element models constructed of flat or curved shell elements of constant or varying thickness can be converted into an equivalent 8, 16, or 20 node solid elements model using NISASSC program. This way one can make a shell model of a three dimensional solid structure by representing the model by its midsurface only and convert it to the desired solid model of varying thickness. Also many design changes due to changes in the thickness of the structure can be readily accomplished by NISASSC.

• *Material Properties*

Temperature dependent material properties can be specified for static, dynamic, and heat transfer analysis. Isotropic, orthotropic and anisotropic (layered or sandwich composite) properties can be specified for all elements of NISA element library for static and dynamic analysis. NISA has a unique feature for specifying orthotropic material properties. Orthotropic material may be specified on the global level or the element level. The direction of orthotropy may be different for each element or each node.

• *Data Checking*

In addition to the interactive graphics programs to verify and check the model, a set of comprehensive data checks is also available in a pre-processing program NISAICE. Improper format, illegal operation, incomplete data can all be detected. Crosschecks are also performed. Elements are checked for repeated or negative node numbers, missing coordinates and unreasonable distortions. The length, area or volume of an element and its total mass are also computed. Geometry plotting can also be done at data checking level. Checks of data during execution are also available in NISA itself and it gives appropriate error messages before abnormal termination.

NISA AXISYMMETRIC ELEMENTS FOR NON–AXISYMMETRIC LOADING

One of the most powerful capabilities of the NISA program is that NISA has elements which can be used to model non-axisymmetrically loaded axisymmetric structures.

The modelling and computer time required to analyze a structure using these elements is typically 1/10th that required for solving the same structure using 3–D solid elements. This is because:

★ Such axisymmetric elements have fewer degrees of freedom.

★ The 2–D axisymmetric finite element model has a drastically reduced wavefront or bandwidth compared to the 3–D solid model.

★ An axisymmetric model using these elements also requires much less computer memory than the solid model. Thus, turn around time is much reduced and one can often make several daytime runs in lieu of a single overnight run on crowded data centers.

PROBLEM : HOLLOW CIRCULAR CYLINDER SUBJECTED TO NON-AXISYMMETRIC LOADING

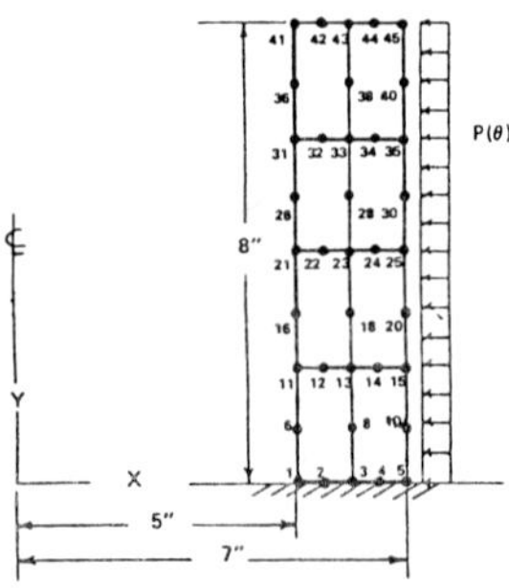

2–D MODEL

Eight 8-node axisymmetric elements for non-axisymmetric loading model.

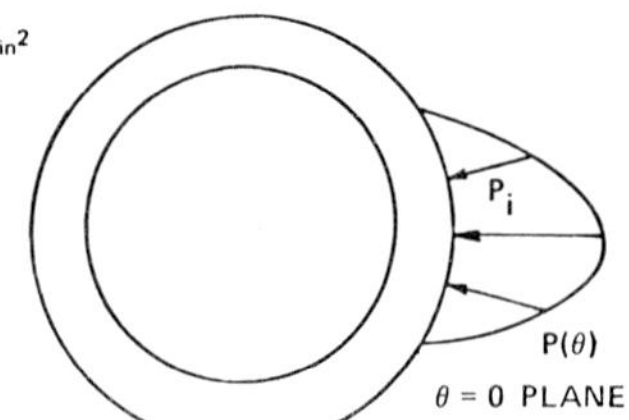

TOP VIEW

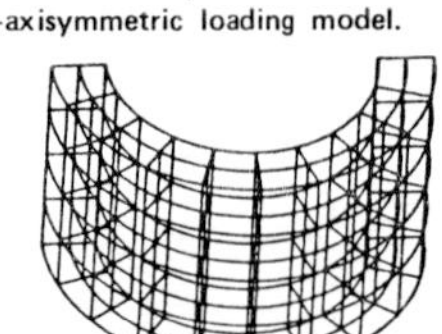

3–D MODEL

Eighty 20 - node solid elements model.

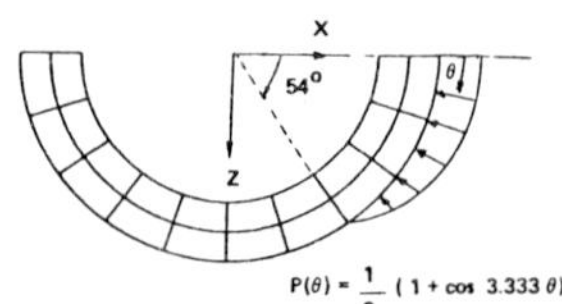

TOP VIEW

COMPARISON OF RESULTS OF A 3–D SOLID MODEL VS 2–D MODEL

	2–D MODEL	3–D MODEL
NO. OF ELEMENTS	8	80
NO. OF NODES	37	577
TOTAL D.O.F	111	1731
MAX. WAVEFRONT	30	153
CPU SECOND (PRIME500)	197.85	2661.9 sec.

VON MISES EQUIVALENT STRESS AT NODES (1, 2, 3, 4, 5)

AT ANGLE	ELEMENT TYPE	NODAL POINTS STRESS (PSI)				
		1	2	3	4	5
0°	AXIS	7197.0	4815.0	4075.0	8160.0	12487.0
	3–D SOLID	7309.0	5232.0	5052.0	7970.0	11948.0
18°	AXIS	6530.0	4401.0	3529.0	6630.0	10157.0
	3–D SOLID	6499.0	4624.0	4243.0	6454.0	9688.0
90°	AXIS	2005.0	1778.0	1973.0	2827.0	3864.0
	3–D SOLID	2009.0	1828.0	2032.0	2729.0	3722.0
180°	AXIS	111.0	90.03	94.25	125.6	168.9
	3–D SOLID	125.2	101.7	98.25	123.4	176.0

ANALYTIC CAPABILITIES

NISA employs a highly efficient, wavefront solution method for solving static, dynamic, and heat transfer problems. The inherent advantages of this method are:

★ Arbitrary assignment of node numbering

★ Economic processing of multiple load cases

★ Resolution of decomposed stiffness matrix

■ STATIC AND HARMONIC ANALYSIS

Forces, displacements and stresses in a given structure due to body forces, concentrated forces, pressures, temperature and centrifugal forces, can be obtained. Multiple load cases can be done in a single run. The results can be obtained either in global or in rotated coordinate system.

- *Boundary Conditions*

Boundary conditions accomodated fall into three principal categories: Specified nodal displacements (zero or non-zero), coupled displacements (two or more nodal displacements are specified equal), and multi-point constraints (specified degrees of freedom are related linearly in a general manner). The coupled displacement feature can also be used to introduce releases, such as pin or ball joints, within a structure. Multi-point constraint equations are generated automatically for rigid elements.

- *Special Features*

  ★ Substructure analysis **

  ★ Geometrical stiffness (stress stiffening effect)

  ★ Coupled displacements (two or more nodal displacements specified equal)

  ★ Multipoint constraints **

  ★ Rigid Elements **

  ★ Capabilities to simulate gaps, interfaces (breaking of contacts after application of loading) including friction; and compression only or tension only members **

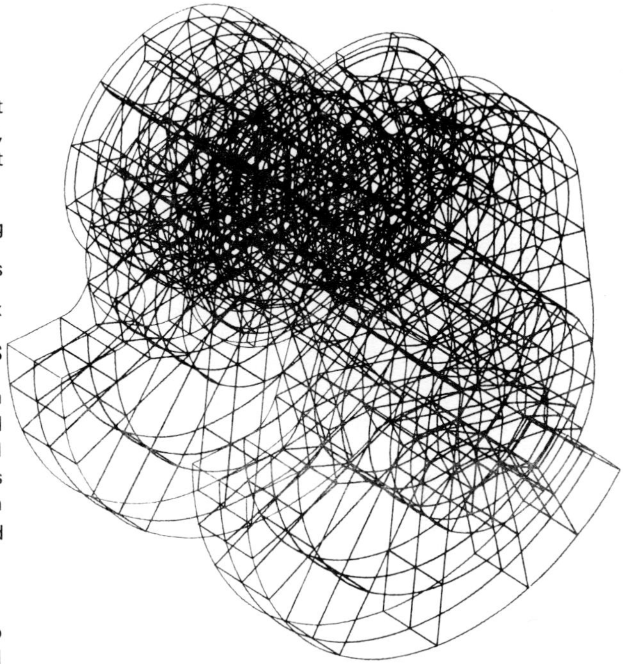

NISA Finite Element model of one throw of a four cylinder crank shaft using 20 node isoparametric solids

NISA SHELL ELEMENT COMPARISON

A McAuto comparison study of all structural engineering programs on their computer systems in respect to shell elements and the NISA shell element (general shell & super shell are provided)

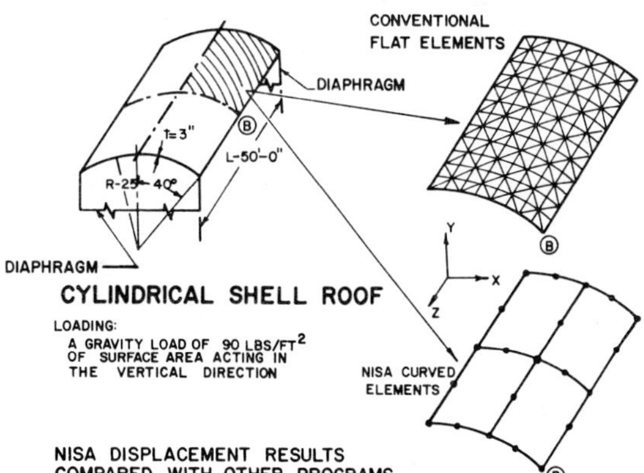

NISA DISPLACEMENT RESULTS COMPARED WITH OTHER PROGRAMS

	TYPE OF ELEMENT	NUMBER OF ELEMENTS	TOTAL DOF	UY DELF. AT Ⓑ	% ERROR	COST RATIO	MACH. USED
EXACT	–	–	–	3.703	–	–	–
<u>NISA</u>	SUPR-SHL	4	87	3.674	–.7	1.00	IBM 168
NISA	GNL–SHL	4	126	3.532	–4.6	1.10	IBM 168
ANSYS	STIFF-63	24	210	3.677	–0.9	1.21	CYB 74
NASTRAN	CQUAD4	25	216	3.769	1.8	1.55	CYB 74
SAP 4	P/S QUAD	96	613	3.403	–8.6	1.07	CYB 74
STRUDL	PBSQ2/PBST2	96 / 192	702	3.306	–10.9	3.22	IBM 168
DANUTA	3D–BRICK	20	720	3.726	.6	3.59	CYB 74

★ Rotated local coordinate system can be specified at nodes to apply loads and boundary conditions in any arbitrary direction

★ Use of a combination of rotated local coordinate system and coupled displacements to create cyclic symmetric effect

★ Extensive restart capabilities

★ Extensive capabilities to simulate sandwich or layered composite structures

★ Simulation of axisymmetric structure for unsymmetric loading using the most accurate and efficient library of linear, parabolic, cubic and combination elements (see NISA element library)

- STATIC OUTPUT – PRINTED

NISA offers a number of output options to meet individual needs. The user may, at his discretion, select only a few of the options and select additional output through a restart after the displacement solution. Options are:

★ Displacements (in global or local directions)

★ Internal forces and strain energy

★ Reactions (in global or local direction)

★ Gauss point and node point stress in the local coordinate system and the direction cosines of the local axes

★ Global stresses at gauss points and node points

★ Average nodal stresses (Global)

★ Principal stresses with direction cosines

★ Maximum shearing stress

★ Von Mises equivalent stress

★ Octahedral shearing stress

★ Tabulation of nodes, in ascending order, outside a specified stress range

OUTSTANDING PERFORMANCE OF NISA SUPER SHELL ELEMENTS

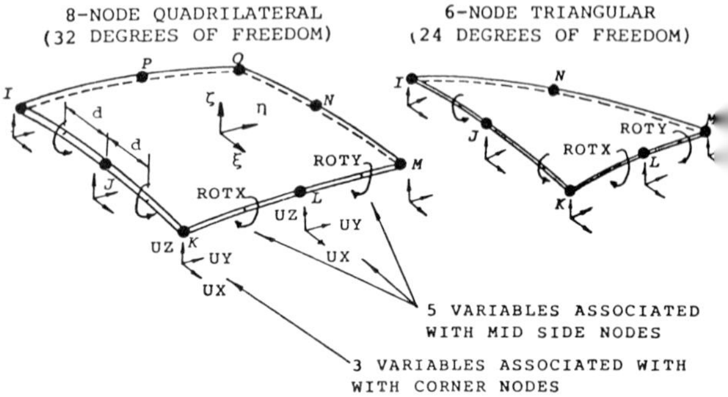

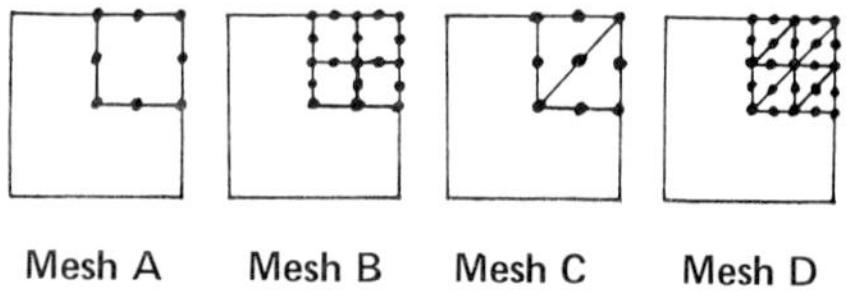

MAXIMUM DEFLECTION AT CENTER OF PLATE

TIMOSHENKO	MESH A	MESH B	MESH C	MESH D
0.00406	0.00409	0.004046	0.004062	0.004046

UNIFORMLY LOADED SIMPLY SUPPORTED SQUARE PLATE ANALYZED USING SUPER SHELL ELEMENTS

OUTSTANDING ADVANTAGES

★ It is the latest and best doubly curved thin shell element compared to all plate or shell elements of ANSYS, NASTRAN, SAP, STARDYNE, STRUDL Programs

★ It satisfies all the convergence criteria

★ It can easily and efficiently model any thin shell structures, including those with sharp corners and multiple junctions (branches).

★ Unlike most other shell elements it has no dummy inplane rotational degrees of freedom. Consequently;

a) It has less variables per element, (for the same degree of accuracy). This also means smaller wavefront and fewer variables, to solve (32 DOF for quadrilateral and 24 DOF for triangular elements)

b) No need for the user to constrain the inplane rotation at nodes surrounded by coplanar or nearly coplanar elements.

★ Elements exclusive to NISA only (amongst all commercially available programs in U.S.A.)

• STATIC OUTPUT – GRAPHICS

NISA provides a complete graphics package to help the user develop and check out the model, and to display output in the most convenient form for each analysis type. Plotting options available are:

GEOMETRY PLOTTING

★ Element plotting(2D and 3D)

★ Arbitrary viewing direction

★ Total or partial model plotting based on constrained volume

★ Selective element plotting according to element number range or element type

★ Plotting the following in any combin– ation: symbols at node, nodal point numbers, element numbers

★ Plot material ID and/or element type

★ Concentrated mass display

POST PLOTTING

★ Deformed structure plotting (option to plot all mesh lines or only boundaries)

★ Displacement contour plots

★ Stress contour plots for components of stress tensor, principal stresses, Von Mises, octahedral and maximum shear stresses

★ Stress survey plot for composite shell – most critical stress ratio in each element is printed, as a percentage, on a plot of the undeformed geometry

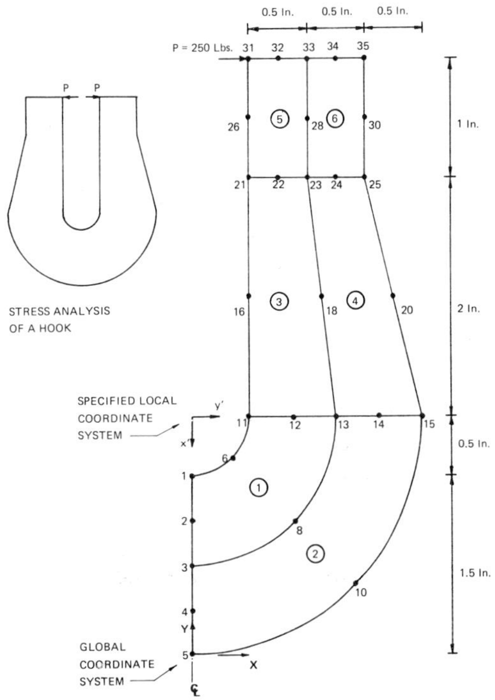

Figure B.1. NISA Static Analysis Example

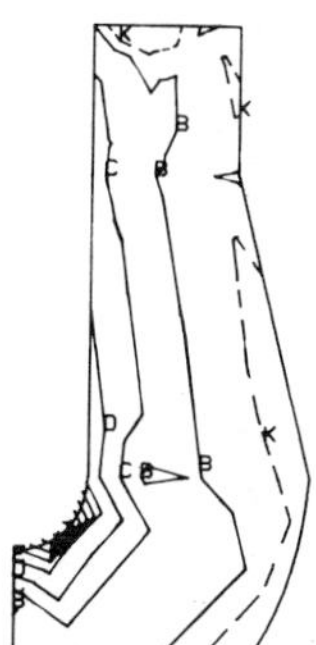

LEGEND
A = -3.9541726E+3
B = +2.2096897E+3
C = +8.3735520E+3
D = +1.4537414E+4
E = +2.0701277E+4
F = +2.6865139E+4
G = +3.3029001E+4
H = +3.9192863E+4
I = +4.5356726E+4
J = +5.1520588E+4
K = 0.0000000E 0

NISA STATIC ANALYSIS EXAMPLE
PLØT NØ. 4
S2 CØNTØURS

CONTOURS OF MAXIMUM PRINCIPAL STRESSES

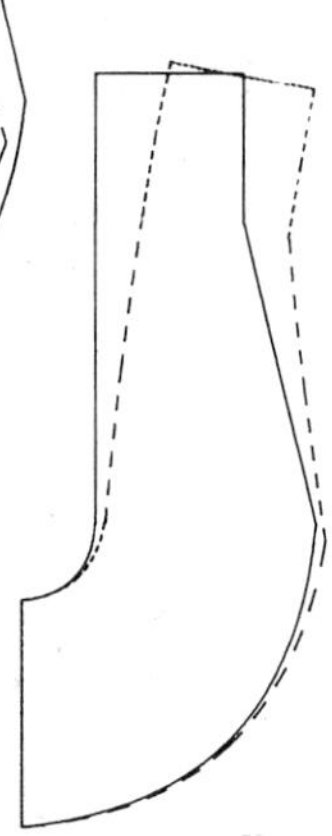

NISA STATIC ANALYSIS EXAMPLE
PLØT NØ. 1
DEFØRMED STRUCTURE

DEFORMED GEOMETRY PLOT
SUPERIMPOSING BOUNDARIES ONLY

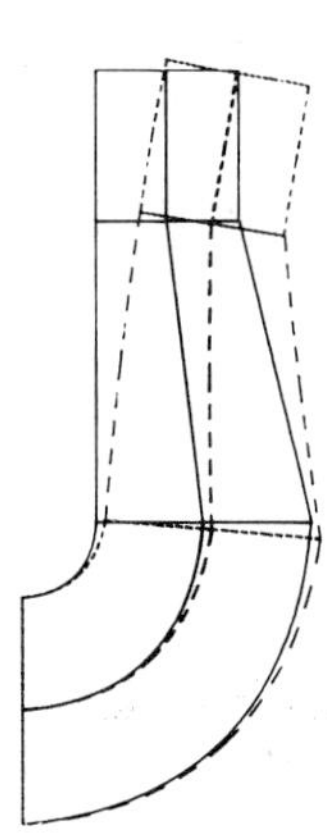

NISA STATIC ANALYSIS EXAMPLE
PLØT NØ. 2
DEFØRMED STRUCTURE

DEFORMED GEOMETRY PLOT
SUPERIMPOSING ENTIRE MESH

■ DYNAMIC ANALYSIS

NISA has most outstanding capabilities to solve a wide variety of problems encountered in dynamic analysis. It uses the wavefront technique with the obvious advantage that it can handle large problems efficiently and accurately.

- *Eigenvalue and Eigenvector Extraction Techniques:*

NISA provides three different solution techniques to find the natural frequencies and corresponding mode shapes of a given structure. All these three techniques are well proven as very efficient and accurate to solve for a large number of frequencies and mode shapes.

- *Subspace Iteration:*

This method is an out of core solution technique. It is used to extract the natural frequencies which lie between zero and the upper frequency limit as specified by the user. This technique is very efficient to extract the first few natural frequencies.

- *Inverse Iteration with Sturm Sequence:*

This method can be used to extract eigenvalues within an arbitrary range bounded by the cut off frequencies supplied by the user. A user specified number of frequencies at the low end of this range is calculated. The method first isolates each eigenvalue by means of Sturm sequence - based bisection process and then applies inverse iteration technique.

- *QR – Householder:*

This method is an in - core solution technique which is very fast for small size problems. It gives all eigenvalues and eigenvectors of a given structure. For large size problems, this method can be used in conjunction with Guyan reduction.

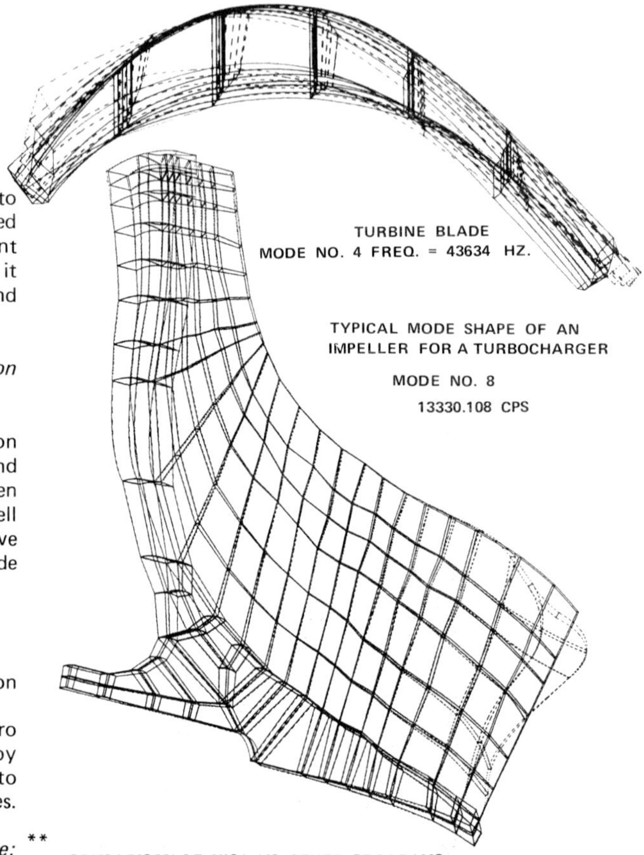

TURBINE BLADE
MODE NO. 4 FREQ. = 43634 HZ.

TYPICAL MODE SHAPE OF AN IMPELLER FOR A TURBOCHARGER
MODE NO. 8
13330.108 CPS

**

COMPARISON OF NISA VS OTHER PROGRAMS FOR NATURAL FREQUENCIES AND MODE SHAPES

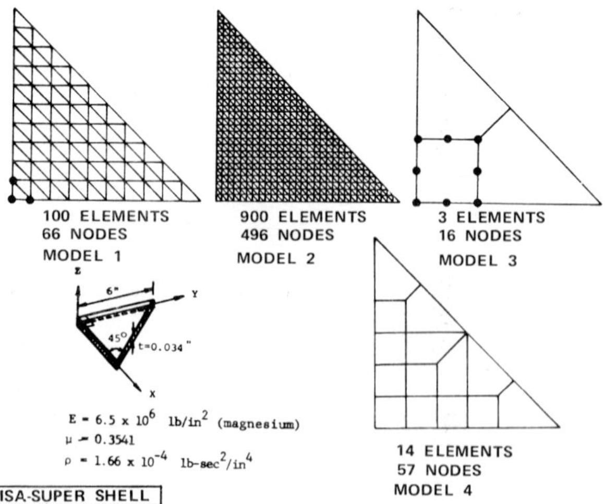

Frequency (HZ)	NASTRAN		ANSYS	NISA-SUPER SHELL	
	Model 1	Model 2	Model 1	Model 3	Model 4
1	55.6	55.9	55.9	54.27	55.76
2	205.5	210.8	210.9	215.41	209.50
3	283.2	292.1	293.5	303.69	289.80

NATURAL FREQUENCIES OF A CANTILEVER TRIANGULAR PLATE

- *Guyan Reduction:*

The size of the original structural problem can be reduced by specifying a set of master degrees of freedom which will characterize the structure properly. After reducing the size of the problem, the program follows the QR – Householder algorithm. The user has the option to allow the program to select the master degrees of freedom or to specify those master degrees of freedom which he considers as representing the true character of the system or can exercise both of these options at the same time.

- *Transient Dynamic Analysis:*

This can be used to find the response of the structure (displacements, velocities, accelerations and stresses) to dynamic loads which may be of the following forms:

  ★ Time dependent concentrated nodal forces

  ★ Time dependent pressure loads which may be uniformly distributed or any other variation as specified by nodal intensities.

  ★ Base excitation

- *Shock Spectrum Analysis:* **

To find RMS response of structures subjected to arbitrarily oriented base shocks. The input to the structure is the maximum response (Displacements, velocity or acceleration) of a single degree of freedom system subjected to the same base shock for various natural frequencies of the single degree of freedom system

- *Digital Calculation of Response Spectra from Earthquake Records:*

This program is an aid to the shock spectrum analysis. The raw data of an earthquake record is used as an input and the output is obtained for the spectral values of displacement, velocity and acceleration defined over a frequency range or natural period range for each specified critical damping coefficient.

VERIFICATION PROBLEM

TITLE: Transient response of a cylindrical tube to a suddenly applied load.

ELEMENT TYPE: Axisymmetric parabolic elements

PROBLEM: A simply supported cylindrical tube is subjected to a suddenly applied load as shown below. Compute the natural frequencies and the time history response of the cylindrical tube.

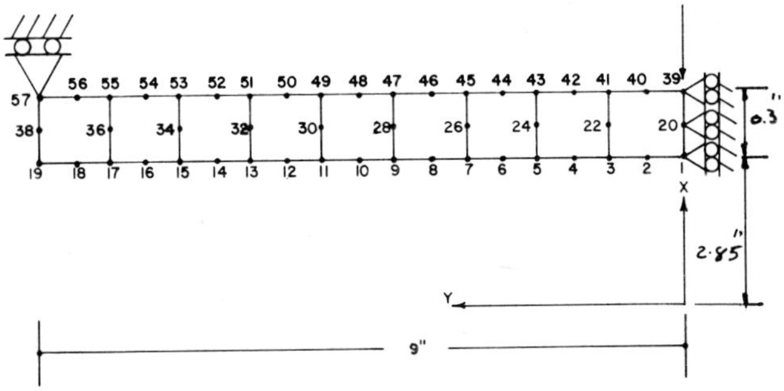

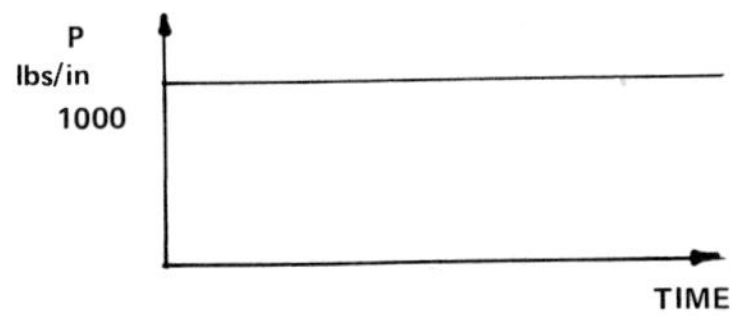

FORCE – TIME HISTORY

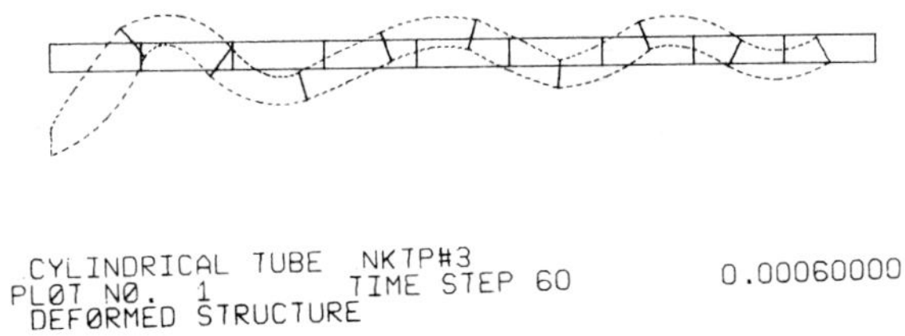

Mode number	Natural Frequency (cycles/sec)	
	NISA	SAP4
1	782.3	781.9
2	1480.0	1472.0
3	1532.2	1520.0
4	1616.9	1601.0
5	1618.8	1609.0
6	1795.2	1775.0
7	2103.8	2070.0
8	2568.2	2492.0
9	2569.4	2556.0
10	3214.3	3032.0

- *Frequency Response Analysis:*

To find the steady state response of a structure subjected to harmonic loads of constant frequency and varying phase angles and amplitudes. The amplitude and phase angles are defined by spectrum curves over frequency range of interest. Also the actual response at user specified phase angles and frequencies can be determined.

- *Random Vibration Analysis:*

The analysis employs matrix methods to calculate statistical measurements of response (displacement, velocity, acceleration and stress) for complex structures subjected to random loads of earthquake excitations, forces, pressures and torques.

- *Boundary Conditions:*

Same as in STATIC Analysis

- *Special Features:*

Same as in STATIC Analysis

- DYNAMICS -- OUTPUT PRINTED AND GRAPHICS

Same as in STATIC plus the following additional features

★ Eigenvalues (natural frequencies) and Eigenvectors (mode shapes)

★ Node point displacement, velocity and acceleration vs time

★ Mode shape plotting

★ Stresses and displacements printed at specified time intervals

★ Displacement and stress contour plotting at specified time intervals

★ Deformed structure plotting at specified time intervals

★ Stress survey plots for composite shells at specified time intervals

TRANSIENT RESPONSE OF A CYLINDRICAL TUBE

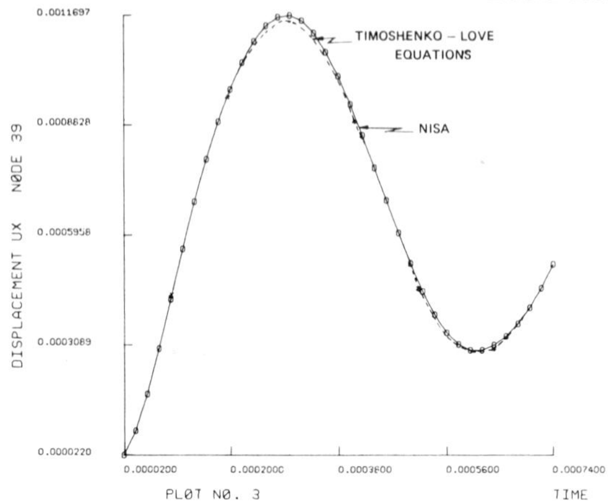

DISPLACEMENT HISTORY RESPONSE OF NODE 39

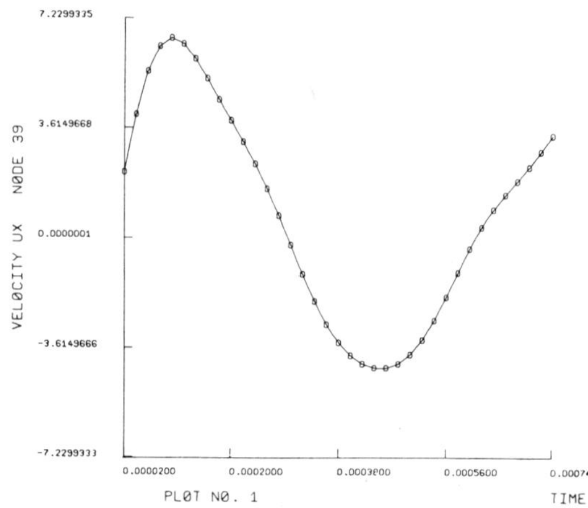

VELOCITY HISTORY RESPONSE OF NODE 39

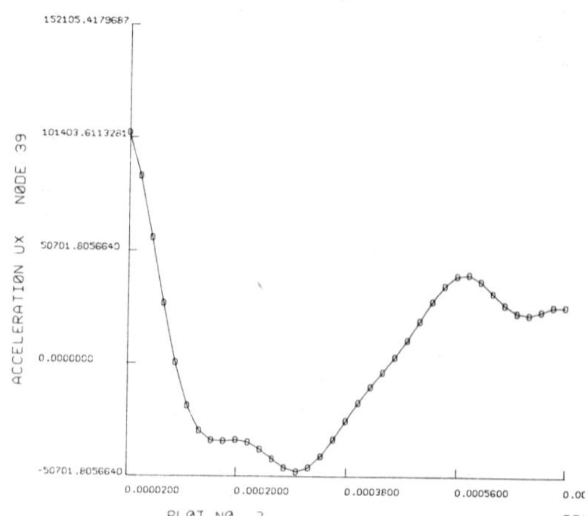

ACCELERATION HISTORY RESPONSE OF NODE 39

★ *Random Vibration:* **

RMS displacements, velocities, accelerations and stresses

Printout and/or plots of PSD (power spectral density) of displacement, velocity and acceleration vs frequency of selected degrees of freedom

★ *Frequency Response:* **

Steady state displacements, velocities, accelerations and phase angles at specified frequencies of excitation

Plots of actual displacements, velocities, accelerations and stresses at specified phase angles and frequencies

Plots of frequency vs phase angle, frequency vs steady state displacements, velocities and accelerations

★ *Shock Spectrum:* **

Generalized displacements, velocities and accelerations

Option to print RMS (Square root of the sum of the squares of the modal responses), PRMS (Maximum absolute modal response added to RMS of remaining modal responses) and PEAK (sum of absolute values of modal responses) responses for displacements, velocities and acceleration

Option to print modal components of RMS, PRMS and PEAK responses for displacements, velocities and accelerations of selected participating modes

Option to print RMS, PRMS and PEAK stresses of the elements of the finite element model

Option to print modal components of RMS, PRMS and PEAK stresses of the elements of the finite element model for the participating modes

NISA RANDOM VIBRATION ANALYSIS (NISARVA)

NISARVA program can be used to analyze the response of a multi degree of freedom linear elastic system subjected to stationary ergodic random excitation. Only the loading functions are assumed to be random. The technique for solving random vibration problems is based on modal analysis. The program will compute the nodal RMS displacements, velocities and accelerations. The power spectral density curves can be obtained at selected nodal degrees of freedom and the stresses for each NISA element type can also be obtained.

A cantilever solid beam shown below is subjected to a random loading at nodes 206 and 208 in the Z direction. The PSD versus frequency of the loading is given in Table 2.

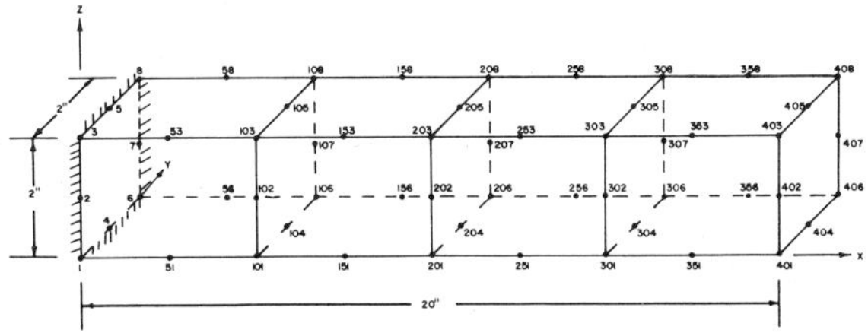

A comparison of the RMS displacement at the end of the cantilever with STARDYNE is given below.

	NISA	STARDYNE
RMS displacement at node 408 in Z direction	0.02005	0.02013

TABLE 2: RANDOM LOADING

Frequency (HZ)	PSD Value (lb^2/HZ)
0.1	0.3
250.0	0.3

SHOCK SPECTRUM ANALYSIS OF A THREE–STORY FRAME

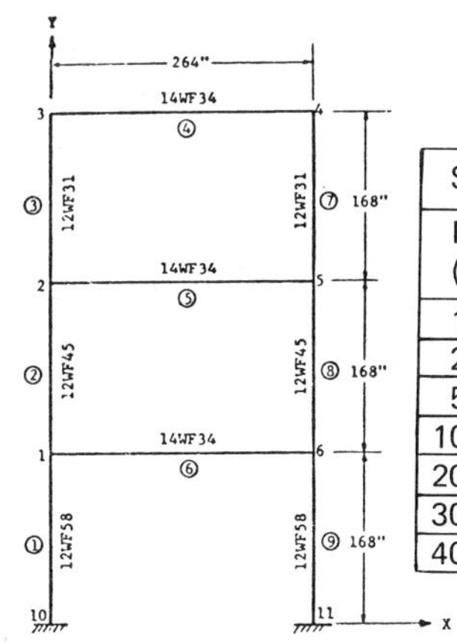

Shock Spectrum Loading	
Frequency (CPS)	Acceleration (FT/SEC^2)
1	27.646
2	50.265
5	62.832
10	50.265
20	25.133
30	3.7699
40	2.5133

Elastic Modulus = 30×10^6 psi
Poisson's Ratio = 0.3
Mass Density = .000735 $lb\text{-}sec^2/in^4$

NODE	UX		UY		ROTZ	
	NISA	STRUDL	NISA	STRUDL	NISA	STRUDL
1 and 6	.267390	.267404	.002359	.002383	.001877	.001870
2 and 5	.680360	.680384	.004031	.004083	.001632	.001626
3 and 4	.959571	.959598	.004743	.004837	.000702	.000739

RMS DISPLACEMENTS (GLOBAL COMPONENTS)

- HEAT TRANSFER

NISA can be used for both, the steady state and transient heat conduction analysis. Steady state heat conduction problems are analyzed with NISA in 1D, 2D and 3D configurations using the wavefront method of solution. Transient heat conduction problems can be studied using an unconditionally stable, time integration technique. Boundary conditions can vary with time. Output temperatures can be stored and used for thermal stress analysis. The heat transfer capabilities of NISA can also be used for other field problems governed by the quasi-harmonic equation.

- STEADY STATE OR TRANSIENT THERMAL ANALYSIS

  ★ Concentrated nodal heat flows

  ★ Distributed heat flux, variable as defined by nodal intensities

  ★ Convective heat flow at surfaces

  ★ Radiation boundary condition

  ★ Internal heat generation, average and distributed, can vary with time and temperature

- SPECIAL FEATURES : Transient Heat Transfer

  ★ Boundary conditions such as specified nodal temperatures, convective heat coefficients, ambient temperatures and heat flux may be varied between time steps.

  ★ All thermal properties including conductivity, specific heat and convective coefficients may be temperature - dependent.

  ★ Thermal loads e.g. nodal heat flows, heat flux and internal heat generation may vary with time.

  ★ Time steps may be unequal

  ★ An unconditionally stable, time integration technique is used in the analysis.

STEADY STATE HEAT CONDUCTION IN A SQUARE PLATE WITH A CIRCULAR HOLE

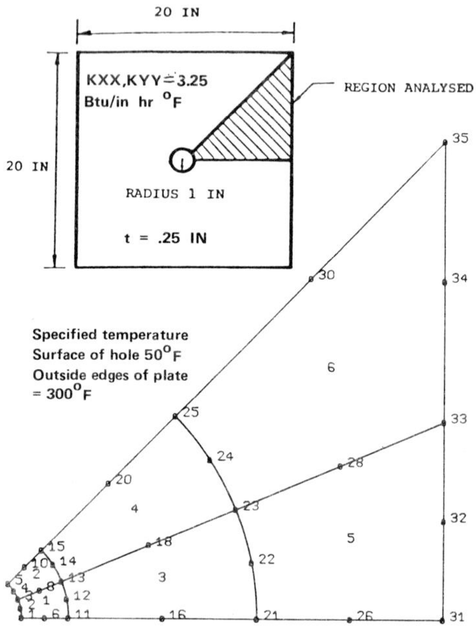

STEADY STATE HEAT CONDUCTION IN A SQUARE PLATE WITH A CIRCULAR HOLE
PLOT NO. 1

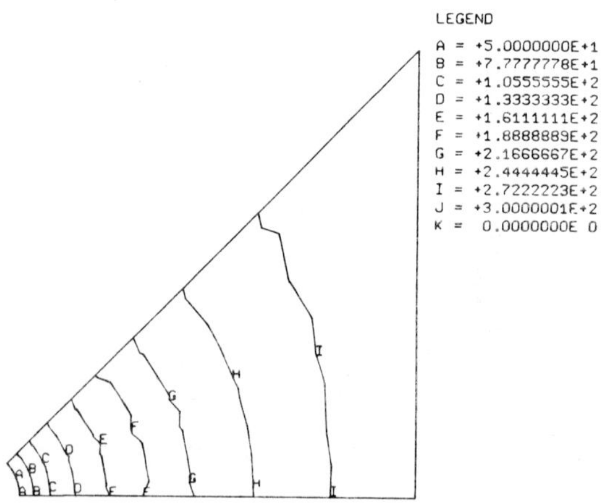

STEADY STATE HEAT CONDUCTION IN A SQUARE PLATE WITH A CIRCULAR HOLE
PLOT NO. 1
ISOTHERMAL LINES CONTOURS

- Includes interlaminar shear effects
- Exact distribution of interlaminar shear stress is found
- Contour plots of layer stresses and stress resultants
- Survey plot of critical stress components in all layers

▪ NON-LINEAR CAPABILITIES **

Non–NISA is a finite element computer program for nonlinear (geometrical and material) analysis. The program has two- and three-dimensional isoparametric elements. At present the program has 4 & 8 node isoparametric elements for plane stress, plane strain, and axisymmetric elements for two dimensional analysis. For three dimensional analysis, 16 node isoparametric thick shell and 8 and 20 node isoparametric solids are available.

Large displacement kinematics (geometric nonlinearity) is based onthe total Lagrangian formulation. A number of material models such as linear elastic, linear elastic orthotropic, nonlinear elastic-plastic and nonlinear elastic incompressible (Mooney-Rivlin material) are included. In elastic-plastic model, Von-Mises yield condition is being used with several hardening rules like isotropic, kinematic, combined isotropic-kinematic, and mechanical sublayers. Both static and dynamic analysis are possible. In dynamic analysis, Wilson's Theta and Newmark's time integration methods are available.

▪ RESTART FEATURES

NISA has extensive restart capabilities at various stages of solution. Job execution can be stopped and restarted at various points to obtain displacements, stresses, temperatures, transient response, random response, frequency response etc. Some of the restart options are described as follows:

- Save displacement or temperature vector and restart to obtain stresses and post-plots; save element stiffness matrices and restart to obtain post-plots; save the decomposed matrix and make restart to get displacements, stresses and plots.
- Save eigenvalues and eigenvectors and restart to get the plots.

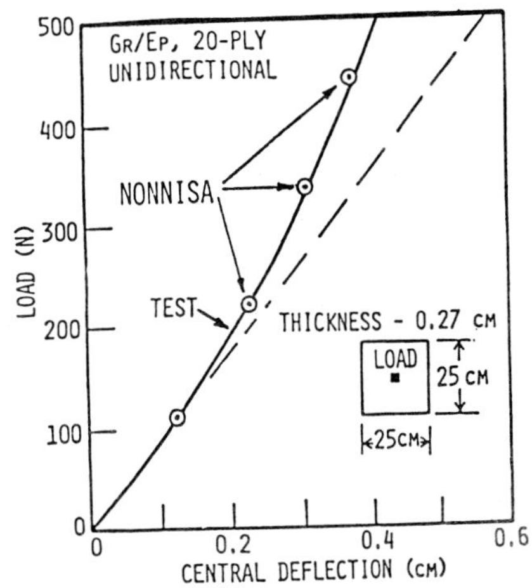

NONLINEAR LOAD-DEFLECTION RESPONSE OF A SIMPLY SUPPORTED COMPOSITE PANEL COMPARING NONNISA FINITE ELEMENT RESULTS WITH TESTS DONE AT GENERAL MOTORS *

* Design Analysis of Automotive Composite Structures by M.F. Kowalski, D. S. Fine, and R. K. Herrmann; SAE 3rd International Conference on Vehicle Structural Mechanics 1979.

NON LINEAR ANALYSIS OF SPHERICAL CAP

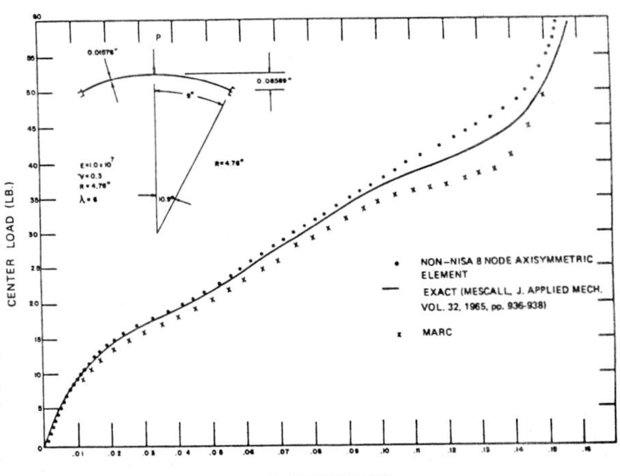

- OUTPUT FEATURES

  ★ Nodal temperature – average value at the midsurface of the shell elements

  ★ Linear temperature gradients at the nodes calculated from convective heat transfer

  ★ Heat values at the element nodes

  ★ Heat values at the nodes with specified nodal temperatures

  ★ Convective heat calculations for the element faces. Positive values indicate heat into the structure

  ★ Isothermal contour plots

  ★ Nodal temperatures at selected time intervals

  ★ Isothermal contour plots at selected time intervals

  ★ Temperature vs. Time plots for selected nodes

- NISA - COMPOSITES

NISA - Composites which is part of NISA is tailored specifically for the accurate, efficient analysis of a wide range of composite structures.

- Plate/shell and solid elements available for modelling complex composite structures.
- Fiber directions may be specified globally.
- Composite layers may be isotropic, transversely isotropic, orthotropic or anisotropic.
- Arbitrary layup with multi-materials, any number of layers
- Can model sandwich construction
- Same number of degrees of freedom as isotropic elements
- Includes bending-extensional-twist-shear coupling even for flat plates
- Smooth variation of lamination parameters (thickness, fiber angles, etc.)

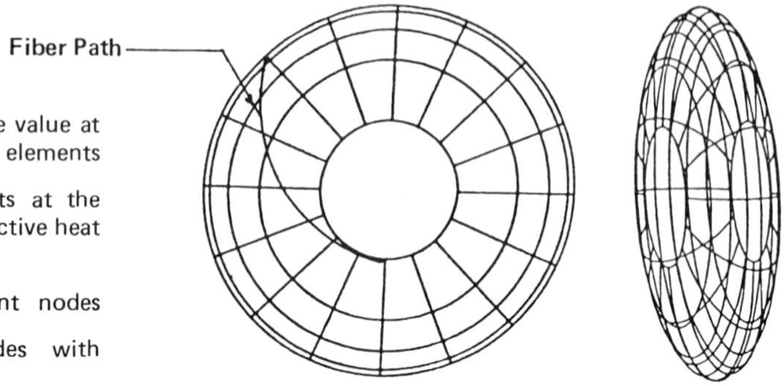

Some composite structures, as this fiber wound helicopter driveshaft coupling, have fibers whose orientation changes rapidly. Exactly modelling complex fiber paths will also be useful in molded composites where fiber angle and layer thickness are changed due to molding pressures.

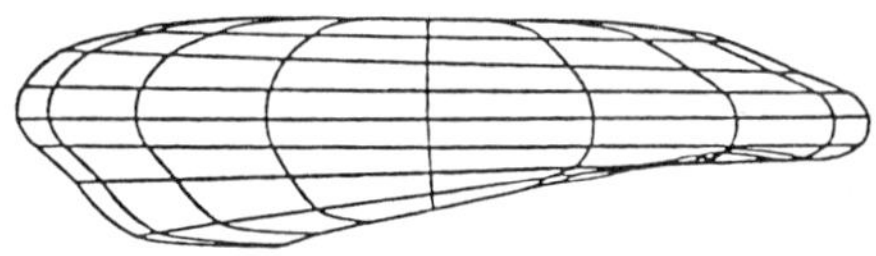

NISA includes comprehensive plot output, including deformed geometry (above) and layer stress contours (below).

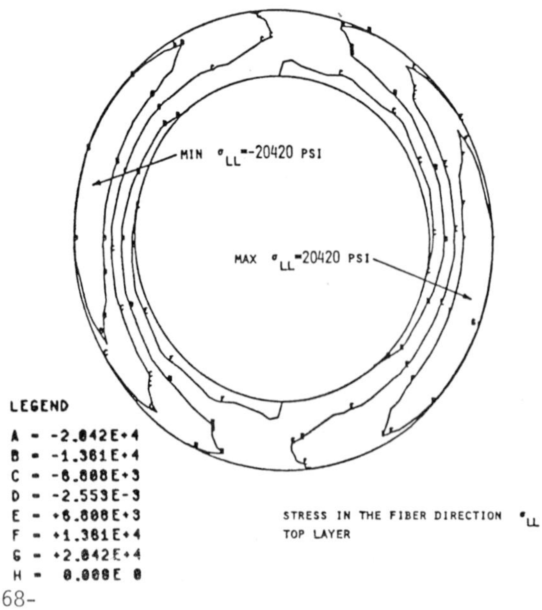

- Save eigenvalues and eigenvectors and restart to get time history response for transient dynamics.

- Save element matrices and restart to do eigenvalue or transient dynamics analysis.

- Save the decomposed stiffness matrix and restart to do eigenvalue or transient dynamics analysis.

The restart features are also convenient for analyzing economically the symmetry and antisymmetry conditions; and for combining these to get effect of unsymmetric loads.

■ MULTIPLE LOADING SOLUTIONS

The NISA program allows the execution of more than one load case in a single run. Multiple load cases can also be executed in conjunction with some restart options. The results can be stored and used for further processing. Combinations of results from various loading cases can be performed using the post-processing program NISACOM.

■ AVAILABILITY OF NISA

NISA and all the pre- and post-processing and other related programs are entirely developed by Engineering Mechanics Research Corporation (EMRC). The programs are used by many large corporations throughout the world. The programs are available through the computer network on royalty basis or can be leased or purchased outright in binary or source version from EMRC, P.O. Box 696, Troy, MI 48099, U.S.A. EMRC can also provide brochures, general introduction and manager's manual, user's manual, demonstration problems manual and verification problems manual.

■ SYSTEM REQUIREMENTS AND PROBLEM SIZES

The feature of dynamic core allocation and selective loading in NISA reduces the amount of core required to load the program thereby making it possible to solve much larger problems.

NISA does not have any limit on the number of elements or number of nodes that can be used in a problem. The size of the problem that can be solved on a given computer system depends on the core storage and file space available.

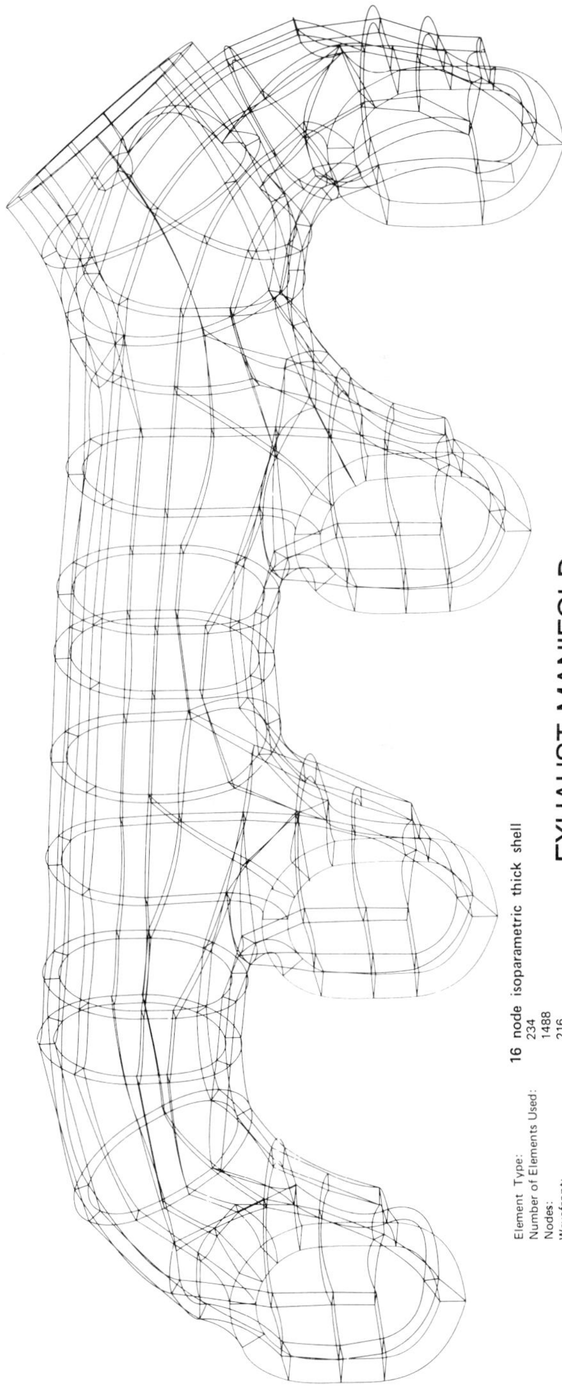

EXHAUST MANIFOLD

Element Type: 16 node isoparametric thick shell
Number of Elements Used: 234
Nodes: 1488
Wavefront: 216

NISA ELEMENT LIBRARY

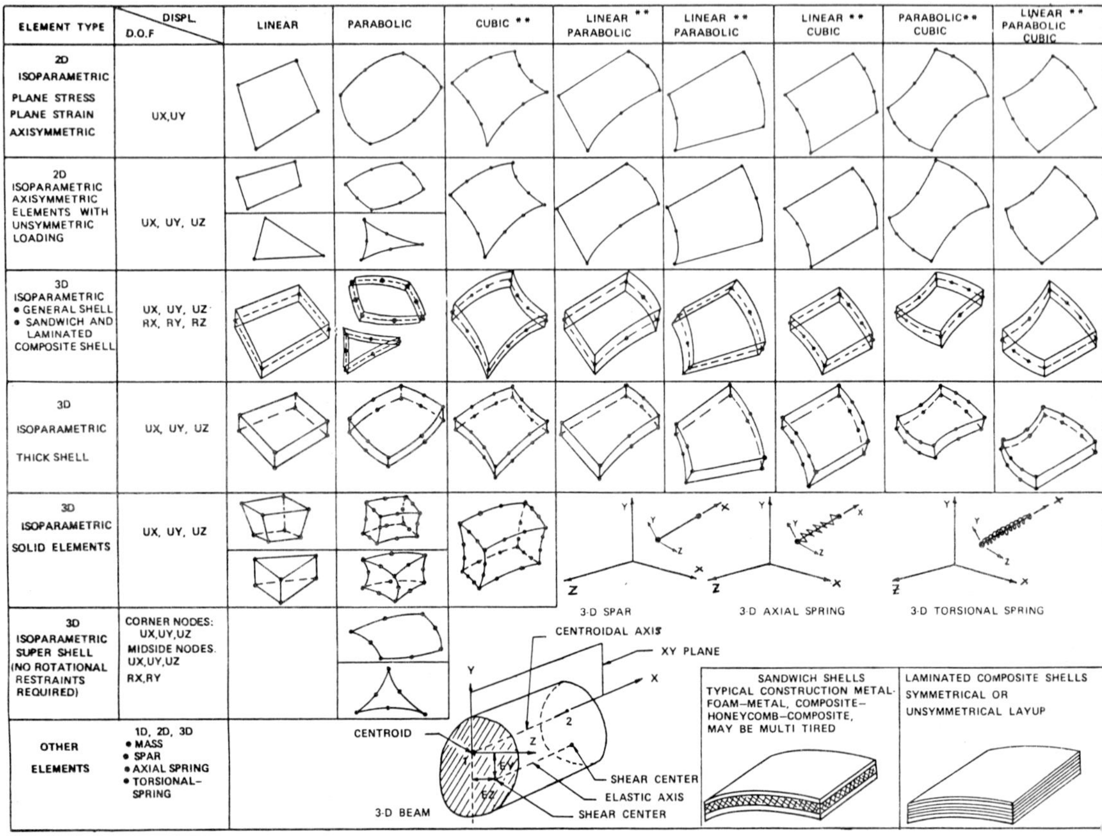

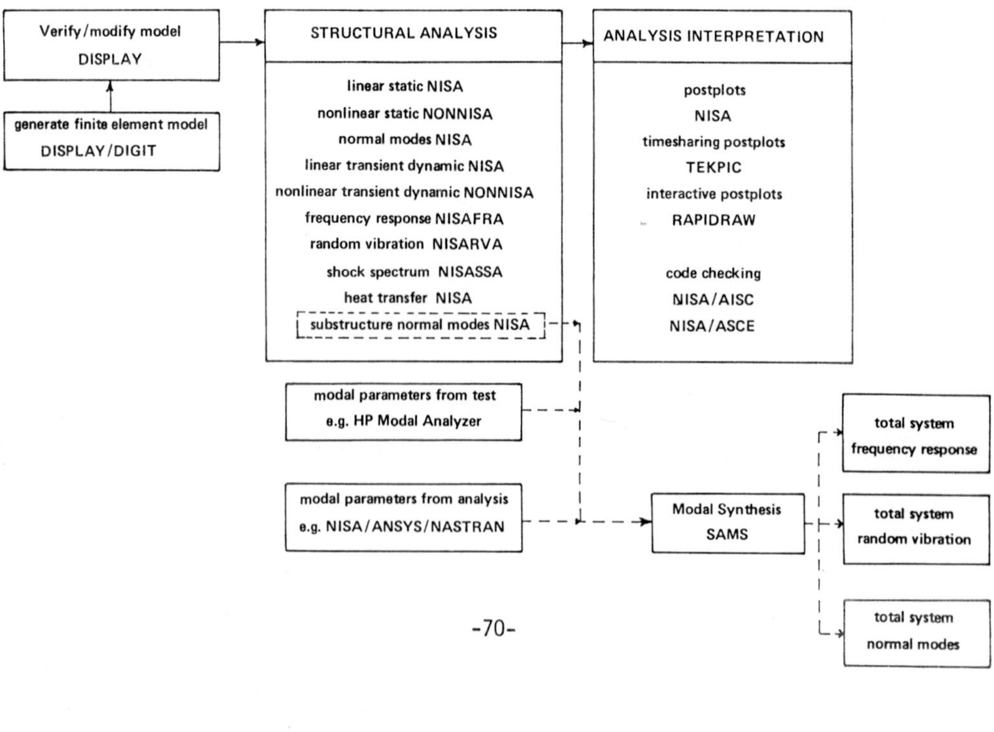

DISPLAY/DIGIT

DISPLAY and DIGIT are two interactive graphics programs which are extremely helpful to the users of finite element methods in the preparation and review of bulk data of a model. These programs permit the user to create nodes and elements, to display for checking and to modify the errors by conversing directly with the graphics terminal. One of the most useful features of this software is its automatic generation capabilities in both two- and three- dimensions. The user need only digitize enough nodes to define the *structure,* as distinct from the finite element *discretization* of the structure. This may be thought of as defining superelements, within which a desired mesh in two or three dimensions may be generated automatically.

DIGIT automates the process of generating input data directly from a drawing. For three dimensional models DIGIT merges any two orthogonal views and produces visual display of the model on the screen as desired. Current versions of DISPLAY and DIGIT have easy-to-use menu structures, powerful editors and various automatic mesh generation capabilities. Also a portion of the model can be isolated, enlarged and rotated about any system of axes until all errors are detected. The user has access to literally all sorts of information about his model in a matter of seconds. These capabilities make the task of constructing finite element models easier and cost effective.

DISPLAY/DIGIT allows one to:

- Digitize elements and nodes of a model from drawing,
- Merge two views to create a three-dimensional model and define three-dimensional elements,
- Select elements, nodes or element type for plotting,
- Isolate a portion, enlarge it or scale it down and display rotated views,
- Interactively edit element and grid point data using cursors, digitizing tablet and keyboard,

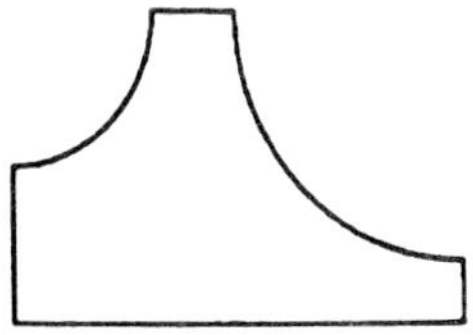

Just Enough Nodes Digitized from Engineering Drawing to Represent the Structure

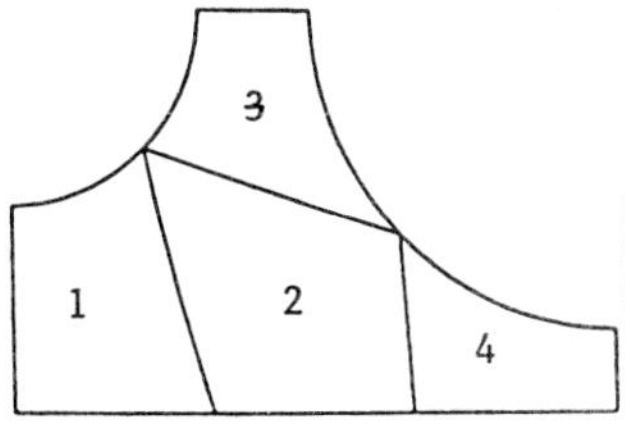

The Structure is Defined by Four Super Elements

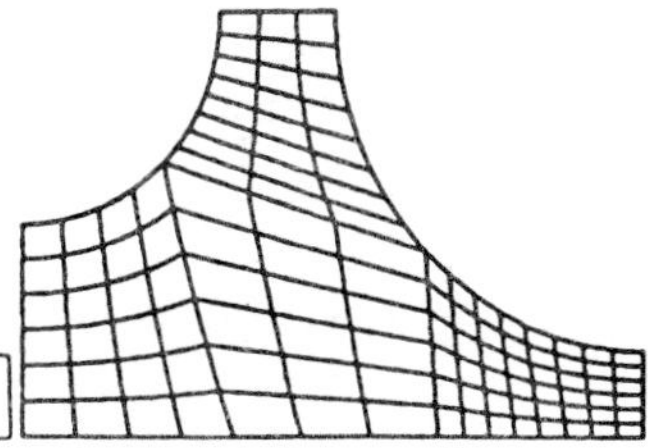

Desired Mesh Generated Automatically

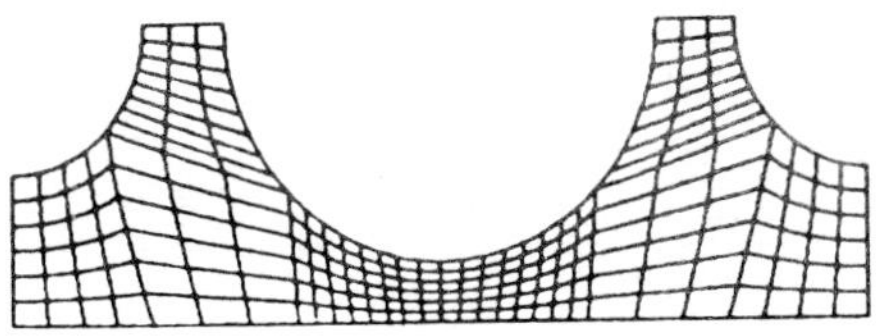

Mirror Image of the Model is Created

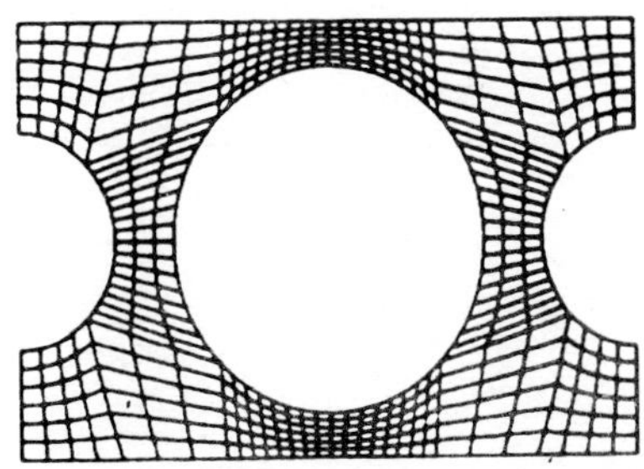

Symmetric Mesh is Generated Once Again

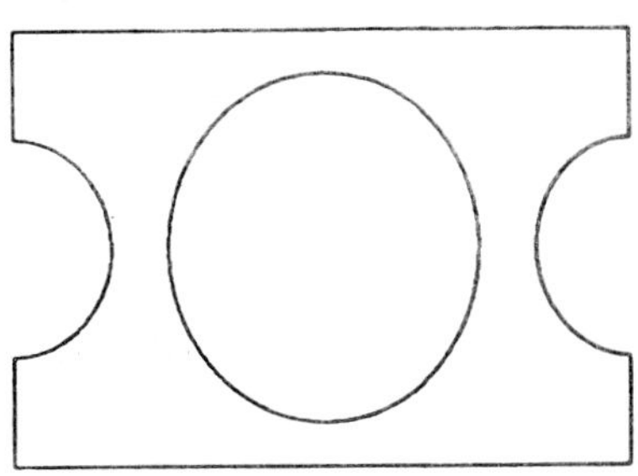

Boundary of the Structure Displayed for Detecting Missing Elements or Applying Boundary Conditions

- List interactively a summary of the available options,
- Locate element or node numbers from an arbitrary view,
- Display boundary of the structure with or without node numbers,
- Automatically generate a two- or three-dimensional mesh,
- Check for wavefront or bandwidth of the current model,
- Eliminate hidden lines or display hidden lines as dashed lines,
- Generate a symmetric mesh about an arbitrary plane in rectangular or cylindrical coordinates,
- Choose the data format for the desired analysis program,
- Draw exact curved boundary by using shape functions,
- Convert lower order elements into higher order elements.
- Model any complex geometry using an extensive library of linear and higher order beams, shells, solids etc.

All these features offer tremendous flexibility that allows one to prepare a finite element model faster and more cost effectively. Using this software, the manpower requirements in setting up a finite element model can be drastically reduced.

- DISPLAY has greatly simplified *checking* of finite element models.
  - ★ It offers an option whereby four different views can be displayed on the screen at the same time. Between two successive views the user can rotate the model, scale it down or magnify it, and select elements or nodes for plotting.
  - ★ Missing elements may be detected by activating the option for a display of the structural boundary only.
  - ★ A plot of the boundary with node numbers simplifies the task

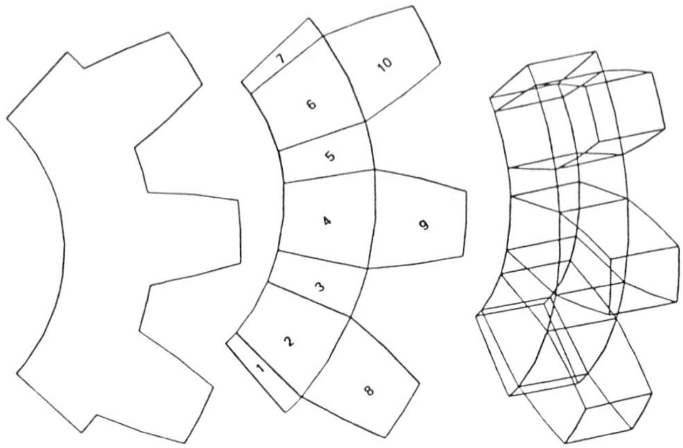

Boundary of the Structure is Displayed and Modeled by Ten Thin Shell Elements. Automatic Conversion of 8- Node Thin Shells into 20-Node Solid Elements.

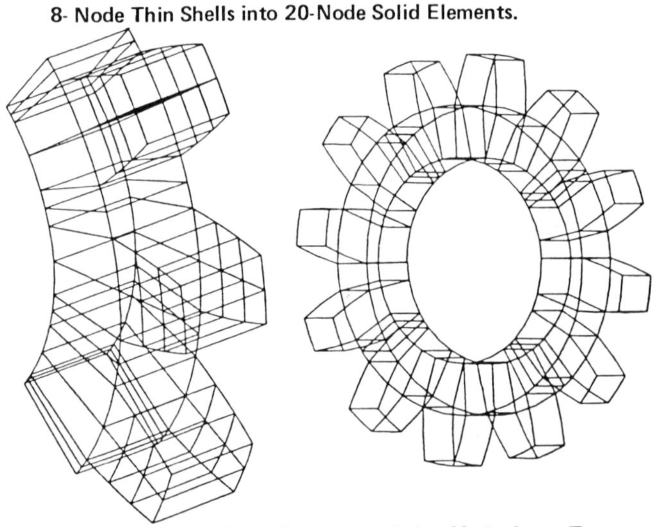

Further Automatic Refinement of the Mesh from Ten 20-Node Solids into Thirty-Two 20-Node Solids. Symmetric Mesh Generated to Build up the Entire Model.

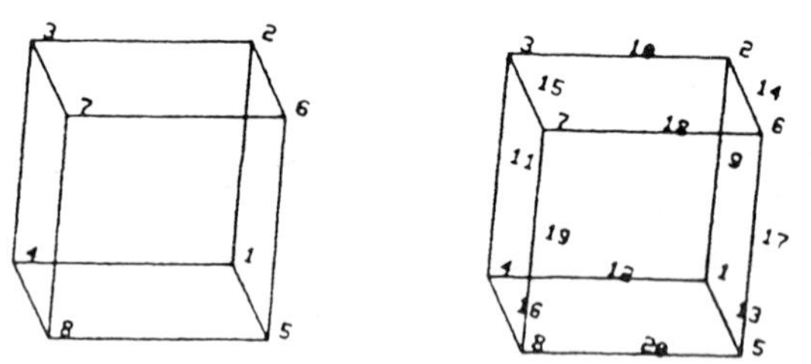

Using Mid–Point Generation Feature, Lower Order Elements can be Converted into Higher Order Elements Automatically

of specifying boundary conditions.

- ★ Any node number in the model can be identified from an arbitrary view using the terminal cursors.
- ★ The coordinates of a specific set of nodes and element connectivity can be listed by calling the editor of the program.
- ★ Elements and nodes can be added easily using the keyboard and/or the cursors.

- ■ The most powerful feature of DISPLAY is its *automatic mesh generation* capabilities for both two- and three dimensional structures.
  - ★ Input data for this option are the element number within which mesh is to be generated, density of the mesh in three directions and type and order of the elements desired.
  - ★ If a structure is geometrically symmetric, only one portion of it need be modeled and the rest of the structure can be created using reflection or cyclic symmetry any number of times.
- ■ The task of building models has been made easier by introducing *midpoint* generation capability in both DISPLAY and DIGIT. The user needs only to model the structure with corner nodes and then use midpoint generation to obtain higher order elements.
- ■ *Editing* of nodal and element data in DISPLAY and DIGIT can be carried out in several ways. The user can re-digitize a particular node, delete undesirable nodes and elements or modify nodal coordinates using cursors. Editor also permits new nodes and elements to be added to the existing model.
- ■ DISPLAY allows *rotations* to be performed about global as well as about an arbitrary cartesian coordinate system.

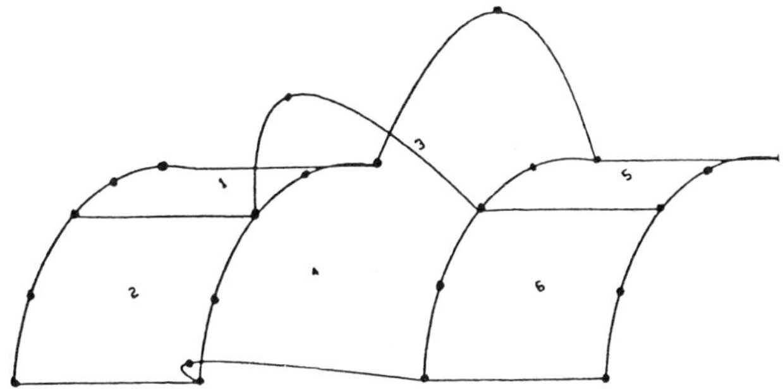

One Quarter of a Doubly Curved Structure is Modeled Using Six Parabolic General Shell Elements. The Unique Feature of the DISPLAY Program to draw Exact Curved Boundary by Usage of Shape Functions is Illustrated here.

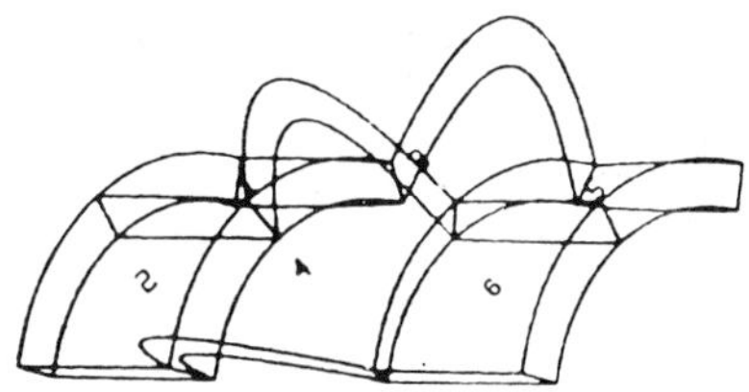

Automatic Conversion of Parabolic General Shells into Twenty Node Solid Elements.

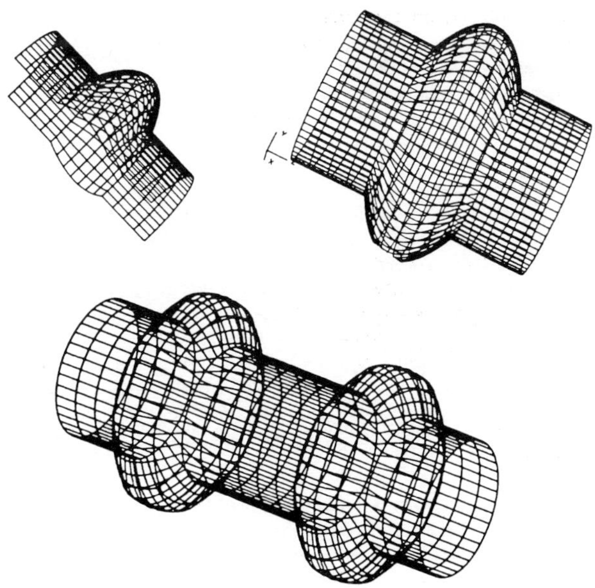

Rotation and Symmetric Mesh Generation of Three Dimensional Parabolic Shell Elements.

- In DIGIT nodes can be digitized in both *cartesian* and *cylindrical* coordinate systems.

- Another interesting feature of DISPLAY is its ability to convert doubly curved thin shell models with variable thicknesses into an equivalent three dimensional solid model. From a basic shell model, solid models of different thicknesses can be generated to analyze design modifications involving thickness changes.

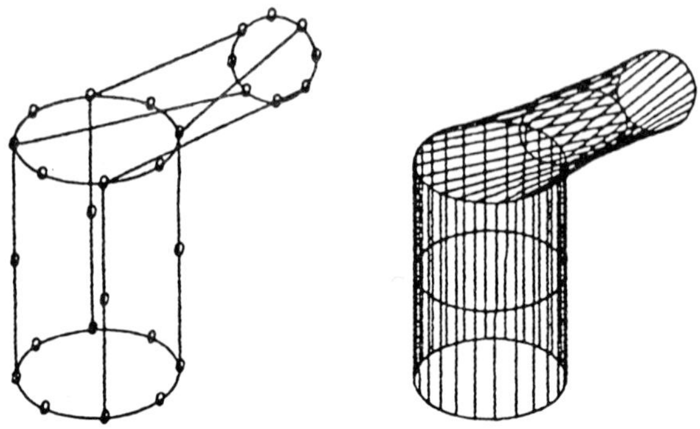

Automatic Mesh Generation of Intersecting Pipes from Eight Parabolic General Shell Elements

The digitizing program DIGIT, automates the process of generating geometry data from engineering drawings for finite element analysis. It is an interactive computer program that can be used to define nodal coordinates and element connectivity from any two-dimensional view of a finite element model, using a digitizing tablet and a CRT terminal.

Nodal coordinates are generated from the digitizing tablet. Element connectivity is defined by using the terminal screen with cross-hairs, or the digitizing tablet, or via keyboard input. The nodes and elements are displayed on the screen for immediate verification by the user. Any errors may be corrected by redefining the nodes or elements. Nodal coordinates from the two views of the model are merged to obtain three-dimensional nodal coordinates.

At present, the program generates data files in any desired input format for the NISA, NASTRAN, ANSYS, SAP, STRUDL, STARDYNE programs. However a very minor modification will be required to generate data files for any other inhouse or commercially available finite element code. Both of these programs have restart capability which will enable the user to stop digitizing and restart the program at any node point.

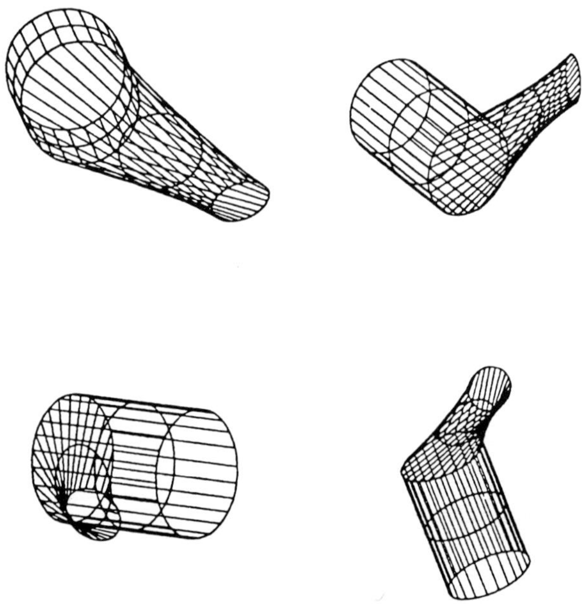

Simultaneous Rotations and DISPLAY of the Structure in the Four Quadrants of the Screen

Both DISPLAY and DIGIT require 25 K words of computer storage space and can be implemented on a minicomputer or any other computer with minimum amount of memory requirements.

production drafting of the 1980's

Hector Holquin, P.E.

Holguin & Associates, Inc.
P. O. Box 12990
El Paso, Texas 79912

One of the greatest challenges of the 1980's will be for the United States to recover its dynamics of production. The greatness of this country was developed by the innovative skills of people coupled to the abundant wealth of natural resources.

The miracle of Japan must be a strong indicator of the importance of modernizing our industrial base. We must begin by tapping the most significant technological advantage that we have - the computer. This paper will present one of the applications that can best be served by the computer - the world of drafting.

You must recognize that every product manufactured today must first be produced by a draftsman or designer on paper. The drafting tools of scales, triangles, etc. must be replaced by computerized tools. These tools must be presented to a drafter or designer in a format that he can readily understand and apply. These tools must be an extension of his own skills and experience. He cannot afford the time that it takes for him to become a sophisticated computer operator or programmer.

This paper will present the elements essential to developing a system tailored to the needs of the draftsman and designer. We will begin by documenting the basics of computerized drafting and the growth curve to the sophisticated world of interactive design and three dimensional modeling.

W - A D D S :

INCREASE PRODUCTION

THE FOLLOWING DRAWINGS WERE PRODUCED
BY DRAFTERS WITHOUT ANY TRAINING IN
PROGRAMMING OR COMPUTER OPERATING SYSTEMS

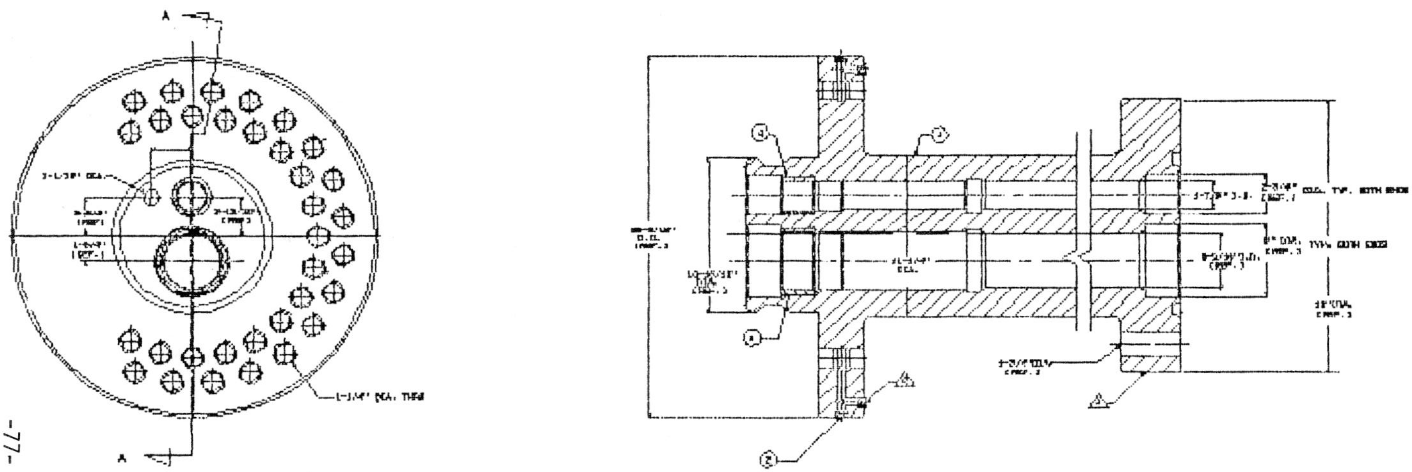

THIS DRAWING CAN BE PRODUCED 3 TIMES FASTER
AND AT 1/2 THE COST OF MANUAL DRAFTING OPERATIONS

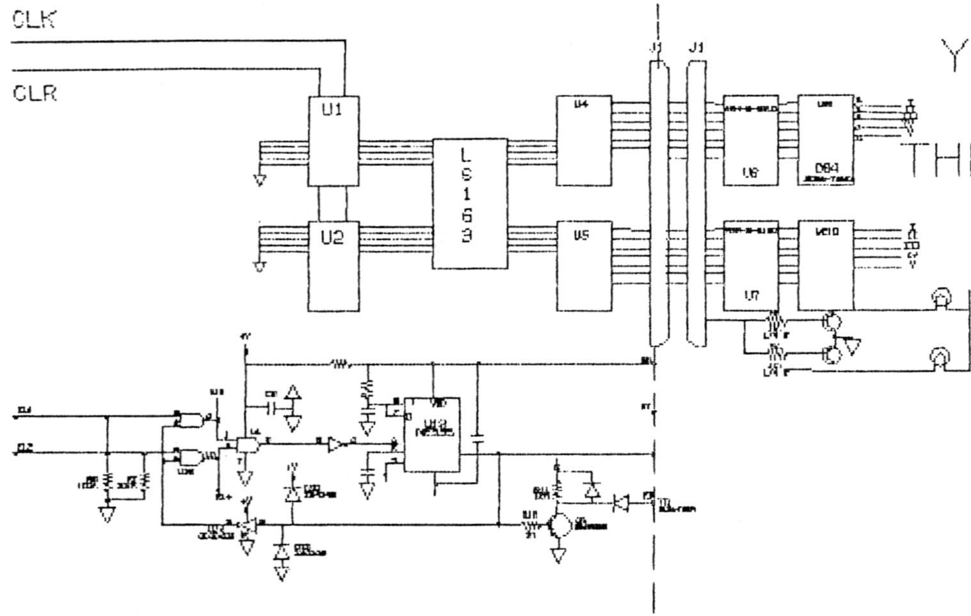

YOU CAN BUILD

THE MOST COMPLEX

OF

SCHEMATICS
DIAGRAMS
FLOWCHARTS
PATTERNS
ETC.

YOU ARE ONLY LIMITED BY YOUR IMAGINATION

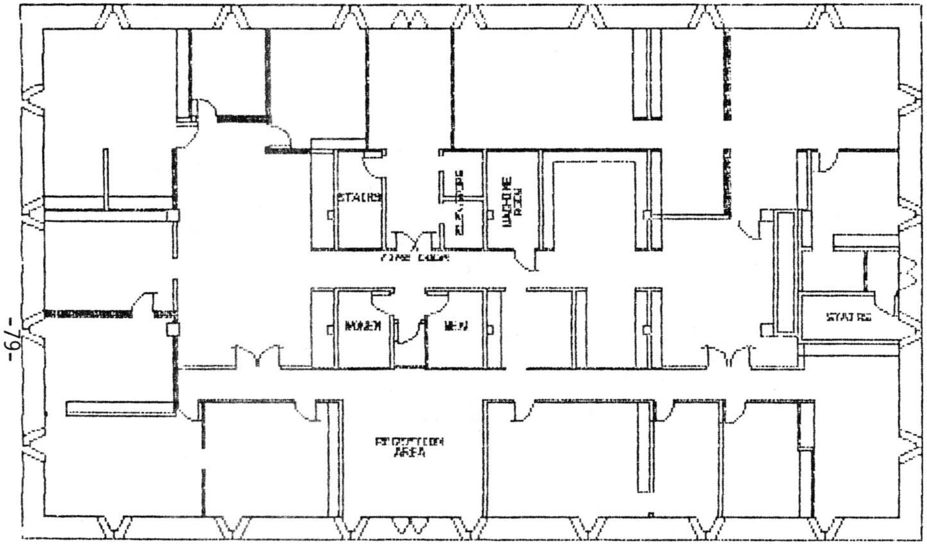

* ARCHITECTURAL DESIGN
* ASSEMBLY LAYOUTS
* GRAPHICS DESIGN
* LOGOS
* MACHINE DESIGN
* MECHANICAL DRAFTING
* PIPING DIAGRAMS
* PC BOARDS
* SCHEMATICS
* STRUCTURAL DESIGN
* UTILITY NETWORKS
* WIRING DIAGRAMS

Simple, dynamic construction lines are used to replace your drafting tools. Construction lines are temporary lines, linear or curvilinear, that are used to build any drawing. These guidelines can be readily displayed at any location and orientation on the Graphics Screen. You eliminate the typical drafting errors and "eyeball accuracy" characteristics of manual drafting operations. Construction lines are set to precise dimensions and precise relationships.....YOUR SKETCH PAD BECOMES A PRECISE DESIGN TOOL.

A. REFERENCE LOCATION

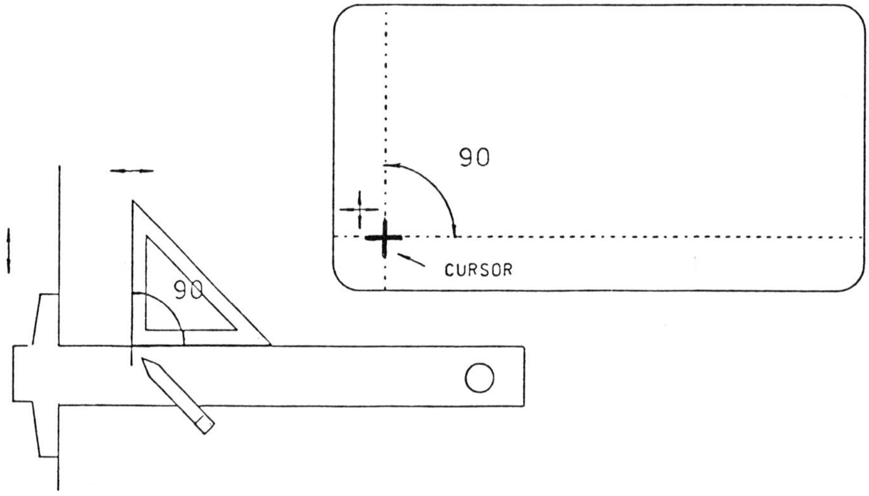

The Graphics Cursor is used to locate the initial pair of construction lines (reference location); this cursor can be moved to any location on the Graphics Screen.

B. ANGULAR MEASUREMENTS

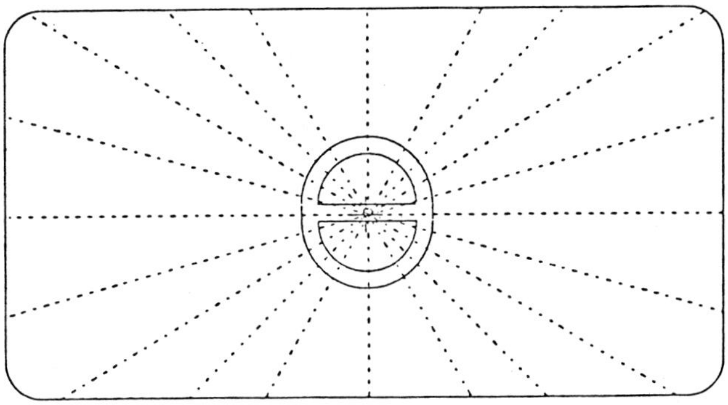

Construction lines can be set at any angular direction. You are not restricted to the eyeball accuracy of compass readings; you can establish construction lines at precise angular measurements (degrees - minutes - seconds or fractions thereof).

C. PARALLEL LINES

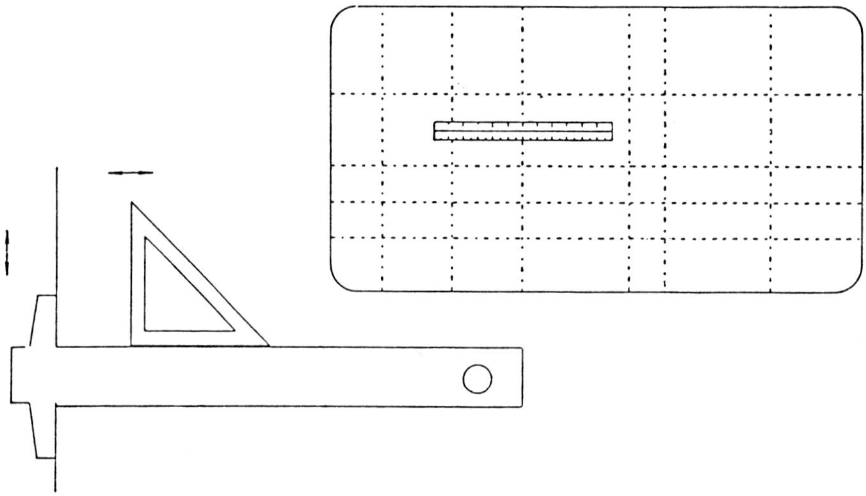

Any number of parallel construction lines can be processed using a common or variable distance measurement. Distances are entered to your specifications of precision.....up to 6 significant digits. You select the units: inches, feet, centimeters or meters. The parallel lines can be set at any location and orientation; you are not restricted to a horizontal and vertical axis (X-Y).....parallel lines can be set at any angle.

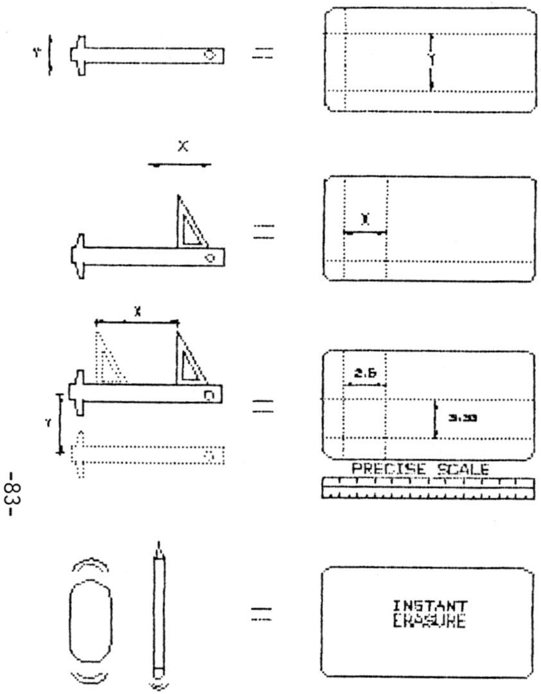

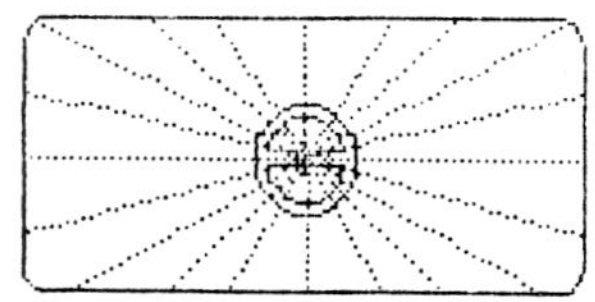

DYNAMIC

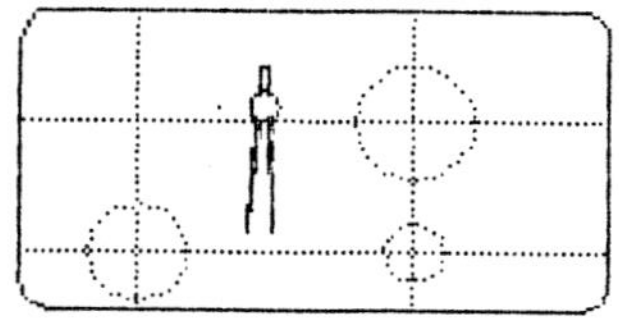

PRECISE

CONSTRUCTION LINES

REPLACE "E Y E B A L L"

ACCURACY OF MANUAL

DRAFTING TOOLS

W-ADDS offers a series of user-selectable parameters to enhance the "tailored to your specifications" environment of its design and drafting operations. Each parameter is set to a value selected by the user; this value remains in effect until changed by the user. You can readily reproduce the same drawing to different specifications by simply changing these parameters. Most firms will use the identical parameters from drawing to drawing; therefore, this feature will dramatically increase the automation and efficiency of the W-ADDS operations.

THE PARAMETERS ARE:

USER-SELECTABLE INPUT AND OUTPUT UNITS

USER-SELECTABLE END POINTS FOR DIMENSION LINES

USER-SELECTABLE LABELING POSITIONS

USER-SELECTABLE DIMENSIONING ACCURACY

USER-SELECTABLE DECIMAL OR FRACTIONAL OUTPUT

USER-SELECTABLE ORIENTATION OF TEXT

USER-SELECTABLE CHARACTER HEIGHTS AND SPACING

The W-ADDS dimensioning system offers unique concepts of automation in the production of final drawings. The entire dimensioning process is automated except for those parameters required by the user to tailor the system to his specifications. Most of these parameters are common within a given drawing. Therefore, once set to the user's specifications, these parameters could remain constant and contribute to the enhancement of automated production.

Automatic generation of each dimension to its precise value and location as determined by identifying its construction points.

User-selectable units: inches, feet, centimeters, meters.

Automatic placement of each dimension; automatically centered in relation to its dimension line.

Automatic dimension lines and arrowheads (optional: slash mark or dot). Dimensions can be placed above, below or within any dimension line.

Notes can be added at any location and orientation. Automatic placement of any note with right, left or center justify alignments.

DIMENSION:

** METRIC

** IMPERIAL

INCHES
FEET
FEET & INCHES

** UNITS

DECIMAL
FRACTIONAL

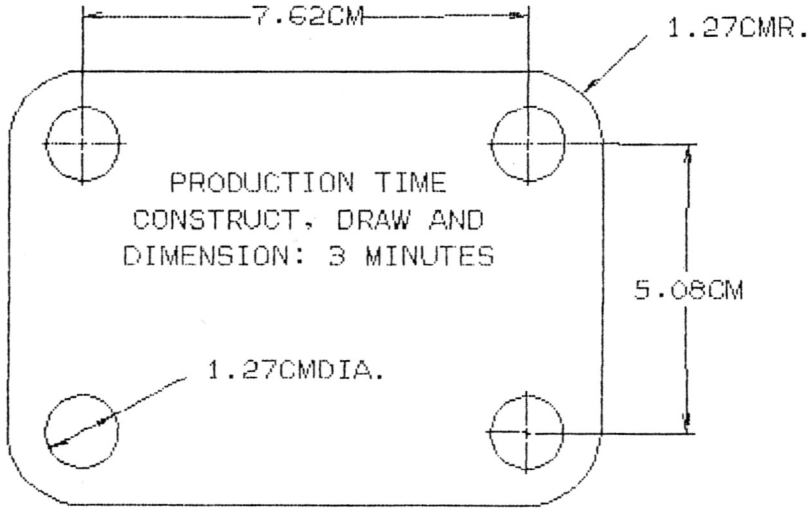

THE EDIT CONTROL SYSTEM offers the following features:

INSTANT EDIT of any drawing

CHANGE, CORRECT, INSERT or ADD any line or series of lines (linear or curvilinear)

INSTANT EDIT of scale or orientation

INSTANT EDIT of any module

INSTANT EDIT of any Text, from a single line to a series of lines

INSTANT EDIT of line types

INSTANT EDIT of pen types (pen sizes)

INSTANT MOVE to a new location for any text, line(s), modules, etc.

INSTANT DELETE of any part of a drawing

INSTANT REPEAT of any portion of a drawing to a new location(s); any number of copies

You can build a library of thousands of modules or modular combinations. The W-ADDS MASTER MODULE SYSTEM offers you instant recall of any drawing in the W-ADDS LIBRARY to build another drawing. Modules can be dynamically reproduced and "tailored" to your specifications; instant reproduction at any scale, orientation and location. You can easily define and store your standard details, patterns, symbols, overlays, text, etc. You have total control over the development and use of modules; you are only limited by your imagination.

The W-ADDS library is dynamic and unlimited in scope. Even if a drawing is to be used as a module in 1,000 different drawings, you only have to store it once......unlimited reproduction of any module or derivative thereof; you can recall any combination of drawings from storage as modules, build a new drawing and store it in a new location in the library. ANY DRAWING STORED IN THE W-ADDS LIBRARY IS AVAILABLE TO BECOME A MODULE FOR INSTANT RECALL AND REPRODUCTION (WITH OPTION TO EDIT) TO BUILD A NEW DRAWING.

The futuristic concepts of MASTER MODULES offers you the total freedom and independence of creating and controlling your own design and drafting modules. W-ADDS is "your" computerized partner; you are not dependent on anyone to fulfill your design and production requirements.

W - A D D S :

R E D U C E   C O S T S

SINGLE WORK STATION: $7.50 PER HOUR

TWO WORK STATIONS: $5.00 PER HOUR PER STATION

FOUR WORK STATIONS: $3.00 PER HOUR PER STATION

** OPERATING COSTS ABOVE ARE BASED ON STANDARD 5 YEAR AMORTIZATION OF W-ADDS SYSTEM COST

COST SAVINGS

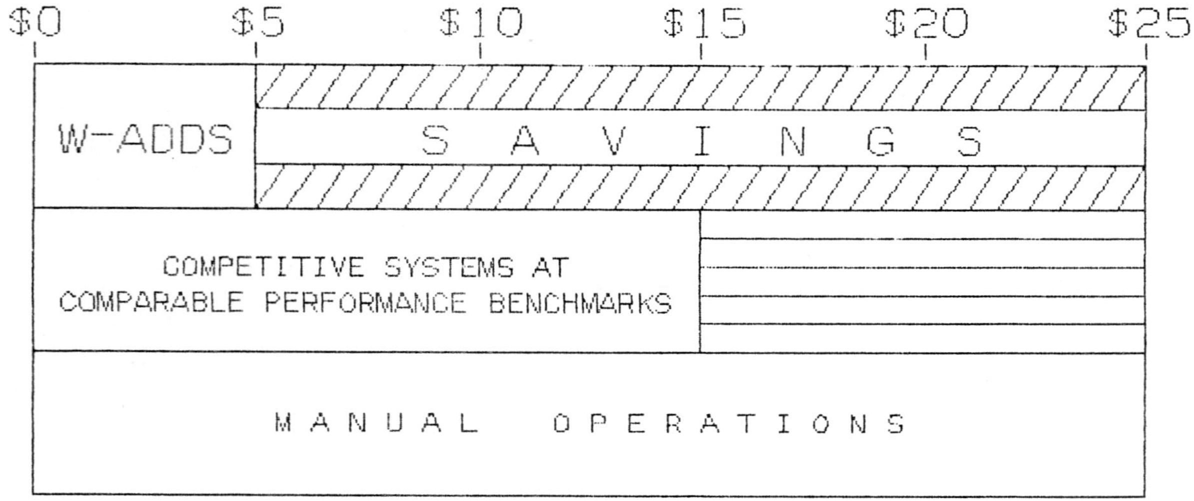

OPERATING COSTS PER HOUR:
W-ADDS OPERATES AT 1/2 TO 1/5 THE COST OF ALTERNATE METHODS

Z O O M

TO ANY ELEMENT
OF A DRAWING

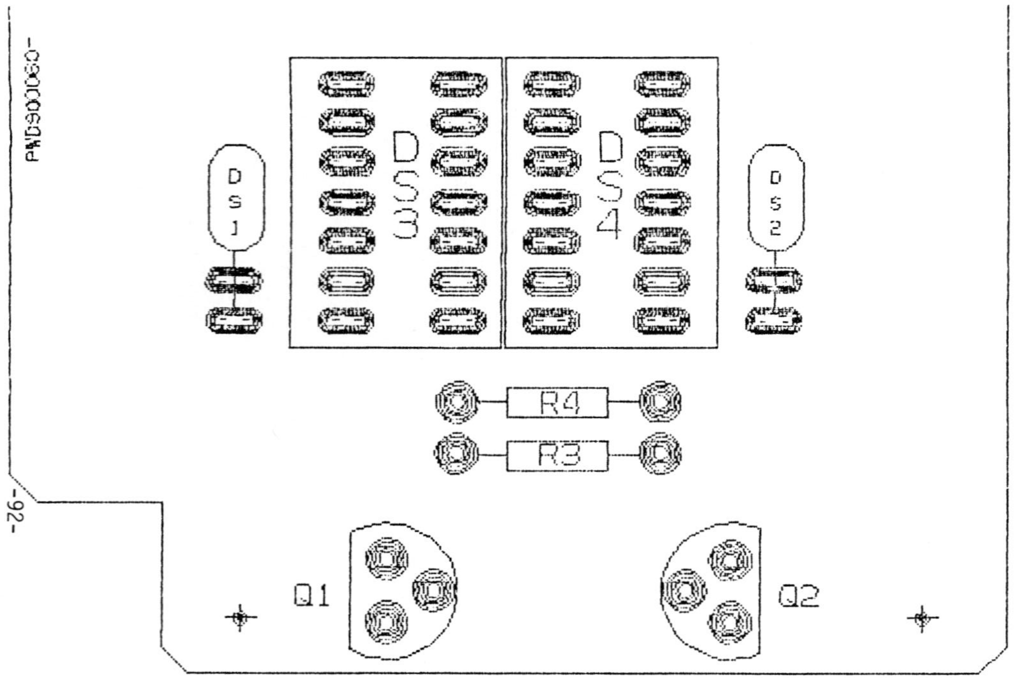

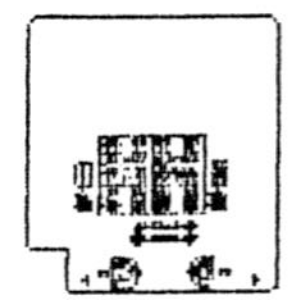

PC BOARD

Z O O M

THRU YOUR DESIGN OPERATIONS

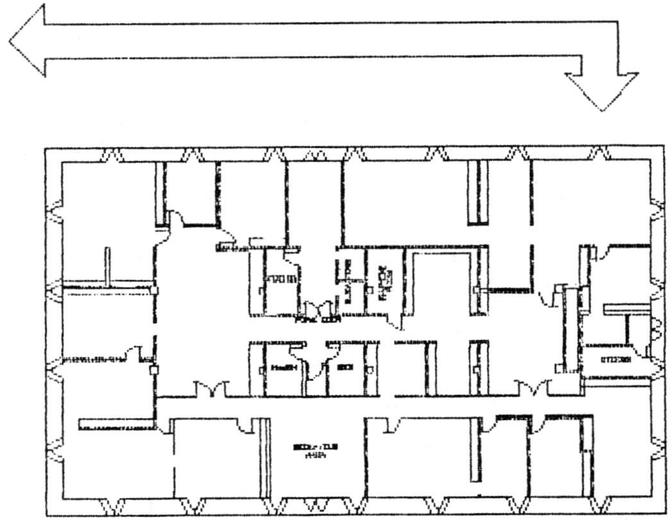

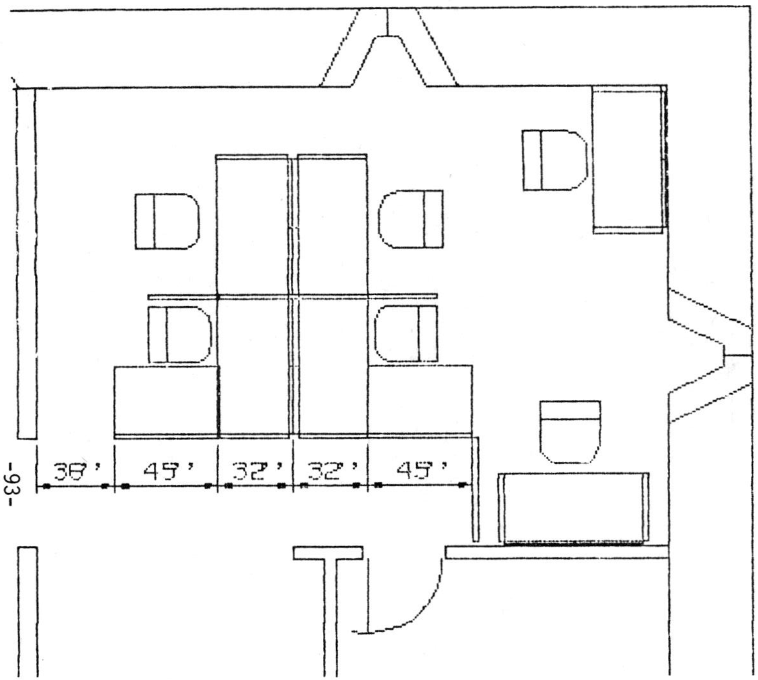

a real-time performance analysis system for computers

Daniel I. Kolody
Hewlett-Packard Company
1900 Garden of the Gods Road
Colorado Springs, Colorado 80907

ABSTRACT

Computer systems are generally organized to provide adequate performance for a wide variety of applications. Rarely is a particular computer optimal for specific requirements of the customer. Consequently, the user is left with the task of determining how well the computer performs under various workloads, and, if possible, how to improve this performance. This paper describes a new tool, a Logic Analysis system, and how the performance of a computer system can potentially be improved by a very large factor - even after the system has been designed and implemented.

The concept of performance is defined and discussed relative to the most common user requirements. Typical performance indices such as throughput rate, response time, instruction mix, and component overlap are introduced and followed by examples of how these indices are measured and displayed.

Finally, the analysis system is discussed from the viewpoint of measurement accuracy, and a methodology is presented for assuring user-defined confidence levels and intervals.

INTRODUCTION

In the more traditional forms of engineering, the design of electronic or mechanical products is generally followed by rigorous characterization. The potential user can typically study data sheet specifications to evaluate bandwidth, sensitivity, horsepower, frequency response, or other parameters to assess the products suitability for th required application. Such characterization by the designer is rarely performed on computer systems. The reason is simple -- computer user requirements are complex and vary dramatically from user to user. The performance of a particular computer system operating in a batch processing mode with SPOOLing and manual memory management can be accurately evaluated for throughput with specific

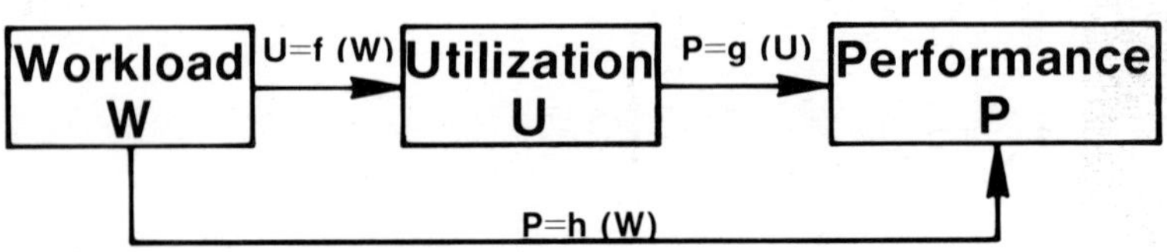

Figure 1. In practice, performance is a function of utilization and workload, although the form of the functions f, g, and h are unknown. The primary purpose of computer performance evaluation is to determine the values of the functions.

workloads. However, the same computer system running the same workloads would probably have significantly different throughput with an interactive mode in a multiprogramming environment and virtual memory. Consequently, the user must ultimately assess the suitability of a particular system. The most prevalent reasons for computer performance evaluations (CPE) are:

A. COMPUTER SYSTEM VS COMPUTER SYSTEM COMPARISONS
    1. Lease/purchase new hardware or software
    2. Select a supplier of computer services
    3. Classify existing systems
    4. Evaluate performance changes relative to hardware or software changes

B. ANALYSIS OF A COMPUTER SYSTEM VS SYSTEM PARAMETERS OR SYSTEM WORKLOAD.
    1. Tune existing systems
    2. Maintain or control system performance
    3. Design or implement new systems

A CPE CONCEPTUAL MODEL

The fundamental quantities used in performance evaluation are workload, utilization, and performance. Their relationship is shown in Figure 1. The performance indices that are measured to describe those quantities have been previously described by several authors. The indices have been either grouped according to their dimensions of volume, time, or ratios of volume or time (1), or according to the level of system structure and function (2) where the categories of effectiveness, efficiency, and workload are used. A matrix that combines both groups is shown in the Appendix.

The value of the matrix is to provide a selection overview of the indices and to indicate the type of metrics required by the analysis system. An example of the interrelationship of performance and workload is shown in Figure 2. This is an example of tuning where the quantitive values of performance and workload could be capacity (maximum throughput) and job CPU time, respectively.

GRAPHICAL INTERPRETATION OF TUNING

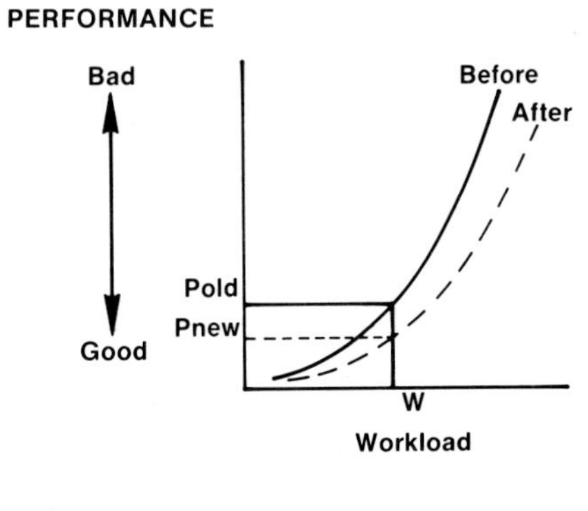

Figure 2. Many indices can be used to described performance and workload. An example for tuning could be capacity (maximum throughput) and job CPU time, respectively.

The first step of the CPE process is to select the performance measures appropriate to the analysis required. The second step is to actually quantize the performance of the system-under-test. It is important to stress that the resultant values must always be analyzed with respect to system structure and workload. A subtle difference in two apparently identical computer systems (such as memory access times) would have a significant effect on indices as CPU productivity or response time. The third aspect of the evaluation process is the assignment of qualitative values to the different levels of performance. Improvement in a systems throughput by 30% might be perceived to be of high value to specific users, but the operations manager could assess the 30% improvement as hardly justifiable and of low value when considering the cost of implementing the change.

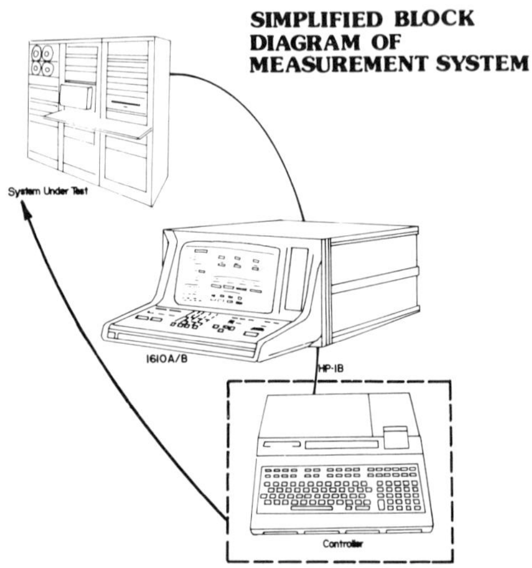

Figure 3. The key element in the measurement system is the Logic Analyzer, which can be optionally controlled by the system under test or another external controller.

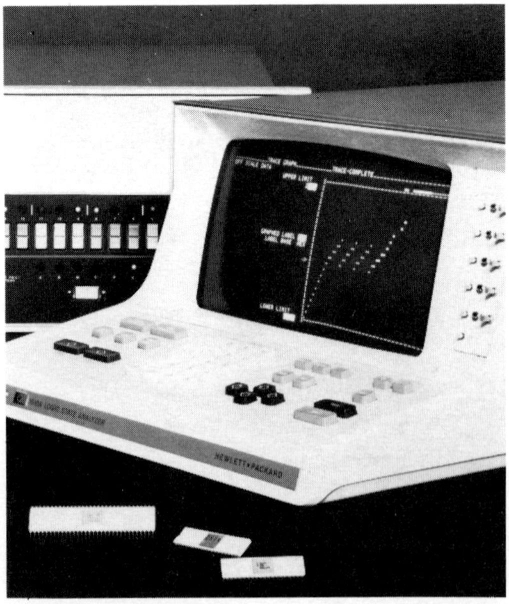

Figure 4. The Model 1610A/B Logic State Analyzer is used in analysis of computer systems.

The Measurement System

The measurement system is shown in Figure 3. The key element is the Logic Analyzer (Figure 4) which can act as a stand-alone measurement tool, or can be controlled remotely via an HP-IB (IEEE-488) bus. The controller can be implemented using a desktop calculator, another computer, or can be a program running within the system-under-test. In the latter case, it should be noted that the

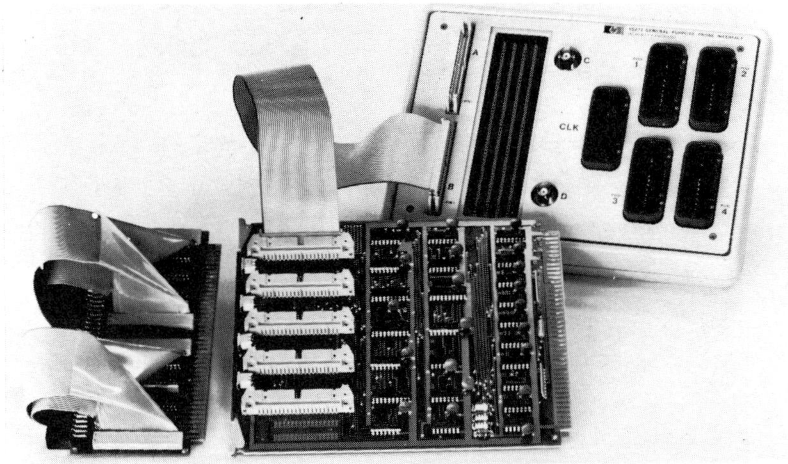

Figure 5. The Model 10278A Interface for an HP 1000 M, E, and F series computer connected to a Model 10277A/B General Purpose Probe Interface allow the mechanical and electrical connection to the computer.

"control" program could represent a measurement artifact and perturb the measurement accuracy. The physical connection (mechanically and electrically) to the computer is implemented with dedicated probes that plug directly into a memory or I/O slot. Figure 5 shows the HP Model 10278A Interface for HP 1000 M, E, and F series computers, and a Model 10277A/B General Purpose Probe Interface.

The measurement system, as described, is a transparent, real-time data acquisition analysis tool. It can be configured via the Analyzers Format Specification menu (Figure 6) to monitor address, data, or control signals within the computer.

All memory, I/O, or DMA transactions can be acquired and measured. The analyzer can be instructed to trace specific program paths, and to measure time or counts (state-events) (Figure 7).

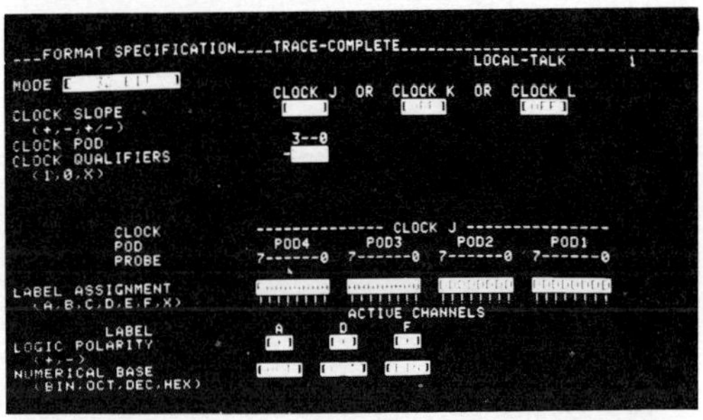

Figure 6. The Format Specification menu allows the user to configure the analyzer to monitor address, data, and control signals.

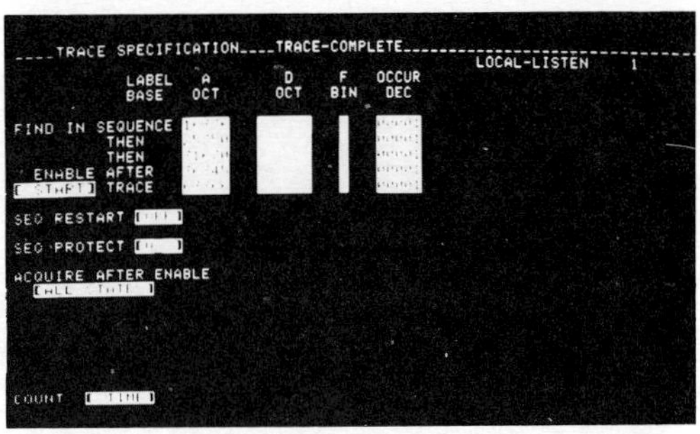

Figure 7. The Trace Specification menu determines where programs will be traced and what activity will be measured.

The resultant trace can be displayed as a list with the time or state-count shown in either an absolute or relative format. (Figures 8 and 9). These measurements can be made using the Analyzer as a stand-alone tool. Versatility can be greatly increased, however, when using a controller. The analyzer can be remotely configured, given execution commands, and then used to acquire and store the required activity. This information can then be post-processed by the controller to create histogram displays (bar-charts), branching probability matrices, or other user-definable displays.

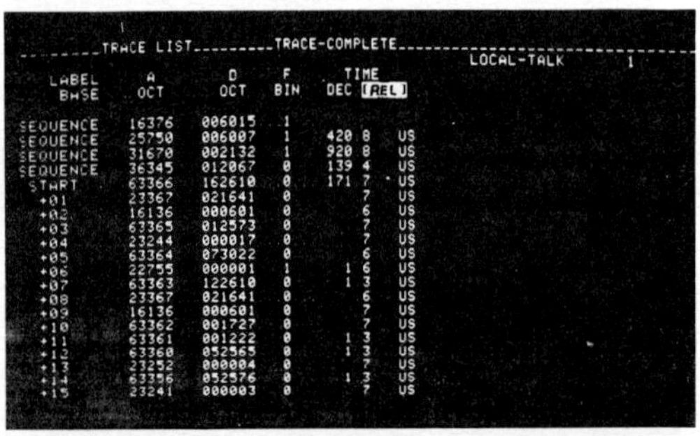

Figure 8. A Trace List of state flow with the differential times between states.

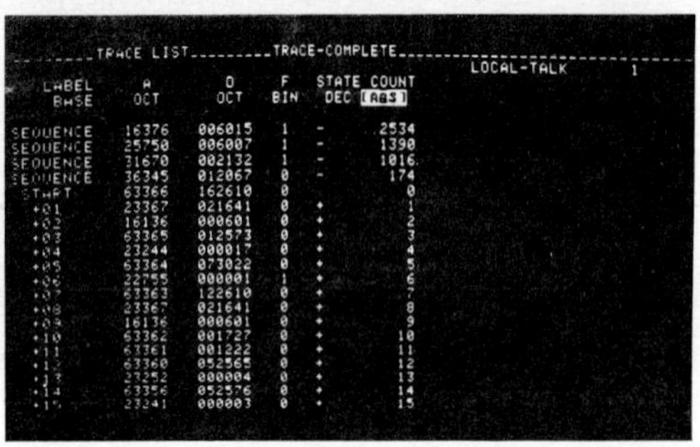

Figure 9. A Trace List of state flow with an absolute count of states shown relative to the start of the trace.

Measurement Examples

From the performance indices table in the Appendix, a selection of four popular indices was made that represents all of the dimensional groups (productivity, responsiveness, and utilization) and all of the functional groups (effectiveness, efficiency, and workload). These indices are: (1) throughput (volume/time), (2) response time (time), (3) component overlap (time/time), and (4) instruction mix (volume/volume).

Throughput

From the perspective of useful work completed by the CPU, a definition of throughput is shown in Figure 10. For this measurement, the Logic Analyzer was instructed to monitor all activity but only store events X_1' and X_2' and

Throughput: Amount of useful work completed per unit of time with a given workload

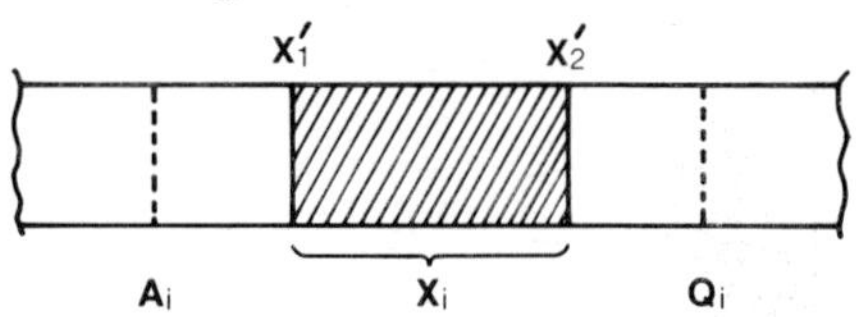

A_i = **Arrival time of Job i**
X_i = **Execution time of Job i**
Q_i = **Completion time of Job i**

$$\text{Throughput} = H = \frac{n}{\sum_{i=1}^{n} X_i}$$

where n = number of jobs

Figure 10. Throughput -- a performance index that is the amount of useful work completed per unit of time with a given workload.

the differential time for each CPU execution, X_i. After many jobs, the controller post-processed the accumulated measurements and displayed the information in a histogram (Figure 11). This display gives an overview of the throughput for all jobs. It can be seen that most job execution times per range were in the range of 32.9 to 39.4 milliseconds, with fewer execution times in ranges 13.6 to 20.1 and 58.7 to 65.1 milliseconds.

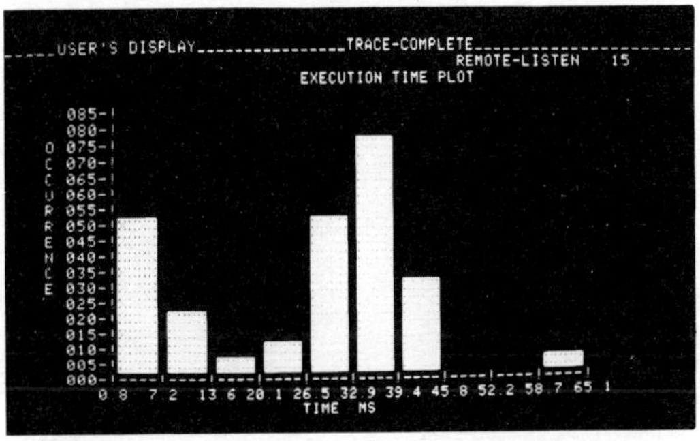

Figure 11. A display of Throughput that shows the volume (occurrences) of jobs that were executed within specific time ranges.

Response Time

For this example, a particular subroutine execution time was measured. The Analyzer was configured to measure the differential time(s) between addresses 1_8 (A_i) and 71400_8 (Q_i), and to store only these states and time differences. The response time is Q_i-A_i. The mean response time is

$$t_e = \frac{1}{n} \sum_{i=1}^{n} (Q_i - A_i). \qquad (1)$$

The output display for five executions of the subroutine is shown in Figure 12.

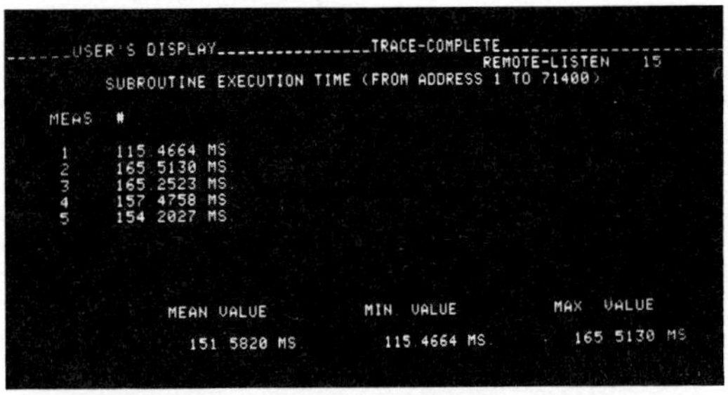

Figure 12. A display of Response Time that shows minimum, maximum, and mean values for five program executions.

Component Overlap

The requirement for this measurement was to monitor three signal lines (flags) and to detect when a transition occurred on any line and to time-tag that event. The output display was to be a horizontal histogram (Gantt chart). The Logic Analyzer was configured to have three data input lines connected in parallel with three clock lines. The clock edge selection was set to (+/-) to allow data storage on any transition on any line. Note that only the HP model 1610B analyzer can be used for this measurement.

The output display, after post-processing is shown in Figure 13.

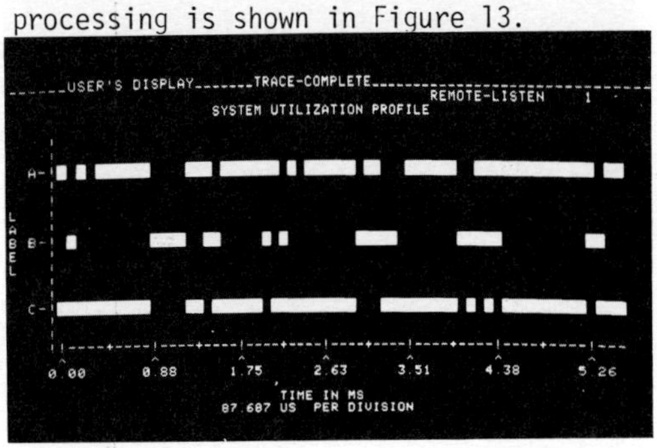

Figure 13. A display of Component Overlap of three resources in a computer system.

Instruction Mix

The objective of this measurement is to determine the ratio of each instruction executed to the total of all instructions executed. In this example, the analyzer is set to "free-run" but acquire only instruction activity. Since a process can have millions of instructions and the analyzer only has a finite memory (64 states for a Model 1610A/B), it was necessary to sample the process instruction stream and to "project" what the instruction mix values were for the process population. The sampling methodology implemented in the controller is explained in the following section, Measurement Accuracy. The resultant output display of the measurement is shown in Figure 14.

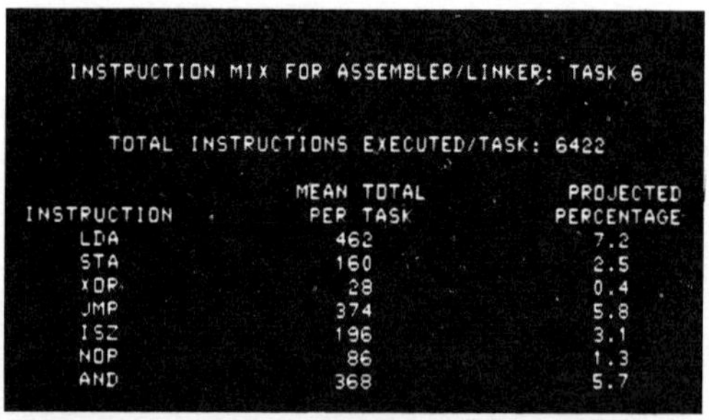

INSTRUCTION MIX FOR ASSEMBLER/LINKER: TASK 6

TOTAL INSTRUCTIONS EXECUTED/TASK: 6422

INSTRUCTION	MEAN TOTAL PER TASK	PROJECTED PERCENTAGE
LDA	462	7.2
STA	160	2.5
XOR	28	0.4
JMP	374	5.8
ISZ	196	3.1
NOP	86	1.3
AND	368	5.7

Figure 14. A partial display of the estimated Instruction Mix for a specific task.

MEASUREMENT ACCURACY

When a measurement system samples a population in order to project certain characteristics of the population, critical factors are sample size, confidence level, confidence interval, and the distribution of the population. When a population has a normal distribution, it is possible to calculate what sample size is required for a particular standard deviation and variance. In general, however, we cannot assume that a program or process has a normal distribution of variables such as instruction mix, occurrences within an address range, or state transition probabilities. What must be known is that if we estimate a value $\hat{\rho}_1$ of a population, how much different is this value from the actual value ρ_1? The question of sample size can be stated as "what is the minimum number of samples such that the

probability of $\left[(|\hat{\rho}_1 - \rho_1| \leq e)\right] \geq K$"

where:

$\hat{\rho}_1$ = Sample mean = $\frac{1}{n}\sum_{i=1}^{n} a_i$

ρ_1 = Actual mean

K = Confidence Level

2e = Confidence Interval

and a_i = Observations of statistically independent samples.

This inequality states that the difference of our estimate and actual value be less than or equal to a specific error, e, and that the probability of this being the case is greater than or equal to K. Figure 15 depicts the confidence interval, 2e, of the mean value estimate $\hat{\rho}_1$.

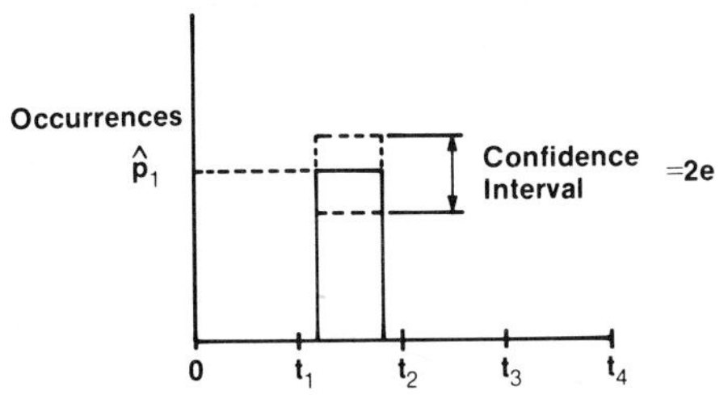

Figure 15. The Confidence Interval of an estimated variable is used to determine the size of the sample.

An important theorem in mathematical statistics, the Central Limit Theorem, shows that regardless of the form or shape of a population distribution, the sampling distribution of the mean of random samples "approaches" a normal distribution as n (sample size) increases. It is this theorem that allows the implementation of a sampling algorithm using a controller and Logic Analyzer.

From the Central Limit Theorem,

$$n \geq \left(\frac{\sigma_1 z}{e} \right)^2 \text{ (normal distribution) } (2)$$

Where n = number of samples

σ_1 = standard deviation of the population being sampled.

z = value from t distribution table reflecting choice of K and n-1 (degrees of freedom)

In general, σ_1 is not known, but can be approximated by:

$$\hat{\sigma}_1 = \left(\frac{\sum_{i=1}^{n} (a_i - \hat{\rho}_1)^2}{n-1} \right)^{1/2} \quad (3)$$

The essence of the sampling methodology is to have a_i be a mean value of the sampled variable, and $\hat{\rho}_1$ would be the mean of the a_i's. A "RUN" can be defined to be ten (arbitrary) analyzer traces, and a_i would be the mean of the variable for this run. Each "RUN", then, must be statistically independent.

At the beginning of a measurement, the user merely inputs to the controller the desired error (2e) and confidence level (K). After the measurement starts, the controller tests each variable for convergence to a value less than or equal to the user-defined specification. Substituting $\hat{\sigma}_1$ equation (3) for σ_1 in equation (2), the resultant inequality (4) describes the interative test of the sampling process.

$$\underbrace{\frac{1}{n} \left[\sum_{i=1}^{n} \frac{(a_i - \hat{\rho}_1)^2}{n-1} \right]}_{\text{dynamic variable}} \leq \underbrace{\frac{e^2}{z^2}}_{\text{user defined}} \quad (4)$$

This algorithm was implemented in several sampling measurements. The results of a sampling measurement which created a state branching probability matrix is shown in Figure 16. In this example, the confidence interval (2e or % Error) was 0.50 and the confidence level (K) was 0.90. The number of traces/run was set at three. One run is treated as a datapoint which for 22 datapoints required 66 traces. The system being analyzed was a 21MX RTE-4B operating system. The elapsed time

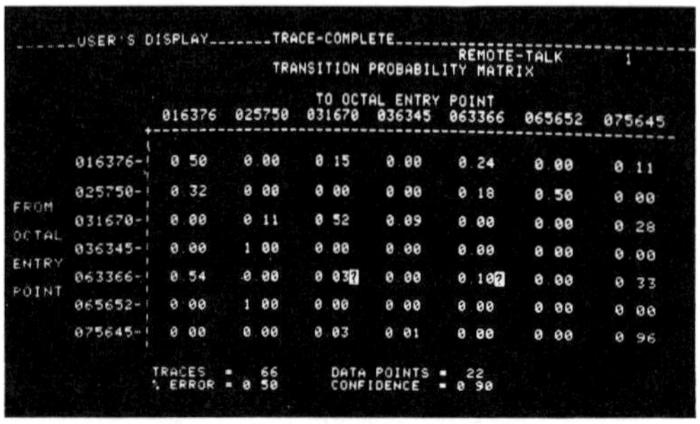

USER'S DISPLAY — TRACE-COMPLETE — REMOTE-TALK 1

TRANSITION PROBABILITY MATRIX

FROM OCTAL ENTRY POINT	TO OCTAL ENTRY POINT 016376	025750	031670	036345	063366	065652	075645
016376	0.50	0.00	0.15	0.00	0.24	0.00	0.11
025750	0.32	0.00	0.00	0.00	0.18	0.50	0.00
031670	0.00	0.11	0.52	0.09	0.00	0.00	0.28
036345	0.00	1.00	0.00	0.00	0.00	0.00	0.00
063366	0.54	0.00	0.03?	0.00	0.10?	0.00	0.33
065652	0.00	1.00	0.00	0.00	0.00	0.00	0.00
075645	0.00	0.00	0.03	0.01	0.00	0.00	0.96

TRACES = 66 DATA POINTS = 22
% ERROR = 0.50 CONFIDENCE = 0.90

Figure 16. The question marks next to the values in the branching probability matrix indicate that the values have not yet met the user-defined confidence level or interval.

to reach the level of convergence shown was about 4.5 minutes. The presence of the question mark next to the probability value indicates that the variable has not yet converged to the user-requested confidence level or interval.

CONCLUSION

A systematic method of computer performance evaluation is now available using Logic Analyzers. Connection to the system-under-test is greatly simplified by using the computer interfaces dedicated to Logic Analysis. Acquiring the necessary parameters of volume (counting states) or time has been shown to be an easy task for the current generation of logic analyzers. Post-processing the acquired data into useful outputs using a controller is a simple yet versatile process, limited only by the imagination of the user. The accuracy of the measurement is also user-definable. A sampling methodology has been shown that allows the measurement system to assess the accuracy of its data, and to indicate to the user when the results are valid.

REFERENCES

1. Ferrari, D., Computer Systems Performance Evaluation, Prentice-Hall, Inc., 1978.
2. Svobodova, L., Computer Performance Measurement and Evaluation Methods: Analysis and Applications, American Elsevier Publishing Co., Inc., 1976.

APPENDIX

	EFFECTIVENESS	EFFICIENCY	WORKLOAD
PRODUCTIVITY (VOLUME/TIME)	Throughput (rate) Production (rate) Capacity/Capability Data processing rate	Page fault frequency Instruction execution rate Page swaps Stack accesses	Job I/O requests Memory requests Subroutine access Utility requests Interrupts Job requests
RESPONSIVENESS (TIME)	Turnaround time Response time System/Activity Enable/Disable	Reaction time I/O wait time CPU wait time Disk seek time Handshake cycle Page swap time Memory access time	Job CPU time CPU service time I/O service time Interarrival time Blocked time User response time Locality of reference
UTILIZATION (DIMENSIONLESS)	Relative throughput Availability	CPU productivity Component overlap System utility Overhead Gain factor ETMF/ITDF	Instruction Mix
OTHER		Queue length Stack depth Memory usage	User intensity Number simultaneous users Number in system Working set size Priority

COMPUTER PERFORMANCE INDICES

RTE panel

Chairman - Marvin McInnis
(McInnis-Skinner & Associates)

The panel was formed to discuss the present and future directions of RTE. The panel members and their topics were:

1. Mike Manley (Hewlett-Packard Co.)
   RTE Future Directions
   (paper not available)

2. David Kitson (Gerber Systems Technology, Inc.)
   Variations on a Theme (RTE) by Hewlett-Packard

3. Larry W. Smith (Hewlett-Packard Co.)
   Circumventing RTE System Memory and Disc Restrictions

variations on a theme (RTE) by hewlett-packard

David H. Kitson

Gerber Systems Technology, Inc.
40 Gerber Road East
South Windsor, CT 06074

ABSTRACT

The paper describes an RTE-IV based "operating environment". Although capabilities similar to those of RTE-IVB session monitor are imbedded in this system, a number of significant differences exist. Those differences considered to be of general interest are addressed in this paper.

The alternate implementation is described in the light of what can be achieved using "RTE-like" systems and with the implication that some of the features discussed should be considered as candidates for implementation by Hewlett-Packard.

I. INTRODUCTION

A. Overview

The subject of this paper is a software system of RTE-ancestry. The software structure of the system will be described in terms of "layered" software. Descriptions of the software components comprising the system will be directed to those features considered to be unique to this implementation and of general interest to the user community. The overall goal of the paper is to present an interesting variation of Hewlett-Packard's Session Monitor product, to perhaps stimulate your imagination, and to suggest some novel features for HP to consider integrating into their product.

B. Brief History of System Evolution

The system was conceived and developed by a group of systems programmers in the mid-1970's who needed a system to support CAD/CAM applications. Some of the unique customer requirements were the stimulus for many of the novel features built into the system.

The initial baseline for the system was RTE-III (Rev. 16--). Working from source listings alone (no RTE Technical Specifications or PICS!), this software group built the system into a successful data management system.

C. Current System Status and Usage

Today the system is RTE-IV-based (Rev. 1840) and soon to be upgraded to RTE-IVB (Rev. 2001). It has aged very gracefully - maintaining its outward appearance, but at the same time learning (bug fixes) and growing (enhancements) as it matures.

It is used as a general purpose program development system, as a data manager, and as the resource allocator in CAD/CAM graphics systems.

II. SYSTEM SOFTWARE STRUCTURE

A. Software Layers

The global structure of the system is graphically presented as a series of concentric software "layers". The criterion for relative layer position being the natural one - the innermost layer of software (the operating system) is a software resource shared and used by all programs in the system. The outermost layer is applications software. By definition, applications software is a user of system resources - both hardware and software. It does not "support" any other body of software in the system.

All remaining software lies somewhere between these two layers. Among this body of "systems" software is:

1. disk-resident software libraries
2. file management system
3. interactive terminal interface programs
4. program development utilities (editor, language translators, loader, etc.)

There is more, but you get the idea. Figure 1 shows a layer diagram built around these ideas.

B. Modified Real Time Executive

In order to support some of the unique system features, modifications to the operating system were required. The philosophy toward modifying HP's code has been and continues to be to enhance wherever required and not remove existing capabilities. In other words, retain compatibility with HP code. These modifications, then, added new capabilities to the system but did not remove or interfere with existing features.

One of the most important objectives was to give the interactive terminal user a greater degree of independence from the rest of the system. Toward this end, we visualized every terminal user as having their own set of "local" logical units. These are to be distinguished from "system" logical units - the logical unit numbers established at system generation time.

The user is permitted to establish a "mapping" between his set of local logical unit numbers and a subset of the available system logical unit numbers. (In some cases, the user may not have this power - a "system administrator" may define this correspondence for him.)

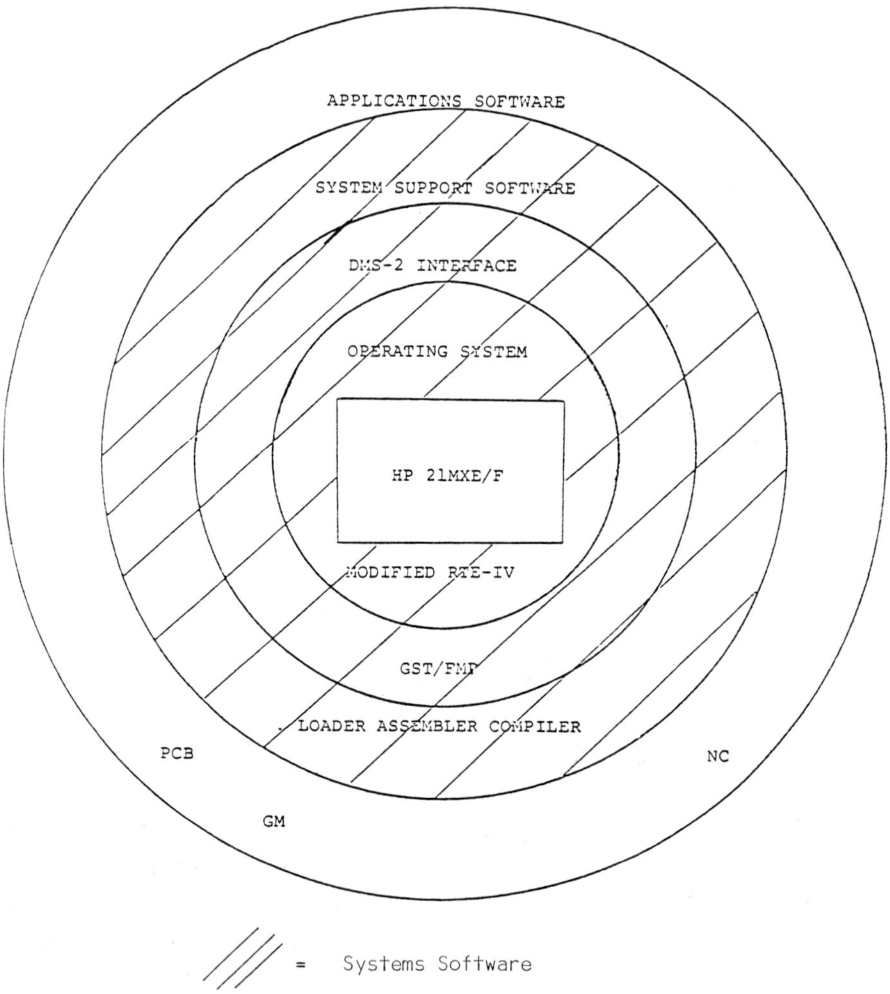

Figure 1: Software Layers

Another capability we wanted was the ability to monitor CPU usage to allow customers to keep track of system usage and to permit accurate billing. This feature was implemented via a "software clock" maintained by the operating system.

In many cases, interactive terminals may not be in close proximity to the rest of the system and/or other system users. This makes sharing of "serial-use" peripheral devices difficult, if not impossible. To alleviate this problem, a more powerful logical unit lock scheme was built into the system. This implementation protects software from "non-cooperating" software.

C. Enhanced File Management System

The area of file management is very important to system as a whole. Security of disk file data was one of the original design goals of the system and greatly influenced the internal structure of the file management system and the interactive terminal handlers.

The system provides for data security at two levels - logical disk cartridge and file. In order to access a particular cartridge, the user must be authorized to do so (by the system administrator).

Files have two levels of protection. First is a sixteen-bit "user code" which establishes whether a particular user has access rights to this file. If the user codes to not match, then the file essentially does not exist relative to that user. The second level of protection is the conventional security code, a'la HP.

D. Interactive Terminal Handlers

For each interactive terminal in the system, a "terminal handler" is assigned. The purpose of the handler is to provide a convenient man-machine interface for the interactive user. Since this part of the system is the subject of a separate paper, it will not be discussed here.

E. Subsystems

Several software subsystems may/may not be part of the system, depending upon customer needs. Among these are:

1. program development
2. backup/archive
3. data base management

4. Remote Job Entry

(and others)

Since these subsystems are not germane to the subject matter of this paper, they will not be discussed here.

F. System Utilities

As is usually the case at a software installation, we have, through the "ages", developed a set of utility programs to assist with various specific problem situations.

The utilities to be addressed here all deal with various aspects of system resource management (i.e., ID segments, system track pool, etc.). Since these problems are generic to RTE systems, I would like to share them with you.

III. REAL TIME EXECUTIVE MODIFICATIONS

A. Logical Unit Translation

The logical unit translation capability required that modifications be made to the Executive Central Control Module (EXEC4) and the RTE-IV Input/Output Control Module (RTI04). When an operating system service is requested (i.e., EXEC call), bit 14 of the request code word is saved for use by the translation logic in RTI04. This bit enables (Ø)/disables (1) the translation logic.

When control is passed to RTI04, the translate flag is interrogated. If no translation is desired, RTI04 proceeds using the logical unit supplied in the call. If translation is desired, validity checks are made, the user logical unit translation table address is determined, and the translation by direct table look-up occurs.

The translation tables are allocated in table area 2 of the system and are set up and maintained by the terminal monitor program (see Figure 2).

B. Software Clock

This feature was implemented via minor changes to the Real Time Clock - Time List Processing Module (RTIME). When the time base generator (TBG) "ticks", an interrupt is generated which results in transfer of control to the RTIME module of the operating system. The logic added will determine the address of the ULUT table entry for the current process (if any). It then increments a double-word integer value contained in the ULUT table.

When the user logs off the system, the terminal handler uses the software clock to update (on a disk file) the cumulative CPU usage value for that user.

C. Logical Unit Lock

To implement the logical unit lock feature required changes in RTI04, the LURQ system library subroutine, the allocation of a "lock" table, and some new commands for interactive users. The logic for this feature in RTI04 is shown in Figure 3.

The scheme is considered an improvement over the HP implementation in that it ensures cooperation in the use of non-sharable devices because the lock is attempted whether the user requests it (via LURQ) or not. The set of system logical units which are "lockable" is configurable and can be easily modified by the system administrator.

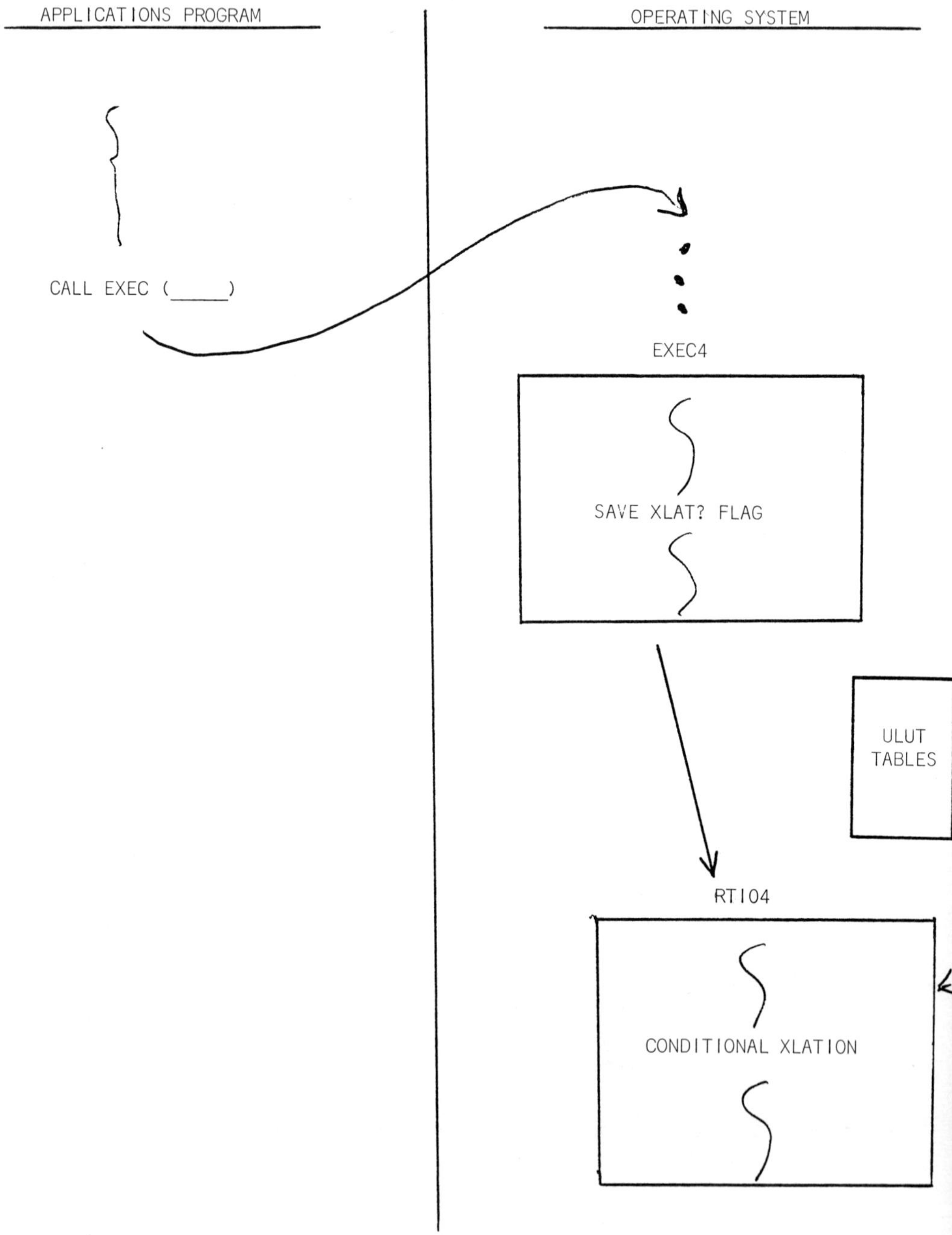

Figure 2: Logical Unit Translation

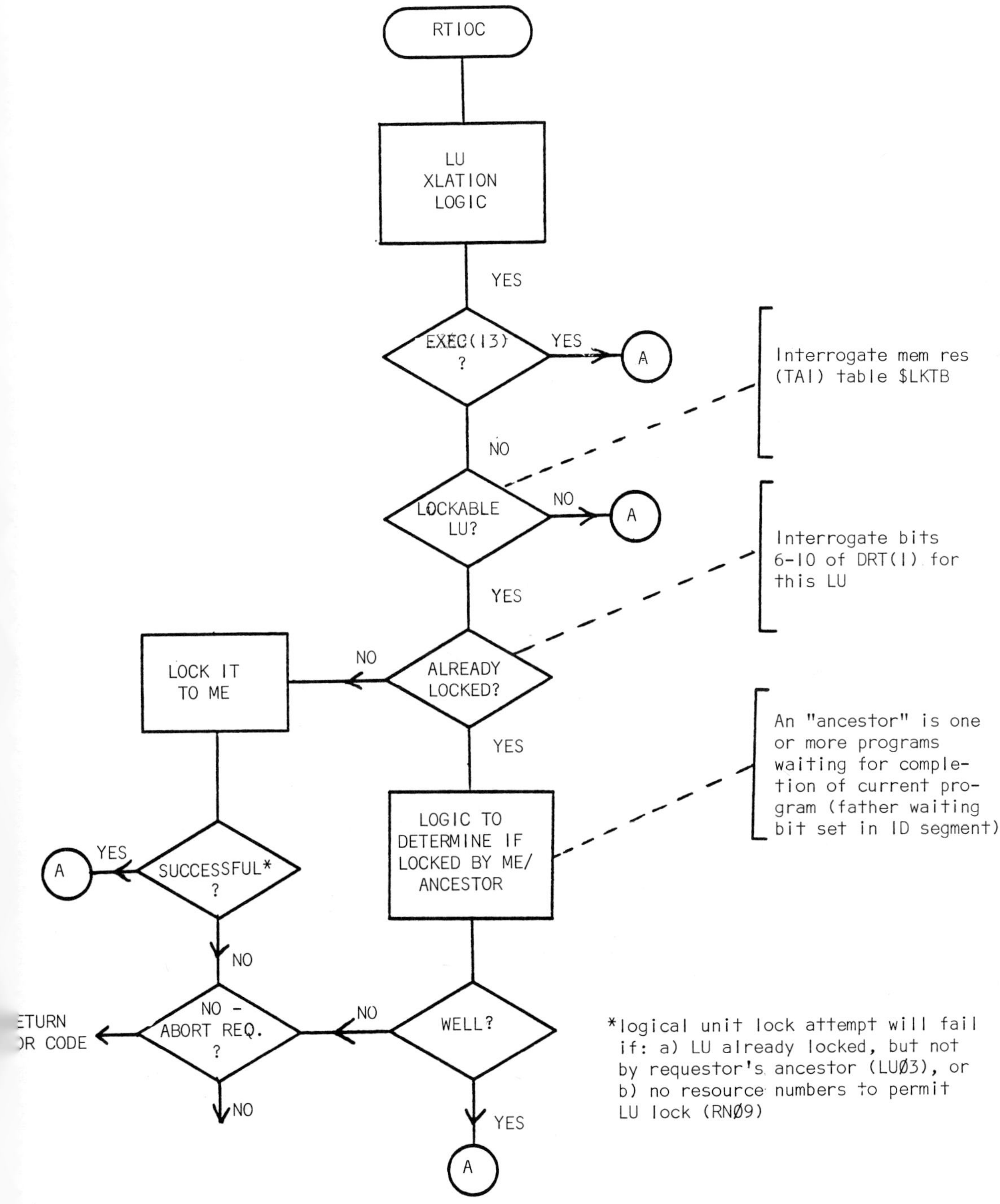

Figure 3: Logical Unit Lock Logic

IV. FILE MANAGEMENT SYSTEM

The File Management System (FMS) is very similar to the HP FMS from a user software point of view. In fact, user software which runs on HP-1000 systems can be run on this system as long as it does not use the contents of the DCB. However, it does contain very significant and valuable extensions which provide for file security as well as increasing the "usability" of the system.

A. Extended Directory Entries

Cartridge and file directory entries are 128 words in length (see Figures 4 and 5) versus 16 words for HP. This extra space is used to accommodate the following features (among others):

1. thirty-character filenames
2. fifty-character file descriptors
3. date and time coding for file creation
4. date and time coding for last file open
5. date and time coding for last file modification
6. file size/extent information

B. Linked Extents (RTE-IVB Release Only)

File extents are linked in a one-way list originating with the master directory entry. The disk address of the next extent is contained in the file directory entry.

This feature permits much faster access to file extents because serial searching of the file directory for the next extent is not necessary.

C. Extendable Type I Files

Additional logic was added to the FMP to permit type I files to have extents.

D. File Security

File security is provided at two levels: logical cartridge and individual files. In order for a particular user to access a cartridge, he must be granted that right by the system administrator. This is achieved by maintaining in each cartridge directory entry a list of (up to 100) user ID's having access rights (see Figure 4).

At the time access to a particular cartridge is attempted, the directory manager program will check the user ID of the user against the list of user ID's in the cartridge directory. If no match occurs, then an error return (-6) occurs.

Individual file security is provided in a similar fashion. Transparent to users of the file management system, the user ID of the file creator is carried along as part of the filename. In order to access a particular file, the user ID's must again match.

Words	Contents
1	BIT 15 = 1, BIT 14 = Ø Remaining bits = CARTRIDGE NUMBER
2 16	30-CHARACTER CARTRIDGE LABEL
17	RESERVED
18	FIRST TRACK FOR FMP
19	NUMBER OF SECTORS/TRACK
20	NEXT FMP TRACK
21	NEXT FMP SECTOR
22	LAST FMP TRACK +1 (LOWEST DIRECTORY TRCK)
23	NUMBER OF DIRECTORY TRACKS
24	DATE DISC LAST SECURED
25	TAPE DISC LAST SECURED ON
26	USER ID INITIALIZED TO THIS DISC OR -1 IF ALL (GLOBAL CARTRIDGE)
27 125	SAME AS 26 FOR UP TO 100 USERS TOTAL
126 128	RESERVED FOR FUTURE USE

Figure 4: Cartridge Directory Format

Words	Contents
1 . 15	30 CHARACTER FILE NAME
16	2 CHARACTER USER ID CODE
17 41	50 CHARACTER KEYWORD ID FIELD
42	SECURITY CODE
43	BLOCKING DELIMITER
44	USER FILE TYPE CODE
45	FILE TYPE WORD (see Section 4.2.9)
46	FILE STATUS WORD (see Section 4.2.11)
47	STARTING TRACK
48	EXTENT NUMBER *STARTING SECTOR
49	NUMBER OF SECTORS IN THE FILE
50	RECORD LENGTH (TYPE 2 FILES)
51	DATE CREATED ((YEAR-1975*1000)+JULIAN DAY)
52	TIME CREATED IN MINUTES
53	DMS VERSION NUMBER
54	USER VERSION NUMBER
55	LIBRARY # LAST ARCHIVED TO
56	LIBRARY # LAST BACKED UP TO
57	OM* OPEN FLAGS (ID SEGMENT ADDRESSES)
64	OM* UP TO 8 USERS MAXIMUM
	OM = 1 = EXCLUSIVE OPEN FOR READ/WRITE ACCESS
	OM = 0 = NON-EXCLUSIVE OPEN FOR READ ONLY
65 72	ACCOUNT NAME
73	DATE FILE LAST OPENED
74	TIME FILE LAST OPENED
75	DATE FILE LAST MODIFIED
76	TIME FILE LAST MODIFIED
77 128	RESERVED

Figure 5: File Directory Format

V. SYSTEM UTILITIES

In this section, I would like to address some system resource management problems which have been successfully dealt with in this system and which are applicable to HP-1000 systems.

A. Track Pool Fragmentation

The operating system manages a "pool" of tracks on logical units 2 and 3 (if present) which are available to user programs. One of the "user" programs which is a heavy user of these tracks is the LOADR program. When programs are loaded, they reside on tracks allocated from the track pool. If the program is loaded as a temporary program, the tracks used by the program will be returned to the pool of available tracks when the system is rebooted. If the program is loaded as a permanent program, the system "remembers" that the program occupies those tracks from one system boot to another.

The fragmentation problem is that over a period of time, as many programs are loaded (permanently), the pool of available tracks tends to become sprinkled with groups of tracks allocated to permanent programs. This has the effect of decreasing the size of the largest group of contiguous tracks available for allocation. Eventually, this size becomes so small that the editor program cannot execute because there are no groups of tracks (contiguous) large enough to satisfy its minimum request. (Same for LOADR).

Our solution to this problem is a program which is scheduled from the "Welcome" file at boot time. This program "packs" the system disk by moving all permanent programs to lower track address where possible, packing them as tightly as possible. We never have problems with track pool fragmentation!

In order to use disk space on LU2 as efficiently as possible, we do not abide by the HP convention of always starting a permanent program at sector Ø of a track. We pack them "head to tail". As a result, we have made a minor modification to the track deallocation logic in the loader program. When a permanent program is purged, the tracks are checked for other "residents" prior to deallocation!

B. Shortage of ID Segments/System Available Memory

The problems to which we turn our attention now need no introduction for those who have worked on an HP-1000 system which is heavily loaded. So on to our solution.

The objective of the solution was to permit segmented programs to execute in a system using only one ID segment. So for a program with, say, 200 segments (don't laugh - there are some!), we would save the need for allocating all those precious ID segment slots to a single program plus we could make more SAM available by reducing the number of ID segments in our system. Figures 6 and 7 illustrate the standard Hewlett-Packard program segmentation scheme and the alternative scheme we have developed.

C. System Configurability

As a supplier of turnkey graphics systems, we find ourselves in the position of having to satisfy quite a diverse range of system configuration requirements. In order to minimize the number of system builds we perform, we have developed a number of techniques and procedures for making our systems quite flexible in terms of logical unit/equipment table configuration and disk subchannel layout.

D. System Generation Considerations

The following practices are observed for all our system generations:

1. include all I/O drivers which might be needed (ever)
2. define the maximum number of disk subchannels allowed
3. allocate the maximum number of EQT's and LU's
4. set up a "skeleton" EQT for each different driver entry point

E. Configuration at Boot Time

In the Welcome file, all system LU's (except 1, 2, and 3, of course) are set up. A special utility program called IOCC is used to copy EQT's and set up slot numbers. Peripheral disk subchannels are defined via a utility program called DIOCC. This program patches the appropriate track map tables.

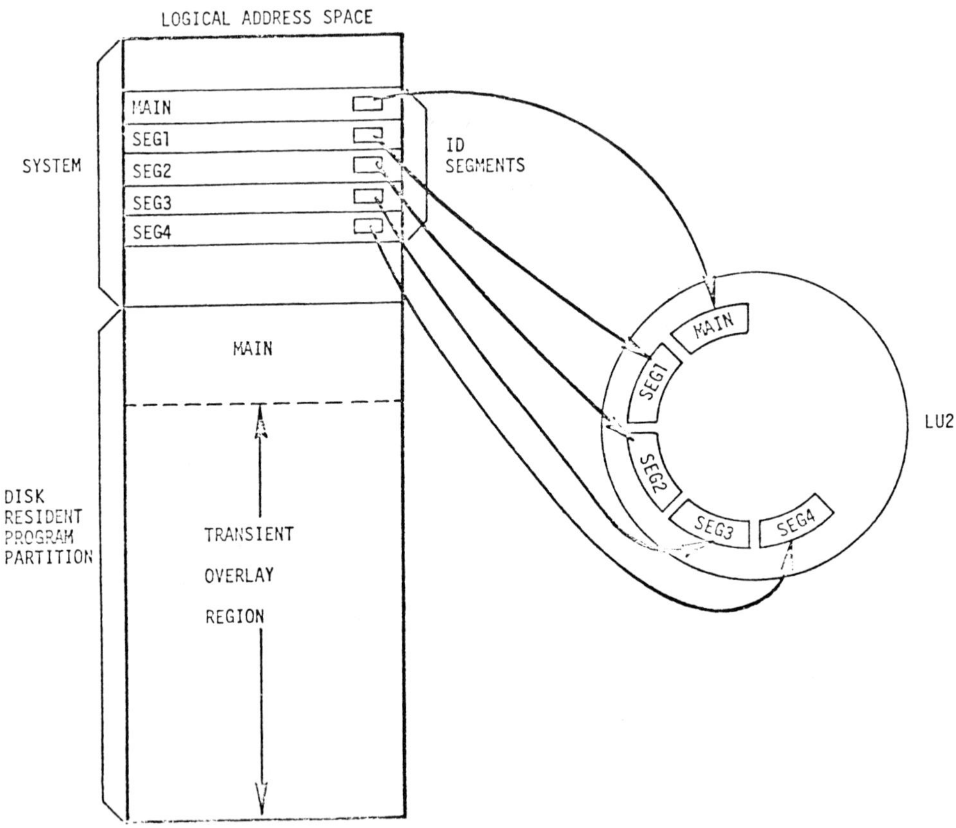

Figure 6: Standard HP Segmentation

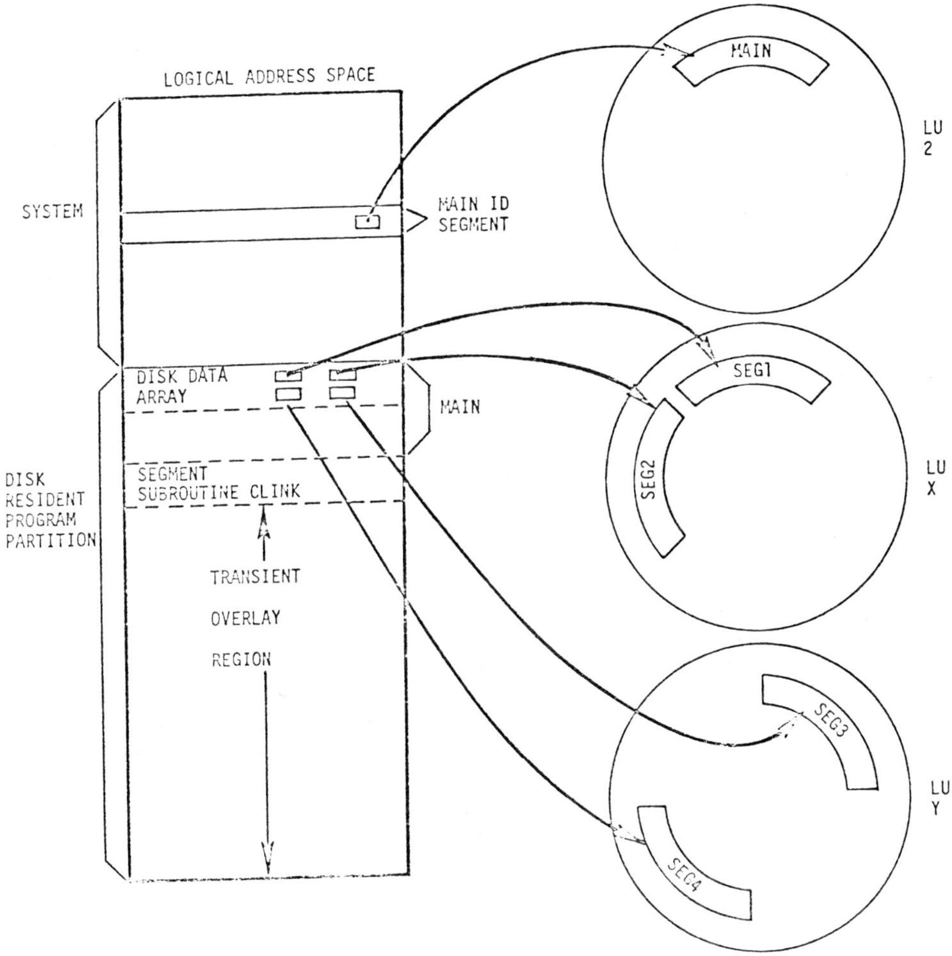

Figure 7: Alternate Segmentation Scheme

VI. WRAP-UP

I hope that you have found the "variation" presented interesting, if not pleasant, to the "ears" of your programming mind. The RTE nucleus offers a good base from which to build all kinds of interesting systems.

I also would like to request that Hewlett-Packard consider some of the utility program/procedures for incorporation into their product.

In addition, some more "food" for thought:

1. Make system building faster and easier.
2. Use more sophisticated searching techniques in system software to improve performance.
3. Add an "immediate" operand instruction format to the HP-1000 base set. This would save space and time.
4. Issue guidelines/offer courses on system tuning.

circumventing RTE system memory and disc restrictions

Larry W. Smith

Hewlett-Packard Co.
Fullerton, CA 92631

Introduction

An operating system is much like a politician; each serves the interests and desires of others. Hewlett-Packard's Real-Time Executive Operating System (version RTE-IVB), unlike a politician, delivers solutions within a marketplace that is both diversified and changing at a very fast pace. To discover that a particular operating system is not all things to all people can be somewhat disappointing at first, but after all, this is quite normal. The simple fact of the matter is that any operating system is nothing more than a general purpose collection of tools explicitly designed to offer a wide range of services within a certain area of application. Furthermore, its designers are also people and quite frequently users of the system that they are developing. All in all and perhaps for the sake of brevity, RTE is like a box of crescent wrenches--each wrench aids in solving a particular problem. It could further be said that the HP 1000 system with RTE is a project machine capable of solving a variety of different problems.

Summary

This paper will cover two major areas where significant system restrictions have been placed upon the user that cannot be overcome without specially designed software. These areas are as follows:

1. Extending EMA usage (making it shareable)

2. Adding extra segment loading flexibility (removing system LU 2 & 3 constraints)

With the addition of these two capabilities RTE becomes as powerful as most large mainframes and in the first area much more powerful.

In most RTE applications that put stringent demands on standard HP supplied software, the above two problems are very common and seem to eventually surface at some point during the application. This is why these two areas were chosen by the author such that solutions can be presented accompanied with program listings.

I think that you will find the remainder of this paper interesting and hopefully something you can take back with you and implement into your application.

Summary

Extending EMA Usage

Some Real-Time applications require fast response time. In general, the faster the response required usually means that time critical functions be put in memory rather than on other devices such as a disc in order to achieve desired speed. These functions could be in the form of programs, subroutines, data areas, or RTE system routines.

We will discuss a technique involving making large data areas available for sharing amongst several executing programs. The author has coined this capability as SHEMA/1000, which means shared-EMA. The software modules developed for SHEMA/1000 are contained in PLUS/1000 under the category of and as program number E08001.

EMA was a significant enhancement to RTE and the 16-bit architecture as a whole as it gave the user the capability of using the rest of physical memory as one large data area, the maximum being about 915K words in a minimally generated system. In addition, HP supplied a set of firmware routines to increase access time of data items within the EMA area. The user can obtain this large data area by using the EMA option during compile or assembly time and produce a relocatable object module containing all the proper EMA calls to access the data. Thus, a large area of memory can now be used for time critical functions instead of a slower speed media such as disc. But unfortunately EMA is only accessible on an individual program basis, unlike data on disc. Therefore, this would immediately eliminate any schemes of directly sharing an EMA area with other programs residing in other partitions, which is usually what most applications using EMA demand.

The user is now faced with the problem of discovering the feasibility of implementing a shared-EMA capability into the system without modifying the standard software. This will require a thorough understanding of EMA firmware and operating system internals to launch an investigation into the feasibility of sharing EMA.

Implementation of Shared-EMA

Fortunately, the RTE system was designed from day one with a variety of flexible tables that are used to manage its basic resources--CPU, memory, and devices. Matter of fact, the majority of restrictions placed upon a user can easily be overcome by simply manipulating information contained within these tables. Without this type of operating system design, it is quite possible that a scheme such as shared EMA could not have been developed without modifying system code.

As it turns out, an easy-to-use and quite flexible on-line solution was found that has five prime advantages to the potential user:

1. Requires no disc or system memory code changes. This means that your software and any subsystems remain supported by HP.

2. Does not degrade system performance assuming proper precautionary steps are taken.

3. Uses standard means of declaring EMA at the language level.

4. Any area of memory (declared or undefined) can be shared.

5. One or more shared areas can be partitioned among several programs.

In addition, individual execution times remain relatively the same and the extra code needed within each program to set up shared access is insignificant.

A typical application could consist of two programs, say SCANI and AQUIR, that both require access to the same 80K word area of memory. This is pictorially shown below in Figure 1.

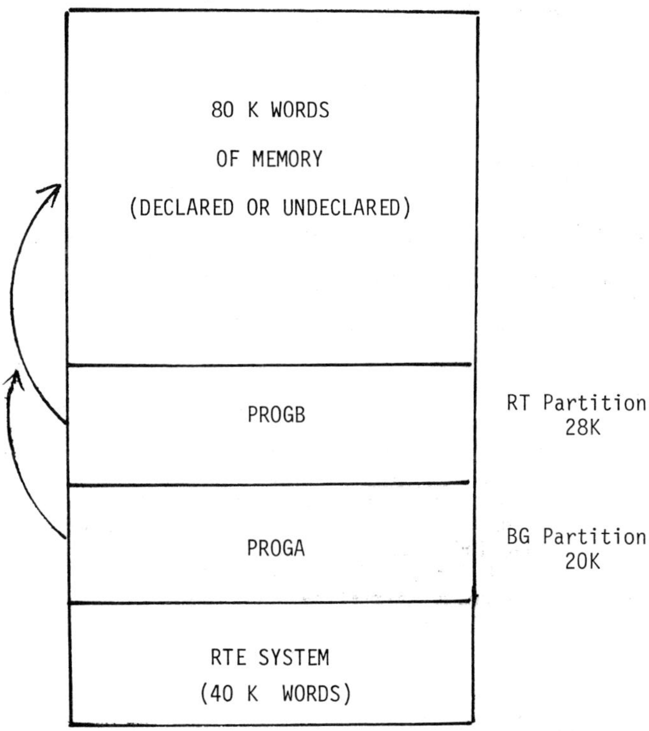

Figure 1

AQUIR collects a series of high-speed analog readings and stores them in the shared area of memory. The program SCANI scans the raw data readings, converts selected ones to engineering units, and schedules another program, UPDAT, which saves the converted results into a disc file.

The solution described later not only allows as much memory as possible to be shared in any increments, but also all program types (1, 2, 3, 4, 5) can be used.

In order to implement shared-EMA, two tables must be manipulated in order to overcome three major system restrictions:

1. The scheduler and dispatcher have to be fooled into thinking that a program does not have EMA requirements. This involves manipulating information in a program's main ID segment.

2. Each program participating in sharing an area of memory has to be set up to point to the proper starting page number. This involves manipulating information in a program's ID extension.

3. The scheduler and dispatcher have to be un-fooled prior to program execution of any EMA code. This entails manipulating data again in a program's ID extension.

Once the appropriate tables have been modified and all participating programs dispatched, sharing of the EMA area is automatic.

There are three basic steps that must be taken by the user in order to successfully be able to share memory as mentioned above. The steps are as follows:

Step 1: Load a program pre-processor into the system.

Step 2: Load all participating programs into the system.

Step 3: Schedule each participating program

Step 1

Since each participating program must be compiled and loaded with EMA requirements, a means must be found to schedule each program into a normal Real-Time or background partition instead of a mother partition which reflects the size of the EMA area declared by the program. A program called "SHEMA" was written that has the function of nulling a program's EMA requirements in word 28 of its ID segment and then scheduling it without wait, thereby allowing it to be dispatched into a normal partition. Word 28 of a program's ID segment contains two types of information

15 — 10	9 — 0
ID Extension No.	EMA Size
Ordinal position in ID extension table. A value of 3 would indicate the third ID extension.	Maximum number of EMA pages declared at load time.

The ID extension table is in Table Area II of the system and is accessed by an entry point name of "$IDEX". SHEMA must retrieve this address and pass it to the participating program along with the original contents of ID word 28. The participating program must then call another subroutine called "IDMAP" to restore ID word 28 and get in the starting physical page number of the desired area to be shared.

To load SHEMA, use the following sequence:

```
:RU,LOADR
/LOADR: RE,%SHEMA
/LOADR: RE,%IDEXT
/LOADR: END
```

SHEMA can be scheduled into any partition except a partition within the shared area of memory.

Step 2

The second step is to load all participating programs along with a subroutine called "IDMAP" as you would normally. A typical program loading sequence would be as follows:

```
:RU,LOADR
/LOADR: RE,%PROG
/LOADR: RE,%IDMAP
/LOADR: END
```

Once each program has been loaded into the system, SHEMA must be run once for each program prior to actual execution such that the original contents of ID word 28 can be restored.

The structure of each participating program is extremely important. The basic sequence of events must be as follows:

```
FTN4,L
$EMA(I,0)
      PROGRAM TEST
      COMMON/I/J(32000),K(32000)
      DIMENSION IPARM(5)
        .
        .
        .
      CALL RMPAR(IPARM)                        IPARM(1) = Starting
        .                                                 physical
        .                                                 page #
        .                                      IPARM(2) = Original
      CALL IDMAP(IPARM)                                   contents of
        .                                                 ID word 28
        .
        .
        .
```

```
CALL EXEC(13,1,IDUM)
   .
   .
   .
(...user code that can now access EMA area...)
   .
   .
   .
END
END$
```

The dummy EXEC status request is only necessary when a mixture of subscripted and unsubscripted variables are used within the shared EMA area. This ensures proper mapping.

Step 3

The final step involves scheduling the pre-processor once per program. The purpose of this step is to allow SHEMA to save and zero out word 28 of the program's main ID segment such that the RTE system will dispatch it into a normal (or mother) partition without knowing about its actual EMA requirements, and to put the starting physical page number into bits 0-9 of word 2 of the program's ID extension. This is required by the EMA firmware. For example, SHEMA would be run as follows:

```
:RU,SHEMA,PROGA,88
:RU,SHEMA,PROGB,88
```

To obtain and verify proper results, we would run SHEMA as follows:

```
:RU,SHEMA,,,-1
PROGRAM ADDRESS CONTENTS
------- ------- --------

EMA1    27077   000050
EMA2    27201   002050
```

SHEMA terminates with saving resources and saves all ID words for possible later restore (IFUN>0). A word of caution should be noted:

> If a participating program is loaded permanently, it must not be reloaded without first restoring its main ID.

Conclusion

Although shared EMA has a wide range of possible applications, the user should proceed with caution and investigate the application before implementing SHEMA/1000. Some limitations are as follows:

1. The usage of EMA variables creates bigger program sizes than non-EMA variables. This can be partially reduced by the use of EQUIVALENCE statements.

2. Caution must be taken that a program's declared EMA size does not exceed the total amount of physical memory. If this is done, a value of zero will be returned.

3. A dummy EXEC status request must be made to ensure proper mapping is done when a mixture of subscripted and unsubscripted variables are used within the shared area of memory.

4. There is no memory management such as lock-out between programs accessing the same areas of memory.

Summary

Adding Extra Segment Loading Flexibility

Segmentation is the most efficient means of logically extending the size of the largest loadable program. This type of program extension offers three major advantages to the potential user:

1. Allows the program to more directly manage segment loading during execution.

2. The number of segments is limited only by the amount of available disc space.

3. Requires the least amount of operating system overhead.

The overall effectiveness of each of the above advantages depends upon how the segmentation scheme is implemented. As a general rule, segmentation is usually more overall effective than other methods such as virtual storage and code segments.

The RTE relocating loader allows automatic loading of most segmented programs by creating absolute memory image modules on the system and/or auxiliary disc work areas. At the end of a successful load, the loader fills out blank ID segments for the main program and each segment that is later used by the operating system. The ID segments, a type 2, 3, or 4 for a main program and a type 5 for a segment, are used as a table look-up scheme for program scheduling and dispatching and segment loading. Since all ID segments are kept in a contiguous block of memory in Table Area II of the system, the user has an extremely expedient means of loading segments and dispatching programs.

The current method of segmentation places some rather significant restrictions on the user. Some of these are as follows:

1. All segments (as well as main programs) must reside on LU = 3 in either the work area or in an FMP file.

2. The total number of loaded (or RP'd) programs and segments is 254.

3. The maximum number of tracks on LU = 2 and LU = 3 is 512, minus the size of the operating system and any FMP tracks.

All of these limitations are due to the internal structure of ID segments and other related system tables. If it were not for issues such as upward compatibility and the long evaluation of RTE as a system, program segmentation and other important system areas could be greatly enhanced.

Let's take a look at the existing system and see why such limitations as those discussed above exist. To begin, there are two primary tables in RTE that are used to manage programs and segments:

Keyword Table
ID Segment Table

The keyword table is constructed of one-word entries, each of which contains an address which points to the first word of a main ID segment or the first word plus 12 of a segment's ID segment (called a short ID). This table is built by the system generator, is fixed-length with a maximum of 256 entries, and is terminated by a value of zero. The head of the keyword table is an address contained in base page location 1650 octal. The ID segment table is also contructed by the system generator, is fixed-length, and consists of two types of entries:

Long ID's - 33 Words Each for Main Programs
Short ID's - 9 Words Each for Segments

RTE uses the ID segment as a scratch area to manage the life of a program as it changes from state to state in Real Time. The relationships between these tables can be shown as follows:

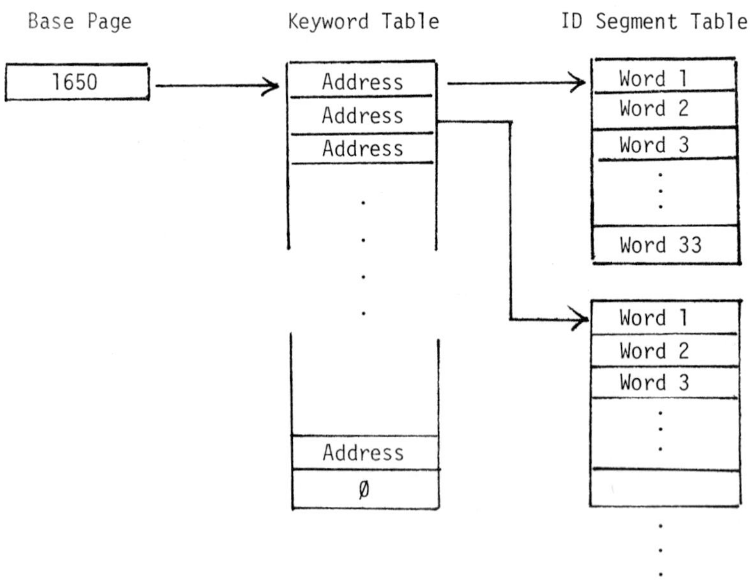

Other system tables such as the Memory Allocation Table and the Class I/O Table are constructed around the maximum length of the Keyword Table and would have to be significantly changed in order to accommodate greater flexibility. When one program schedules another, bits 0-7 in main ID word 21 of the father program--contain the ordinal position in the Keyword Table of the program it scheduled. Furthermore, there are a number of standard HP supplied software subsystems that access ID segments and pointers in other tables referencing ID segments.

Loading Segments from FMP Files

In order to overcome the limitation of the maximum number of short ID segments, a method of directly loading the contents of an SP'd segment into the segment overlay area must be found. The advantages of this approach would be as follows:

1. Unlimited number of segments.
2. Segment can be located on any disc LU.
3. Built-in FMP file protection.
4. A short ID segment is never used (nor needed).

The user is now capable of loading as many segments as disc space will allow, and any system table dependency is eliminated.

To implement this capability, it would be desirable to replace the "CALL EXEC" with a call to a subroutine, say "SLOAD". SLOAD would accomplish the segment loading and transfer of control to the segment. In order to accomplish this, the structure of a type 6 file must be known. The format of an SP'd type 6 file is as follows:

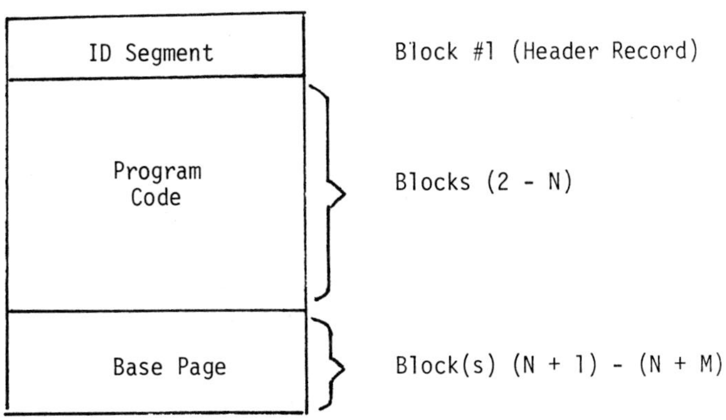

Block #1: Words 23-24 Contain Program Length - 1
Words 25-26 Contain Base Page Length - 1

The SLOAD subroutine reads the header record to retrieve program and base page bounds. The program area can then be directly read into the segment overlay area since this part of the user's partition is unprotected. The base page area is then loaded by reading a record at a time, calling an assembly language subroutine named "BPMOV" to move the record onto base page in privileged mode, and finally transferring control to the segment via a "JSB Ø,I" instruction. The segment could then save the return address and return to the main at the point of call.

Conclusion

The above method of loading segments is an effective way to overcome any system restrictions placed on program segmentation. If you are a user with a very large number of segments, you will have to make two or more loads with the main program (or root), the largest segment, and the other remaining segments. Similar loading capabilities exist in HP standard supplied software in a program called "APLDR" in RTE-M and a subroutine called "SEGLD" in RTE-IVB. The "SEGLD" subroutine is very limited and induces a considerable amount of system overhead. Other methods of loading segments could be developed by performing an EXEC input directly onto the base page area or by using $XSIO calls.

I would be extremely interested in hearing from you if you can use anything in the paper. Please phone or write to:

Larry W. Smith and Associates
2641 Franki St.
Orange, CA 92665

Phone: (714) 974-5638 Home
(714) 870-1000 Business

MUCH MUCH THANKS TO:

Gene Hathaway

For so professionally preparing this paper.

Dean Millett

My boss for allowing preparation time.

Bob French & Bill Grist

For their time and technical assistance.

I THANK YOU

(And BRUNO Thanks You)

COPY OF LECTURE OVERHEAD SLIDES

LARRY W. SMITH

TOPIC AREAS:

A. Sharing EMA

B. FMP Segment Loading

$ $

The universal solution

to any computer

problem is ___

B M M

$ $

BUY

MORE

MEMORY *

* *Known within HP circles as "Meyers Universal Solution"*

EMA: Can it be shared?

Standard EMA:

A. Extends memory data area to 2 mega-bytes.

B. Several programs can each have their own EMA area.

C. EMA firmware greatly increases access time.

D. Runs on RTE-IVA or IVB.

E. EMA cannot be shared.

Shared EMA:

A. Any number of programs can share same or over-lapping areas of memory.

B. Uses standard means of declaring EMA at the source level.

C. Standard means of program loading.

D. No system code changes.

E. No hardware memory lock-out or protection between participating programs.

Steps for implementing shared–EMA:

1. Modify programs main ID segment before it is scheduled.
2. Program must then restore it's main ID segment.
3. Program issues a dummy status request to any LU.

EMA is now shareable

Shared EMA Pre-Processor

Purpose: To schedule a program as if it does not have requirements.

Operation:

RU,SHEMA,program,page#,ifun

Program Name to be Scheduled

Starting Physical Page Number To Be Shared

Program Function:

(–) – Restore all ID's

(0) – Enter a program

(+) – List all prog's

SHEMA Processing

1. Terminates with saving resources for IFUN#0.
2. Performs extensive error checking:
   a. Program loaded?
   b. Program disc-resident?
   c. Program dormant?
   d. Program loaded with EMA requirements?
3. Schedule program immediate without wait.

Applications for shared EMA:

1. CAD
2. CAM
3. Simulation
4. Graphics
5. Fast Real-Time data acq.
6. Political Redistricting.
7. Word Processing.
8. Text Editing.

   .
   .
   .

B. FMP Segment Loading

Standard Program Segmentation:

A. Segments must be self-contained on LU=2 or 3 in either the work area or an FMP file.

B. Total number of loaded (or RP'd) segments is 254 minus any main programs.

C. Maximum number of tracks on LU=2 and LU=3 is 512 minus operating system and FMP areas.

Loading Segments Directly From Any FMP File Area

A. Number of segments limited by available disc space.ed

B. Segments can be located on any disc LU!

C. Built-in FMP protection.

D. Short ID segment not used.

E. Automatic return to main.

SLOWER BUT MORE FLEXIBLE

SLOAD Relpaces 'CALL EXEC(8,...)'

CALL SLOAD(IERR,name,sc,cr)

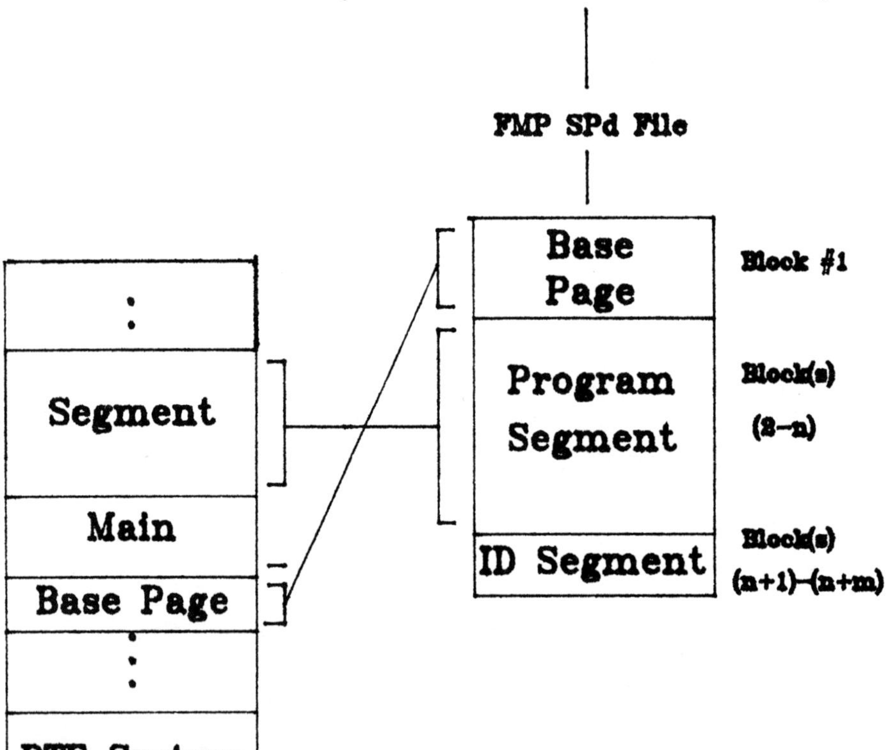

PROGRAM STRUCTURE

```
FTN4,L
      PROGRAM MAIN
            .
            .
      CALL SLOAD(IERR,'SEG1',ISC,ICR)
      IF(IERR)99,100
   99 <...File Open Error...>
            .
            .
  100 <...Segment Return...>
      END
      END$
```

SLOAD Subroutines:

FREAD, BPMOV, SJUMP

CALL FREAD(IDCB,IERR,IADRS,IL,LEN,NREC)

Reads a record from an FMP file into the specified address contained in 'IADRS'.

CALL BPMOV(IBUFR,IDRES,NWORDS)

Moves a block of data in 'IBUFR' of 'NWORDS' words onto base page.

CALL SJUMP(IADRS)

Transfers control to the loaded segm at address 'IADRS'.

the gerber data management system: a powerful operating environment based on RTE

John J. Robinson

Gerber Systems Technology, Inc.
40 Gerber Road East
South Windsor, Connecticut 06074

ABSTRACT: In the area of Computer Aided Design and Manufacturing, there is a need for capabilities which are not available in the standard HP File Manager or Session Monitor. The purpose of the Gerber Data Management System (DMS) is to expand and enhance the capabilities provided by HP. This is accomplished by replacing the actual File Manager/Session Monitor with the DMS. It provides similar functions, but communicates with the user in easily understandable terms and prompts for required information. It also provides varied levels of security as well as maximum flexibility in changing system configuration. Since many users write their own application programs, DMS allows easy integration of those programs into the system command structure so that they can be provided with the same interface as the standard DMS commands.

USER INTERFACE

The DMS system is oriented toward ease of user operation. Toward this end, the DMS commands are English language like. A few examples are given below.

COMMAND	DESCRIPTION
??	LIST COMMANDS...??(,COMMAND)
LIST	LIST FILES......LIST,NAMR(,FORMAT)(,REC#)(,#RECS)
DELETE	DELETE FILES....DELETE,FILE NAME
COPY	COPY FILES......COPY,FROM NAMR,TO NAMR(,ID)(,FORMAT)

Further, a command exists to display to a user all the commands that are available to him at his terminal, along with a brief explanation and syntax for each command. Parameters within parentheses are optional and will be set to default values if not entered.

This feature can save a user the trouble of having to go through a manual to look for the command syntax to accomplish the function that he wants.

For the case where a user remembers the command name, but cannot remember the order in which some required parameters are entered, there is a prompting mode. For example:

```
User:   COPY
DMS:    COPY FROM?
User:   ABC::2
DMS:    COPY TO?
User:   ABC::3
```

Again, this feature can save the user a trip to the manual. Prompting mode is activated only when data, which has been designated as necessary to the processing of the command, has been left out. This feature allows a beginner to get all the help he needs to use the system, yet as he becomes more familiar with the system and remembers more of the commands, the prompting feature becomes less used until he is using the system without any prompts whatsoever. The DMS matches the amount of prompting to the needs of the individual user.

ARCHITECTURE

The Gerber Data Management System was designated to be functionally modular. This guarantees that someone making changes to one function will not damage the operation of some other function. It also allows a user to remove or add certain functions with a minimum of effort and without disturbing the rest of the system. This modular design allows an extremely simple system structure, as can be seen in FIGURE 1.

The DMS mainline was written to be as small as possible so as to provide the maximum amount of partition space for the segments (see FIGURE 2).

PROGRAM COMMON	1285 words
DMS MAINLINE	48 words
DMS SEGMENT OVERLAY AREA	8192 words

FIGURE 2 DMS PROGRAM PARTITION USAGE

It only contains the common module and the instructions to schedule the initialization processing.

Each terminal on the system has its own copy of the DMS. When the system is up and running, it waits in the command monitor segment. (Refer to FIGURE 1 for the following discussion.) This segment prompts the terminal and then waits for the operator input. Every input is checked to see if it is a valid DMS command. If not, an appropriate error code is output to the terminal and the prompt is re-issued. When a valid command is entered, the command monitor schedules the appropriate overlay

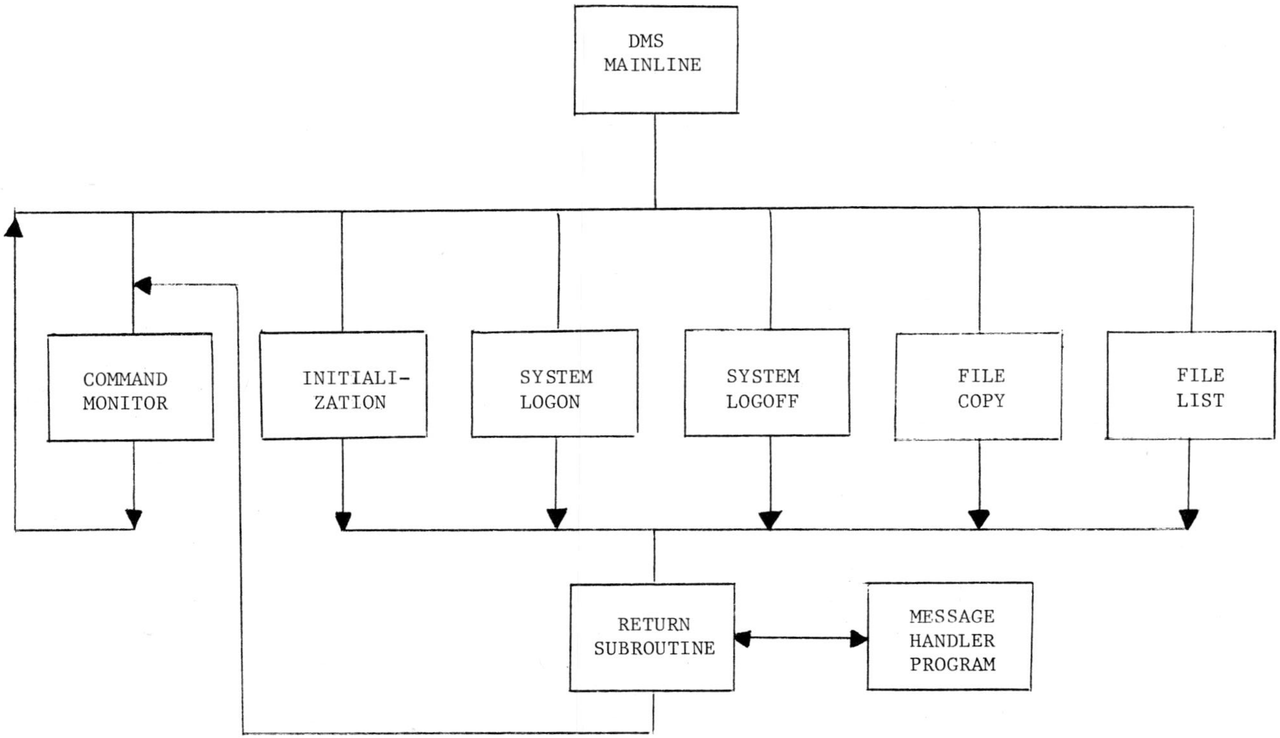

FIGURE 1 DMS FUNCTIONAL FLOW

segment to do the processing. The segment contains calls to the FMP subroutines and EXEC functions, if needed, to accomplish this task. When the segment has completed its task, it calls a special return subroutine to return to the command monitor segment. This subroutine, which is used by all the DMS segments, not only provides a standard return path, but also provides the function of inter-terminal message handling. This function allows an operator at one terminal to send a message to an operator at another terminal. The return subroutine schedules a special program which checks to see if any messages are queued for this terminal. If there are, the messages are displayed and control returns to the subroutine which then schedules the command monitor segment. This completes the processing of a DMS command. It should be noted that the FMP subroutines used are modified versions of the standard HP routines. The modifications were made to support the DMS 30 character file name, as well as the other information included in the 128 word DMS file directory. This was done through the addition of new entry points to existing HP FMP subroutines. The old entry points remain the same except that when called, a 6 character file name is padded with blanks to create a 30 character file. This allows programs, which were written on an unmodified HP system, to work successfully on a DMS system without having to alter any source code.

SYSTEM SECURITY

One of the main features provided by the DMS is its multi-level system security. This feature prevents unauthorized people from accessing the system, as well as preventing users from accessing system resources which they do not have clearance for (see FIGURE 3). The first block to unauthorized use is the fact that a person must logon to the system to access any of its resources. The logon sequence consists of supplying a valid ID and password to the system. The system checks this entered data against its table of valid users, and if a match is found, it also checks a code associated with the user's ID to determine if he is allowed to logon to this terminal. The user's ID carries with it a code which determines what type of terminals his ID is valid at. He may be allowed access to plotting stations and edit stations, and denied access to any other type of terminals. If all of these checks match, the user is logged onto the system. The ID also carries with it an access level. This code determines what level of commands are available to the user. Since each command carries with it an access level code, the user is denied access to any commands which have a higher access code than that associated with his ID. As an added security feature, commands can be limited to certain types of terminals. It would be highly undesirable for someone who is logged on to an edit station to be able to execute commands which could access a plotter. The plotters should be under the control of the plotting station.

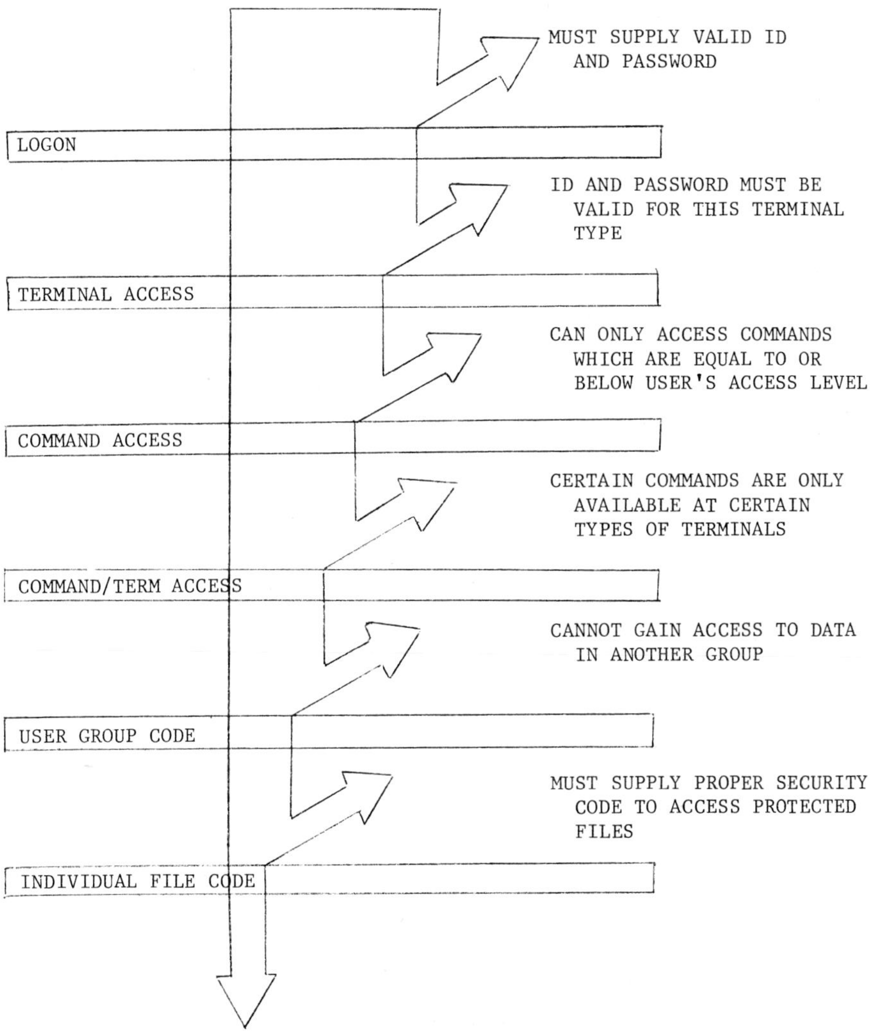

FIGURE 3 LEVELS OF DMS SECURITY

Since there can be many unrelated tasks being performed on the system at one time, it is advantageous to be able to separate the data to prevent one group from inadvertently damaging the data of another group. This is accomplished by assigning a single word user group code to each ID. This group code is used whenever a file access is performed. The group code is appended as the last word of every file name on the system, but is transparent to the user. The FMP subroutines have been modified to check the user group code of the logged on user's ID with the last word of the file name. If they don't match, the user is not able to access the file for read or read/write. This makes it appear to the user that his group is the only one on the system, since he can't see any of the files in other groups. This also allows files in different groups to have the same file name, since the system appends the user's group code to the end of the file name, thus making the name unique. A user who created a file named "AB" in group number 4, and another user who created a file named "AB" in group number 5, would both see their file "AB", but the system would hold them as "AB....4" and "AB....5", respectively. Since a system administrator would want to be able to access all files, he is given a special user group code of "-1" which allows him access to all files.

Another feature of the system is that certain files are able to be accessed by users in any user group. This is accomplished by another special group code. The code "Ø" applied to a file name means that any user group is allowed access to this file.

Lastly, the DMS provides the same individual file security as provided by the HP File Manager. That is, a zero file security code means that the file is not protected, a positive or alpha security code means that the file is write-protected, and a negative security code means that the file is read/write protected.

COMMAND FILE

One of the major advantages of the DMS is its ability to easily add or delete functions from the system. To add or delete a function involves adding or deleting the segment which processes the function, as well as adding or deleting the commands which provide access to the function. This is an extremely easy operation since all the valid DMS commands are contained in a disk file, which is maintained by a utility program.

This file not only makes command maintnenance easy, but it is also an important factor in the overall system flexibility. Each command in the file contains all of the necessary information about the command to enable its processing. The command file is large enough to contain 256 commands (see FIGURE 4). Each command entry contains the command key word, which can be up to 10 characters long, followed by 2 words of "bit map" which specify what types of data are permitted for each of the 8 optional input parameters. This provides the first level of com-

COMMAND 1 (5 WORDS)
⋮
COMMAND 256 (5 WORDS)
BIT MAP 1 (2 WORDS)
⋮
BIT MAP 256 (2 WORDS
TERMINAL TYPE SCHEDULE TYPE ACCESS LEVEL 1 (1 WORD)
⋮
TERMINAL TYPE SCHEDULE TYPE ACCESS LEVEL 256 (1 WORD
SCHEDULE NAME 1 (3 WORDS)
⋮
SCHEDULE NAME 256 (3 WORDS)
PASSED PARAMETERS 1 (5 WORDS)
⋮
PASSED PARAMETERS 256 (5 WORDS)
COMMAND DESCRIPTOR 1 (32 WORDS)
⋮
COMMAND DESCRIPTOR 256 (32 WORDS)
QUESTION SETS 1 (128 WORDS)
⋮
QUESTION SETS 256 (128 WORDS)

FIGURE 4 DMS COMMAND FILE

mand error checking, which assures that the data entered is of the proper type (for example, NAMR, Numeric, etc.). This data is followed by another "bit map" which specifies for which types of terminals the command is valid. The DMS can have edit stations, plotting stations, graphic stations, a virtual batch station, and a main console attached to it. The next field in the command file entry is an access level. Since each logged-on user has an access level associated with him, his access level is compared to the access level of the commands. If his access level is not greater than or equal to than that of the command he has entered, he is denied access to that command. The command file entry also contains the name of the segment, program, or JCL file to be scheduled in order to process the command, along with 5 command-dependent parameters. These parameters can be used to distinguish between two different commands using the same piece of software for processing, or to set some default values which can easily be changed without editing the source code, recompiling, and then reloading the software module, etc. Next is 32 words, which is available for specifying the syntax of the entire command string. This is available for when an operator requests information from the system about a particular command. In response, the system can display the entire command syntax. Lastly, the file contains "question sets" for up to 8 questions for each command. These "question sets" allow the system to prompt the operator for the data required to process the entered command. An operator need only enter the command name and the system will prompt him for each required piece of data. If all the required data is entered with the command string, no prompting occurs. With all these features, the system is extremely easy for a beginner to use, while still allowing an experienced operator to bypass the time-consuming process of prompting.

FIGURE 5 contains a functional flow chart of the DMS Command Monitor. The figure illustrates how the DMS implements the processing of commands.

DEVICE FILE

On the DMS, a user does not deal with system logical unit numbers. The DMS contains a translation table for each of its 48 possible terminals (see FIGURE 6). This table contains information as to what type of terminal it is, how many lines per page it has, as well as assigning 63 DMS user logical unit numbers to any of the available system logical unit numbers. This allows terminals to have standard device configurations regardless of the logical unit assignment in the system generation. For example, all terminals are user logical unit number "1" regardless of their system logical unit number. This translation table can be easily modified permanently by use of a utility program, or the assignment can be changed temporarily by a DMS command. The table can also be set up to prevent certain terminals from accessing certain devices. If a particular system logical

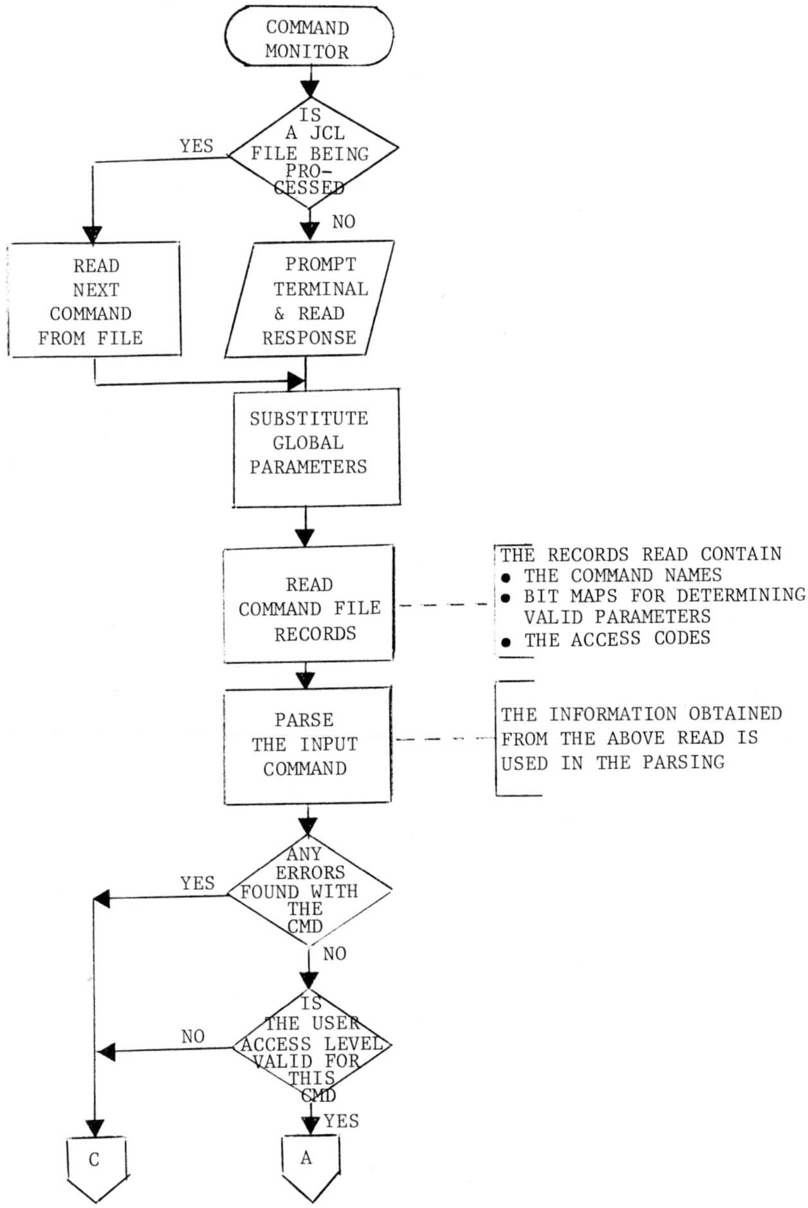

FIGURE 5 DMS COMMAND MONITOR FLOW (1 OF 3)

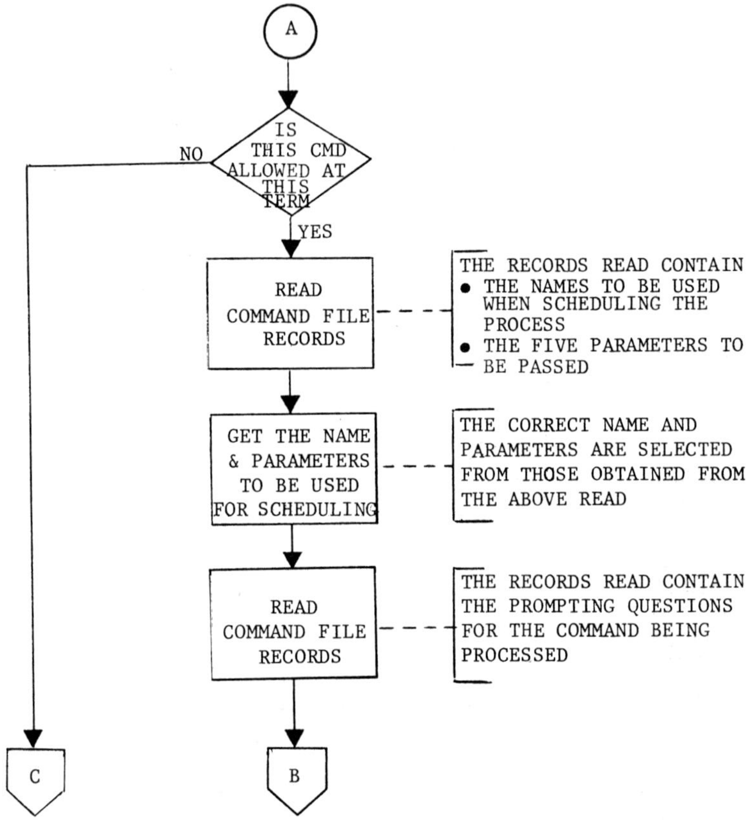

FIGURE 5 DMS COMMAND MONITOR FLOW (2 OF 3)

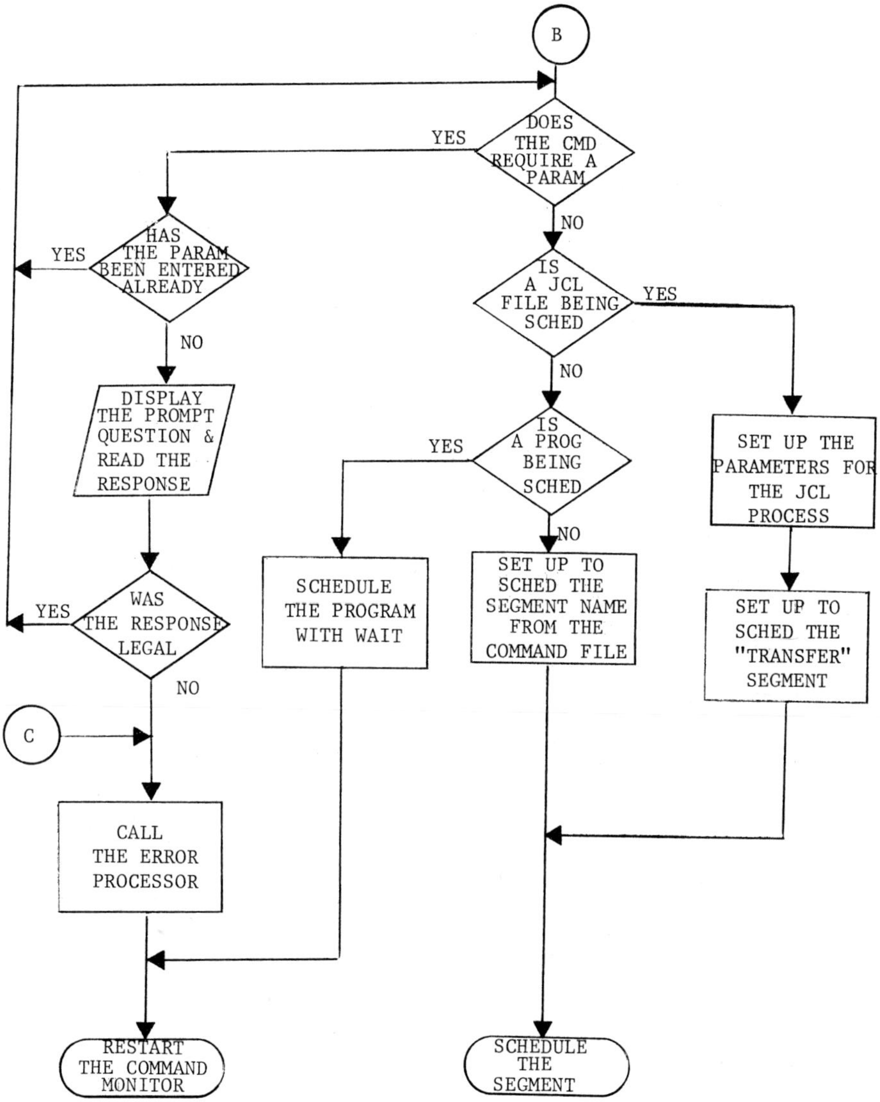

FIGURE 5 DMS COMMAND FLOW (3 OF 3)

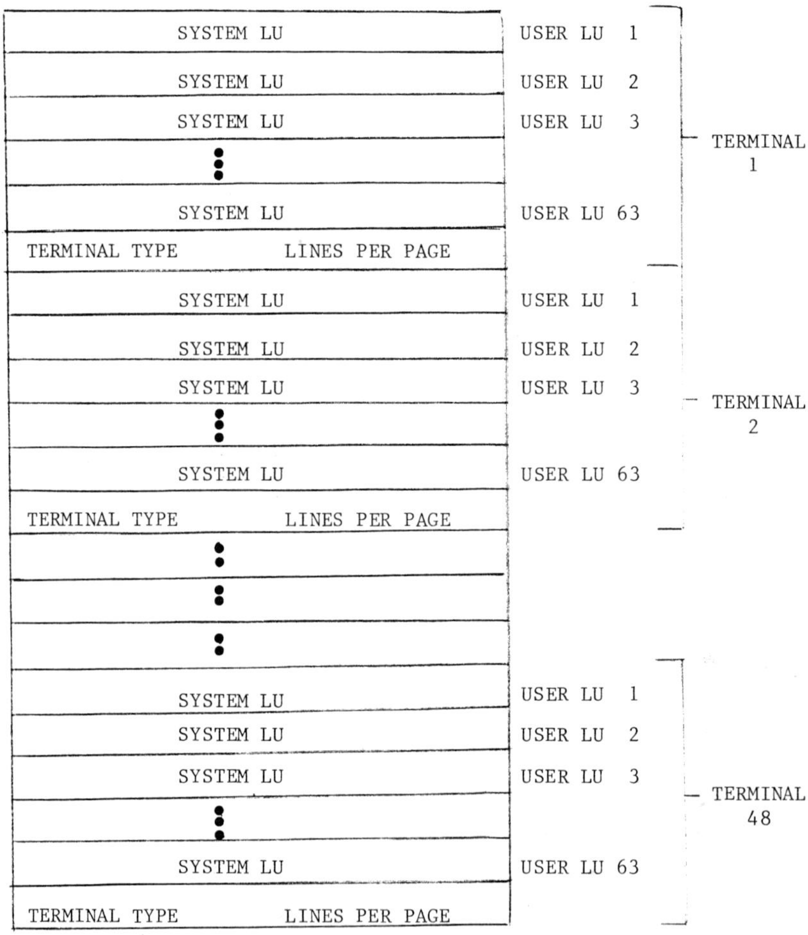

FIGURE 6 DMS DEVICE FILE

unit number is not assigned to one of the 63 DMS user logical unit numbers, the device is not accessible. This also allows certain common devices, such as a line printer or magnetic tape drive, to always have the same user logical unit number regardless of the system generation. Whatever the system logical unit number is, it can be assigned to the same DMS user logical unit number.

This function is supported by modifications to the RTE operating system. At terminal start-up time, the translation table is taken from a disk file and put into a table in the operating system. Every time an I/O request is made, the operating system takes the logical unit number passed to it and uses the translation table to change it to a system logical unit number. The I/O operation is then performed. Since there are times when the software may not use the logical unit number, but may know the system one, there is a calling sequence which will suppress the translation of the logical unit supplied and will use it directly.

Changes made by the utility program are considered permanent since the disk file is modified and therefore, every time the terminal is started-up, the modified device file is read in off the disk. Changes made by the DMS command only modify the table in the operating system and therefore are considered temporary, since a terminal start-up will bring in the unmodified translation table from the disk.

All programs which are scheduled from the DMS program are sons and therefore, also use the translation table of the father.

USER ACCOUNT FILE

All the valid user ID's and passwords for the DMS system are held in a disk file. This file is maintained by a utility program which allows easy addition or deletion of ID's. This file, in addition to containing the ID's and passwords, contains a code which specifies what types of terminals are valid for this user. It also contains the command access level and the user group code for each user. For accounting purposes, the file also contains the CPU time accumulated by the user and the accumulated real-time the user spent on the system. There is room in this table for 256 users (see FIGURE 7).

FILE DIRECTORY

The file directories of the DMS are 128 words long, as opposed to the 16 word directories on HP systems. All this extra space is used to hold pertinent information about the file. This information consists of, but is not limited to, the following items:

- 30 character file names
- user group code
- 50 character file descriptor

USER ACCOUNT NAME 1 (5 WORDS)
USER PASSWORD 1 (3 WORDS)
USER'S ELAPSED REAL TIME (2 WORDS)
USER'S ELAPSED CPU TIME (2 WORDS)
DATE ACCOUNT INSTALLED (1 WORD)
DATE ACCOUNT TIMES CLEARED (1 WORD)
TERMINAL TYPES ACCESS LEVEL (1 WORD)
USER GROUP CODE (1 WORD)
USER ACCOUNT NAME 2 (5 WORDS)
USER PASSWORD 2 (3 WORDS)
:
:
:
USER ACCOUNT NAME 256 (5 WORDS)
USER PASSWORD 256 (3 WORDS)
USER'S ELAPSED REAL TIME (2 WORDS)
USER'S ELAPSED CPU TIME (2 WORDS)
DATE ACCOUNT INSTALLED (1 WORD)
DATE ACCOUNT TIMES CLEARED (1 WORD)
TERMINAL TYPES ACCESS LEVEL (1 WORD)
USER GROUP CODE (1 WORD)

FIGURE 7 DMS USER FILE

- file type word specifying the type of data contained in the file(ASCII, EIA, binary, etc.)
- date/time created
- date/time last accessed
- date/time last modified
- account ID of person creating, accessing, and modifying the file
- DMS version # on which the file was created.

This information allows a user to better manage his data files:

- Inactive files can easily be found.
- Actual part numbers can be used as file names.
- File classification codes can be placed in the 50 character descriptor, to be used in file searches.

This information is used by certain DMS commands, as will be seen below.

SPECIAL SYSTEM FEATURES

The following section describes some of the many features which have been designed into the DMS. Its purpose is not to go into a detailed discussion, but to give a very brief overview of what DMS can be made to do.

The DMS system contains a command to find and display a list of files based upon a search of the file directories. Information contained within the directories is used as a key in the search. For example, a user could search for all files created after a certain time, on a certain date, and created by a particular user. The list of files which met this criteria could be displayed in different formats. One format would display all the information held in the directory for each of the found files. Another format would only display the file name and cartridge number of the found files. This would allow the list to be easily made into a transfer file, which could be used to do some operation on these files (for example, purge them from the system). The option also exists to obtain the file name list in alphabetical order. This function was implemented using an in-house written subroutine which searches through the directories and returns appropriate 128 word file directory entries. It is also dependent upon the modifications to the Directory Manager, which supports the creation and maintenance of 128 word file directory entries.

Another enhanced DMS feature is the Cartridge List command. In addition to supplying the standard information, such as system logical unit number, cartridge number, and last track, it also supplies the following information:

- Number of free tracks remaining on the cartridge.
- Number of directory entries remaining on the cartridge.
- Number of free tracks available if the cartridge is packed.
- Number of directory entries available if the cartridge is packed.

This information provides a system administrator with the necessary tools to manage his disk cartridges more efficently.

Through one of its subsystems, DMS can communicate with other DMS's and Gerber CAD/CAM systems. Data files can be copied from one system's disk or device to another system's disk or device. This allows data to be created on one system, quickly transferred to another system, and then used there. The capability also exists for a user to make his terminal operate as a local terminal to a system that is remote to him. It would appear to the operator that his terminal was connected directly to the remote system. After logging on to the remote system, he could have access to all the resources permitted someone local to the system. The capability also exists to communicate with a large scale host computer, such as an IBM 370. Batch jobs can be constructed on the DMS and then sent, via modem link, to the host for processing. The output of the processing is then returned to DMS through this link.

SYSTEM MODIFICATIONS

Since the DMS command interface is very desirable to have, it has been made very easy for users to add new commands to the system. A user who wishes to add some of his own functions to DMS can do so with a minimum of extra effort. All that is required is to write a segment for the function, load it with the DMS mainline, and then add the command to the command file.

An operator's interface to this function would be the same as any DMS function, including all the security features associated with it.

Since the DMS commands can be made to schedule JCL files, some new functions can be made without writing any new software. This is accomplished by creating a "transfer file", which uses DMS commands and has global variables as the inputs to these commands. A user executing one of the "JCL" commands would not be aware that the function was being performed in JCL rather than in software.

An example of a JCL command would be as follows:

Function "MOVE" - To copy a file from one Namr to another and then delete the original file.

Command Syntax:
MOVE,From File,To File

Transfer File:

COPY,=G1,=G2
DELETE,=G1

In the command monitor, the two input parameters (From File and To File) are moved into the global variables G1 and G2, respectively. When control is transferred to the JCL file, and its commands are executed, the input parameters are substituted for the variable names =G1 and =G2.

It should be noted that access to the MOVE command would have to be as restrictive as the sum of all the restrictions on the commands in the transfer file. For example, the MOVE command could not be allowed from a plotting terminal if the DELETE command was not allowed.

BACKUP/ARCHIVE

Since interfacing programs to DMS is fairly easy, one of the DMS's major subsystems is a separate program. This subsystem is the Backup/Archive Subsystem. Its main purpose is to be able to store files off on magnetic tape, and keep a directory to these files on disk for rapid searches. The Backup function is intended for routine data protection. Files Backed-up to a magnetic tape can be restored whenever needed, and the file will be restored as belonging to the original owner. The Archive function is intended for inactive files, which are not needed anymore and are being removed from the disk to free up space for active development. Files archived to magnetic tape, when restored, become the property of the system administrator and cannot be accessed by other user groups. The DMS system allows multiple Backup/Archive libraries on the systems with each library containing a maximum of 50 magnetic tapes. Each library has its own directory on disk as well as saving a copy of it on the last tape in the library. This is to protect the data on the tapes in the event of a disk failure and loss of the disk directories.

Backup/Archive library directories can share disk cartridges with FMP data and directories. When this is desired, the beginning tracks of the cartridge are reserved for the libraries and then the FMP data area starts after them followed by the FMP directory area (see FIGURE 8). Special subroutines are used to manage the disk space allocated to the Backup/Archive subsystem. Since the cartridge is initialized using FMP routines to start at a track after the library tracks, there is no contention between the DMS and Backup/Archive for disk space. Backup/Archive library directories are very similar to the DMS directories in that they can be easily mounted, dismounted, initialized, packed, and searched.

Each magnetic tape in the library contains a header record which contains information as to what library it belongs to, what tape number it is, and whether it is a Backup or Archive library tape. The data is stored in variable length records with a maximum size of 2177 words. The first word of each record contains information as to the record number and whether or not the record is the start of a new disk data file.

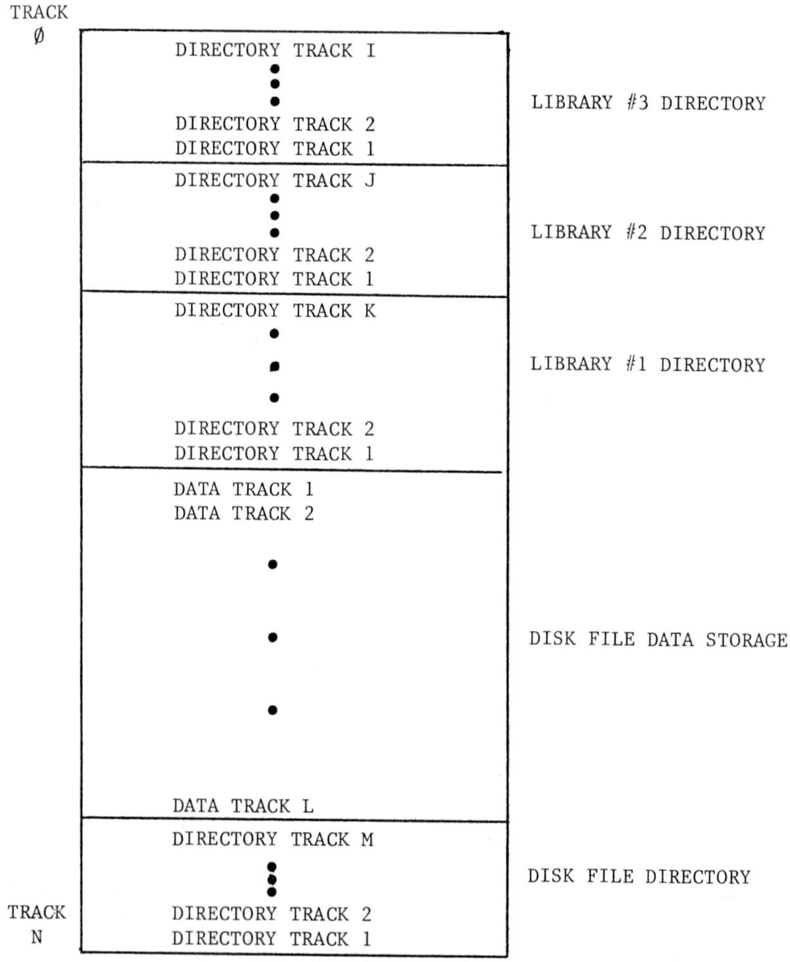

FIGURE 8 DISK LAYOUT FOR DISK FILES AND LIBRARIES

In order for the system to be able to rapidly obtain a file on tape, the library directories contain the number of the tape where the file exists and its record number on that tape. If a user wished to restore a particular file, he would first execute a command to search the libraries for the file. The system would display information as to what library, tape number, and record number the file resided on. He would then execute a command to restore the desired file from the indicated library. The system would automatically ask the user to mount the correct tape on the magnetic tape unit. It would then space out to the proper record and restore the file to the disk.

The Backup/Archive subsystem, even though it is a separate program with its own segments, appears to the user to be part of the DMS since it is interfaced through the DMS command structure. All of its commands are given the same security protection as any of the DMS commands.

CONCLUSION

As can be seen by this paper, the basic HP system has the necessary ingredients to be made into a very sophisticated, yet user-oriented, system. With certain changes to the operating system and FMP subroutine package, the DMS system has been made easily configurable, very secure, and presents its many varied functions to the user in a standard format. The DMS system is currently in use at Gerber installations in the United States and internationally. It is continually being updated to add new features and to improve old ones, as well as being modified to keep it compatible with the current release of the RTE operating system.

ultra low level programming using a high level language

Steven E. Ashcraft

Corporate Computer Systems, Inc.
Aberdeen, N.J.

KEYWORDS:

systems programming, high level languages, programmer productivity, I/O drivers, C language

ABSTRACT:

This paper describes the techniques used in writing a low level program using a high level programming language. The program that was written is a driver for use with terminal type devices interfaced to the HP 12966A interface card. This driver operates in the RTE-IVB operating system on a Hewlett- Packard HP1ØØØ mini computer. Included is a discussion of the advantages and disadvantages of doing systems programming in a high level language, as well as the working code for the driver written in C.

1. INTRODUCTION

Systems programming such as I/O driver writing has historically been done in the assembler language of the target machine. This has been because most high level programming languages have not offered the necessary efficiency and machine control.

The purpose of this paper is to explore the feasibility of and problems associated with doing systems programming on the Hewlett-Packard HP/1ØØØ computer system in a high level language.

The specific task of writing a driver for the HP 12966A buffered asynchronous data communication interface card was chosen as the test case. An I/O driver was chosen because writing a driver for the HP1ØØØ entails using most of the tools necessary for doing systems level programming.

2. SYSTEMS PROGRAMMING

Although the distinction between systems programming and applications programming is sometimes fuzzy, some of the features necessary for systems programming may be ennumerated [4]:

a) Time and space efficiency are very important
b) All features provided by the hardware must be accessible

The programmer must be able to:

1) invoke any of the functions native to the machine including any I/O instructions or memory mapping functions.
2) access absolute memory address in the machine.
3) manipulate words, bytes, bits, or any other data structure native to the machine.

All of these capabilities are necessary as they characterize a great many of the functions that operating systems must perform as well as provide the programmer the necessary tools to extract maximum performance from the machine.

c) Programs should be structured and readable to make maintenance easier and faster.

d) A reasonably high level language is necessary to make program writing and modification faster and easier.

In the past, items a and b have been available only in the assembly language of the machine.

In recent years, systems programming languages such as PL360[4], BLISS[4], MODULA[1], SDL[2], C[3], etc., have been developed to provide programmers with the necessary features of assembler languages yet also provide the features of high level languages. After all, high level languages such as FORTRAN, PL/I, and ALGOL were developed to increase programmer productivity so why not use the same ideas to do systems programming? This increase in productivity is the result of providing programmers with the tools to describe complex data structures (i.e. records in PASCAL, structures in C, etc.) and the necessary control constructs (i.e. if then else, repeat while, case of) to use structured programming techniques.

Finally, programs written in a high level language tend to be more self-documenting, portable, and maintainable than an equivalent program written in assembler.

3. CHOOSING A LANGUAGE

Given the task of writing an I/O driver for the HP1000 and having decided to use a high level language, a language must be chosen. Currently, the high level languages available are FORTRAN, ALGOL (no longer supported by HP), PASCAL, and C. FORTRAN and ALGOL were eliminated because of their inability to directly describe complex data structures (i.e. records in PASCAL and structures in C). This ability is essential when trying to access the data structures that exist in the RTE operating system. In the case of drivers, the data structures of interest are the equipment table entries. PASCAL was eliminated because of the large run-time package and its lack of an efficient interface to the machine language of the HP 1000.

C was chosen because it allows the programmer to exercise control over the computer that is found in assembly language, and yet it retains the advantages of a high level language.

C provides the user the capability to define data structures which may then be mapped onto existing RTE system tables so that characters, bits, double integers, etc. may be directly accessed. A full complement of logical operators (AND, OR, NOT, EXCLUSIVE OR) as well as a set of shift operators are provided in C to enable the programmer to do the data manipulation at the bit level whenever necessary.

Because of these tools, the efficiency of a programmer is increased and at the same time the program becomes more readable and thus more maintainable. The language allows the programmer to write code in which the flow of control is easily understood, the variable names may be chosen to make the program self documenting, and the data structures aid in gaining access to system tables.

As an example, the fourth word in the RTE equipment table (referred to as EQT4 in HP documentation) contains a number of bit fields which must be accessed. The process of breaking this word apart is normally done by the assembly language programmer as a series of mask and shift operations. However, in C, EQT4 may be mapped into a data structure in which the bit fields are directly accessible, as shown in the following program fragment.

```
struct EQT4 {                    /* define the fields          */
            dcpc_bit    :1;/* dcpc required              */
            b_bit       :1;/* use buffering              */
            p_bit       :1;/* process power fail         */
            t_bit       :1;/* process time outs          */
            timed_out   :1;/* device timed out           */
            s_chan      :5;/* device subchannel          */
            select_code:6;/* select code                 */
           };

struct EQT4 *status;
status = *(int*)01663;      /* absolute address of EQT4
if ( status->timed_out) {.....};      /*test time out bit */
```

In this example, the operating system sets bit 5 in the fourth word of the equipment table to indicate if the device timed out. In order to access the bit, the programmer need only reference the variable status-> timed_out.

In Appendices A and B, a complete listing of the driver is included and numerous examples of this technique of mapping C structures onto RTE-IV system tables are shown.

4. DRIVER COMMENTARY AND DISCUSSION OF C

In this section we will discuss the implementation of the driver itself and some of the features of the C language which were used to complete the project.

C is essentially a block structured language with structures, pointers and data types which match those found in the HP/1000. Two essential features of C which we use heavily are the macro processor and embedded assembly language.

C's macro processor allows the programmer to define macros which are then used directly in the C source code. This ability enables you to insert code in-line, yet maintain a high degree of readability. In addition it allows all of the program's "magic" numbers to be gathered together in one place and be assigned names. For example consider:

```
mode = 0400;
```

This C statement will assign an octal value of 400 to a variable named mode. In the middle of a program this operation (even with a comment) would at best be difficult to understand. In addition if, for some reason, the value would be redefined to be octal 500, it could potentially be difficult to locate all of the uses of the value. C's macro processor allows you to write:

```
#define  TRANSMIT  0400
    :
mode = TRANSMIT;
```

The "#define" tells the macro processor to associate the value 0400 with the name TRANSMIT. When the value 0400 is to be used we may use the word TRANSMIT instead. If we must change the value, then only the define line need be changed.

C also allows embedded assembler language. This is very important in DVC00 since the RTE was designed with the intention that all drivers would be written in assembler. This means that the entry/exit sequences are not general purpose in nature (.ENTR). By itself embedded assembler is not necessarily a good thing, but coupled with the macro processor, it becomes a safe and workable tool. Consider the macro to do an "OTA."

```
#define OUTPUT(sc, data) asm { \
    lda  +5; \
    and  =0177740; \
    ior  sc; \
    sta  +2; \
    lda  data; \
    ota  0;      }
```

What we have done is essentially extended the C compiler by providing a new "OUTPUT" type of statement. The definition, of the semantics of the statement has been given in assembler language. From now on, whenever we write OUTPUT(x,y), the assembler language code for outputting character y on subchannel x will be generated by the compiler. The really nice part is that the OUTPUT statement is much easier to read than all of the assembler language, and it is easier to change if the I/O design of the computer changes (pronounced 21LC).

The macro processor also allows an "include" file. This enables the C programmer to gather together all of his common macro definitions (or anything for that matter) into one central file. This file may then be included by the compiler at compile time. By doing this we centralize all of the basic definitional items which may be used in several different source files. All C based drivers, for example, will probably use the same basic RTE system interface macro set. All of the driver macros can then be stored in a file called "dvrmacs" and at the start of each C driver we would use the statement:

```
#include "dvrmacs"
```

From that point on, we could use the defined macros. If we wish to port the drivers to another machine we can change the dvrmacs file for the new computer and recompile.

We have done just that with the file !DVC00. That file is our macro definition file. In the source for DVC00 you will find an #include statement which references the !DVC00 file. Note that it is C programming custom to spell macro names in capital letters. By doing this, the reader can easily see extensions to the language through the use of macros.

To enable you to more easily read the driver code we point out the following C syntax features or abnormalities depending on your viewpoint.

1. All subroutines have () after their name. If the subroutine passes arguments, then the arguments are inclosed in the () pair. If there are no arguments, then the () pair must still be there. You can think of it as a "post fix" call statement.

2. C contains the "points to" operator which is written as "->". This function uses a pointer as its left argument and a member of a structure as its right argument. For example the base page location EQT4 is a pointer to the 4th equipment table entry. We can use the points at operation to get the power_fail bit by writing:

   ```
   EQT4->power_fail
   ```

   That expression will return an integer equal in value to the power fail bit. It may appear on the left of the equal sign (an uncomfortable notation at first) to allow us to store into the power fail bit. For example the C statement to set the power fail bit to 1 would be:

   ```
   EQT4->power_fail = 1;
   ```

   Really if we are going to be "good" programmers we should not use the "raw" 1 constant but rather use a macro:

```
#define ON 1
    :
EQT4 -> power_fail = ON;
```

That reads much better and is easier to understand.

3. Comments in C are inclosed in /* and */ pairs. New blocks are inclosed in { } pairs. This is just like begin and end in ALGOL. Unfortunately for programmers forced to use PASCAL and C, the PASCAL comment convention uses the { } pairs.

4. The C switch statement has a format:

   ```
   switch(expl) {
     case xx:
          statement;
     case yy:
          statement;
   }
   ```

   The expression "expl" is evaluated first. Its result is then compared to the xx and yy of the case statements. If any of the case statements match the result of the expression, then control is passed to the statement labeled by the case prefix.

   An optional label "default" may be used. Control will go to the default when none of the case statements match the result of the expression.

5. The C "for" statement is like a FORTRAN do loop only quite a bit more flexible in its operation. The syntax of the for statement is:

   ```
   for(expl; exp2; exp3) statement
   ```

   The semantics are: The expression "expl" is evaulated once. This is usually referred to as the initialization expression. Next expression "exp2" is evaluated. If its result is true (non-zero) then the statement following the closing) is executed. The statement may be a complex statement inclosed in a { } pair. When the statement is finished, exp3 is executed and then exp2. In this way exp2 is called the "test expression" and exp3 is called the "increment expression." The following example of a for statement is the same as the FORTRAN written next to it:

   ```
   for(i=1; i<=10; i=i+1)           DO 150 I = 1,10
     s = s + x[i];            150   S = S+X(I)
   ```

   The syntax may appear odd at first, but remember there are no restrictions on the contents of expl, exp2 and exp3. They can make loops go forward, backward or may involve linked lists or function calls.

To help the reader understand how the aforementioned features of C aided in the development of the driver three sections of the code will be examined.

Probably the most complex function performed by the driver is the process of emptying the FIFO (first in first out) buffer on the 12966A card during a read operation. The driver is scheduled to empty this buffer when a special character is received, the FIFO is full, or a parity error occurs. In this driver the carriage return and backspace characters have been designated as special characters (see the function setram.) As the characters are removed they must be placed in the user's buffer in the correct place and a count of the number of characters received must be maintained.

The function empty (lines 309-325 in Appendix A) perform this task. The REPEAT macro in line 312 indicates that the main body of the function will be repeated forever. Obviously there must be an exit someplace as we shall soon show. The first action in the loop is to read the next character from the FIFO using the macro INPUT. Next the input character (actually a 16 bit word is read in with the low order bits containing the character and the upper bits containing status information) is checked to see if the FIFO has been emptied. This is indicated by bit 15 of the input word being equal to Ø and consequently the input words value being greater than or equal to zero. If the FIFO is empty a zero is returned to the calling module otherwise the input word is checked to see if it contains a special character. This is done by inspecting the bit represented by the constant SPEC_CHAR. If a special character has been detected then it is returned to the calling module. Finally if neither the buffer is empty nor a special character has been found the driver checks to see if the character should be inserted into the user's buffer. This is done in lines 321-322.

An English description of the function of lines 321-322 is: If the number of characters input that have been input from the terminal (eqt1Ø->char_count) is less than the length of the user's buffer (eqt8->buff_length) then put the input character into the user's buffer. The postfix operator ++ increments the character counter after the comparison. After putting the character into the user's buffer (eqt12->ptr points to the correct location) the ++ operator bumps the pointer to the next location so that the pointer will be correct for the next input. This process is repeated until an exit is taken from the function because of an empty buffer or a special character.

The reader might note that the C code is as easy to understand and read as the English description. This same process in an assembler language might not be.

A second example will demonstrate the use of the C switch statement to determine the flow of control. Three types of requests are processed by the driver: reads, writes, and control requests. One of the first acts of the driver in the initiator section is to determine the type of request that is being processed and then take the appropriate action. The switch statement which encompasses lines 67 to 132 illustrates how a program might use the switch statement to direct the flow of control. After extracting the type of request from bits Ø and 1 of the sixth word of the equipment table (This information is in the variable eqt6->function.) the driver uses the switch statement to branch to one of the case statements (READ, WRITE, CONTROL, or default). This is a good example of how structured programming makes for very readable code.

As a third example, let's examine the function clear_status on lines 347 to 359. This function is an example of how to clear the status bits 1 to 7 in the fifth word of the equipment table. Since each of the variables eqt5->statusi (i=1 to 7) corresponds to a single bit in eqt word 5 the function of the code is self-evident. This function is a very inefficient way of clearing these bits but at the same time the code is very easily understood.

Finally the reader should note that all function calls in this driver contain no arguments. This was done because the C compiler generates very efficient code for invoking and returning from functions with no arguments (i.e no calls to a parameter passing function like .ENTR are generated). The disadvantage to making most of the variables global is the possible misuse of a variable in some function that doesn't know that some other function is also using the same variable.

5. CONCLUSIONS

After writing a driver for the 12966A card using C, the following conclusions were drawn:

A) Programmer productivity is greatly improved. The time to design the driver and to write the code was approximately 5 man days spread over a period of two weeks. Of this time, two days were spent designing the driver and developing the flow charts.

B) The code is more easily read and understood than most drivers. Compare the program listings in Appendix A with any of the I/O drivers in the contributed library PLUS/1000.

C) Additions and modifications to the driver are easily made. As an example of this, adding additional control functions entails adding an additional case statement. This is easily done and the programmer doesn't have to worry about "interesting" side effects.

D) Drivers written in a high level language currently use more memory than drivers written in assembler. DVC00 is 954 words long. An equivalent driver in assembly would probably be 20%-30% smaller and would consequently execute faster. This disadvantage should be viewed in the light of constantly increasing processor speed and decreasing memory costs. In addition, as compilers get better the code will become more efficient and so without rewriting the driver, the driver will become more efficient. Improvements in compiler code generation are typically cheaper than increases in processor speed.

E) The amount of embedded assembler code in this driver is due to

a) the calling sequence used to invoke drivers in the RTE. If a standard calling sequence were used, drivers would become subroutines.

b) the architecture of the HP1ØØØ series of processors. If memory mapped I/O were available an OTA would become an assignment operation.

The amount of assembler needed in systems programming will approach zero as computer architects and compiler writers collaborate more.

F) More sophisticated tools for debugging systems programming code need to be developed. This driver was debugged using a stand alone machine level debugger similar to HP's DBUGR. This entailed becoming too familiar with the code generated by the compiler and the frustration of working with a 27 page mixed listing. Driver development would have been faster if a source level debugger similar to the one available for use in debugging C programs in the RTE had been available. An alternative would be an emulator on which to run RTE and then debug the driver using a debug package running on the emulator.

6. THOUGHTS ON FUTURE WORK

From this initial experience, a further interesting concept became apparent. It appears that drivers, or any systems level software, should be written with the attitude that the software will be ported to a new machine. If all operating systems were written in a language like C with portability in mind, perhaps the wheel would not be reinvented quite so often. In addition, when confronted with implementing a sophisticated algorithm to solve a complex problem in a complete manner or using a simplistic method that gets the job done, the programmer might choose the right way. Complex algorithms are more easily implemented in a high level language than in an assembly language.

Operating systems could be written and debugged using simple emulators in a host machine and then transported to the target machine.

This could be accomplished by dividing the code into two levels: logical and physical. The logical code would address the algorithms such as process to process communication, file management, or process scheduling. The physical code would be concerned about machine dependent operations such as memory mapping, or I/O operations.

All of this code would be written in a high level language and when the op system was to be ported only the physical code would need to be changed.

This opens up a world where users would be able to use the same op system on a wide class of machine.

C has proven to be a good choice for systems work as is evidenced by the work at Bell Laboratories. The UNIX operating system, originally written for a DEC PDP-11 was written almost entirely in C, has now been successfully ported to the Perkins Elmer's Interdata 8/32 which is a 32 bit machine. [5]

The porting of an operating system from one machine to a dissimilar machine is probably the best argument for using high level languages for writing operating systems. Not only can the original operating system be written more quickly, but when the state of the art dictates throwing away an old architecture, the operating system and all of the software base that is dependent on a particular op system will not have to be tossed away.

Wouldn't it be nice to implement a resource management system for a processor without learning the assembly language for that processor?

ACKNOWLEDGEMENTS

My appreciation must be expressed to my co-workers Tim Chase, Dave Boskey, and Larry Hinderks without whose C compiler, driver debug package, and excellent advice this paper would not have been possible.

REFERENCES

[1] Wirth, Nicklaus, "MODULA: A Language for Modular Multiprogramming", Software Practice and Experience, January 1977.

[2] Dietrich, R.W., "A Machine-Independent Systems Programming Language", Microprocessors, Microprogramming and Minicomputers, Western Periodicals Company, 1977:

[3] Kernighan, B.W. and Ritchie, D.M., The C Programming Language, Prentice-Hall Software Series, 1978.

[4] Bergeron, R.D. et al, Systems Programming Languages. Advances in Computers, Vol 12, 1972.

[5] Johnson, S.C. and Ritchie,D.M., "Portability of C Programs and the Unix System", The Bell System Technical Journal, Vol. 57, No. 6, Part 2, July-August 1978.

APPENDIX A

```
HPC,1,m,w,nr,"DVC00  DRIVER FOR 12966A 07-04-80 SEA(CCS)";

/*
 * PROGRAM:    DVC00
 * CREATED:    6-1-80
 * AUTHOR:     STEVE ASHCRAFT (CCS)
 * LAST MOD:   7-4-80
 *
 * DVC00 is a standard RTE-IVB driver for the HP 12966A BACI card.
 * Calls to the driver are standard EXEC calls as described in the
 * RTE-IVB Programmer's Reference Manual.
 * The driver supports reads, writes, and two control functions.
 * The control functions are:
 *        0      -     reset the card
 *       30B     -     enable the driver to schedule a program
 *                     on interrupt. The option parameter is
 *                     the address of the ID block of the program
 *                     to schedule.
*/
#include !dvc00
dvc00()
{
/*  this is a test module for developing drivers using C  */


/* debug stuff for driver development (only included if DEBUG is defined)*/

#ifdef DEBUG
DEBUG_STUFF(i);
#endif


/*
 ***************************************************************************
 *
 *  entry into the initiator occurs here
 *
 ***************************************************************************
*/

 INITIATOR(sc);
 SET_EQT_ADDRESSES;      /* set the eqt table addresses */
 INT_CLEAR(sc);          /* clear any old interrupt status bits */

#ifdef DEBUG
 CALL_DEBUG(dummy);      /* if DEBUG is defined initiate the debugger */
#endif



/* if this is the first time into the driver the special character ram
 * needs to be set up to acknowledge:
 *     1)  carriage return
 *     2)  backspaces
 * as special characters
*/

 if (!eqt5->status0) {
    setram();
    eqt5->status0 = ON;
 }

 baud = baud_table[eqt11->baud_code];    /* set the baud code */

 /* switch on the type of the request READ, WRITE, or CONTROL */

 switch (eqt6->function) {
  case READ:
       set_charactercount();
       mode = RECEIVE;
       setup();                           /*set up card to receive */
       eqt11->special = NOTSET;           /*clear special char flag */
       START_TRANSFER(sc);
       NEED_INTERRUPT_EXIT;

  case CONTROL:
       /*
        *  Only 2 control functions are currently implemented:
        *        clear card
        *        enable card to schedule program
        *
        *  The other obvious choices (set baud rate, parity, etc.)
        *  are left as an exercise( ha-ha ) for the reader
       */
       switch (eqt6->subfunction)  {
          case CLEAR:      /* issue a reset all to the card */
             INT_CLEAR(sc);
             setram(); /* need to reset ram if powerfail occurred */
             IMMEDIATE_COMPLETION;

          case ENABLE:     /* enable driver to schedule a program */
             eqt13->id_address = eqt7->buffer;
             IMMEDIATE_COMPLETION;

          default:    /* ignore all other requests */
             BAD_CONTROL_COMPLETION;
       }

  case WRITE:

        set_charactercount();  /* set up the char counter */
        mode = TRANSMIT;
        setup();               /* set card for transmission */

        /* output the user's buffer to the card */
```

```
        buf_ptr = 2*(eqt7->buffer);
        for ( i = 0; i < eqt8->buff_length; i++) {
          character = *buf_ptr++;
          if( (character=='_') &&
                  (eqt10->char_count+1 == eqt8->buff_length)){

            /* if the last output character is _ do not output CR LF */

            START_TRANSFER(sc);
            NEED_INTERRUPT_EXIT;
          }
          OUTPUT(sc,character);
          eqt10->char_count++;          /* bump character count */
        }

        /* output a carriage return and linefeed */

        character = CARRIAGE_RETURN;
        OUTPUT( sc, character);
        character = LINEFEED;
        OUTPUT( sc, character);
        START_TRANSFER(sc);
        NEED_INTERRUPT_EXIT;
 /*  INVALID REQUEST TO THE DRIVER */
  default:  BAD_CONTROL_COMPLETION;
 }

/*
 ************************************************************************
 *   continuator section begins here                                    *
 ************************************************************************
*/
CONTINUATOR(sc);
GET_STATUS(sc,status);                  /* get current status */
card.stats = status;                    /* map status into bit fields */
INT_CLEAR(sc);                          /* clear any interrupts*/
SET_EQT_ADDRESSES;                      /* set address of eqt */
baud = baud_table[eqt11->baud_code];

/* determine the cause of the interrupt  */

 if (card.status_bits.breaks) {         /* break key was pressed */
     schedule_program();                /* schedule a program if enabled */
     CONT_EXIT;
 }
 else {

    switch (eqt6->function) {          /* READ or WRITE? */
      case READ:
        /* are we processing a interrupt from a write that was due to
         * having received a special character?
        */
        if( eqt11->special == NOTSET) {

/* no this is an int from a read operation */
   if( card.status_bits.special_char ){ /* special character int? */

      /* get special character and empty card into user's buffer */

      eqt11->special = spec_type = (empty(eqt10,eqt12) & 0177);
      mode = TRANSMIT;        /* set card for transmit mode */
      setup();
      switch (spec_type)  {
        case CARRIAGE_RETURN:
          character=LINEFEED;
          OUTPUT(sc,character);
          START_TRANSFER(sc);
          CONT_EXIT;

        case BACKSPACE:

          /* process a backspace by:
           *  if (within user's buffer)
           *    decrement transmission log
           *    replace character with a null
           *  backspace cursor
           *  output blank
           *  backspace cursor
          */

          cptr = bs_buf;
          while( *cptr  != NULL) {
              character = *(cptr++);
              OUTPUT(sc,character);
          }
          if( eqt10->char_count >0)
            if( eqt10->char_count-- <= eqt8->buff_length)
              *(--eqt12->ptr) = NULL;
          START_TRANSFER(sc);
          CONT_EXIT;
      }
   }
   else {
    /* not a special character so must be
     *          buffer full or
     *          interrupt due to a parity error
    */
       if( card.status_bits.ov_parity) {
          empty();       /* empty fifo */
          if (eqt10->char_count >= eqt8->buff_length)
             /* buffer is full  so xfer is done */
             clear_status();
          else eqt5->status1 = PE;   /*  had a parity error */
          SET_TRANSMISSION_LOG;
          /* b has transmission log */
          COMPLETE_TRANSFER;
       }
       else ERR_COMPLETION;   /* driver is confused */
```

```
            }
        }
        else {
            /* coming back from an int from a write operation */
            spec_type = eqt11->special;
            eqt11->special = NOTSET; /* clear special flag */

            if( card.status_bits.ov_parity){  /* check for parity error */
              eqt5->status1 = PE;
              SET_TRANSMISSION_LOG;
              COMPLETE_TRANSFER;
            }
            else
              switch (spec_type) {
                case CARRIAGE_RETURN:
                  /* set up the transmission log in the b register */
                  SET_TRANSMISSION_LOG;
                  COMPLETE_TRANSFER;
                case BACKSPACE:
                  /* continue read operation */
                  mode = RECEIVE;     /* set card to receive */
                  setup();
                  START_TRANSFER(sc);
                  CONT_EXIT;
                default: ERR_COMPLETION;    /*can't happen so 12966 is dead */
              }
        }
      case WRITE:
            /*
             * determine which kind of interrupt we are handling
            */
            if (card.status_bits.empty_buff) {
               SET_TRANSMISSION_LOG;
               COMPLETE_TRANSFER;          /* completion exit */
            }
            else ERR_COMPLETION;
      default:  ERR_COMPLETION;     /* should never happen */
    }  /* end of switch (eqt6->function) */
 }
}


/*********************************************************************
 *
 *   support subroutines for dvc00
 *
 *********************************************************************
*/

setram()
/*
 * setram sets up the special character ram on the 12966A card
*/
{
 /*
  * set default baud rate
  */
 eqt11->baud_code = baud_table[b9600];
 character = SENDMODE;
 OUTPUT(sc,character);    /* establish transmit mode */


 /* set all characters to not special */
 for( i = 0; i < 256;  i++)
     {
      character = i + NOTSPECIAL;
      OUTPUT(sc,character );
     }

 /* now make backspace and carriage return special characters */
 character = BACKSPACE + SPECIAL;
 OUTPUT(sc,character);
 character = CARRIAGE_RETURN + SPECIAL;
 OUTPUT(sc,character);
}

/*
 *  schedule_program uses a system call to $LIST to schedule the
 *  program whose id block address is found in eqt 13
 */

schedule_program()
{
 int  id ;
 id = eqt13->id_address;
 if ( id != NULL) {
     SCHED (id,sc  );    /* schedule program and put sc in B register */
   }
}

/* empty empties the fifo on the 12966 card into the user's buffer
 * the pointer into the user's buffer and the character counter
 * are updated in the equipment table
*/

empty()
{
 int data;    /* holds data as it comes from fifo */
 REPEAT
   {
    INPUT(sc,data);
    if (data >= 0)    /* fifo is empty */
       return 0;
    else
       if ( (data & SPEC_CHAR) == SPEC_CHAR )  /* found a special char*/
          return data & 0177;   /* return special character */
    else
       if ( (eqt10->char_count)++ < eqt8->buff_length)
```

```
          *(eqt12->ptr++) = data;
   }
}

/* setup  setups up the card by
 *              1) resetting all
 *              2) setting parity
 *              3) setting character size
 *              4) setting baud rate
 *              5) setting echo
 *              6) setting parity
 */

setup()
{
  int word;   /*  temp to hold word to be output to 12966 card */
  int type;   /*  mode of card TRANSMIT or RECEIVE */
  type = mode;
  word = RESET_ALL;
  OUTPUT(sc,word);     /* issue a reset all command */
  word = WORD3 + ECHO  + SEVENBITS + EVENPARITY + CHECKPARITY;
  OUTPUT(sc,word);
  word = WORD4 + baud + type;
  OUTPUT(sc,word);
}

/*  clear status   clears the status bits in eqt 5     */

clear_status()
{
  eqt5->status7 = 0;
  eqt5->status6 = 0;
  eqt5->status5 = 0;
  eqt5->status4 = 0;
  eqt5->status3 = 0;
  eqt5->status2 = 0;
  eqt5->status1 = 0;
}
/* set_charcount  puts the number of characters to
 * move into eqt10,  changes the buffer length in eqt8 into a positive
 * character count, and sets a pointer to the user's buffer in
 * eqt 12  ( this is a character pointer ).
*/

set_charcount()
{
 if ( eqt8->buff_length > 0)  /* user  specified word count */
    eqt8->buff_length *=  2;  /* convert to character count   */
 else
    eqt8->buff_length *= -1;  /* convert to positive char count */
 eqt10->char_count = 0;
 eqt12->ptr = 2 * eqt7->buffer;
}
```

APPENDIX B

```
#define DEBUG 1
int mask = 0177740;
#define  NULL  0
#define  ON    1
#define  NOTSET 0
static int immediate = 4;   /* immediate completion code */

/*  absolute addresses for the equipment table entries */
#define SET_EQT_ADDRESSES \
eqt1 = *(int *)01660;\
eqt4 = *(int *)01663;\
eqt5 = *(int *)01664;\
eqt6 = *(int *)01665;\
eqt7 = *(int *)01666;\
eqt8 = *(int *)01667;\
eqt10= *(int *)01671;\
eqt11= *(int *)01672;\
eqt12= *(int *)01771;\
eqt13= *(int *)01772;

#define INPUT(sc,data)  asm {  lda  *+4;    \
                               and  mask;   \
                               ior  sc;     \
                               sta  *+1;    \
                               lia  0;      \
                               sta  data;   \
                             }
#define LINEFEED  012
#define CARRIAGE_RETURN 015
#define ERR_COMPLETION      asm {  lda d4;  jmp "CC00,I";}
#define BAD_CONTROL_COMPLETION asm { lda d2; jmp "CC00,I"; }
#define COMPLETE_TRANSFER   asm {  cla; jmp "CC00,I";}
#define CONT_EXIT   asm {  isz  "CC00"; jmp "CC00,I";}
#define BACKSPACE  010
#define SCHED(id,eqt4)  asm {  "   EXT   $LIST";      \
                                   ldb  id;           \
                                   stb  *+4 ;         \
                                   jsb  " $LIST";     \
                                   oct "001";         \
                                   def  *+2;          \
                                   nop ;              \
                                   nop ;              \
                                   sza ;              \
                                   jmp  *+5;          \
                                   ldb  id;           \
                                   adb  d10;          \
                                   lda  eqt4;         \
                                   sta  "1,I";        \
                                   nop;               \
                             }
static int d10 = 10;
static int d4  = 4;
static int d2  = 2;
#define CALL_DEBUG(dummy)  asm{" JMP XXX,I";}
#define DEBUG_STUFF(dummy) asm{" EXT  ODT   ENTRY POINT INTO DEBUGGER";\
                               "XXX   DEF  ODT+0";\
                               "      ENT  .BPT.  BREAK POINT LINKAGE";\
                               "      EXT  PC     BREAK POINT LINKAGE";\
                               ".BPT. JSB  XX,I   BREAK POINT LINKAGE";\
                               "XX    DEF  PC+0   BREAK POINT LINKAGE";\
                               }
/*
 * structure for each of the EQT words used by the driver
*/

struct EQT1 {
                          :1;   /* bit reserved for system use   */
          req_list        :15;  /* request list pointer          */
        };

struct EQT4 {
          dcpc_bit        :1;   /* dcpc required                 */
          buffering       :1;   /* device buffered               */
          power_fail      :1;   /* driver process power fail     */
          time_out        :1;   /* driver process time outs      */
          timed_out       :1;   /* device timed out              */
          sub_chan        :5;   /* last subchannel addressed     */
          select_code     :6;   /* select code                   */
        };

struct EQT5 {
          av              :2;   /* i/o controller availability   */
          eq_code         :6;   /* equipment type code           */
          status7         :1;   /* status                        */
          status6         :1;   /* status                        */
          status5         :1;   /* status                        */
          status4         :1;   /* status                        */
          status3         :1;   /* status                        */
          status2         :1;   /* status                        */
          status1         :1;   /* status                        */
          status0         :1;   /* status                        */
        };

struct EQT6 {
                                /* control word                  */
          call_type       :2;   /* type of call                  */
          unused          :3;   /* unused                        */
          subfunction     :5;   /* subfunction                   */
                          :4;   /* unused                        */
          function        :2;   /* control function              */
        };

struct EQT7 {
          int  buffer;          /* address of request buffer     */
        };
```

```
struct EQT8 {
                int  buff_length;   /* length of request buffer      */
              };

struct EQT10 {
                char_count;         /*-number of char left to transmit
                                       or receive                    */
              };
struct EQT11 {
                baud_code     :3;     /* index into baud rate table */
                              :5;
                special       :8;     /* last special character received */
              };

struct EQT12 {
                char  *ptr;           /* pointer into user's buffer  */
              };

struct EQT13 {
                int *id_address;      /* pointer to id block to program
                                         to schedule on interrupt */
              };
/* baud table -  contains bit patterns to be sent to the card to
 * establish the baud rate
 */

static int baud_table[] =   {  0317,     /* 9600 baud  */
                               0315,     /* 4800 baud  */
                               0313,     /* 2400 baud  */
                               0311,     /* 1200 baud  */
                               0306,     /*  300 baud  */
                               0303,     /*  110 baud  */
                               0300,     /*  EXT       */
                               0300,     /*  SPARE     */
                            };
#define BREAK   0100
#define  b9600  0
#define  b4800   1
#define  b2400   2
#define  b1200   3
#define  b300    4
#define  b110    5
#define  bEXT    6
#define  RESET_ALL   0150077
#define  WORD3   030000
#define  SEVENBITS  2
#define  ECHO     020
#define  REPEAT while(1)
#define  PE   01
#define  CLEAR  0
#define  EVENPARITY 4
#define  CHECKPARITY 010
#define  WORD4   040000
#define  TRANSMIT 0400
#define  RECEIVE  0
static char bs_buf[] = " \b";  /*buffer for backspacing */
/* the a register */
#define  AREG     (int *)0
/* the b register */
#define  BREG     (int *)1
#define  READ        1
#define  WRITE       2
#define  CONTROL     3
#define  ENABLE      030
#define  INITIATOR(sc)    asm {" ENT IC00";"IC00  NOP";  sta sc;}
#define  CONTINUATOR(sc)  asm {" ENT CC00";"CC00  NOP"; sta sc;}
#define  IMMEDIATE_COMPLETION  asm {  lda immediate  ; " JMP  IC00,I" ;}
#define  NEED_INTERRUPT_EXIT   asm {  cla ;" JMP IC00,I" ;}
#define  START_TRANSFER(sc)   asm { lda  *+4; and mask   ; ior sc;\
                                     sta  *+1; " STC  0,C";}
/* max length of user's buffer */
#define  MAX_LENGTH  128
#define  OUTPUT(sc,data)                     \
                             asm { lda   *+5;  and  mask;  ior  sc;\
                                    sta   *+2;  lda  data;     ota  0;}
#define  SENDMODE   040500
/* mark character as special */
#define SPECIAL  060400
#define SPEC_CHAR 040000
/* mark character as non-special */
#define NOTSPECIAL 060000
/*  get the status of the card
 *    sc  =  select code
 *    status  = status word on return
*/
#define GET_STATUS(sc,status)   asm {                  \
                                      lda  *+8;       \
                                      and  mask;      \
                                      ior  sc;        \
                                      sta  *+5;       \
                                      lda  *+5;       \
                                      and  mask;      \
                                      ior  sc;        \
                                      sta  *+2;       \
                                      clc  0;         \
                                      lia  0;         \
                                      sta  status;    \
                                   }
/*
 * define a union to map the status word of the 12966 into a set
 * of bit fields
*/
static union u  {
        int  stats ;   /*word to hold status */
        struct s  {
           device_int        :1;  /* device interrupt  */
           special_char      :1;  /* special character */
```

```
                                 :1;  /* unused              */
           spare_rec             :1;  /* spare receiver      */
           test                  :1;  /* test bit            */
                                 :1;  /* unused              */
           half_full             :1;  /* buffer half full    */
           full                  :1;  /* buffer full         */
           empty_buff            :1;  /* buffer empty        */
           breaks                :1;  /* breaks set          */
           ov_parity             :1;  /* buffer overrun or
                                       * parity error        */
         }.status_bits;
     } card;


/*
 * clear the interrupt bits on the card
*/
static int xclear=050077;
#define INT_CLEAR(sc) asm{    lda  *+9;            \
                              and  mask;           \
                              ior  sc;             \
                              sta  *+6;            \
                              lda  *+6;            \
                              and  mask;           \
                              ior  sc;             \
                              sta  *+3;            \
                              lda  xclear;         \
                              ota  0;              \
                            " STC  0,C";           \
                          }


/*  support functions   */

 static int set_character();    /* function to set up character counter */
 static int clear_status();     /* function to clear eqt5 status bits   */
 static int empty();            /* function to empty user's buffer */
 static int setup();            /* function to set transmit/receive mode */
 static int mode;               /* current mode  TRANSMIT or RECEIVE     */
 int schedule_program();        /* function to schedule a program */
 static int spec_type;          /* type of special character */
 char *cptr;                            /* pointer into output buffer */

 /* pointers to eqt structures */

 struct EQT1  *eqt1;
 struct EQT4  *eqt4;
 struct EQT5  *eqt5;
 struct EQT6  *eqt6;
 struct EQT7  *eqt7;
 struct EQT8  *eqt8;
 struct EQT10  *eqt10;
 struct EQT11  *eqt11;
 struct EQT12  *eqt12;
 struct EQT13  *eqt13;

 static int  sc;           /* current select code */
 static int  baud;         /* current baud rate code word */
 static int  status;       /* current status */
 static int  i;            /* loop counter */
 static int character;     /* character to output */
 int  setram( );           /* function to set up special character ram */
 static int  buffer_length; /* user's buffer length */
 static char *buf_ptr;     /* pointer to user's buffer */

#define SET_TRANSMISSION_LOG \
               if(eqt10->char_count < (*BREG = eqt8->buff_length))\
                    *BREG=eqt10->char_count
```

STAR — a stream generator for the HP/1000

Frank Hall

Hewlett-Packard, Corvallis Division
1000 NE Circle Boulevard
Corvallis, Oregon 97330

ABSTRACT: Programming capabilities at the control command level are imperative for a user-oriented operating system. If they are implemented only in system command interpretation modules, size and speed considerations necessarily limit certain crucial capabilities, as is the case with RTE's transfer file mechanism. A powerful, efficient, and more generally useful solution is to implement them through a stream generation utility, although ideally this requires control command stacking, which is absent from RTE. This paper describes STAR, a stream generator designed for RTE which provides command-level symbolic string manipulation, logic and loop control, and interactive dialog as input stream(s) are transformed into output file(s) and/or a subsequently executed transfer file.

SECTION 1. WHAT STREAM GENERATORS ARE AND WHY WE NEED THEM.

An operating system's control language is usually interpreted by system modules which must be compact, fast, and possibly core-resident. For this reason, programming capability at the control language level is typically very limited. However, an operating system user needs the ability to combine a frequently used series of commands into a single unit that can be called by an arbitrary name, like a control language "subroutine." Most operating systems attempt to provide this "procedure" capability, as it is often called, with varying degrees of refinement. Some of the more important refinements are:

1. Parameter passing to the procedure.

   Parameter values are substituted at places specified symbolically in the procedure's commands.

2. Indefinite embedding or recursion.
   A command within a procedure may invoke the same or a different procedure.

3. Procedure logic and loop control.
   These are usually used in conjunction with the symbolic values of (1).

4. Output stream diversion.
   Besides generating a stream of control commands, a procedure mechanism allows generation to devices, or to files which may then be used as input by programs invoked by the procedure.

5. External symbol modification.
   Procedure symbols may be set or modified by input from a device or file. With (4), this allows interactive dialog during expansion.

6. Abend entrapment.
   In order for a procedure to be able to end cleanly if an execution error is encountered, there must be a mechanism to allow control to transfer to another command in the procedure after an abort. With control command stacking, this is usually implemented as a special control command (e.g., EXIT) that is searched for whenever an abend condition is encountered. If the special command is found before exhausting the remaining control commands of the job or session, execution resumes with the next following control command. Otherwise, the job or session receives normal abend processing.

These refinements provide a powerful control command programming capability. To implement them in an operating system, there are two basic choices:

A. Implement them all in the system's command interpretation modules. Procedure execution is then a one-step process of "stream interpretation." The disadvantage of this method is that it places the burden on modules that have high size and efficiency constraints. Consequently, the above refinements are implemented in a very restricted fashion, or not at all. Unfortunately, this was the method chosen by RTE, implemented by the File Manager transfer file mechanism.

B. Implement most of them in a utility program that has less restrictions on size and speed, and implement in the basic operating system only those features necessary for the utility to do its job. Apart from capability (6), the only other necessary operating system features are control command stacking, with the ability for a properly authorized program to insert commands at the top (next out) of its session's or job's command stack. Procedure execution is then a two-step process of stream generation and command insertion. Unfortunately, RTE does not have control command stacking.

The advantages of method B over A are its greater power, and the fact that the utility's output stream diversion capability allows it to be used also as a general purpose stream generator for applications that need only text files produced.

1.1 A STREAM GENERATOR, SOMEDAY, NAMED STAR

STAR has not yet been written. The design outlined in this paper is to be considered only a working draft. My purpose in presenting it here is to generate dialog about what features are most needed in an RTE stream generator.

STAR is designed for RTE as if method B had been implemented. Because RTE chose method A, the command stream produced by STAR cannot be inserted in the control command stack since there is none. The command stream is written instead to a spool pool file whose LU is passed back to the FMGR command level in global parameter 10G, whereupon it may be executed as a transfer file.

The following design for STAR is derived from DEFCCM, an excellent stream generator for the CDC 6600 developed in the early 1970's by Dr. John Howard at the University of Texas at Austin Computation Center. Parts of the following section have been adapted freely from the UT Computation Center User's Manual (1977), which is in the public domain. My debt to Dr. Howard and my former co-workers at the Computation Center is hereby gratefully acknowledged.

SECTION 2. STAR: DETAILED DESCRIPTION.

STAR command macros are simply files consisting of FMGR commands (or other text lines) and directives to modify them. They are called macros because, when processed by the STAR program, they typically expand into a sequence of commands that can be subsequently processed by the RTE File Manager. STAR macros are therefore useful in defining "canned" general sequences of commands that can be automatically tailored to each application of the sequence. They expand RTE's FMGR transfer file mechanism, and are analogous to the HP/3000 User-Defined Commands (UDC's) and the "catalogued procedures" of the IBM 360 and 370 systems.

STAR command macros are created and executed as follows:

1. The user creates a STAR macro, which is a text file consisting of directives, text, and special lines.

2. The user runs program STAR to interpret and expand the macro:

   :RU,STAR,<macro file>,<parameter list>

   STAR takes as input parameters the name of the macro file and a list of parameter values for use in the macro expansion. For brevity, after STAR is loaded on the system, it may be SP'ed (saved) onto a Type 6 file which may be renamed "*". The command

   :RU,*,<macro file>,<parameter list>

   may then be used instead.

3. As STAR creates the FMGR commands, it writes them onto a spool file which it has requested from the RTE operating system. When STAR is finished, it sets the value of global parameter 10G equal to the logical unit number of the spool file containing the control commands.

4. The user then issues the command:

   :TR,10G

   to execute the expanded command sequence. The commands in steps 2 and 4 can be combined into a transfer file named "*", and invoked by the simple command:

   ::*,<macro file>,<parameter list>

2.1 THE EXPANSION PROCESS

When STAR expands a macro, it first reads the entire macro file into memory, making the following changes:

1. Lines with the characters "*." in the first two columns are discarded as comments.

2. Columns 73 and beyond of all lines are discarded.

3. Any line with a comma (,) in column 1 is taken to be a continuation of the preceding line. STAR appends columns 2 through 72 of the continuation line to column 72 of the preceding line.

4. Any line beginning with the letters "LABEL" is immediately parsed as a LABEL directive without expansion. Labels are stored in memory separately as pointers and not as line images.

Note that the entire macro is read and expanded before FMGR is allowed to process the first FMGR command the expansion contains.

2.1.1 PARAMETER BINDING

After the macro file has been read into memory, parameter binding occurs. This process associates actual parameters from the <parameter list> on the run string with formal parameters from the MACRO directive, which occurs at the start of the macro file. The bound values of these formal parameters can then be referenced later in the macro expansion by causing "evaluation" of a formal parameter in the same way that other symbols are evaluated during expansion.

2.1.2 SYMBOL REFERENCES AND EVALUATION

A symbol name is a string of one to ten alphanumeric characters. If a longer string is used, only the first 10 characters will be taken as the symbol name. A symbol reference is an occurrence of the symbol name followed by optional suffixes which specify the field number and character position within the symbol value which is to be referenced. Any of the following combinations are valid symbol references:

```
name
name[n]
name[n]{m}
name{m}
```

where n is the field number and m is the character position. These suffixes will be described in the next section. In the following description, the word "symbol" will represent any of the above valid symbol references.

Symbol evaluation may occur at two different phases in the expansion of a macro line. Recursive evaluation, which occurs early in the expansion, is denoted by placing a dollar sign before the symbol reference:

```
$symbol
```

Delayed evaluation, which occurs late in the expansion and is not recursive, is denoted by placing a less-than sign (<) between the dollar sign and the symbol reference:

```
$<symbol
```

Delayed evaluation is useful when dealing with symbol references whose values may contain special characters (such as $ in FMGR file names) which are not intended to be interpreted as recursive symbol evaluation.

Separation of a symbol reference from arbitrary following characters is accomplished by placing the evaluation delimiter character (>) immediately after the symbol reference in the symbol evaluation. Delimitation is necessary when the character immediately following the symbol reference would otherwise be interpreted as part of the symbol reference (e.g., [or { or an alphanumeric character that might otherwise become part of the symbol name). These, then, are the four methods of symbol evaluation:

```
$symbol        ::=  simple evaluation, no explicit delimiter
$symbol>       ::=  simple evaluation with explicit delimiter
$<symbol       ::=  delayed evaluation, no explicit delimiter
$<symbol>      ::=  delayed evaluation with explicit delimiter
```

2.1.3 SYMBOL VALUES

Symbols acquire values in four different ways:

1. By binding of parameter values specified in the run string to parameter symbols in the MACRO directive.
2. Directly as a result of certain directives such as SET.
3. Automatically at the beginning of the expansion process. These predefined symbols describe the environment in which the expansion is being performed.
4. By lack of definition. A symbol which has not been defined will yield a null value when evaluated.

A symbol value is an arbitrary character string with length between 0 and 256 characters, inclusive. A symbol value can be broken into a series of up to 16 fields (using the SET directive), any of which may contain from 0 to 256 characters. Symbol value fields may be evaluated all together (yielding the total symbol value), or individually (yielding only the value of the referenced field). This feature is useful in dealing with FMGR file name records (FNAMR´s) and their subparameters.

A symbol value field is evaluated individually by placing the field number n in brackets ([n]) immediately after the symbol name in the evaluation:

```
$name[n]
$<name[n]
```

If n is 0, null, or non-numeric, the total symbol value is yielded. If n is numeric but not between 0 and 16 inclusive, the null value is yielded.

In addition, each character of each symbol value field can be referenced individually by placing the character number m in braces ({m}) immediately after the symbol field specification in the evaluation:

$name[n]{m}

If m is 0, null, or non-numeric, the entire value of $name[n] is yielded. If m is numeric but does not correspond to an occupied character position of $symbol[n], the null value is yielded.

Any of the following combinations are therefore valid evaluations:

$symbol	or	$<symbol	::=	total symbol value
$symbol[n]	or	$<symbol[n]	::=	value of nth symbol field
$symbol{m}	or	$<symbol{m}	::=	mth character of total symbol value
$symbol[n]{m}	or	$<symbol[n]{m}	::=	mth character of nth symbol field value

For the remainder of this description, the above combinations will be referred to collectively as $symbol, and referred to simply as symbol evaluations.

2.1.4 PREDEFINED SYMBOLS

These symbols are defined at the beginning of every macro expansion. They characterize the environment in which the macro is being expanded, and provide detailed access to the syntax of the run string.

Symbol	Format	Meaning
DATE	DD MMM YYYY	Date at start of expansion.
LOGLU	nn	Logical unit number of current Log device (nn is a session LU if in session).
Q0,Q1,...	character	Qi is the punctuation following Si, either comma, blank, or equal sign.
R0,R1,...	long string	Ri is the run string image starting after Q(i-1) and extending to end of the command. R0 is the run string beginning with the macro file name.
S0,S1,...	symbol	Simple symbols from the run string. S0 is the macro file name, S1 is the first parameter symbol, and so on. Note that none of these simple symbols are broken into subfields, and that run string keyword parameters (of the form XXX = YYY) are

		represented as two successive simple symbols.
TIME	HH:MM:SS	Time at start of expansion.
U1,U2,...	symbol	Unrecognized positional parameters from the run string (for a positional parameter to be recognized, it must be formally defined by the MACRO directive).

2.1.5 LINE EXPANSION RULE

Here is a precise definition of how a macro line is expanded to become the next sequential directive or text line:

1. Start with a macro line that has been read into memory, with all continuation lines already appended.

2. Find the leftmost character string of the form:

   $symbol

   where "symbol" is a valid symbol reference (see Section 2.1.2).

3. Replace the dollar sign ($) and the symbol reference by the defined value of the symbol, or by the null string if the symbol reference is undefined.

4. If the symbol reference was immediately followed by the evaluation delimiter character (>), delete the delimiter.

5. Repeat steps 2 through 4 until no further dollar signs followed by valid symbol references are found on the line.

6. Scan once across the line starting from the left. Wherever there is a dollar sign followed by the delayed evaluation character (<) followed by a symbol reference, replace the dollar sign, delayed evaluation character, and symbol reference by the defined value of the symbol reference, or by the null string if the symbol reference is undefined. If the symbol reference was immediately followed by the evaluation delimiter character, delete the delimiter.

7. Scan once again from left to right. Wherever there is a dollar sign followed by the evaluation delimiter character (<), delete the delimiter character.

EXAMPLE: Suppose the following symbols, and no others, are defined:

Symbol	Value	
CC	>	
LISTFILE	ABC::-9:4:48	
FILE	ABC//-9/4/48	(where "/" only delimits fields)
ONE	1	
Q	P	
P1	Y	
X	LIST	
Y	FILE	

The expansion of macro line:

```
$$CC>Q,$<$X$Y,$$$$Q$ONE>>>[3]{$ONE}
```

proceeds as follows. After recursive pass 1 (steps 2 through 4):

```
$>Q,$<LISTFILE,$$$P1>>[3]{1}
```

After recursive pass 2:

```
$>Q,$<LISTFILE,$$Y>[3]{1}
```

After recursive pass 3:

```
$>Q,$<LISTFILE,$FILE[3]{1}
```

After recursive pass 4:

```
$>Q,$<LISTFILE,-
```

After delayed evaluation (step 6):

```
$>Q,ABC::-9:4:48,-
```

After final pass (step 7):

```
$Q,ABC::-9:4:48
```

2.2 SYNTAX OF THE MACRO FILE

A macro file is a sequence of line images, but only columns 1 through 72 of each image are used. The first line of a macro file must be a MACRO directive if formal parameters are to be defined for the macro. If a MACRO directive is encountered anywhere else in the file, it is ignored.

The line images in a macro file are classified into three types:

1. Special (lines with a comma (,) in column 1, or with the comment-line identifier (*.) in columns 1 and 2.) These lines are processed as the macro is read into memory, and are either discarded or merged with other macro lines.

2. Directives (lines which, after line expansion, have an alphabetic string in column 1 that matches one of the directive verbs). Directives cause special processing to occur as the macro expansion proceeds.

3. Text (all other lines). After line expansion, a text line is copied to the file being generated by the macro expansion.

2.2.1 SPECIAL LINES

Special lines are processed as STAR reads the macro file into memory:

*.text

Lines with an asterisk (*) in column 1 and a period (.) in column 2 are taken as comments by STAR. These lines are listed in the STAR expansion listing (if the listing is requested by the OPTIONS directive), but are otherwise completely ignored and in no way affect the expansion.

,text

A line with a comma (,) in column 1 is a continuation of the previous line. As the macro file is read into memory, columns 2 through 72 of the continuation line are appended to column 72 of the preceding line image, without any further modification. Up to 9 continuation lines may be appended to a single line image. However, the expansion process truncates the expanded line image after 300 characters. But this limitation does not apply to the MACRO directive, which is not expanded in the normal manner.

2.2.2 DIRECTIVES

A directive is a line that starts with one of the STAR commands listed in Section 2.3. It calls for special processing during macro expansion.

2.2.3 TEXT LINES

A text line is one which is not a special line and which, after line expansion, is also not a directive. Text lines are copied to the FMGR command file or other file being generated by the macro expansion.

2.2.4 STAR DIAGNOSTICS

Besides reporting system errors encountered during the expansion process, STAR produces the following error messages on the current log device and in the STAR expansion listing:

```
** STAR ERROR **  MORE THAN NINE CONTINUATION LINES.
                  Too many continuation lines.

** STAR ERROR **  DUPLICATE LABEL - XXXX
                  Two label directives use value XXXX.

** STAR ERROR **  EMPTY MACRO FILE.
                  The macro file contains nothing.

** STAR ERROR **  NULL LABEL.
                  A label directive is given no value.

** STAR ERROR **  TOO MANY LABELS.
                  The macro contains more than 400 labels.

** STAR ERROR **  LABEL NOT DEFINED IN MACRO - XXXX
                  A JUMP directive used an undefined label.
```

2.3 DIRECTIVES

MACRO directives have basically the same syntax as FMGR commands, except that they do not begin with a colon (:), they sometimes use longer parameters or quoted strings, and they accept other characters besides a comma (,) as separators.

Any character other than a letter or digit can be used as a separator. Blanks are separators when not next to other separators.

Extra parameters in directives are ignored. When the end of the expanded line image is encountered, any subsequent symbols or strings are taken to be null (length 0), and any subsequent integers are taken to be unsigned zeros.

Quoted strings are written in the form:

string

where the asterisk (*) represents a string quote character, which may be any non-alphanumeric character, and "string" is a sequence of arbitrary characters not containing the string quote character. In each instance, the two string quote characters must be the same. A blank may be used as a string quote character provided that the string is null or starts with a letter or digit. The string quote also serves as the punctuation that separates the string from other parameters. Two adjacent strings share the same quote character, being written:

*string1*string2*

where each asterisk (*) here represents the same quote character, which does not appear inside either string1 or string2.

In the following descriptions of individual directives, commas (,) are used for separators and asterisks (*) for string quote characters in order to illustrate the syntax.

The following parameter symbols are also used:

Parameter	Format and Meaning
symbol	A valid symbol reference (See Section 2.1.2): One to ten alphanumeric characters, optionally followed by a field specification enclosed in brackets ([]), optionally followed by a character position specification enclosed in braces ({}). Note that most directives will also allow a null string in place of a symbol reference. The value of the "null" symbol is always null, and any attempts to alter it are ignored.
string	An arbitrary sequence of characters other than the character used to quote the string. String lengths may be from 0 to 256 inclusive.
compound-string	A group of one or more strings joined by the same quote character, and interpreted as a single parameter. Compound-strings are used to define symbol fields.
n	An unsigned decimal integer.
label	A name used as a jump location in the macro. See the JUMP and LABEL directives.
name	One to ten alphanumeric characters used to define labels and formal parameters.

filename	A FMGR file name record (FNAMR). Unless specified otherwise, a logical unit number can also be used in place of a filename.
lu	A device logical unit number. A filename cannot be used in place of an lu.
text	Arbitrary text used to define a generated text line.
conditional	A description of actions to be performed, based on the outcome of a test. There are three forms of conditional: the null string, an unsigned integer, and a non-null directive or text line other than an unsigned integer. If the conditional is null, no action is performed. If the conditional is an integer n, the next n lines (not counting comments) are skipped if the test is false. If the conditional is a non-null directive or text line other than an unsigned integer, it is processed only if the test is true.

2.3.1 COMPUTE,symbol=expression

Define $symbol to be the computed value of "expression". The syntax of a compute expression is:

```
<expression>  ::=  <letters>|<expression><sum><letters>

   <letters>  ::=  <null>|<letters><letter>

       <sum>  ::=  <term>|<sum>+<term>|<sum>-<term>

      <term>  ::=  <integer>|<term>*<integer>|<term>/<integer>

   <integer>  ::=  +|-|<digit>|<integer><digit>
```

Blanks within an expression are ignored, except that a blank may be used to separate two adjacent integers (when the second is unsigned). The value of an expression is converted to string form by computing the value of each sum using integer arithmetic (treating division by zero as division by one), expressing the sum using integer arithmetic, expressing the sum as a decimal integer, and concatenating characters to eliminate blanks. For example,

Expression	Value
P5-6	P-1
5/0	5

```
5/2A-5/2B-5/-2            2A-2B2
6*5/3 + 1+2*3-7           10
1 2 3 + 4 5               1275
A+1+B2+2C3-5D6E0007F      A1B4C-2D6E7F
```

2.3.2 DEFAULT,symbol*string*

If $symbol is undefined, define $symbol=string.

2.3.3 GENERATE,filename,OVERWRITE

Close out the file being generated, then start generating command file whose lu will be passed back in parameter 10G. The OVERWRITE parameter must be present and correctly specified if the named file is allowed to already exist. Otherwise, STAF will abort with a FMGR -002 (DUPLICATE FILE NAME) error.

2.3.4 IFEQ *string1*string2* conditional

```
IFNE *string1*string2* conditional
IFLT *string1*string2* conditional
IFGT *string1*string2* conditional
IFLE *string1*string2* conditional
IFGE *string1*string2* conditional
```

Compare string1 with string2 and process the conditional accordingly. String comparisons use lexigraphic ordering based on ASCII character codes, with the shorter string filled with zero bits on the right. Thus:

+ < - < 0 < 1 < ... < 9 < A < ... < Z < a < ... < z

Note that this is not arithmetic ordering, for:

-1 < -2 < 10 < 9

To compare integer values, use the sequence:

```
COMPUTE DIFFERENCE = $I - $J
IFLT *$DIFFERENCE*0* conditional action for i < j
```

2.3.5 IFJUMP,label,conditional

Test to see if label is defined, and process the conditional accordingly.

2.3.6 INCLUDE,filename

Copy "filename" to the file being generated. Macro expansion is not applied to the data copied. The copy proceeds until the end of file is reached.

2.3.7 INCREMENT,symbol

Add 1 to the low-order numeric portion of $symbol, inserting a zero (0) beforehand if necessary. For example, a symbol value of "U" when incremented would yield "U1", and when incremented again would yield "U2". This command is equivalent to:

COMPUTE,symbol=$symbol+1

2.3.8 JUMP,label

Break the sequential flow of expansion by jumping to the LABEL directive defining "label". If there is none, STAR aborts with a diagnostic message.

2.3.9 LABEL,name

Define "name" as an allowable target for a JUMP. LABEL directives are interpreted, without expansion, when the macro file is read into memory. They are only valid in the macro file, and are ignored if encountered while expanding a process file (see the PROCESS directive).

2.3.10 MACRO,paramdef,...,paramdef

Like LABEL, the MACRO directive is interpreted, without expansion, during STAR's initialization phase. It formally defines the parameters accepted by the macro, and must be the first line in the macro file (it is ignored elsewhere). If it is omitted, all positional parameters are unrecognized and can be accessed through the $U1, $U2, ...,$Un predefined symbols. The paramdef fields may have the following forms:

name/default

This form defines a positional parameter, whose value may be referred to by $name. The default value is "default", which must either be a name, or null. If default is null, the intervening slash (/) can be omitted.

name=default-simple/default-implicit

This form defines a keyword parameter, whose value can be referred to by $name. The value of the keyword parameter can be specified in the run string by either of these two ways:

name = value
name

The first method results in "explicit" binding of the value to $name. The second method results in "implicit" binding, or binding of an "implicit default" to $name. The implicit default for a keyword may differ from its simple default, which is bound to $name only if "name" is completely omitted from the run string.

The parameter values "default-simple" and "default-implicit" represent the simple and implicit defaults of the keyword parameter. Both must be a name, or null. If "default-implicit" is null, the intervening slash (/) may be omitted. If both defaults are null, the equal sign (=) must still be retained.

The binding process that associates actual parameters with these formal parameters consists of the following steps:

1. Make a list of the formal parameters.

2. Scan the actual parameters from left to right.

3. For an equated actual parameter (X=Z), first define $X to be Z. Then cross off the leftmost, if any, formal parameter whose name matches X (X=D1/D2 or X/D).

4. For a simple actual parameter (X), first find the leftmost, if any, formal keyword parameter (X=D1/D2) whose name matches X. If one is found, define $X to be D1, and cross off the formal parameter. If one is not found, find the leftmost remaining formal positional parameter (Y/D), define $Y to be D, and cross off the positional parameter. If neither a formal keyword nor positional parameter are found to match, create a dummy formal parameter Ui, taking it from the sequence U1, U2, ..., and define $Ui to be X.

5. After all the actual parameters have been scanned, go through the surviving formal parameters from left to right and define their default values as follows. For keyword parameters (X=D1/D2), define $X to be D2. For positional parameters (Y/D), define $Y to be D.

For example, the directive:

```
MACRO,IN/1,OUT,CODE=ASCII/ASCII,REWIND=NO/YES
```

when called with the following run string:

```
:RU,STAR,<macro file>,A,B,C,D=E,REWIND,F
```

will yield the following symbol values:

$IN	=	A
$OUT	=	B
$U1	=	C
$D	=	E
$REWIND	=	YES
$U2	=	F
$CODE	=	ASCII

2.3.11 OPTIONS,LIST=filename

This command defines the expansion mode. Currently the only option available is the LIST option, which specifies a file or lu onto to which a listing of the macro is written, including STAR comment lines, as it is read into memory. During expansion, the TRACE directive can be used to write debug information to the list file. Expansion errors are noted on the list file whether or not the TRACE directive is in effect.

The OPTIONS directive must immediately follow the MACRO directive, if one is present, or be the first line in the file if the MACRO directive is omitted. An OPTIONS directive occurring elsewhere is ignored.

2.3.12 PROCESS,filename

Read the next lines to be expanded from "filename" until the end of file is reached, or a JUMP directive is encountered. Continuation lines are appended and comment lines discarded as in expansion of a normal macro file. However, any PROCESS, LABEL, or MACRO directives encountered in this file are ignored. When the end of the process file is reached, expansion continues in the macro file with the next line following the PROCESS command. If a JUMP directive is encountered before the end of the process file, it is closed and expansion resumes in the macro file at the referenced label.

2.3.13 PROMPT,lu*string*

Write the string to lu if lu is interactive.

2.3.14 QUOTE,text

Place "text" in the file being generated. QUOTE could be used for every line generated but is necessary only for lines that would otherwise be taken as directives or special lines.

2.3.15 READLINE,lu,symbol

Read a line from lu, and set $symbol to the line read. An end of file condition on lu returns a null value.

2.3.16 SET,symbol,*compound-string*

Define $symbol to have the value of the compound-string. Field 1 of $symbol is set to the first string of the compound-string. Field 2 is set to the second string, if any, and so on out to 16 fields. For example, the following commands read a filename from a terminal and parse it to isolate the cartridge reference number of the file:

```
READLINE $LOGLU LISTFILE
SET FNAMR :$<LISTFILE:
SET CRN $FILE[3]
```

2.3.17 TERMINATE

Close out the file being generated, and terminate macro expansion. STAR exits normally. Every macro ends with an implicit TERMINATE directive. An alternate form is:

```
TERMINATE,text
```

This form results in an error termination with the message "text" displayed to the log device. The initially generated FMGR transfer file is returned to the system, and the value ":*:" is returned in global parameter 10G.

2.3.18 TRACE

Turn on the macro debugging trace mode, in which each macro line is copied to the listing file after line expansion. If the listing file has not been defined by the OPTIONS directive, the warning message

```
** STAR WARNING ** LIST FILE NOT DEFINED FOR TRACE.
```

is written to the log device, and the command is ignored. To turn off the trace, use:

```
TRACE,OFF
```

Any parameter value but "OFF" turns on the trace.

SECTION 3. SAMPLE MACRO

As an example, let us take a macro that gets around the RTE LOADR's inability to accept library names in the run string. Suppose the following macro is on a file named "LOAD":

```
MACRO,PROG,L=1/6,LB=/LB,BG=/BG
*. LOAD $PROG
:RU,LOADR,TEMP,,$L,$LB$BG
*. SP PROGRAM
PROMPT $LOGLU "SP THE PROGRAM?"
READLINE $LOGLU ANSWER
IFEQ *$ANSWER{1}*Y* :SP,10G
*.........................
*. CREATE LOADR COMMANDS .
*.........................
GENERATE TEMP OVERWRITE
SET LIB U0
LABEL LOOP
INCREMENT LIB
IFNE +$<$LIB++ LI,$<$LIB
IFLT *$LIB*U4* JUMP LOOP
RE,$PROG
EN
```

Executing the commands:

```
:RU,*,LOAD,%X,LB,$PLIB,$IOLB,L
:TR,10G
```

would perform interactively what is often done only in batch:

```
:RU,LOADR,5,,6,LB
LI,$PLIB
LI,$IOLB
RE,%X
EN
:SP,10G
```

SECTION 4. CONCLUSION.

STAR has been designed to provide more programming power at the FMGR command level by effectively enhancing the transfer file mechanism of RTE. By use of the GENERATE directive, STAR also becomes a powerful generator of line streams intended for purposes other than FMGR transfer files.

It is hoped that STAR can be implemented fairly soon using the new PASCAL/1000 compiler, and that future RTE system developments will be designed with a mind toward making command stream generation a simpler task on RTE. Interested parties should feel free to contact the author.

BIBLIOGRAPHY

University of Texas at Austin Computation Center.
1977 "Control Command Macros". Computation Center User's Manual, Volume 6, Section 2.

future directions of the HP/1000

John Moss

Data Systems Division
Hewlett-Packard
11000 Wolfe Road
Cupertino, CA 95014

Abstract

This paper overviews the entire HP 1000 product program in an effort to put the products in perspective. Current and future directions of the HP 1000 are discussed with respect to the hardware and software features technical computer buyers seek, as well as a review of the elements of TOTAL cost of ownership, which also affect the buying decision.

INTRODUCTION

The HP 1000 Computer product program has never been more exciting or has ever had a more promising future!

During this User's Group Conference, you are hearing about a number of exciting, in some cases new, industry leading products such as RTE, PASCAL, FORTRAN 4X, DISTRIBUTED SYSTEMS, IMAGE and the new L-SERIES, to name a few.

In the next 25 minutes I want to try to put these products in perspective, as they are only part of what we consider to be a superior line of products which is continuing to grow and improve. I will talk about our current products, some of which you may not be familiar with, and the general directions in which we are developing them. I will first discuss our product line with respect to the HP 3000, Desktops, and other HP minicomputers, then HP 1000 software and hardware, and finally, some thoughts regarding the TOTAL cost of ownership of any computer.

PRODUCT LINE DIRECTION

Hewlett-Packard has long used itself as the source of inspiration for new products as well as the early test site; we call this "The Next Bench" Program. Consequently, in computers as well as instruments, we orient our product strategy around the needs of manufacturing companies, as that is what we are.

If one takes the typical computer applications in a manufacturing company, they might be arranged in a spectrum (SLIDE 1) ranging from the most business oriented, such as accounting and payroll, to the most technical, such as engineering computation or manufacturing. In general, the target market of the HP 1000 is the bottom two thirds of this spectrum. Naturally, the general characteristics of the HP 1000 allow it to be used in a far wider range of applications, but this spectrum is how we orient our design objectives.

If one regards the world of computers as a two dimensional spectrum, it might look like this (SLIDE 2). The horizontal axis represents computational power from the smallest micros to the largest mainframes. The vertical axis is the same as the previous slide, representing the spectrum from business to technical applications. The blobs on this slide should indicate to you the relative positioning of the HP 1000.

SOFTWARE/FIRMWARE PRODUCTS

Real Time Executive Operating System

RTE is, of course, our real-time, event-driven operating system which, in its various forms, runs on all our HP 1000 systems, from the low cost L-Series up through the M- and E-Series to the high performance F-Series.

(SLIDE 3)

The primary objective of RTE is to provide a real-time, fast response, priority interrupt scheme suitable for responding to external events or for controlling external processes. But RTE does a great deal more than that, managing the total resources of the system and providing time slice and batch capabilities.

Sessions VI and VII this morning dealt extensively with RTE, discussing many of its capabilities, some ways to extend those capabilities, and a little of its future direction. For those of you who were not there, let me comment on these areas.

In these days of ever larger and more complex applications software packages, the natural desire is for larger data addressing, larger program addressing and extended data accuracy; some computer users feel that the only way to achieve these capabilities is with a wider word machine. However, in 1978 RTE-IV introduced the Extended Memory Area, which allows the user to access data anywhere in the full physical memory, up to nearly two megabytes. RTE-IV also gave the user double word, 32-bit integer and 64-bit floating point, instructions and arithmetic. As for computational accuracy, the algorithms used in the HP 1000 are as accurate as any in the industry.

We at HP are confident that it is possible to improve not only the speed and price performance ratio, but also the ease of use of large data addressing. We are also confident that software innovations such as multi-level segmentation and load on call techniques will provide the user an easy way to achieve large program addressing without the expense of wider word hardware. We expect that the HP 1000 will continue to be the leader in these areas.

Software Development

Another growing strength of the HP 1000 is in the area of software development tools which run under RTE. Technical languages, editors, profilers, logic analyzers and the Session Monitor are among the offering of Hewlett-Packard. In addition, important contributions are coming from third party software houses and the HP 1000 Users Group. Let me discuss each of these topics briefly.

FORTRAN and BASIC are undoubtedly the most widely used technical computer languages today, with PASCAL growing rapidly into third place. The recent announcements of the greatly enhanced FORTRAN 4X compiler and PASCAL/1000 should be indicative of the recognition by HP of the importance of having a really strong, modern language package for the HP 1000. In the last two years we have assembled an outstanding language development lab in Data Systems, and you can expect a continuing flow of technical language enhancements.

A new screen editor, EDIT/1000, was introduced in June, after two years of development and usage within HP. We believe that this new editor will prove to be a truly great productivity enhancer for HP 1000 programmers. Not only does it enable the programmer to use the local screen capabilities of the terminal, but EDIT/1000 also introduces powerful commands for string manipulation, text moving and copying, file backup and providing HELP when the user needs it.

The RTE Profile Monitor, introduced earlier this year as part of the ACCEL/1000 package and to be offered as a standalone product on October 1st, was originally developed to help our software development lab identify troublespots in their code. The Profile Monitor allows them to monitor and analyze the execution of the code to determine where the computer is spending the most time. Once isolated, inefficient routines can be recoded to run faster; often, just recoding in the original high level language doubles the speed of execution, while recoding in Assembly or Microassembly may improve it by an order of magnitude. Enhancements, such as the ability to monitor the Operating System as well as applications programs or compilers, are under development.

The HP 1610 Logic Analyzers offer a level of capability unequalled on the market today. If you are not familiar with logic analyzers and did not attend Session V yesterday afternoon, these instruments, when used with the appropriate L-Series or M/E/F-Series interface, provide the capability to monitor memory, I/O and DMA transactions within the computer to capture desired activities in order to ascertain that the computer is executing as desired. This type of analysis accelerates the development of software by helping the programmer debug more quickly or avoid altogether many software problems. HP is putting in the Users Group Library a set of FORTRAN programs which will simplify and speed the use of the analyzers and the analysis of the resulting data. We at HP feel that these types of software development and optimization tools are crucial to technical computer users, and we intend to maintain our leadership position.

The Session Monitor in RTE-IV is intended for multi-user systems where program development and production activities are taking place concurrently. The Session Monitor provides an orderly, accountable access to the system which acts to limit undesirable or unauthorized use of system resources. At the same time, it provides a generally simpler, friendlier interface for the user. Given the multi-user, multi-task, multi-lingual capabilities of RTE, Session Monitor is the way that the computer can be tailored to the user, so that the HP 1000 can approach the friendliness of a desktop computer. We have come a long way toward this goal and intend to go much further.

In addition to our own development capability within HP, we have also initiated a Third Party Software program, to leverage the efforts of our customers. We publish a directory of our OEMs and software houses which cross-indexes their products by application and type. Third party products of general usefulness to other customers may be submitted for publication in the Crosstalk column of our OEM newsletter On-Line. We have also bought the right to sell at least one software development tool, the "C" language compiler, from Corporate Computer Systems. This compiler is being presented by CCS right now in Session XI; you can still make it if you hurry.

Another important source of software development aids is your own Users Group Contributed Library, PLUS/1000. Many useful programs are available in PLUS/1000, not the least of which are the logic analyzer programs I mentioned a few minutes ago and WOLF, the document processor and formatter I used to prepare this paper. I look forward eagerly to see what new goodies you have put in it when the library is released this fall.

Data Base Management System

(SLIDE 4)

Tomorrow morning in Session XVIII you will have an opportunity to meet and interact with the HP product team responsible for IMAGE/1000. Since its introduction a few years ago, HP's IMAGE Data Base Management System has won wide acclaim as a cost effective, highly usable general purpose package. Until this month, IMAGE/1000 has always included our high powered inquiry and report generating facility QUERY. However, as many of our customers prefer to write their own inquiry and report generating programs, we have just introduced a new product IMAGE/1000 (without QUERY) at a reduced price, along with enhancements to the IMAGE portion of both products.

The whole theory of data base management is, of course, advancing and the HP 1000 development lab is investigating the applicability of these new concepts to the HP 1000.

Distributed Processing

As you are probably aware, HP was among the first to offer a distributed processing capability. Since then we have developed and enhanced DS/1000 and this month we are introducing DS/1000-IV, the fourth generation product. Session IX this morning discussed this product in detail. Let me just say that at this point in time, there are more DS/1000 nodes installed and working than any other vendor's. The HP 1000, with a memory-based or execute only version of RTE, is particularly well suited to be a disc-less or run-only node. Here again, DS/1000 is an area where we are the leader and we are going to continue to be the leader.

Applications Software

Hewlett-Packard probably offers the broadest selection of graphics peripherals of any manufacturer in the business. In recognition of this growing business, the GRAPHICS/1000 family of graphics software is being developed. The first package, Graphics Plotting Software (GPS), contains 53 device independent plotting subroutines and the device drivers to support virtually every graphics peripheral offered by HP. In Session XIX tomorrow morning, you will have an opportunity to hear more about this exciting area, as well as two new Users Group Contributed Library programs, BRUNO, which gives the HP 1000 an unusually friendly, high level capability to generate overhead slides and illustrations, and PENNY, which gives the user the ability to create schematics on the system. We feel that graphics capability is a key element of success in the future, and the HP 1000 is going to continue to be a leader in this area.

(SLIDE 5)

In 1978 HP introduced DATACAP/1000, a real-time data capture support package using the HP 3070 family of Data Capture Terminals, to collect data at the point where it is generated. For example, DATACAP can be used to collect labor data, clock-in clock-out times, test results and track work in progress throughout a factory floor and to put it in a data base or to send it to the EDP computer. The DATACAP package is general purpose enough to be widely useful and is easily tailored, using menu forms, to the user's application. DATACAP represents an area of considerable importance in computer aided manufacturing, and the large development lab team assures me that DATACAP is only the first of many such HP 1000 application specific packages.

In fact, the increasing importance of application-specific software in today's world is well appreciated by HP. Trade journal articles appear regularly showing that demand for programmers is and will continue far exceeding the available supply. The value of the investment in software outweighs the investment in hardware in many installations; in order for users to stop reinventing the software they need, software suppliers must supply and computer users must use applications-oriented software which is easily adapted to the customers requirements. HP has as a goal the development of high level, application specific software tools and expects them to become a major portion of our business in the 1980's. For the HP 1000 the application areas we concentrate on will continue to be in the broad categories of computer aided design and manufacturing.

HARDWARE PRODUCTS

(SLIDE 6)

I would now like to turn my attention to some of the major hardware capabilities of the HP 1000.

Given that the HP 1000 is a "technical" minicomputer with its primary applications focus in the lab and manufacturing, there are certain hardware attributes, complementing the software already discussed, which are key to its continuing success. These fall into the broad categories of internal performance and I/O capability.

Internal Performance

Internal performance is something that everyone wants but nobody wants to pay for, so it is most important for a computer manufacturer to offer a wide range of compatible computers. The HP 1000 M-Series was introduced in 1974 as our first mapped memory machine, capable of addressing two megabytes of memory. The E-Series followed two years later and, using 30% faster components plus a variable cycle speed, was able to double the internal performance of the M-Series. In 1978 the F-Series, with its floating point hardware, increased floating point performance two and one half times.

The development of Large Scale Integrated circuits has enabled the computer industry to lower prices and/or increase performance. The L-Series, introduced earlier this year, gives performance comparable to the M-Series at a much lower cost. Very Large Scale Integrated circuits assure that the trend toward physically smaller, lower cost, higher performance HP 1000 computers will continue. Other hardware innovations such as lower cost high performance memory, very high speed cache memory and wider paths to memory assure that memory intensive operations can be speeded up. Wider microinstructions allow more operations to be done in a single machine cycle. HP 1000 Users should rest assured that there is a large hardware development lab in Data Systems which is dedicated to broadening the HP 1000 family and keeping it viable for the foreseeable future.

I/O Capability

One of the most important contributions made by the L-Series is its distributed intelligence I/O. A microprocessor on every L-Series I/O board gives every interface direct memory access capability and offloads much of the CPU interaction previously required. This is one reason the L-Series, which has a somewhat lower cycle speed than the M-Series, approximates the M-Series in overall performance and exceeds the F-Series in I/O performance. Obviously, future HP 1000 processors will use this distributed intelligence I/O system.

One of the most important attributes for a technical minicomputer is that it be designed for easy interfacing with a very wide range of devices, processes and computers. Both the L-Series and the M/E/F-Series have or will have a multitude of analog and digital interfaces, serial and parallel interfaces and, of course, HPIB for interfacing directly with processes, peripherals, instruments and measurement & control front ends. DS/1000 and RJE/1000 software packages support the necessary interfaces to give the HP 1000 unequalled computer-to-computer communications capability. Session XVII tomorrow morning will discuss real world considerations for DS and Data Communications users.

All this I/O capability would be a whole lot less exciting without the broad range of HP peripherals currently available and to be introduced in the future. Time does not allow me to go into detail here, but HP has probably the broadest range of computer peripherals of our own manufacture offered by any computer company now, and there are remarkable new products coming in every category. Most of these will be supported on the HP 1000.

TOTAL COST OF OWNERSHIP

(SLIDE 7)

One of the key criteria that any HP 1000 product development team considers is the TOTAL cost of ownership of a proposed new product. Total cost of ownership includes not only the highly visible costs, such as initial purchase price and monthly maintenance charges, but also the less obvious ones, such as site preparation and monthly energy costs, and the harder to measure costs such as compatability, availability and modularity.

The first and easiest cost to compare when considering a variety of computer products is the bottom line on the purchase price of the set of products required to do the job. The HP 1000 is, by design, usually very competitive on a price performance basis, particularly if the buyer can state the performance, rather than architectural features, sought. For example, the RFP should state that large data addressing is required, rather than a wide word architecture.

Second, and equally obvious, the projected maintenance or support charges over the useful life of the system need to be considered as part of the price performance calculation. Here again, HP has a reputation for reliable products and our monthly support charges generally reflect this lower failure rate.

Often, it is not obvious when comparing a number of alternative computer proposals, what, if any, modifications will need to be made to the site to make it suitable for the system. The usual preparations are special electrical power and air conditioning, but occasionally noise barriers, raised floors and special access are required. These costs can make a tremendous difference to the customer, so the HP 1000 has been designed to minimize them.

Clearly, if a particular computer requires special power and/or air conditioning, the monthly costs of these requirements need to be added into the total cost equation. With electrical energy at five cents a kilowatt-hour and rising, the overall effect on price/performance can be significant. Here again, we feel that the HP 1000 comes away a winner.

I am sure everyone in this room recognizes the importance of compatibility when moving from one system to the next and the cost of reprogramming if it's not there, so let me just say that it always has been and will continue to be a very important criterion to maintain upward compatibility among HP 1000 systems. In fact, code written for the 2116A, HP's first computer, is compatible with the L-Series, our most recent. Where we have not in particular; now that the magnitude of the problem is understood, we are committed to doing a better job.

Here in the factory, availability has in the past been thought of as synonymous with reliability or mean time between failures. Any customer who does not have a resident customer engineer, which is the majority, I believe, recognizes that the real measure is availability. Fixing the problem in 5 minutes doesn't count if it took two hours for the CE to get there. Consequently, we are now working on techniques for doing remote diagnosis and repair, for doing substantial self test and logging of non-critical problems, for turning intermittent failures into hard failures, and for increasing MTBF on our systems, so that system availability can approach 100%.

(SLIDE 8)

Modularity to us simply means offering our products packaged the way our customers want them. In general this means we offer most of our HP 1000 computer products as boards (for hardware oriented volume users), boxes (for customers who mix and match) and systems (for buyers who want a fully tested, VDE and UL approved package).

Compatibility, availability, and modularity obviously have direct effects on the cost of an installation but measuring the magnitude of the effect is difficult. We at HP are not so interested in measuring the costs as we are in minimizing them. You can plan on this emphasis continuing in the years to come.

CLOSING

I hope that this paper has helped put the HP 1000 program in perspective and has reaffirmed in your mind that Hewlett-Packard is committed to the ongoing development and success of the program.

Thank you for your attention.

Any questions?

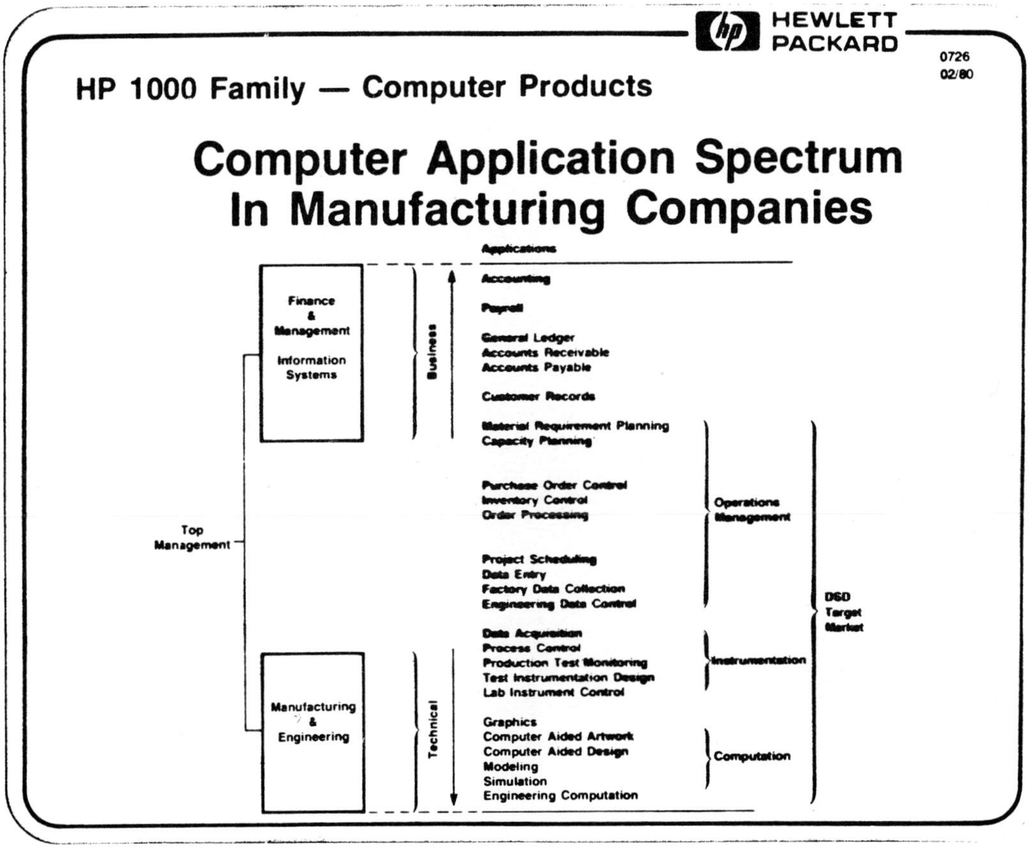
HEWLETT
PACKARD
0726
02/80
HP 1000 Family — Computer Products
Computer Application Spectrum
In Manufacturing Companies
Finance
&
Management
Information
Systems
Top
Management
Manufacturing
&
Engineering
Business
Technical
Applications
Accounting
Payroll
General Ledger
Accounts Receivable
Accounts Payable
Customer Records
Material Requirement Planning
Capacity Planning
Purchase Order Control
Inventory Control
Order Processing
Project Scheduling
Data Entry
Factory Data Collection
Engineering Data Control
Data Acquisition
Process Control
Production Test Monitoring
Test Instrumentation Design
Lab Instrument Control
Graphics
Computer Aided Artwork
Computer Aided Design
Modeling
Simulation
Engineering Computation
Operations
Management
Instrumentation
Computation
DSD
Target
Market

SLIDE 1

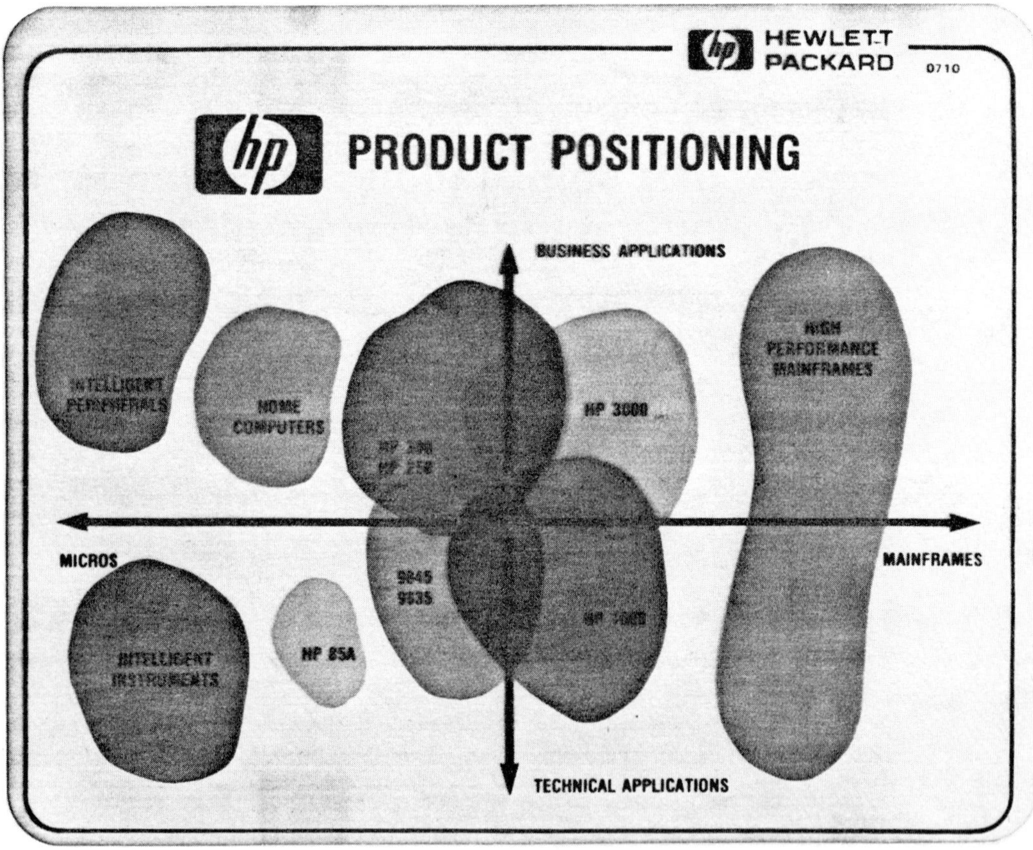
HEWLETT PACKARD
0710
PRODUCT POSITIONING
BUSINESS APPLICATIONS
INTELLIGENT PERIPHERALS
HOME COMPUTERS
HP 3000
HIGH PERFORMANCE MAINFRAMES
MICROS
MAINFRAMES
9845
9835
HP 85A
INTELLIGENT INSTRUMENTS
TECHNICAL APPLICATIONS

SLIDE 2

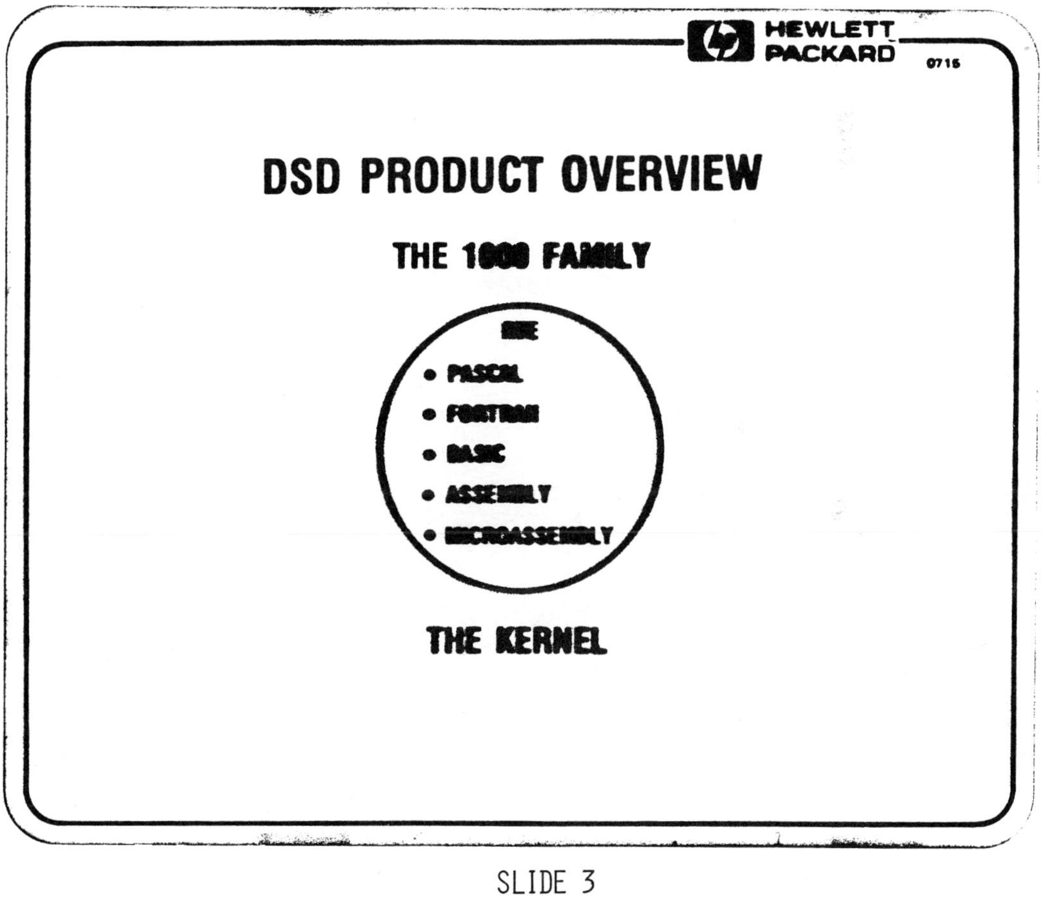
HEWLETT PACKARD
0715
DSD PRODUCT OVERVIEW
THE 1000 FAMILY
• PASCAL
• FORTRAN
• BASIC
• ASSEMBLY
• MICROASSEMBLY
THE KERNEL

SLIDE 3

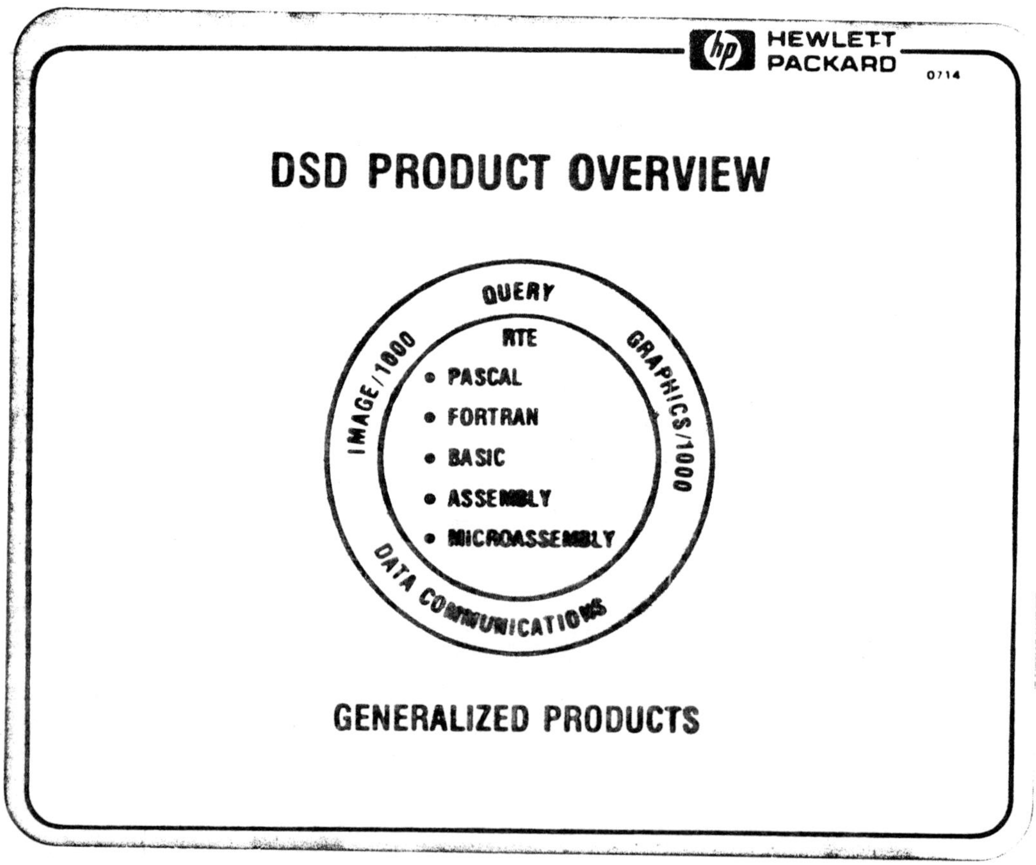
HEWLETT PACKARD
0714
DSD PRODUCT OVERVIEW
QUERY
RTE
IMAGE/1000
GRAPHICS/1000
• PASCAL
• FORTRAN
• BASIC
• ASSEMBLY
• MICROASSEMBLY
DATA COMMUNICATIONS
GENERALIZED PRODUCTS

SLIDE 4

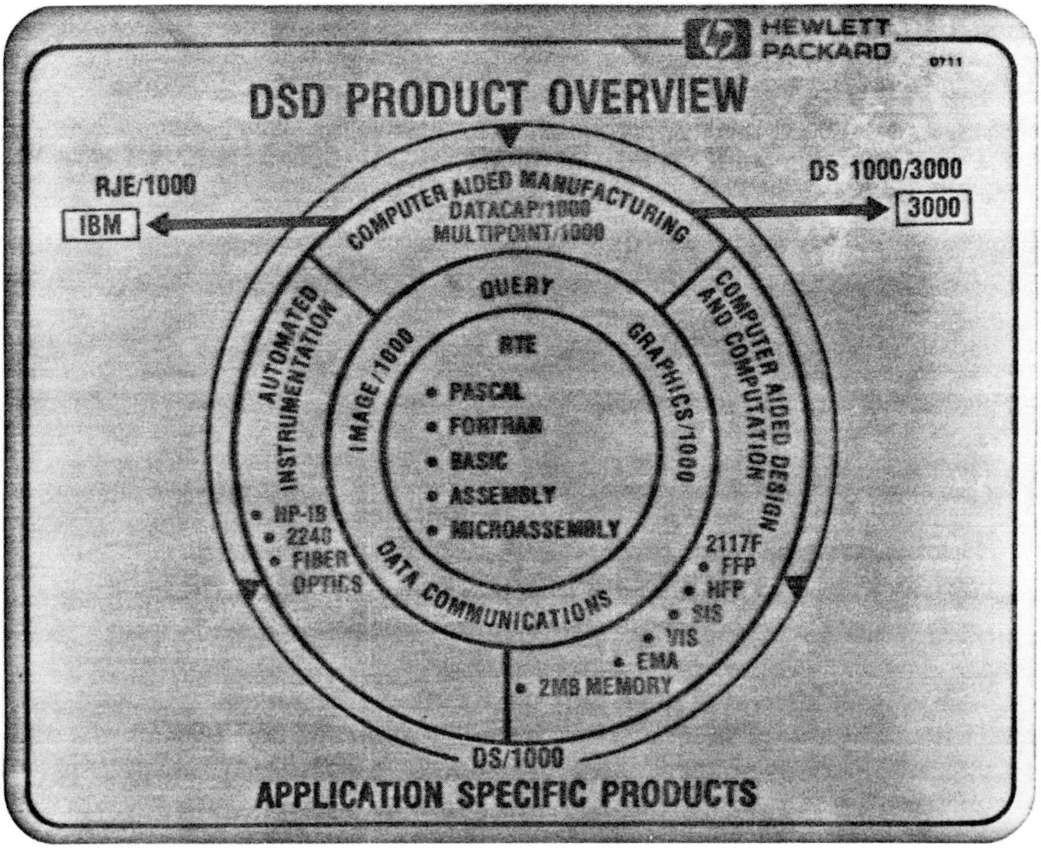
HEWLETT PACKARD
DSD PRODUCT OVERVIEW
RJE/1000
IBM
DS 1000/3000
3000
COMPUTER AIDED MANUFACTURING
DATACAP/1000
MULTIPOINT/1000
AUTOMATED INSTRUMENTATION
• HP-IB
• 2240
• FIBER OPTICS
COMPUTER AIDED DESIGN AND COMPUTATION
2117F
• FFP
• HFP
• SIS
• VIS
• EMA
• 2MB MEMORY
QUERY
IMAGE/1000
GRAPHICS/1000
DATA COMMUNICATIONS
RTE
• PASCAL
• FORTRAN
• BASIC
• ASSEMBLY
• MICROASSEMBLY
DS/1000
APPLICATION SPECIFIC PRODUCTS

SLIDE 5

HEWLETT PACKARD

0730
02 80

HP 1000 Family — Computer Products

Comparative Specifications

	L-SERIES	M-SERIES	E-SERIES	F-SERIES
Base Instruction Set Execution Speed	300,000 IPS	500.000 IPS	1.000.000 IPS	1.000.000 IPS
Floating Point Processing Speed	2,000 OPS	40.000 OPS	80.000 OPS	200.000 OPS
Instruction Set	HP 1000 Base Set	Extended Instruction Group	Extended Instruction Group	Extended Instruction Group plus SIS & FFP
Instruction Cycle Time	Not applicable	325 ns (fixed)	175 280 ns (variable)	175 280 ns (variable)
Memory Cycle Time	681 ns	650 ns (std perf)	595 ns (std perf) 350 ns (hi perf)	350 ns (hi perf)
Direct Memory Access Rate	2.7 megabytes/sec	1.2 megabytes sec	1.8 megabytes sec (sp) 2.3 megabytes sec (hp)	2.3 megabytes sec
Maximum Memory Capacity	64 kilobytes	2 megabytes	2 megabytes	2 megabytes
Number of DMA Channels	All (per channel)	2	2	2
User Microprogrammable	No	Yes	Yes	Yes

SLIDE 6

TOTAL COST OF OWNERSHIP

PURCHASE PRICE
MONTHLY CHARGES
SITE MODIFICATIONS
ENERGY COSTS
REPROGRAMMING
DOWN TIME
PACKAGING

SLIDE 7

HEWLETT PACKARD
0717
DSD PRODUCT OVERVIEW
THE 1000 COMPUTER FAMILY - PACKAGING
L M E F
SYSTEMS
BOXES
BOARDS

SLIDE 8

what you should know about computer site planning

Marcia Jefferies

Inmac
2465 Augustine Drive
Santa Clara, California 95051

ABSTRACT

With a relatively small investment in time and money, preplanning of a computer facility will result in a well organized installation with less downtime and increased efficiency.

I'd like to share with you some thoughts on the importance of computer site planning.

In our experience, users who plan well and solve many of the potential problems up-front, benefit from higher efficiency and productivity. Because our expertise is in minicomputer supplies and accessories, we have often been involved in helping customers design and layout their computer rooms.

We've seen sites that were fairly neglected be transformed from looking like this....to this! With a relatively small investment in time and money, the result is a well organized installation with less downtime and increased efficiency. However, for the remainder of this discussion I will assume you are about to either add a system or receive shipment on your first system. The planning process is the same whether you're up-grading or starting from scratch. Our experience has shown the need for a comprehensive guidebook on how to maximize the efficiency and productivity of a computer room through proper planning. As a result, in September we are publishing a Computer Site Preparation Guide as a service to the industry.

I'd like to review some of the highlights with you today. I will point out briefly some key points for consideration in proper planning for optimum efficiency of a computer facility. They include:

1. Plan ahead on the physical layout of the proposed site;
2. Provide an adequate air-conditioning system;
3. Plan for an adequate power and electrical system;
4. Plan for adequate data storage requirements;
5. Allow time for a final site verification before completing the installation of your computer system.

First, planning the layout of the site. This is an extremely important factor, not only from the standpoint of functional productivity, but also employee motivation. The tools you'll need include grid paper, a ruler, a triangle, possibly a compass and a template with cut-outs of equipment commonly found in a computer room.

You need to start by preparing a grid of the floor plan of the proposed area, showing location and arrangement of all equipment and accessories to be included. Be sure to ask yourself these six questions when making your floor plan;

<u>Question 1</u>: Do corridors and entryways to the site allow clearance for equipment? Be sure to discuss the hardware's dimensions with a consultant or with the vendor's customer engineers.

<u>Question 2</u>: Does the floor plan allow for system expansion? According to some industry experts, about 75 percent of those buying a computer add hardware within 2 years. Rapid changes in hardware and software systems can dramatically affect room requirements, department size and interrelationships. Both systems and physical space should be adaptable and expandable.

<u>Question 3</u>: Is enough space provided for personnel safety, comfort and freedom of movement? We feel it is especially important to prepare a work-flow diagram which follows the step-by-step movement of people, materials and documents. Actual steps taken by computer room personnel in transporting printouts, tapes, disks, and other media should be included in the diagram. Here, we have used a different color to indicate traffic patterns and access required by: Field Service, the System Manager, the Programmer and the clerk. By placing often-used materials at the fingertips of those employees who will use them, you will eliminate wasted steps, time and money, thus improving the operating efficiency and productivity of your computer operation. People need sufficient space to work effectively and safely. But you can be creative. For example, the use of a simple idea like a lazy susan can save you the cost of an extra, often infrequently used terminal. And increase the productivity per square foot utilized.

<u>Question 4</u>: Have provisions been made for an adequate fire protection system? Other emergency systems? Plan to install smoke detectors and fire detectors. Be sure to include Halonated hydrogen extinguishers at

strategic locations to fight any fire that may develop. They are available in various sizes and, according to fire officials, Halon is the best material available for fighting computer room fires. It is safe, even in a closed computer room. It is a stable chemical that won't corrode your electronic components, and it won't cause static. It's not cold like the CO_2 type of extinguishers that can harm your computer's sensitive PROM's or chips. It is harmless to material like plastic or delicate fabrics. Mark all locations clearly, and train personnel to use the extinguishers. Regular sprinkler systems and water extinguishers are unsuitable for computer room use. If there is no way to avoid a water sprinkler system, fit protective cowls on sprinklers located over computer equipment. All on-site records or stored data should be housed in fire-proof, theft-proof safes or cabinets. Keep as few records as possible in the computer room, and duplicate all data kept there. Store the redundant data off-site as an added security measure.

Question 5: Does the floor plan indicate the position of all cabinets, files, doors, windows and other permanent structures? Make sure it shows the location of the power distribution panel; provides enough space for cabinets, files, and dividers; allows for proper clearance (about 36 inches) at the front and rear of equipment for proper servicing; and indicates the location of all supporting posts and columns. For optimum visibility of lighted displays and indicators, brilliant illumuniation should be avoided. Direct sunlight is not recommended and window locations will affect placement of equipment.

Question 6: Will the floor withstand the distributed weight load estimated for the computer system configuration -- plus all auxiliary equipment? The specifications accompanying the floor plan should indicate the weight of clusters of equipment. The weight of the system and the possible necessity for a raised floor to accommodate cables should be taken into consideration. Raised floors are a great expense and can be avoided in most modern buildings by proper layout. If raised flooring is used, heavy pieces of equipment should be separated by enough distance to avoid unnecessary concentrations of weight loads. Consideration must also be given to allowing for service and repair access without requiring that heavy equipment be moved.

The second key area, an adequate air-conditioning system, is mandatory. Attention should be given to the following three steps:

Step 1: With the help of an expert, calculate the total heat dissipated by the computer system, lights, people and accessory equipment. Since the computer system, consisting of the central processing unit and peripheral devices, is a major heat source in itself, you must determine your air-conditioning requirements on the basis of heat dissipation by equipment and people; the rate of heat transfer through walls, windows, and ceiling; plus the effect of climate. Generally, computer systems can operate in any environment suitable for human occupancy so long as no moisture condenses within that environment. Check with an air-conditioning expert to determine your specific needs. The MTBF (mean time between failure) of your computer system will be directly related to the adequacy of your air-conditioning system.

Step 2: Verify that the site's air-conditioning system is adequate to maintain a constant room temperature range of 60 to 85 ambient degrees Fahrenheit and a relative humidity range of 50 to 80 percent. To monitor the computer room temperature and humidity levels, use a hygrometer or temperature-humidity meter. These readings can be checked regularly and at a glance.

Step 3: Provide for installation of dust-abatement devices. Excessive dust in the computer room can cause equipment failures and heat build-up. To protect the CPU and peripherals, it may be necessary to install dust-abatement devices at air-conditioning outlets. After consulting the specifications on the equipment regarding air-borne particles, ask the same air-conditioning expert about double filtration methods that will eliminate the problem if one exists.

Key area number three, determination of an adequate power and electrical system, is one of the most important considerations in advance planning. To determine the requirements, you will need answers to these nine questions:

Question 1: Is proper and adequate power available to the site (both voltage levels and sufficient amperage)? Be sure to determine if the computer area is supplied with adequate, regulated AC power. If requested, many power companies will install testing equipment to see if any additional line regulation is needed. Testing can also be done by an electrical specialist using a line-transient recorder. You can avoid many subsequent power problems by discussing your specific needs with one or more vendors before installing your equipment. It may be necessary to have a dedicated power line brought in directly to your computer room.

Question 2: Have tests been conducted to determine voltage fluctuations through-out the day?

Question 3: Have plans been made for voltage regulation equipment?

Question 4: Have provisions been made to protect the system against power surges? Remember that voltage spikes can cause a system to malfunction or lose data, so question an expert on electrical power line interference. Also ask him about alternative solutions such as inexpensive power surge protectors, which can control line voltage transients that can damage a computer unit and associated peripherals.

Question 5: Are sufficient electrical power or digital communication receptacles available in your computer facility? Consult a qualified electrician to determine what additional receptacles may be needed for peripheral devices and service equipment. Shown is an EIA wall plate permanent installation.

Question 6: Are lighting requirements met? New task-lighting systems, in which fixtures are mounted on work stations to direct light on the work surface provide a selective, high-quality light source that is economical, effective and energy saving. As we have said before, brilliant illumination should be avoided. The electrical circuits for lights should be separate from those used for the computer system, and local electrical codes must be considered when determining the final lighting layout.

Question 7: Has a cable layout been completed showing the location and approximate length of system cables? Determining cable requirements is another vital consideration. Computer cables, due to the speed or rate at which information is transmitted, are more sensitive than cables used on other electrical machinery. The length of a cable, as well as environmental factors, can have a lot to do with preventing data loss or scrambling due to electrically caused interference. Cables should not be too short and prohibit movement of peripherals; they also should not be too long, because data mismatch, or attenuation of signal strength between input and output devices, can occur if excessive length exists. Special signal amplifiers or peripheral interface logic may be required if excessive cable lengths are required (over 100 feet), especially for equipment with high-speed data transfer. It may be necessary to have a raised floor, or you may simply be able to use cable bridges that meet OSHA requirements to protect the system's interconnecting cables. This is another instance where you should discuss your system needs with your vendor's customer engineers to get advice.

Question 8: Have equipment power connectors been obtained? Each manufacturer uses different power plugs -- make sure you have the right one in the wall before the system is delivered.

Question 9: Has the terminal or data communications interface equipment (modem, acoustical coupler, or leased line) been installed?

Storage requirements, key item number four, is perhaps the real key to efficient utilization of computer room space. Storage facilities should be considered on three levels; work stations, active files and archival. Disk cartridges, disk packs, tape cartridges, magnetic tapes and diskettes should be stored in or near the areas where work is performed. Be sure to plan for convenient, attractive storage furniture specially built to store these media. This might include special cabinets to protect and store the media, with shelves designed for printer paper, binders and disk packs. Be certain there is adequate shelf space for supplies like ribbons, media products, and emergency items such as cables. To further ensure programmer and operator productivity, consider products such as system manual racks, copy holders and stackable, 132-column printout trays for easy access. Second, departmental storage of active materials: the use of safe, secure cabinets in a location convenient to all will reduce everyone's steps and anxieties. Finally, to assure adequate space for growth, archival materials should be stored elsewhere. Convenience and security can be assured with the proper planning of storage facilities designed especially for computer rooms.

Final site verification, key item number five on our list of key areas, should be a final checklist. Be sure you prepare one to make sure you haven't forgotten anything. This list should include such items as:

1. Is the floor covered with anti-static material? Static electricity can shock personnel and cause equipment to malfunction. Inexpensive shock-absorbing mats will prevent electro-magnetic interference from reaching conductive objects.

2. Is the air-conditioning system adequate and operable?

3. Is the electrical power system adequate and properly regulated?

4. Are all local electrical, fire, construction and building codes maintained?

5. Is the ceiling covered with sound-absorbing material? Total system noise will depend upon room acoustics. You can minimize the system's noise effect on the environment with acoustical tiles and draped walls.

6. Are data-phone lines and other necessary equipment installed?

7. Are modems installed, and is line-conditioning performed?

8. Are all emergency systems provisions installed and operable?

Whether it be a relatively small facility like this one, which is at one of our branches, or a larger installation like this site maintained by one of our customers, or a very large site like the one we visited recently...I'm sure you'll find these tips on site preparation useful and productive.

Thank you...

experience with an HP/1000 computer in a small consulting engineering firm

G. E. Santee, Jr., R. A. Dimenna and Staff Members

Intermountain Technologies, Inc.
1400 Benton, P. O. Box 1604
Idaho Falls, Idaho 83401

ABSTRACT

The use of a Hewlett-Packard 1000 21MX E-Series computer in a small consulting engineering firm is discussed in terms of the acquisition of the system and the application of software to remote I/O operations, engineering problem solution, and utility functions.

INTRODUCTION

Intermountain Technologies, Inc. (ITI) of Idaho Falls, Idaho, is a small consulting engineering firm specializing in the field of nuclear engineering. A significant service to our clients is the use of remote computers to run large computer codes for analyzing nuclear reactor systems. To perform the remote I/O operations, a Hewlett-Packard 1000 21MX E-Series computer system is used. In addition to the remote I/O operations, the HP/1000 system is used for local processing. This paper discusses the application of the HP/1000 system to the particular needs of ITI.

The selection of the HP/1000 system was made to satisfy several requirements. Utmost was the ability to communicate with remote computers. Further requirements were the ability to save and edit disc files and the ability to plot CALCOMP files generated by remote computers. To meet the specified requirements, a line printer, a card reader, a plotter, an additional terminal for editing, and a 4800-baud modem were acquired with the basic HP/1000 computer system.

As the number of users increased from seven to fifteen, the HP/1000 computer system became overloaded, and it became apparent that additional hardware was required. Furthermore, additional needs were recognized. Thus, a tape drive, a 120 Mbyte disc, two more terminals, another line printer, a digitizer, and a 9600-baud modem were added to the system.

As the users have become more familiar with the system, locally developed programs have become more important towards providing service to our clients. Local I/O applications programs are available to interpret CALCOMP plot files generated by remote computers and to allow the user to scan output from a remote computer without actually printing the file. Programs for in-house support include a routine for using the plotter locally, a routine for backing up individual files from disc to tape, routines for word processing, and accounting routines for payroll and record keeping. Technical applications programs currently being run on the system include a continuum mechanics program, a water properties program, and various heat transfer programs. In addition, a generalized graphics package has been purchased and implemented on the system. This program has been used to plot complex shapes and figures both on the flat bed plotter and on the graphics printer.

PHYSICAL ARRANGEMENT

The computer hardware currently used by ITI consists of an HP/1000 21MX E-Series computer, two disc drives (15 Mbyte and 120 Mbyte), two line printers (300 lpm and 400 lpm), a tape drive, a flat bed plotter, and a card reader. Input to the computer is generally via one of four CRT terminals. Both a 4800- and a 9600-baud modem are available for remote site computer communications, and a digitizer is available to enter graphical information directly. All of the hardware are located in a single room in an air-conditioned building separate from the main office building. The fact that the equipment is all located in a single room has a significant drawback in that the background noise level is quite high. However, it is convenient to have the equipment in a single room since all the equipment is operated by the individual users with one exception to be discussed later.

COMPUTER USE

Utility Programs

The principal use of the ITI HP/1000 is for processing I/O operations with remote computers. Input decks for large computer codes are stored locally. The program UTERM, a CDC 200 UT emulator, is used to transmit the input deck card images to the remote job site and to bring the output back to either disc, tape, or printer. A spooling capability provided with the RTE-IVB operating system greatly enhances the efficiency of bringing output back from the remote computers. Printing can take place at maximum printer speed while transmission can take place at the maximum line capability. Transmission line noise does not affect print time unless the printer empties the spool file before the transmission is completed, a relatively rare occurrence.

The drawback with UTERM is the amount of CPU time required by the program. Because UTERM interrupts the HP/1000 CPU every time a character must be processed, it consumes about 60% of the CPU time. This effectively precludes the use of two copies of UTERM simultaneously. Because so much work is done on remote site computers, the inability to connect to two sites at once is a significant hindrance to the local turnaround of jobs at remote computers. ITI has used several schemes to minimize turnaround time for remote site jobs through our HP/1000. To date, the most effective means has been to use a full-time operator to transmit and bring back jobs. This eliminates non-connected time associated with a sign-up list. The use of a full-time operator for remote job submittal is the only situation in which ITI users do not have direct control of the computer.

Local use of the HP/1000 is generally to support work for jobs computed on other machines. Much of the local time is used in editing input decks to be transmitted elsewhere. For this purpose, the Hewlett-Packard program, EDITR, is very versatile. Text editing, single-line data changes, and field scanning capabilities are convenient and easy to learn.

Second to the editor, the plot routines are probably the most heavily used software packages. Plot capabilities include an HP 7210A digital plotter and an HP 2608A graphics printer. The software for the printer is such that plots can be made more quickly on the plotter, although the plotter requires essentially constant operator attention to change paper. Plotting software includes programs to interpret CALCOMP files returned from remote sites and a local program, PANE, to plot directly from files stored locally. The current arrangement requires about three minutes per plot using the plotter, and about four minutes per plot using the printer. The programs to interpret CALCOMP files are simply interpreters to make the CALCOMP plot commands compatible with the HP plotter. The plot format is set by the generating code run at the remote site. Long plot jobs associated with long detailed runs are very tedious and very time consuming.

Programs to assist the user in bringing back long jobs from remote sites include the HP spooling capability and its associated program, GASP, and the local programs PAGE and TAPE. As mentioned above, the spooler serves to reduce the printing time by allowing the spool file to fill at the transmission line rate while it empties at the printer rate. The printer seldom pauses from momentary interruptions in transmission. Transmission time is also reduced because the spool file can accept data at a faster rate than the printer. The HP program GASP is used to manipulate spool files to some extent. It can restart a spool file, change priorities, and reassign spool files to another logical unit. GASP does not give the user complete control over spool files, but it is helpful.

The local program PAGE allows a user to scan a disc file in regular sections with a pause between each section. Parameters specifying the size of each page displayed, display time, and scanning page width can all be user input from the terminal. A principal advantage of PAGE over EDITR is that PAGE can read backwards in a file, eliminating the time required by EDITR to copy the entire file whenever it has to back up. Disposition of the file is also user specified with PAGE, including an option to dump the file to a spool file for printing on whichever printer is specified. The TAPE program is similar to PAGE, but operates on files stored on magnetic tape. Another program called SCAN is used to examine the contents of a tape created by the DUPER program (DUPER is from the LOCUS library).

Tape storage capability is invaluable in providing backup for files stored on disc. In this regard, three programs are currently in experimental use at ITI, STOTAPE, GETTAPE, and LSTTAPE. STOTAPE and GETTAPE complement each other for storing and retrieving data from magnetic tape, while LSTTAPE will provide a directory list of the files stored on tape. STOTAPE will transfer disc files to tape and store redundant tables of contents on the front of the tape and at the end of information. Files are identified with a 9-level hierarchic pathname. Multiple versions with the same file name are allowed, providing an easy means of storing updated copies of frequently used files. Scanning and retrieval of files can be accomplished by specifying a particular pathname, by specifying high level names in the pathname hierarchy, or by specifying any one name in the pathname. All files having the particular portions of the names requested will be retrieved regardless of the names in the other levels of the pathname. Options available in the current tape storage routine, ZUPER (ZUPER is an enhanced version of the LOCUS program DUPER), which are yet to be included into STOTAPE are a write and then purge capability and a general file name specification such as RD----, where all files with names beginning with the characters "RD" will be stored on tape. GETTAPE recovers files stored on tape by STOTAPE and writes them on an available disc logical unit mounted to the user's session.

The local program PANE allows the user complete flexibility in generating plots from a local data file. It is a self-scaling plot routine designed to choose "people-oriented" scales (i.e., reasonable scale values). It can make quick plots for scanning data, or more detailed plots with titles, axis labels, multiple lines and multiple axes for use directly in reports. The program is interactive for maximum flexibility.

ITI has recently installed MOVIE.ARIZONA on its HP/1000. MOVIE.ARIZONA is an interactive program for graphic display of any model composed of triangles and quadrilaterals. The program has the capability of rotating, translating, and/or manipulating different portions of the model as well as specifying colors and display devices. The program will be used at ITI to produce movies of 3-dimensional scientific models.

For this installation, a new program overlay structure was written for MOVIE.ARIZONA which is composed of a root segment and three overlay segments. The program will display a model composed of 530 nodes by utilizing the HP/1000 EMA option and 72 pages of HP/1000 memory. Several new drivers have been written for the program which allow display on additional devices. These are the HP 2608A digital plotter for line drawings, the HP 7210A raster printer for line drawings as well as solid fill, 15-level gray scale, and two DICOMED drivers for black and white as well as color display. ITI expects a heavy usage of this new graphics capability in the future.

In order to utilize the Summagraphics Bit Pad digitizer, a driver had to be written to interface the device with the 12966A buffered asynchronous data communications interface. The Bit Pad and interface communicate using the RS-232-C communications protocol at 4800 baud. A general purpose driver for the 12966A interface could have been used had one been available from Hewlett Packard or the Users Group Library.

Technical Programs

Several ITI users have found the HP/1000 more convenient for certain technical applications than larger computers at remote sites. In general, the convenience of the HP/1000 is the essentially immediate turnaround provided compared to submitting a job to a batch input queue on a large machine. A second advantage of the HP/1000 is the ability the user has to watch the output and terminate a job at any point desired without having to wait for an entire output file to be returned from a remote computer.

Several options which allow a program to be broken into convenient blocks are available on the HP/1000 system. These options are useful in the development of large programs.

The EMA option is used for maximum array storage. The space available for array storage with the EMA option depends on the memory configuration specified by the installation. Various options used in conjunction with the FTN4 statement can be set to provide debug information in the form of load maps, addresses within subroutines, debug printouts, etc.

A major reason to break up a large program is to save time. Usually a large portion of the program is not undergoing any change and needs to be compiled only once. After the block containing the programs that are being changed is compiled, the complete program can be loaded by means of a segmented load procedure. Only the portions of the program being changed need be recompiled each time a trial run is made.

Several representative applications of the HP/1000 to technical problems follow.

For many engineering calculations, the physical properties of steam are required. The generally accepted standard for steam properties is the ASME Steam Tables [1]. The complex equations presented in Reference 1 have been programmed into a set of subroutines called ASTEM [2]. This collection of subroutines forms a self-contained modular set to evaluate the Gibbs, Helmholtz, and saturation line functions for steam. Any of the desired steam properties can be calculated from these functions. This set of routines was originally written in FORTRAN IV for the IBM 360/75 and required 68K bytes of storage. ITI has converted and implemented these routines on the HP/1000 system. The routines have proven useful in several applications. Primarily they are used in conjunction with programs that process, interpret, and evaluate experimental data from thermal-hydraulic systems.

Another use of the HP/1000 was by a staff engineer to develop a very simplified model to calculate the pressure in a hypothetical nuclear reactor containment for a special case. A large, expensive nuclear containment analysis code was being used on a computer service bureau mainframe, using the HP/1000 only as an input editing, I/O communications and printing device. At a point in the analysis, it was recognized that the physical phenomena had become quite simple and that the large mainframe program was a good deal more complicated than was necessary. Also, the contract time and money were beginning to run short. Rather than accept the complication and expense of the mainframe program and the relative problems of the service bureau, a simplified model was written and debugged in a few days and run locally on the HP/1000. The model and program were kept simple enough to fit the configuration of the ITI HP/1000 at that time. Through the use of the simple model on the HP/1000, adequate results were obtained in a timely manner. Subsequent independent checks of the analyses by another consultant verified the results.

A similar application by another user was the use of the HP/1000 to debug a complex continuum mechanics code written for a CDC-7600 computer. Although the complete code could not fit on the HP/1000, the particular subroutines needed for the analysis could be extracted from the main code and run on the HP/1000. The difference in word length on the CDC and HP/1000 was accommodated by using double precision arithmetic on the HP/1000.

With a short driver program to call the subroutines, the analysis of the continuum mechanics code proceeded at a rate which could not be achieved with a remote site computer. Any portion of a long run could be duplicated on the HP/1000 version of the code by entering data from the time step at which the trial run was to begin. With the necessary input data, the HP/1000 results proved to be identical to the results of comparison runs on the CDC computer. The advantage of the HP/1000 was quick turnaround. Twenty-minute turnaround time was typical, compared to 3-4 hours from the remote site. (This relatively slow service from the remote site was due, in part, to the long wait at ITI for a turn to connect to the remote site.) Changes to the code were easy to make and convenient to try. The results of the changes were known in about twenty minutes, making iterations to a proposed solution technique easy to evaluate. Plots of the results were produced automatically and were frequently finished before the printout. The quick turnaround from the HP/1000 meant that most of the project time was spent analyzing the code, and relatively little time was wasted simply waiting for a turn on the computer.

The HP/1000 proved convenient in the development of a heat conduction model to give the best accuracy possible with a minimum number of degrees of freedom (to minimize computation time) for the type of complex problem in which the thermal boundary condition on a surface is in the form of a two-step, staircase function with the position of level change a function of time. An example is a vertical fuel rod partially submerged in water, where the liquid level is a function of time. The convective heat transfer coefficient (h) in this case would be of the two-step staircase function, where h on the two sides may differ by several orders of magnitude. The model developed was based on an application of the Method of Weighted Residuals using the Galerkin approach with regional discretization and a moving mesh system. The methodology is generally termed the Finite Element Method.

The development of this heat conduction model demonstrated the usefulness of the card reader. A program already available on cards had portions which could be used for the heat conduction model development. The program was read into the HP/1000 via the card reader and the necessary portions extracted with the editor. After the model was fully programmed and the output successfully compared with detailed calculations, it was transferred into a much larger program easily. The editor and the file managing capabilities proved very useful in this task.

It is worth noting that ITI does not make extensive use of its card reader. The procedure to use the card reader requires that the computer be turned off and a terminal I/O interface board be replaced by the card reader I/O board. After reconfiguring the computer, the card reader can be used. The entire procedure is then reversed to replace the disconnected terminal. Although ITI makes very little use of card input, the card reader is invaluable when a client delivers input in card form. Once the deck is read in, it is stored on disc or tape. Our HP/1000 system does not have a card punch capability.

Non-technical Applications

Report writing at ITI is facilitated by the word processing routine, BARB, the graphics printer, which will print lower case characters, and the four HP terminals which have lower case character sets. An editor file containing the report text is created in the normal fashion. BARB commands entered in column 1 will then instruct the printing routine to eject a page, start and indent a paragraph, set margins, center text, or double space. Revisions to reports are thus easy to enter. Once final changes are made, a printout of the file can be submitted to a secretary for typing. Additionally, the WOLF program from the PLUS/1000 library has been implemented on the ITI HP/1000 system. In the future, ITI may purchase an NEC spinwriter to use when producing final copy for a report. It is anticipated that a driver will have to be written to interface the spinwriter to the 12966A interface.

Accounting functions do not represent a major use of time on the ITI HP/1000, but they are handled conveniently nonetheless. At present, our primary accounting use of the computer lies in the areas of payroll, distribution of salary charges to job or client accounts, and preparation of various quarterly and annual tax reports.

Our current computer accounting system is composed of four programs and six cassette tapes. The tapes are used to store employee information needed to run payroll and to ensure confidentiality of payroll information.

The accounting programs include a payroll program used to calculate an employee's gross pay for the month, FICA withheld, state and federal withholding, and state and federal unemployment tax. This program produces the paystub given to the employee showing the gross salary, withholding, and net pay. A salary distribution program calculates the direct salary chargeable to each of the clients and to various overhead accounts. This program also determines the overtime for each employee based on completion of normal monthly work hours. The Quarterly Report program is run in April, July, October, and January to produce quarterly and annual reports. It calculates state unemployment, federal unemployment, and federal tax return information on a quarterly basis.

One tape used by these programs contains a record of each employee's name, number, social security number, hire date, hourly rate, monthly salary, date of last raise, marital status, number of exemptions, and monthly charitable donation. Another, the salary accumulation tape, is generated each month and contains the number of the month and each employee's taxes withheld, monthly gross salary, net salary paid, accumulated salary paid, and accumulative charitable donations. A client tape contains the names and account numbers of all clients and overhead accounts. A restart tape is used to permit easy correction of input errors.

In the near future, we plan to eliminate the use of tapes and store all data on a removable private disc. We also plan to gradually computerize the remainder of our accounting and reporting system.

Lastly, the HP/1000 computer is available on a non-interference basis for the personal use of ITI employees. Those studying through the University of Idaho/Idaho National Engineering Laboratory Education Program can enjoy virtually instantaneous turnaround for course-related programming.

PROBLEMS

One of the principal problems associated with the HP/1000 is the use of CPU time. The number of users presently supported by the upgraded system is twenty-five. At times, the system is overloaded. To lessen the overload, more editing terminals may be required. Users are also noticing that the system responds more slowly due to the high CPU utilization. As mentioned above, the program UTERM consumes about 60% of the machine time when it is running. With the extensive amount of work ITI performs at remote sites, and with the availability of two printers, a capability to connect to two sites at once would be extremely useful. The current UTERM arrangement will not allow this, however. A needed improvement is an I/O board with a microprocessor and some storage on it. The microprocessor would store a block of characters on the I/O card and would interrupt the HP/1000 CPU to transfer the entire block, rather than interrupt to transfer each character. This would release CPU time to other uses and allow two or more copies of UTERM to run at once.

The other problem with UTERM is that it requires two I/O ports for each site to which it connects. ITI currently makes full use of all the I/O ports available on the machine. Including another copy of UTERM would require removing some other devices, two terminals for instance. This particular problem can be solved, however, by extending the number of ports past that included with the basic machine with an I/O extender.

HP FORTRAN is quite similar to that used on other computers. There are some inconveniences, however. File usage is awkward in that several statements must be used to access a disc file from FORTRAN. This problem was relieved somewhat with the spooling package of RTE-IVB, but there are instances when the spooling package does not help.

Some users at ITI feel that the file directory could be improved by allowing longer file names. Currently, only six characters are allowed for an editor file, and only five for a program or subroutine name. Another improvement would be to include the creation date and the date the file was last changed in the file directory. The file manager system could also be improved by modifying it to support a tree structure in the file naming convention.

FUTURE ACQUISITIONS

At the present time, new hardware is being considered for ITI's HP/1000 system. In the very near future, ITI anticipates purchasing an I/O extender, another CRT terminal, and an NEC spinwriter.

SUMMARY

During the evolution of the ITI HP/1000 computer system, general problem areas have been identified. Problems with UTERM using too much CPU time are probably the most serious. Other problems of a lesser nature have been identified and some have been solved. File usage with FORTRAN has been improved with the spooling package of RTE-IVB. In general, the problems encountered have been more of an inconvenience than a serious impediment to accomplishing a task.

The benefits of the HP/1000 have far outweighed any minor disadvantages encountered during our use of the system. The system has been very reliable, upgrades in both software and hardware have been timely, and the service to our clients has remained very rapid despite the increasing number of system users.

REFERENCES

1. C. A. Meyer, R. B. McClintock, G. J. Silvestri, R. C. Spencer, Jr., _1967 ASME Steam Tables -- Thermodynamics and Transport Properties of Steam_, New York: The American Society of Mechanical Engineers (1967).

2. K. V. Moore, _ASTEM - A Collection of FORTRAN Subroutines to Evaluate the 1967 ASME Equations of State for Water/Steam and Derivatives of These Equations_, Aerojet Nuclear Company Report, ANCR-1026 (Oct. 1971).

increasing your programming productivity

Dr. Larry W. Hinderks

Corporate Computer Systems, Inc.
675 Line Road
Aberdeen, New Jersey 07747

ABSTRACT

The increasing use of computers in our society places a high demand for more programming man hours. To meet this need, educational institutions are training more programmers. A more economical alternative is to increase the productivity of programmers by providing a total software development environment.

INTRODUCTION

The spiraling cost of software development forces the careful scrutiny of the past techniques used to develop software. This reassessment of the software development cycle is stimulated from two directions. The first is the realization that software development consumes enormous amounts of time to produce disproportionately small amounts of software. The second observation is that much of the software produced today tends to be incorrect and requires constant modification.

This situation has existed from the invention of the computer until the present and is likely to persist for another decade. The examination of this problem and possible solutions are the subject of this paper.

HISTORICAL BACKGROUND

The first computers built were considered engineering marvels because of their ability to perform calculations at amazing speeds. The current trend of computer hardware is to manage more memory, more peripherals, and to execute instructions at an ever increasing rate. Thus the computer itself still continues to be the wonder device it was when it was initially introduced. It has been in vogue to always purchase a new piece of hardware which runs faster and has more memory to solve all computational problems. The years of thinking that the newest piece of hardware will solve all the programming ills, has had a large impact on the decisions which data processing managers have and are making.

Little attention has been paid to the needs of the programmers, designers, and software development teams. It can be especially fruitful to turn attention away from computer hardware and focus on the environment required by the people who build computer software.

The most fundamental and most often overlooked item needed to increase programmers output is their physical environment. The historical "comp center" consisted of floors of immaculate computer equipment with a small window for the programmers give their decks of cards to a computer operator to feed into the machine. Hours later, the output was placed in a bin and the programmer had to keep checking for his output. Most modern computers now have facilities in which programmers can connect to the computer via terminal This on-line environment has decreased the turn around time dramatically.

PROGRAMMER WORKSTATION

The concept of the programmers' workstation is an addition of non-computer hardware which can increase the programmers productivity at relative small costs. A programmers workstation consists of basically a terminal stand, a chair and of course, the one computer related device, the terminal.

The terminal stand must be large enough to hold the terminal at a confortable typing height and wide enough to accomodate the terminal and two sets of listings. The common mistake which managers make is to purchase the narrow tables which hold only the terminal. This causes the programmer find a free chair or two and spread his listings out on them. Sometimes terminals are ordered without thinking about the terminal stand. In this case, the terminal arrives and the terminal is placed on any old desk which is usually the right height for writing but not for typing. The terminal must be placed on a terminal stand which is the same height as a typing table (approximately 28 inches from the floor) to reduce the typing fatigue.

Each workstation should have the reference manuals required by the programmer. A place to hold these reference manuals should be located near the terminal stand or on shelves above it. This keeps the programmer from having to be distracted by the effort of trying to chase down the required manual.

The chair must be posturepedic in nature to reduce back fatique and allow the user to type confortably. So often just any old chair is given to the programmer for their use. Long hours in an uncomfortable chair is torture.

The last and most important ingredient of a programmers workstation is privacy. The workstation should have sound deading partitions on three sides to reduce ambient noise. Most managers have forgotten how hard it is to construct a double linked list in a room full of noisy people. Programming is a tedious art and requires careful concentration. This is to be contrasted with the early stages of software design in which groups of highly interacting people are required.

It is equally important to reduce visual noise as well as audio noise. The visual noise of people walking around is as distracting a people talking. The workstation must have facilities to reduce this visual noise.

The programmers workstation provides an isolated productive setting for the creation, implementation and testing of software.

PROGRAMMER/COMPUTER INTERFACE

The interface between the programmer and the computer operating system helps to increase productivity. Every operating system contains many diverse software modules such as compilers, librarians, editors, linkers and numerous others. These modules usually have evolved over a number of years and were written by various authors and their interface to the programmer is not consistent. For example, some of these modules may use commas to delimit arguments of the commands, while others use blanks. These small but annoying differences increase a programmers entropy (entropy is any effort expended by a programmer which is not directly related to doing his job).

These problems can be easily corrected by introducing a layer of software between the programmer and the system modules. Such a layer is called the shell in UNIX or the command string interpreter (CSI) in TS/21. The characteristics of these packages is to provide a system which can parse the input command, understand what the user wants and construct requests to the various system modules in a format which the module desires.

It is important that this layer be user programmable. This allows the easy modification of the environment which each user sees. If one user likes to type run,editr while another prefers to type just the letter e to cause the editor to execute, the CSI should effect the correct action in both cases. It should be noted that having the capability to execute system commands (transfer files) is only small service which is required.

Once the layer of software is available, many entropy increasing functions which a programmer must do can be relegated to it. In fact such a layer provides the capabilities required to lead a neophyte through his required tasks while at the same time streamlining the efforts of experienced personnel.

PROGRAMMER TOOLS

Once the extensible environment is available, various programmer needs must be met. Typical software engineers are involved in

1. System Design
2. Program Development
3. Program Documentation
4. Program Maintenance

To aid the programmer in all phases of the development cycle, software tools are an invaluable resource. Some typical tools are listed in Table I.

1. TEXT FORMATTER (NROFF,TFORM)
2. SPELLING CHECKER (SPELL)
3. SOURCE LEVEL DEBUGGER (CBUG,FBUG)
4. ASSEMBLY LEVEL DEBUGGER (BUGS)
5. SOURCE CODE CONTROL (SCONS,SCCS)
6. HIGH LEVEL LANGUAGES (BASIC, FORTRAN, PASCAL, MODULA, C)
7. STATIC PROGRAM ANALYSIS
8. DYNAMIC PROGRAM ANALYSIS
9. PROGRAM FORMAT CHECKER

Table I
Programmer Tools

The System Design and the Program Documentation effort require extensive manuscript preparation and revision. This effort can be efficiently done by programmers rather than the once traditional approach of sending it to the typing pool. Programmers are comfortable typing source into files and editing these files. Typical computer systems have high speed line printers which can be used as document printers. This allows programmers to create the required documents in their computer environment. This procedure is greatly aided by a text formatter such as TFORM or the UNIX program, NROFF. Such a text formatter provides justification of the right margin, macro substitution, general registers for counting, etc. Such a software aid removes the tedium associated with page formatting. If a simplified screen editor, such as VEDIT is available, then the editing phase can be accomplished by persons unfamiliar with sophisticated computer text editors.

After the document is finally typed into the computer, the tedious process of proof reading is started. Technical personnel are notoriously bad spellers and any assistance which can help them correct their spelling errors and typing errors should be used to allow them to generate relative spelling error free documents. There are two general classes of spelling correcting programs. The first class is the dictionary lookup program. This program looks up every word used in the text and compares it with its dictionary. More advanced versions of this method remove prefixes and suffixes and compare the root word with the dictionary entries. A typical program in this class is SPELL. A more ambitious method of detecting spelling errors is to look at the digraphs and trigraphs of characters in the words. For example, the digram qq is never allowed in the english languge and is always considered an error. Other combinations of characters are highly improbable and generally constitute a typing or misspelling error. A program in this class prints a list of words which contain improbable combinations of characters in the order of their improbability.

During the program development stage, it is highly desirable to have source level debuggers to decrease the time required to find problems. Source level debuggers such as FBUG (for FORTRAN) and SEBUG (for C) allow breakpoint and variable printing to be done with only the aid of the source program. No mixed listing or load maps are required. Such debuggers completely eliminate the need for the commonly used write statement.

Assembly level debuggers are needed to debug the assembly language programs. Such a debugger should allow the users to read and patch memory locations and machine registers. The registers should be addressed mnemonicly. The debugger should have the ability to handle at least 8 break-points and print memory values as characters as well as in octal and decimal. These debuggers typically require mixed listings of the program unless the program being debugged is in assembly language. Also a load map containing the module location is necessary. A typical debug package is BUGS.

During the program maintenance stage, the problem of source file control becomes significant. Keeping track of various revisions of source files is key to successful product maintenance and enhancement. Ensuring that only one programmer is modifying a source file, the ability to easily keep track of releases and revisions, restricting access of source files by certain users, and the ability to easily compile and list all source files in the library are a few of the important requirements of a source file system. Examples of source file control systems are the UNIX SCCS program and SCONS which runs on the RTE operating system.

Of the various phases of software development, the most understood aspect is the implementation of the design. This is a result of the use of high level languages instead of the more traditional approach of using assembly language. The abundance of these languages provides an almost endless list of choices. The most popular and highly restrictive language today is PASCAL. The language C, has all the modern control constructs as PASCAL, but allows a high degree of control over the machine formally only found in assembly language. FORTRAN and its deratives are not considered useful high level languages for systems programming, but are still dominant in the engineering field.

Another useful tool is static analysis. This is a program which is very much like a compiler but does not produce any relocatable output code. It checks the program for errors or suspicious programming constructs which can be detected at compile time. Static analysis can check for adherence to the standard for the particular language being used if the software is required to be ported to another compiler or if the software is expected to have a relative long life. Static analysis detects such things as a varible being used before it is initalized. Also it can check for the same number of arguments in the calling and called routines. For FORTRAN programs, static analysis can check for the correct common alignment of all the routines in a program. Some commerical compilers perform many of the functions of static analysis. A good example of this type of program is LINT which runs on UNIX and checks the validity of C programs.

Dynamic program analysis is used to examine the action of a program while it is running. Typically these programs "instrument" the target program by inserting special code into the target program. The dynamic analysis can then tell if all paths through the program have been executed and how many times the path is executed. The dynamic analysis tool is extremely useful in eliminating various suprises when untested paths suddenly are executed when the program is out in the field. Dynamic program analysis in its current state has limited application in real time programs in which the program paths are required to be as short in time as possible because of the extra code which is inserted.

With such tools, the development and continued support of software products is greatly streamlined and results in higher programmer productivity.

CONCLUSION

With careful attention to each step of software development, significant increases in productivity can be achieved. These increases usually require a significant amount of initial effort to institute, but are well worth the investment.

interactive generation of narrative text

Steven M. Isenberg

Hewlett-Packard Company
1776 Minuteman Road
Andover, Massachusetts 01810

ABSTRACT

An Interactive Generator of Narrative Text (IGENT) has been developed to provide a method of generating descriptive text having a standardized form and flexible content. The current application is for the generation of summary reports following cardiac catheterization procedures.

The IGENT subsystem allows the user to write programs in the IGENT language, a language which describes both the nature of a report and the nature of the user interaction necessary to construct it. IGENT then interprets the IGENT commands, requests appropriate user responses as necessary, and produces an interim report file. A text formatter, WOLF, prints the final report.

The IGENT language provides constructs which allow the specification of places in the report where a choice may be made from a set of options and inserted into a "blank" in a sentence. Other constructs allow for direct insertion of user text and for control over report formatting.

The purpose of this paper is to describe the structure, function, and operation of IGENT, the Interactive Generator of Narrative Text.

INTRODUCTION

Many processors exist today which transform free-form text containing embedded commands into formalized typewritten pages. Most are intended for the formatting of randomly generated text, and are not well suited for the generation of standardized reports where the emphasis is on consistency of report format, content, and phraseology.

IGENT is an attempt to bridge this "standardization" gap and, in addition, to provide ease of use by freeing the IGENT user from the burden of "computerese". The IGENT user need not be familiar with system commands, file manipulation commands, editor commands, and the like in order to generate reports.

IGENT is available as an option to Hewlett-Packard's 5600M Cardiac Catheterization Data Analysis System (CDAS). The 5600M CDAS uses an HP-1000 computer (the HP-21MX or HP-21MX-E) and runs under the RTE-II operating system.

IGENT TEXT FILES

The IGENT subsystem makes use of files, called IGENT text files or IGENT programs, which contain text fragments that are to be integrated into the narrative report. For example, one IGENT program could contain the information necessary for the generation of a report describing a routine surgical procedure. The basic structure and content of the report is defined in the IGENT program, but this may be modified in several ways through interaction by the user, resulting in a narrative report adapted to a particular circumstance. The IGENT program also contains the information necessary to inform IGENT what to request from the user and what data to retrieve from the database.

By way of the IGENT program, the IGENT subsystem may ask the user to:

- Select from a variety of text files the one which is to be used,
- Specify whether a section of the IGENT text file should be included in, or excluded from, the report being generated,
- Construct sentences within the text file by selecting from a set of applicable text fragments, or
- Type in free format text which is to be inserted directly into the narrative output.

These facilities allow the user to provide diversity and distinction to prewritten text statements in order to adapt the text to the specific case at hand.

The first interaction takes place at the start of an IGENT run. A listing of the various available text files is presented, and the user is asked to choose the one which best serves the purpose at hand.

The second type of interaction allows the user to specify whether or not a section of the IGENT text file should be included in the report. Therefore, the IGENT text file can be constructed of many individually-selectable sections or paragraphs which, in the aggregate, form a complete description of the report topic. For the particular circumstance, however, just the relevant sections are used. For example, a general surgical report might contain a section describing many potential surgical complications, but this section would be omitted by the user in normal cases.

Multi-Choice Sentences

The third type of interaction involves perhaps the most useful feature of the IGENT subsystem. An IGENT text file may contain sentences or sentence fragments containing sets of alternative text fragments. Such a construct is called a "multiple choice", or simply multichoice, sentence. During report generation, the user selects from the list of alternatives the one which is most pertinent. An example of a multichoice sentence is given in Figure 1.

The patient was anesthetized with { lidocaine. / procaine. / novocaine. / xylocaine. }

Figure 1. A Sample Multichoice Sentence

Display Frames

During the processing of multichoice sentences, IGENT creates displays on the user's terminal; these displays are called "frames". A frame presents:

- A sentence or sentence fragment (to provide a contextual reference),
- A "blank",
- A short description of the type of choice requested, and
- A list of alternatives.

An example is given in Figure 2.

```
... The patient was anesthetized with ______

Choose appropriate anesthetic:

1.  lidocaine.
2.  procaine.
3.  novocaine.
4.  xylocaine.

S  other (specify)
N  no choice
-  back up to previous question

CHOICE:
```

Figure 2. Sample Display Frame as Presented to the IGENT User

The user selects one of the alternatives by typing in the number of the choice. IGENT then inserts the chosen text alternative in place of the blank, and stores the resulting sentence in the narrative output.

The user has other options available in addition to choosing from the list of text alternatives presented. Free format text of the user's choosing can be entered instead of the choices listed, or the user can specify "no choice". In the case of "no choice", the sentence or fragment is not altered, and the blank is removed but not replaced with any text prior to its insertion in the narrative output. Additionally, if the user makes a mistake when choosing entries for the report, the system allows the user to easily back up to a previous question to make the correction.

Report Production

Once the user has finished interacting with IGENT and the narrative report has been constructed, IGENT asks the user to specify the number of printed report copies desired. After this is answered, the user's involvement in the report generation process is complete. IGENT then calls a text formatter to produce the finished, formatted report on the system printer. The text formatter used is WOLF, the Word Oriented Line Formatter [1].

TECHNICAL DESCRIPTION

This section describes the IGENT command set and subsystem operation from the IGENT programmer's point of view.

IGENT Text File

An IGENT text file is a source file which contains a list of IGENT blocks. A block is a group of one or more words that IGENT deals with as a unit. A word in the IGENT sense is a string of non-blank characters surrounded by blank characters or line boundaries.

IGENT blocks frequently contain command words which identify sector interactors, IGENT commands, and WOLF text formatter commands. These command words are indicated by the special characters ">", "$", and "\".

There are three types of blocks in IGENT: text blocks, database retrieval blocks, and interactor blocks.

Text Block

A text block consists of a set of words which is added to the narrative output file without user interaction and which normally appear as a continuous narrative paragraph after processing.

The text block also contains formatting commands for the final report. For example, when text is preceded by the word "$", it is output by IGENT at the start of a line which is preceded by a blank line, and text preceded by the word "$$" starts a new paragraph. Words which begin with the back-slash character "\" are commands for the text formatter WOLF. Use of WOLF commands provides the IGENT programmer with control of such things as margins, page numbering, text centering, page headings, etc.

A line which begins with "$AS" (AS-is) puts IGENT into a special processing mode: the lines following the $AS are copied into the narrative output file verbatim, without interpretation by IGENT. The lines typically contain WOLF formatter commands which have a form that must not be altered prior to interpretation by WOLF. This may be used for centering lines or constructing headers. The normal IGENT processing resumes following a line containing the "$EC" (End Condition) command.

Database Retrieval Block

A database retrieval block provides a means to transfer data to the narrative output without involving the user. It consists of the block identifier string "$V" followed by a data identifier string. The data indicated is retrieved from a file which was specified by the user at the start of the narrative report generation and is formatted before being inserted in the narrative output. In the cath data analysis system, this is used to transfer patient information to the report. For example, "$V NA" causes IGENT to retrieve the patient's name and insert it in the narrative input.

Interaction Block

An interaction block, or interactor, directs IGENT to ask the user to supply some direction or text input to the narrative output. This interaction can consist of the decision to include or exclude a section of the IGENT text file, a choice from a list of alternative words or phrases, or the entry of text for direct insertion into the narrative output.

Section Interactor:

A section interactor precedes a portion of the text file that the user may choose to include or exclude from the narrative output. A section interactor is a line in the IGENT text file that has a ">" in column one. The remaining text on the ">" line is the section name. It is this name which is displayed to the user for approval and stored in the narrative output as the section's label.

If IGENT is instructed by the user to exclude a section of the text file, the section name is not placed in the narrative output and IGENT scans forward in the file until the next section interactor is encountered. Text and commands scanned over during this process are ignored. IGENT continues the usual processing with the new section interactor.

An example is given in Figure 3. If the user chooses to include the "complications" section, the text and commands following (the $MC command in the example) are processed by IGENT. If, however, the user excludes the section, IGENT scans forward and resumes processing by asking the user if the "applicable personnel" section should be included.

```
> COMPLICATIONS:

$MC Select applicable complications from the procedure:

   Cardiac arrest
   Drop in blood pressure
   Faintness

$EC
> APPLICABLE PERSONNEL
```

Figure 3. Example of the Section Interactor

Multichoice Interactor:

A multichoice interactor has a set of alternatives that are presented to the user, allowing him/her to choose among them. It is of the form:

```
$MC prompting string
alternative-1
alternative-2
...
alternative-n
$EC
```

The "$MC" identifies this block as a multichoice interactor. The (optional) prompting string is presented to the user along with the alternatives, but is not inserted into the narrative output, as its purpose is to describe the needed choice. Each alternative is listed on a separate line preceded by its choice number. The list of choices is terminated by a line containing the "$EC" (End Choices) command. Figure 4 shows the result of a translation of a multichoice sentence into an IGENT command.

```
The patient was anesthetized with

$MC Choose appropriate anesthetic:

lidocaine.
procaine.
novocaine.
xylocaine.

$EC
```

Figure 4. IGENT Command for Sample Multichoice Sentence

Fill-In Interactors:

The "fill-in" interactor tells IGENT that the user is to be allowed to enter narrative to be stored in the narrative output. The IGENT programmer specifies the method of text entry and WOLF processing of the entered text by the choice of interactor.

The "$FI" interactor is used when a word or short phrase is expected from the user, as IGENT accepts one line of text input. When more narrative is expected, the "$FM" is used. With the $FM, one or more lines of text may be entered. Text entry under $FM control is terminated when the user enters a line containing just a zero in column one. This extra step is not needed with the $FI command.

The $FI and $FM commands instruct IGENT to insert the user-entered narrative in the final report, subject to text formatting by WOLF. The "$FE" interactor provides a way that the user may enter text in a format which is not altered by WOLF. This is useful for entry of lists or tables. Except for this difference, the $FE and $FM are treated alike by IGENT.

The form of these fill-in interactors allows the user to be prompted with a string. "$FM STRING" asks for entry of narrative "on" STRING. For example, "$FM Describe the results of the procedure" will cause IGENT to ask the user to enter as much narrative as necessary to describe the procedure results.

ACCESSING IGENT

In our application, the IGENT subsystem is accessed from a patient data management terminal we call the PIMS (Patient Information Management System) terminal. The user initiates report production by selecting the IGENT option from the menu presented on this terminal. IGENT first asks the user to supply the datafile link which is used in database reference blocks. Then the user is asked to select an appropriate text file from those listed. Finally, IGENT begins processing of the text file.

SUMMARY

IGENT provides a means of generating standardized narrative reports with flexible content in a way which is quick to learn and easy to use. A user-modifiable text file conveys the basic character of the report and contains commands which describe the data required from the user and the database. The IGENT system interprets this text file, asks the user to supply needed information, and calls the WOLF text formatter to produce the final output report.

ACKNOWLEDGMENTS

IGENT is not the first system of its kind. In fact, it is based to a large degree on a system called SELECT [2]. The motivating idea for IGENT arose out of a similar program developed at Stanford University by K. Hamilton and E. Alderman [3].

The author would like to thank Jeff Corliss for his suggestions throughout the development of IGENT, Mark Low for his thorough readings of this paper which resulted in numerous small improvements and clarifications, and Marianne Fox for preparing the final manuscript.

REFERENCES

[1] Evenden, Gerald Ian: Automatic Typing Program. United States Department of the Interior, Geological Survey. 1978. (This is the WOLF program, available on the PLUS/1000 library.)

[2] McLeod, Dennis J. and Meldman, Monte J.: SELECT: An Interactive Mini-computer Subsystem for the Generation of Specialized Narrative Text. Computers and Biomedical Research, 10:91-99, 1977.

[3] Hamilton, Karen K. and Alderman, Edwin L.: An Interactive Generator for the Production of Standardized Medical Reports. Computers in Cardiology, September 1978, pg. 369-372.

CAI — computer aided instruction

Roger Jenkins

Wycliffe Bible Translators
Huntington Beach, CA

Guy Gallaway
Dennis Adams

Dynalectron Corporation
Radar Backscatter Division
RATSCAT Site
Holloman AFB, NM

ABSTRACT

CAI, Computer Aided Instruction, is a software package developed specifically for the HP1000/FMGR/FORTRAN system. It is a learning-testing aid which uses Programmed Instruction techniques. A CAI course consists of Question and Answer sessions where text and questions are presented to the user. User responses are compared against a menu of correct answers. Correct answers result in continuing through the course, incorrect answers can result in hints, review of previous material or scolding.

The software uses standard FMP calls to access CAI material. Each CAI course is a standard type 4 file which contains both the keyword instruction and the interactive dialog material. We have prepared courses to introduce new programmers to RTE-IV, FMRG, the Editor and to our systems. The attributes that we appreciate most are the ease of preparing course material, the acceptance by the users, and the adaptability of the code to implement new capabilities.

Computer Aided Instruction

This software was developed to meet the challenge of training programmers and computer operators on new RTE systems. The RATSCAT Site has a variety of HP computer systems and operates on a 24-hour basis. This presents unique opportunities in training computer users.

RATSCAT is a Radar Test Facility operated by the USAF but located in the Army White Sands Missile Range. The site is located in the southern part of the test range in the center of the gypsum (White Sands) flats which gives the region and the missile range its famous name.

The facility. operated by the Dynalectron Corporation is capable of a large variety of radar tests. This includes a wide range of radar frequencies and the ability to handle large target vehicles.

The role of the HP computers at RATSCAT include:

1. Real time data collection
2. Real time test control
3. Quicklook data processing

There are several computers on site including:

One 2115 turn-key radar system
Several 2100 systems
One 2112 software development system
One 2113 real time system
Two 2117 real time systems

We are currently running under RTE-IVA and IVB on the 2112, 2113 and 2117 systems.

A group of computer specialists, Computer Services Section, is responsible for all software. The need and desire for CAI arose from this section's recognition of the need to train programmers on RTE. This included programmers with minimum experience on RTE system and those familiar with RTE procedures and capabilities but with no HP experience.

The authors, Mr. Jenkins and Mr. Gallaway were convinced that a CAI Programmed Instruction capability could be developed:

1. Without the large system/memory requirements, and
2. without the complex structuring of commands and user dialogs.

We decided to use the first available slack time to develop a very simple CAI capability. The result is this software.

Mr. Jenkins conceived, designed, wrote and implemented this software during two nights of "System-Baby-Sitting". (A new 24 hour a day real time system was put on line.)

We have found this software to be an easy and very effective way of introducing material to programmers and computer operators. The important features and uses include:

1. Reduce demands upon experienced programmers for training new programmers.

2. Introduce the new user to:

   RTE
   The Editor
   File Manager, FMGR
   The Equipment
   Our Conventions

3. Allow us to develop new CAI courses quickly.
   Modify courses easily and quickly.

4. The course material would be standard files.

5. The course programming instructions would be standard files.

The following terms are used in describing the CAI system .

COURSE:

Course material is limited to a single topic or subject. A complete training or testing session which contains the CAI program instructions and the user dialog.

QAS:

Question and Answer Session.

A QAS is the main module of the course. Each course can consist of as many QAS modules as you desire or your disk budget permits.

We have found a Course of 10-15 QAS modules is about the right size in terms user attention span, course preparation, and coverage of a single topic or sub-topic. Topics requiring more QAS modules are covered in two or more courses.

The basic set of CAI commands/instructions includes:

PRINT ASK SEEK HINT FAIL PASS

Each QAS consists of an ordered sequence of these commands.

PRINT	Optional, more than one is permitted
ASK	Required, only one permitted per QAS
SEEK	Required, one only per QAS
HINT	Optional, more than one permitted
FAIL	Required, one only per QAS
PASS	Required, one only per QAS

Each of these commands is followed by the information or dialog desired for that part of the QAS. These dialogs are displayed for the user.

For example:

```
PRINT
     The PRINT command is optional and when used must be the first
     command of the QAS.
ASK
     What optional command begins a QAS?
SEEK
     PR
     PRINT
HINT
     The first letter is P
HINT
     Second letter is R
FAIL
     You weren't paying attention, Charlie!!
     The answer is PRINT
PASS
     PRINT is correct, very good!
```

All records not interpreted as a command are listed to the users terminal as the dialog, except for the SEEK command. The records of a SEEK command are lists of acceptable answers.

We established a fixed protocol for the commands of the QAS. The restrictions of this protocol include:

1. Format of the command word record.

All capitals and first two characters must be first word of the record. That is the software does explicit integer compares when searching for commands.

e.g. IF (BUF(1) .EQ. 2HPR) is a test for PR of PRINT.

2. Dialog records are identified by and must have the first word of the record blank.

e.g. 2H space space

So, a command has the form

COMMAND	(one record)
Dialog	(as many records as desired)
Dialog	

The set of commands includes:

PRINT

This is an optional command and when used must proceed the ASK command. More than one may be used. The PRINT command is used to introduce the course as well as material for a QAS module. No input or response from the user is required.

ASK

This is a required command, only one per QAS. The dialog of the ASK is presented to the user. The user must enter a response.

Questions should be worded in such a way that the answers are simple inputs such as TRUE/FALSE, multiple choice and simple words.

SEEK

The SEEK command is followed by records which are a set of acceptable answers. The composer of the CAI course must be clever in including a wide variety of possible correct answers. There were several possible methods of handling the user anwser and comparing it to the list of correct choice. The method used is a comparison of character strings. The user answer must contain the (an) acceptable answer.

SEEK List	User Response	Pass or Fail
TR	TRUE	Pass
TR	XXTRUE YY	Pass

These pass since the user response contains the required TR.

There is a bug which we have never taken time to fix but just work around. It is, character strings should be WORD size not byte size. That is, use even numbers of characters, (full 16 bit words.)

The SEEK command is required and only one per QAS.

HINT

This command is used to display a dialog to the user when his response to ASK does not match the list of answers in a SEEK. It is an optional command and there may be more than one. The user responds to the HINT as he would to an ASK. This response is handled in the same way, that is, it is compared against the existing list of SEEK answers.

FAIL

This is a required command, only one per QAS. When the users response is wrong, the final time after all HINT's are used, the FAIL dialog is displayed. No user input to FAIL is required.

PASS

This is a required command, one per QAS, no user response required. A correct response by the user advances the disk file and QAS command dialog passed any FAIL or HINT commands and dialogs. The PASS dialog is displayed.

These are the basic commands:

PRINT   ASK   SEEK   HINT   PASS   FAIL

and must appear in the order given. Other commands are:

WAIT   CLEAR   LABEL   GOTO

These four commands do not have to have any associated dialog.

WAIT

An optional command and requires the user to enter a space return. This is an ignored input.

Without the WAIT command, the user would often see a confusing display of information scrolling up his screen. For example, when he entered a correct response he would see:

a. The PASS dialog followed by
b. a PRINT dialog followed by
d. an ASK dialog.

The WAIT permits the user to read displays at his own speed. The WAIT can also be used effectively as a PRINT command that will PRINT and the wait for the user.

CLEAR

This is simply 22 carriage returns used to "clear" the average CRT. It moves the previous displays out of sight.

LABEL and GOTO

These optional commands are used to permit "programming" of the CAI course. Without them the course would be sequential execution of QAS modules. These permit:

a. Looping or repeating QAS modules
b. Skipping QAS modules, an accelerated path

The form is

LABEL, n
GOTO, n

Where n is an integer number

Only QAS modules may be labeled. The LABEL, n proceeds the first non-optional instruction of the module. The GO TO,n follows a FAIL or PASS command.

Two special commands were developed to provide some control of the user and his environment. These two commands are:

ASK,n,t and IF,n,string

ASK, n, t

This optional form of the ASK permits:

A. Time limit on user's input to t seconds.
B. A GOTO, n if a time out occurs.

The command ASK, 250, 5 means:

t = 5 = five seconds
n = 250 = a GOTO, 250

Unfortunately, the user familiar with RTE can get around the limit t by just hitting any key in order to reset the time out clock for that terminal.

IF,n,string

This optional command must follow the ASK and proceed the SEEK. More than one IF command may be used. That is you may

```
ASK
IF
IF
SEEK
```

The form is IF,n,string, where n is a LABEL number and string is possible user response.

Example:

```
IF,300,ME
```

If the user enters ME a GOTO,300 is executed.

As with any programming language there is a need for comments and annotation in the program (commands). With the CAI structure having dialog following the command this need is not as great as the dialog effectively documents program sections. However, the need does exist and can be met by putting two asterisks in the first word of a record.

```
** This is a comment.
```

Command	Required or Optional	Number per QAS	Input Required	Dialog Displayed	Use/Comment
PRINT	Opt	1 or More	No	Yes	Introduce
ASK	Req	1	Yes	Yes	Dialog is question to user
SEEK	Req	1	No	No	Dialog is list of possible acceptable answer
HINT	Opt	1 or More	Yes	Yes	User responds as to an ASK
FAIL	Req	1	No	Yes	The FAIL message is displayed
PASS	Req	1	No	Yes	The PASS message is displayed
WAIT	Opt	1 or More	Yes	Yes	Dialog optional, input is ignored
CLEAR	Opt	1 or More	No	No	22 line feeds
GOTO, n	Opt	1 or 2	No	No	Typically after FAIL and/or PASS
LABEL, n	Opt	1	No	No	At beginning of QAS preceding a non-optional command.
ASK, n, t	Opt Form	1	Yes/No	Yes	User has t seconds, else a GOTO, n
IF, n, String	Opt	1 or more	No	Yes	GOTO n if response is string

SUMMARY OF COMMANDS

SUMMARY

We have found the CAI software and courses to be very beneficial, within limits. It is useful aid introducing and explaining topics such as RTE or conventions used by the site. It is especially useful for operators, engineers, and technicians who have had only limited exposure to computers. They gain familiarity and confidence in using the equipment.

Experienced programmers quickly grasp the CAI command, formats and techniques. After just a few minutes of explaination they are able to write courses quickly and efficiently. The file structure of CAI, with commands and dialog in the same file permits quick and easy modification of any course. Whenever a suggestion about form or material is made, it can quickly be implemented and tested. We hope other users will have as much fun writing and running CAI courses as we have.

SUMMARY OF GOT-CHAS

1. Disk Files

In the mainline, clearly commented, is a section of code identifying the disk CR and security code, S.C. These variables must be set by the user (system manager) to fit his system.

All CAI courses must be on the same disk. If the code is not modified the user gets a TURKEY message to be passed on to the system programmer.

```
SC = 2HCA
IF ( CR  .EQ. - 32767) CALL CRASH
```

2. File Names

We established a file name convention of . namer (period namer) The CAI user types in the five character namer and the software inserts the preface of a period. (These are called DOT files).

3. CAI file processing, performed when executing a course, is essentially brute strength sequential.

4. Byte and Word Boundaries

We never addressed the problem of half-word alignment of character strings. Occasionally the author of a CAI course will believe he has an acceptable alternate answer in the SEEK list which is apparently ignored. This is due to byte (1/2 word) alignments in comparing strings.

CAI COURSES

RTE-IV-A

1INTR (RTE)
RTE, RTE Prompt, CNTRL H,
FMGR, colon, RU
2INTR (RTE
Disk, files, file names,
First character, security code,
CR 66,
3INTR (FMGR)
FMGR, comma, NAMER,
Syntax, options, LI, LL, EX,
ST,??, DU, RN, PU,
4INTER (Editor)
ED.#, file name, arrow, EOF
line, delete, /, G, ER,

CAI

CAI01
PRINT, ASK, SEEK, HINT, FAIL, PASS
CAI02
CLEAR, WAIT, LABLE, GOTO
CAI03
ASK, IF, SUBROUTINES,
CRASH
HOWTO
File name, 4 basic commands
INTRO Required
MENU

General
ELEC1 (D/C Theory)
EMPIR (The Empire Strikes Back)
WARS (STAR WARS)
FILNM (File name conventions)
&, %, X, /, \ ,
#, ?, !, ", ', $,

MOUTH
Safety unit one, mouth-to-mouth breathing

STAR1 (STAR TREK)
STAR2 (STAR TREK)
T500 (Tektronix T500)

* * * COMPUTER AIDED INSTRUCTION * * *
* * * TREE STRUCTURE * * *

```
                                CAI
                                 |
                                 |
                                 |
     ----------------------------|----------------------------
     |              |            |             |             |
     |              |            |             |             |
     |              |            |             |             |
   CRASH          CISUB         DLB          CHRMV         GDATE
                    |
                    |
                    |
      --------------|--------------
      |       |       |       |       |
      |       |       |       |       |
      |       |       |       |       |
    ERRTN   GETR    FIND    PRINT   CSRCH
              |       |       |
              |       |       |
              |       |       |
            ERRTN   ERRTN   ERRTN
```

CAI = COMPUTER AIDED INSTRUCTION LAB

NAME SUBROUTINE DESCRIPTION

CRASH = ERROR PROGRAM TERMINATOR
CISUB = CAI INTEROGATION SUBROUTINE
DLB = DELETE LEADING BLANKS
CHRMV = CHARACTER MOVER
GDATE = GREGORIAN DATE FORMATER
ERRTN = FILE ERROR HANDLING ROUTINE
GETR = GET A RECORD SUBROUTINE
FIND = FIND A COMMAND
PRINT = CAI PRINT TEXT
CSRCH = CHARACTER STRING SEARCH

ACKNOWLEDGMENTS

This implementation of a CAI/Programmed Learning system was designed and implemented by Mr Roger Jenkins. The desired attributes of: easy to program; easy to establish dialogs; easy to modify; improve and update both command and dialog, were more than satisfied. The effort of Mr. Dennis Adams in adding ASK,n,t and IF,n,string have significantly improved the capabilities of the software. The following RATSCAT programmers contributed their time and efforts in the creation of CAI courses which have been both informative and entertaining for the CAI user:

Roger Jenkins, Wycliffe Bible Translators
Mac McFarland, Dynalectron Corporation, RATSCAT
Mike Forsman, Dynalectron Corporation, RATSCAT
Chuck Fugee, Dynalectron Corporation, RATSCAT
Dennis Adams, New Mexico State University
Guy Gallaway, Dynalectron Corporation, RATSCAT

instrumentation panel

Chairman - Dave Hall
(FMC Corp.)

The panel was formed to discuss the problems inherent in interfacing instruments with the HP/1000. The panel members and their topics were:

1. Louis Drake (FMC Corp.)
   Interfacing the HP 2240 in a Process Control Environment
   (paper not available)

2. S. H. McFarlane (RCA)
   Interfacing HP IB Equipment in a Laboratory Environment
   (paper not available)

3. Brice Clark (Hewlett-Packard Co.)
   Some Solutions to Instrument Interfacing
   (paper not available)

4. Barry S. Perlman (RCA)
   PLANA/1000 - Phase Locked Automatic Network Analyzer, Accuracy Enhancement Software for Use With the HP/1000

PLANA/1000 — phase locked automatic network analyzer, accuracy enhancement software for use with the HP/1000

Dr. Barry S. Perlman

RCA Laboratories
David Sarnoff Research Center
Princeton, New Jersey 08540

ABSTRACT

PLANA/1000 is a package of accuracy enhancement software designed to automate the HP-8409 analyzer by using a disc-based HP-1000 minicomputer as the system controller.[1] It provides for hardware calibration, device measurement, complex vector mathematics, and error correction of transmission and reflection measurements, listing and plotting of data output, disc and tape file management, an interactive operator interface, and control of the phase-locked frequency source subsystem and other instrumentation using the HP-IB* interface.

INTRODUCTION

The program incorporates an explicit error correction algorithm based on a regressive 3-, 6-, or 12-vector model. The 3-vector model provides for full error correction of reflection measurements on one-port devices, while the 12-vector model provides for full error correction for bidirectional transmission and reflection measurements. The 6-vector model provides for forward transmission and reflection measurements (i.e. S_{11}, S_{21}) requiring device reversal to acquire the reverse parameters (i.e. S_{12}, S_{22}). The choice of model used is interactive, allowing one to switch models to achieve the highest possible accuracy or minimize the measurement time. Measurement resolutions of 0.02 dB in amplitude, 0.1^{o} in phase, 0.1 ns in delay, and 100 Hz in frequency are achievable. The group delay is calculated from the corrected transmission phase data by computing the derivative of the phase slope.

User options may be entered in alphanumeric format in order to direct program flow, from calibration to measurement, to list or plot, to change frequency lists or reference planes or perform many other tasks. Outputs include S-parameters, VSWR, impedance and admittance, group and phase delay, as well as the maximum available gain and stability of active two-port devices. Output data may be displayed graphically in either polar, S-chart, or rectangular format, listed to a terminal or line printer, or stored into a disc or tape file for use by other programs.

*HP-IB is Hewlett-Packard's implementation of the IEEE 488 instrument bus interface standard.

SOFTWARE DESIGN

PLANA/1000 is written in Fortran IV and is designed to run on a disc-based HP-1000 under the control of the RTE-IVB operating system. It consists of a main program and four (4) overlapping program segments which share a common memory area. A minimum memory partition of 19 pages is required to support the loaded program, which provides up to 81 measurement frequencies and 12 error vector coefficients at each frequency. Frequency data may be linearly related, in multiple bands, or tabulated.

The program is designed to perform four (4) primary tasks which are:

(1) Calibrate
(2) Measure
(3) List
(4) Plot

Each of the four program segments is relegated to perform essentially one of these tasks. A description of the function of each segment is given below:

PLAN 1 This segment is the primary control segment and is responsible for initializing program and system parameters, management of task requests, output parameter and peripheral device selection and calibrating the measurement hardware. Other functions performed here include change of calibration error model, change of instrument settling delay, and specification of output frequency list.

PLAN 2 This segment is responsible for acquiring data from the device under test and reducing that data using an error correction algorithm. Other functions of this segment include saving and restoring the common data block, rotating data to a new reference plane, providing a single or digitally swept frequency mode with A/D diagnostics, and switching the HP-IB to its local mode.

PLAN 3 This segment formats data output to be listed on any terminal, line printer, mag tape or disc file. The disc file can be located on any active node within the DS-1000 network in which the PLANA controller resides. Any combination of columns of listed data is also made available for rectangular raster plotting. S-parameter data smoothing is also performed here.

PLAN 4 This segment is responsible for both soft- and hardcopy graphics. A user's request for either single parameter video plotting or 4-color S-chart pen plotting is handled here. Data is formatted for polar, S-chart or rectangular plots. A plot data smoothing algorithm is also available here.

The program is modular in its design, utilizing subroutines to perform specific tasks such as controlling individual instruments, computing quadrature error coefficients for calibrating the polar display, acquiring polar display DC offsets for the beam center calibration, modeling the open circuit capacitance, parameter selection, rotating reference planes, creating disc files, scaling, smoothing, plotting, etc. Modifications to the software, in order to suit changes in configuration or procedure, are readily performed by replacing the appropriate subroutine. Unique and extensive data reduction or special programming requirements can be readily implemented by adding new segments.

CONTROLLER REQUIREMENTS

PLANA/1000 was designed for use with an HP-1000 having at least 192 Kbytes of memory (256 Kbytes is preferred), a suitable disc and at least one HP-2648 graphics terminal. RTE-IVB is the preferred operating system, although the program may easily be modified to run on other RTE systems. An HP-59310B bus controller is also required. Other peripherals such as a line printer, a hard-copy unit (e.g. Versatec 1640), a flatbed plotter, or the use of DS/1000, are optional.

ACKNOWLEDGEMENT

The author is grateful for the support provided by his many colleagues whose constructive criticism and patience contributed to the development of this program and to Mr. J. Fitzpatrick of the Hewlett-Packard Company, Santa Rosa Division, California, for his advice and encouragement.

REFERENCES

[1] J. Fitzpatrick, "Error Models for Systems Measurement," Microwave Journal, May, 1978.

a computer system for a multi-instrument materials characterization laboratory

S. H. McFarlane, J. R. Woolston

RCA Laboratories
Princeton, NJ 08540

An HP-1000 is used to control and acquire data from several analytical instruments, i.e., Auger spectrometers, X-ray photoelectron spectrometer, secondary ion mass spectrometer, X-ray diffractometers, etc. Interfacing was generally accomplished by using the HPIB and compatible "off-the-shelf" components or the 6942A Multiprogrammer, although a microprocessor system was designed and built for use with one instrument.

The Materials Characterization Research Group at RCA Laboratories operates a central facility to provide expertise and instrumentation for a wide range of analytical techniques. The research staff at the Laboratories provides samples to the group on a routine basis as well as unique special problems. As instrumentation for analysis has become more sophisticated and as the demands on an individual analyst have become greater in terms of both quantity and quality of results, automation has become not only highly desirable but practically mandatory.

This paper will highlight the results of using an HP-1000 to provide a central automation facility for some of the instrumentation in the Materials Characterization Research Group. It should be emphasized that there are instruments not mentioned here that have no computer control, e.g., Electron and Optical Microscopes, or have dedicated computerization, e.g., Fourier Transform Infrared Spectrometer, Gas Chromatograph/Mass Spectrometer, and Energy Dispersive X-Ray Spectrometer.

The general approach to all computerization has been to free the analyst from routine instrument operation to permit him or her to concentrate on problem solving. For example, there has been no attempt to completely automate the identification of peaks in a spectrum of interest. A skilled observer can pick out what is important, what is an artifact, or what is unusual about the result. The computer may be used to acquire the spectrum, smooth the data, compare with known peaks, measure the peak position and size - but the analyst chooses how the power of the computer is to be used.

The computer system has been in use for three years and has expanded to include a 21MX-E CPU with 448 kbyte memory, 15 and 120 Mbyte discs, 5 HPIB cards (HPIB is the Hewlett-Packard implementation of the IEEE-488 interface bus.), 1 card (12566A) for 16 bit communication with a microprocessor, and

DS/1000 links with 4 other HP-1000 systems at the laboratories. Users can access the computer through either impact printers (3 - LA36 DECwriter II and 1 - HP2635) or graphics terminals (2 - Tektronix 4010 and 2 - HP2648) as well as the HP2645 system console. There is also a port for dial-up telephone communication.

There are several ways to approach the actual computer control of analytic instrumentation. One method is simply to buy the entire system - instrument, dedicated computer, software, etc. This becomes more advantageous when the instrument is sophisticated and the required software would require a person-year or more of development effort. An almost opposite approach is to build the instrument, make the interfacing electronics for computer control, and write the system software. A middle ground is to assemble a system from vendor supplied parts, i.e., an analytic instrument for a specific application, HPIB compatible components for instrument control and data acquisition, a computer with an operating system that will support the HPIB, and user written application software.

Although each of these methods has been appropriate and implemented for a given application, most of the instrumentation has been automated using HPIB compatible components. One reason for this is because the initial automation was accomplished using a programmable calculator and the HPIB. This was done so quickly and easily that a second system was placed under calculator control. However, the shift to a computer with multi-user capability was made before there was a proliferation of instruments with dedicated calulator control.

Analytic instrumentation under computer control includes:

- TFA - Auger Electron Spectrometry for Thin Film Analysis
- SAM - Scanning Auger Microanalysis
- XPS - X-Ray Photoelectron Spectrometry
- ISS - Ion Scattering Spectrometry
- SIMS - Secondary Ion Mass Spectrometry
- PDR - X-Ray Powder Film Reading
- XRD - X-Ray Diffractometry (2 systems)
- XRF - X-Ray Fluorescence Spectrometry

Although each instrument is different, there is a logical similarity in that the computer is used to set operating conditions (with relays) and then start a cycle of setting a spectrometer (with a relay or digital-to-analog converter), reading a result (with a counter or voltmeter), displaying the result (on a plotter or graphics terminal), and storing the data on disc. The data acquisition continues for a predetermined time or until the analyst decides that sufficient information has been obtained.

The HPIB approach was used with the TFA, SAM, ISS, SIMS, XRD, and XRF systems. For example, the Secondary Ion Mass Spectrometer [1] was designed and built at RCA, and represents a typical application. The system uses an ion beam to sputter away material from a sample. The ejected ions are guided to a quadrupole mass spectrometer which can detect ions from mass 1 to 300. A given voltage applied to the quadrupole will tune it for a specific mass and the number of ions of that mass can be counted. The usual method of analysis is to select several masses of interest, e.g., boron and silicon in a silicon wafer with a boron implant. The computer switches on the ion beam, sets the quadrupole with a DAC, counts the number of ions detected during a specific time interval, records the result on a plotter, repeats the procedure for each mass of interest (the time interval can differ), and then starts again with the first mass. The result is a multi-element depth profile of the number of ions of each mass sputtered away as a function of time, i.e., depth in the crystal. The data are stored on disc for later recovery and use to determine actual atomic concentration, dose in an implanted sample, and replotting of the profiles in a form suitable for publication.

Recently, the new HP6942A Multiprogrammer II has been used with the HPIB to acquire data from the X-ray fluorescence spectrometer. In this application, extensive mechanical modifications would be required to permit computer control of the instrument. However, if the computer can monitor the output from the X-ray detector at a regular interval, then the X-ray spectrum can be obtained. A counter on the HPIB could not be used directly as this requires the computer to issue a command to read the counter several times a second. Other demands on the computer prevent this from happening on a reliable basis. The solution is to use the multiprogrammer with a counter card, a timer-pacer card to gate the counter at a desired rate, and a 4000 word memory card to store the data until the entire spectrum has been obtained. This means that the computer needs only to send the initial conditions to the multiprogrammer and read the contents of the memory card when the run is complete. Work is in progress to use the multiprogrammer for computer control and data acquisition with a new X-ray diffractometer that has stepping motors to control the spectrometer.

The PDR system to read X-ray powder films is an older home-made system that operates in series with the RS-232 connection of its terminal. It had been in use with a large IBM time-sharing system and the software was transferred to the HP-1000 with little difficulty.

The X-ray photoelectron spectrometer required unique interfacing to the computer because it used a 16-bit DAC (none is available on the HPIB) and needed to have rapid (faster than 10 times/sec) interaction with the computer. The solution was to design and build a microprocessor based system that provided local control, data acquisition, and data storage for the XPS system. (The 6942A multiprogrammer probably could be used for this application, but it was not available when this work was done.) The GRUMP (General RCA Utility MicroProcessor) is based on the RCA CPD1802D COSMAC microprocessor and communicates with the HP-1000 through a 12566A 16-bit I/O card and a custom driver to provide both interrupt and DMA communication. GRUMP provides control of a 16-bit DAC and a 24-bit counter to collect counts from the XPS instrument. The HP-1000 programs GRUMP to scan a given voltage range with up to 4000 steps in the range. At each step, GRUMP collects counts for a programmed amount of time (from 1 msec to several seconds) and stores the result in a 24-bit memory location. The scan is repeated a given number of times with the counts at each step being accumulated in memory. At the end of the run, the data in memory are sent by DMA to the computer. The transfer of 4000 24-bit words takes less than

0.2 sec, in contrast to the 6 seconds required to send 4000 16-bit words from the 6942A multiprogrammer.

The software for the various instruments has been written in Fortran IV and usually involves an integrated system of as many as eight programs or several segments for a given application. The scheduling of the programs is transparent to the analyst who initiates the main program and moves through the steps of an analysis by the input of simple control codes and appropriate operating parameters. During a run the analyst has the option to change operating parameters, terminate the data collection or abort the analysis. This is done by communication between the data collection program and a separate control program through system common. In addition to the programs to replot the data, there are programs for curve smoothing, peak area calculations, and fitting appropriate curves to the observed peaks in a spectrum. Much of the software is the same or very similar for many of the applications. All the software has been developed with close collaboration between the programmer and the analyst. As mentioned previously, the aim is to use the computer as an additional tool for the analyst, not as a system to replace intelligent operation of an instrument and analysis of data nor as a burden which interferes with easy control.

Acknowledgments

The staff person responsible for each instrument has been an important part of the development of the computer system as applied to that given application - E.P. Botnick, SAM; G.L. Fowler, TFA; W.L. Harrington, ISS; C.W. Magee, SIMS; J.T. McGinn, XRD; R.J. Paff, XRF and PDR; R.T. Smith, XRD and PDR; and J.H. Thomas III, XPS. The contributions of J.Y. Avins in the design, building, and programming of GRUMP and B.S. Perlman in the writing of the GRUMP driver are also gratefully acknowledged.

References

1. C.W. Magee, W.L. Harrington, and R.E. Honig, "Secondary Ion Quadrupole Mass Spectrometer for Depth Profiling - Design and Performance Evaluation", Rev. Sci. Instrum, 49, 477(1978).

GEDAP: an integrated software system for experiment control, data acquisition and data analysis

E.R. Funke and N.L. Crookshank

Hydraulics Laboratory
National Research Council of Canada
Ottawa, Ontario, Canada

Michael P. Wingham

DMR and Associates
Ottawa, Ontario, Canada

ABSTRACT

The use of the digital computer for on-line data acquisition and analysis is now widespread in research laboratories. It is, however, still not common to use this same computer for the control of experiments and the real-time display of data. In many situations, the computer system is programmed to perform a specific real-time task and the effort required to develop software for the execution of other functions is often time consuming and costly.

On the other hand, the variety of work which comes into a research laboratory demands a versatile data acquisition, experiment control and data analysis capability, which only a computer can provide. The software system which is described here was designed and developed with this fact in mind.

The features of GEDAP include:

- Multi-user capability
- User description of experiment configuration via HP2645 "forms"
- Semi-automated transducer calibration
- Real-time data acquisition and control of multiple experiments
- Real-time simulated strip chart display of input and output channels
- Graphics editing of data and analysis of results
- Plotting of results on a variety of HP and non-HP devices.

SUMMARY

1.0 STATEMENT OF NEED

The use of the digital computer for on-line data acquisition and analysis is now widespread in research laboratories. It is, however, still not common to use this same computer for the control of experiments and the real-time display of data. In many situations, the computer system is programmed to perform a specific real-time task, and the effort required to develop software for the execution of other functions is often time consuming and costly.

On the other hand, the variety of work which comes into a research laboratory demands a versatile data acquisition, experiment control, and data analysis capability, which only a computer can provide. The software system which is described here was designed and developed with this fact in mind. It has many features which are quite unique and, although it grew out of the special requirements of a coastal engineering research laboratory, the authors believe that it would be applicable to any research situation where acquisition of data, especially in the audio and sub-audio range, is required. It should also be well suited to a university laboratory environment because it is easy to maintain, to learn, and to share.

2.0 METHOD OF SOLUTION

The software system described here was named GEDAP as a snappy abbreviation for Generalized Experiment Control, Data Acquisition, and Data Analysis Package. GEDAP is currently running on a Hewlett-Packard 1000 computing system operating under RTE-IV4B, which permits multi-user, foreground/background activities. Additional peripherals, which are considered to be particularly valuable for the support of GEDAP are the HP2648A video-graphics terminal and the Xerox Versatec 1200A printer/plotter.

The minimum requirements for the operation of GEDAP depend on the number of concurrently running experiments and background jobs, as well as the extent of the data acquisition and control tasks*. The presently used Hewlett-Packard system consists of a 21MX-E computer with 256 K bytes of memory, a 21 MX-F computer with 512 K bytes of memory, two disc drives, one with 20 M Byte and the other with 120 M Byte storage, which are shared by both computers, a Floating Point Systems Inc. AP120B array processor, seven terminals (most of which can be switched manually between one of the two computers or a remote IBM 370), and finally a Xerox Versatec 1200A printer/plotter. The second computer and the array processor were acquired to perform real-time numerical modelling of estuary dynamics and are not essential to the operation of GEDAP.

The analog/digital subsystem consists primarily of a NEFF Series 500 serial data link with remote converters. Two BIOMATION high speed transient recorders have also been interfaced to the computer and integrated into the data acquisition phase. Whereas the particular analog/digital hardware of any system defines the capability of the data

*It is believed that a reasonable minimum configuration would consist of an H.P. 1000 model 45 computing system or equivalent with 256 K Bytes of memory, a 20 M Byte disc and one HP2648A terminal, a suitable hardcopy graphics device, and adequate analog/digital subsystem.

acquisition system, the GEDAP System is not dependent on it. Those components of the software which communicate with the analog/digital hardware must, of course, be changed, but the remainder of the system is not affected.

GEDAP is logically divided into 3 parts: Setup, Real-Time Data Acquisition and Control, and Analysis (Figure 1).

2.1 Setup

The major component of setup is the Experiment Definition program. Through a series of HP2645 "forms" displayed at his terminal, the user interactively defines his experiment control and data acquisition task. This consists of:

- associating a set of parameters with the experiment so that subsequently collected data are properly defined
- defining a system of units and conversion formulae which allows control and acquisition functions to be described in physical units instead of voltages
- describing the hardware configuration, i.e. which transducers and actuators are connected to which I/O channels
- defining control functions for actuators in terms of a formula and/or time series, with optional feedback
- defining a set of "fault" conditions which will be monitored during the experiment, allowing alarms to be generated and/or corrective action to be taken.

Related to the Experiment Definition program are the Transducer Calibration and Time Series Synthesis programs, which allow the user to calibrate his transducers and generate time series for actuator control.

All this information is stored in the Experiment Definition Database, where it can be recalled and updated as required.

2.2 Real Time Data Acquisition and Control

Once the GEDAP user has described his experiment, he runs it under computer supervision via an HP2648 graphics terminal located at the experiment site. He controls aspects of his experiment such as scheduling and terminating actuator control, data acquisition, and on-line display and analysis, by using the function keys at his terminal.

To give the user immediate feedback on the progress of his experiment, input and output channels can be monitored on the HP2648 with the STRIP program, a strip chart recorder simulator. STRIP performs all the functions of a real strip chart recorder such as selection of channels, specification of gain and offset, and adjustment of chart speed. STRIP retrieves the data to be displayed from system common, each channel being mapped to a different location in system common. Thus STRIP can monitor any experiment parameter in any system of units, as long as the value of that parameter is periodically updated in system common. This gives STRIP an advantage over a real strip chart recorder, which can only monitor voltages of input and output channels.

As data is acquired, it is demultiplexed and stored in data files according to a fixed GEDAP format. This standard format allows a library of analysis routines to be shared between different users and applications.

2.3 Analysis

After completion of his experiment, the user would like to review his collected data and extract interesting sections for further analysis. This is accomplished with STRIP, which can review a data file forward or backward, and can store a time interval of data, specified by the graphics cursor, in a separate file.

Analysis consists of scheduling a sequence of programs, each of which performs a specific filtering or transformation operation. The inputs and outputs of each program are all compatible GEDAP data files, hence the programs can be mixed in any order to satisfy the requirements of any application.

The final results are then plotted on a variety of HP and non-HP devices by the GPLOT program. A "menu" is displayed at the user's terminal which allows the user to specify the format of his plot. Depending on the device specified, another program is scheduled which actually outputs the plot. At the moment we have one such program which interfaces with HP devices via GRAPHICS 1000, and another which interfaces with a Versatec plotter via the Versaplot package. A valuable feature of GPLOT is its ability to access the parameters in the header of a GEDAP data file, thus allowing the values of these parameters (time of acquisition, method of analysis, means, peaks, RMS's, etc.) to be displayed along with the data.

3.0 CONCLUSION

The use of an on-line digital computer system operated with the support of GEDAP has significantly contributed to improving the effectiveness of research activities in the Hydraulics Laboratory of the National Research Council of Canada. The following factors are attributed to this:

- greater productivity because of easier and more convenient operation of an experiment
- greater accuracy of measurement
- more sophisticated and complicated measurements are being attempted, and
- staff can execute a greater portion of the experimental research work with less professional supervision.

It is expected that through the increased use of GEDAP by other laboratories, an exchange of analysis and synthesis programs will also lead to a net saving in computer programming activities.

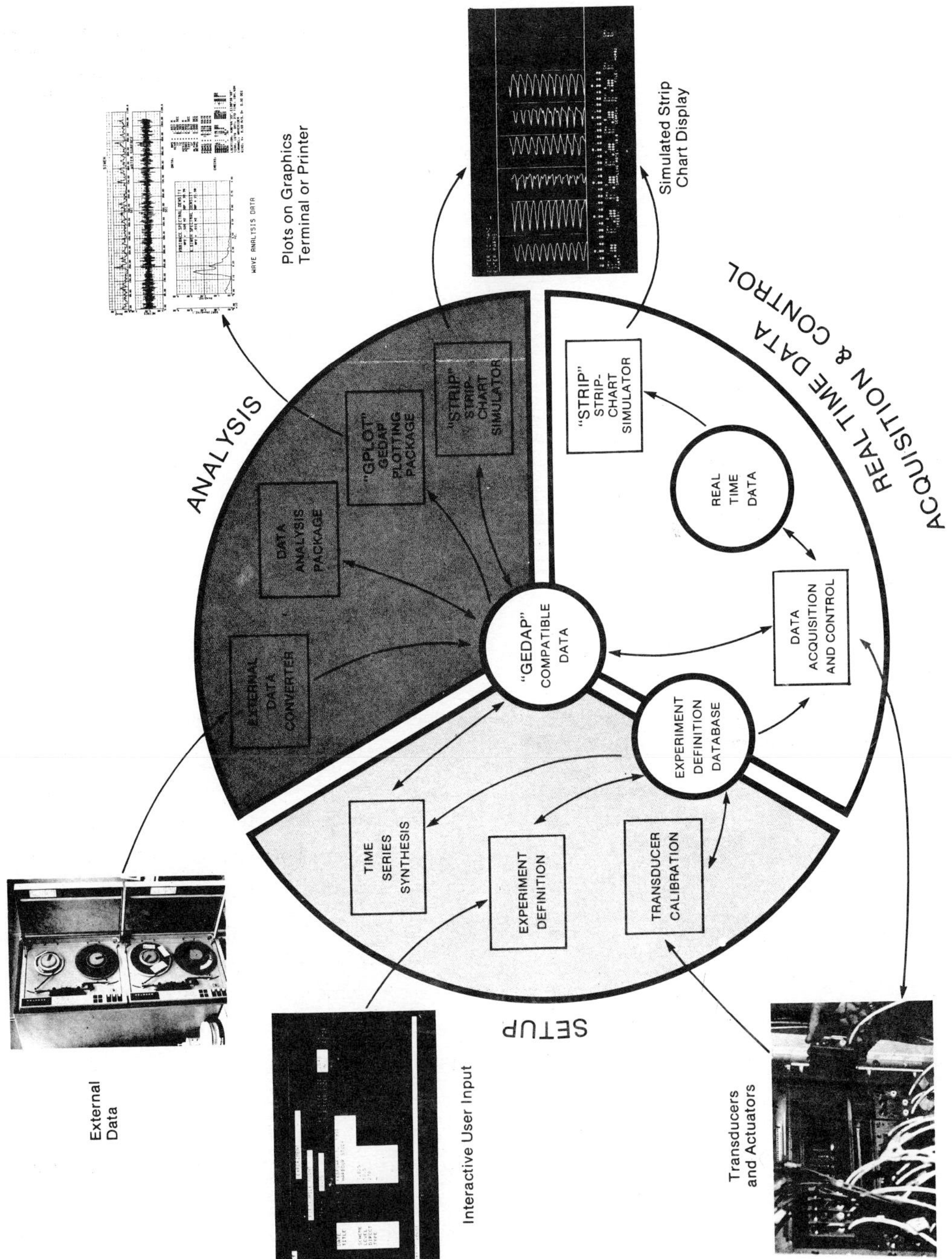
ANALYSIS
EXTERNAL DATA CONVERTER
DATA ANALYSIS PACKAGE
"GPLOT" GEDAP PLOTTING PACKAGE
"STRIP" STRIP-CHART SIMULATOR
"GEDAP" COMPATIBLE DATA
SETUP
TIME SERIES SYNTHESIS
EXPERIMENT DEFINITION
TRANSDUCER CALIBRATION
EXPERIMENT DEFINITION DATABASE
REAL TIME DATA ACQUISITION & CONTROL
DATA ACQUISITION AND CONTROL
REAL TIME DATA
"STRIP" STRIP-CHART SIMULATOR
Plots on Graphics Terminal or Printer
Simulated Strip Chart Display
External Data
Interactive User Input
Transducers and Actuators

FIGURE 1

STRIP: a strip chart recorder simulator

Michael P. Wingham

DMR and Associates
Ottawa, Ontario, Canada

N.L. Crookshank and E.R. Funke

Hydraulics Laboratory
National Research Council of Canada
Ottawa, Ontario, Canada

ABSTRACT

A useful if not indispensable tool in any low frequency (< 10 Hz) data acquisition system is the strip chart recorder. It gives the user immediate feedback on the functioning of transducers in the system, and supplies qualitative information on the data being collected. Its disadvantages, however, are its expense, its appetite for large amounts of chart paper which is often quickly discarded, and its lack of versatility (since most data is stored digitally, the strip data recorder is rarely useful after the data has been acquired). There is a genuine need for a device which presents the same visual information as an analog strip chart recorder, and yet is compatible with digital data. This compatibility would allow the device to be used throughout the entire data acquisition and analysis process.

STRIP is a real-time simulator of an analog strip chart recorder, designed for the HP2648A graphics terminal. In addition to monitoring I/O channels, it can display in real-time the contents of any memory location in system common. STRIP also operates in background mode, where it can review and edit multichannel data files.

SUMMARY

1.0 STATEMENT OF NEED

A useful if not indispensable tool in any low frequency (10 Hz) data acquisition system is the strip chart recorder. It gives the user immediate feedback on the functioning of transducers in the system, and supplies qualitative information on the data being collected. Its disadvantages, however, are its expense, its appetite for large amounts of chart paper which is often quickly discarded, and its lack of versatility (since most data is stored digitally, the strip data recorder is rarely useful after the data has been acquired). There is a genuine need for a device which presents the same visual information as an analog strip chart recorder, and yet is compatible with digital data. This compatibility would allow the device to be used throughout the entire data acquisition and analysis process.

2.0 METHOD OF SOLUTION

The solution is to simulate the strip chart recorder with a graphics terminal. This makes good sense especially if a computer is already being used for data acquisition. The simulator would merely intercept the data after A/D conversion and display it on the graphics terminal. In our case, the simulator (called "STRIP") runs on an HP1000 system under RTE-IVB and uses an HP2648A graphics terminal for display. The program is written entirely in FORTRAN IV. STRIP has all the features of an analog strip chart recorder including:

- simultaneous display of up to 8 channels
- adjustable "chart speed"
- control of channel sampling rate (applicable only to real-time mode)
- adjustable gain and offset for each channel

Figure 1 is a photograph of STRIP in use.

2.1 Real-Time Mode

STRIP operates in either real-time or background mode. In real-time mode, it is the responsibility of an existing data acquisition program to store the acquired data in system common and periodically update it. The user runs STRIP and specifies parameters such as which channels he wishes to monitor (these are mapped to system common), their gains and offsets, the chart speed, and the sampling rate. System common is then sampled and the channels are displayed on the screen, moving from bottom to top. When the top is reached, the screen is cleared and display continues from the bottom. Note that the chart speed specifies the speed at which the traces move up the screen, while the sampling rate specifies how often data is retrieved from system common (affecting the precision of the trace). It is completely independent of the data acquisition sampling rate, although it makes no sense for STRIP's sampling rate to be greater than this. Since in real-time mode STRIP is only used for qualitative information, there is no need to synchronize it with the data acquisition program.

One can give STRIP a great deal of flexibility by transforming the acquired data before it is stored in system common. For example, while an analog strip chart recorder can monitor only the voltage output of a transducer, STRIP can display data in the physical units of the variable (displacement, velocity, temperature, etc.) being measured. This gives the user a more meaningful display, and allows him to visually compare the output of similar channels without worrying about the characteristics of the particular transducers involved. By the same token, physical variables which are a function of several transducers (such as means) can be displayed just as easily. In fact, not only external data, but any variable in the computer system can be monitored, as long as its value is stored in system common and is periodically updated. To maintain the functionality of STRIP, any data transformation is performed by an auxiliary program. STRIP merely displays whatever it finds in system common.

2.2 Background Mode

In background mode, STRIP is used to review and edit data after it has been acquired and stored in multi-channel disk files. In this mode, every point acquired is displayed. All the real-time mode commands (channel selection, gain, offset, etc.) have the same function in the background mode, except for sampling rate and chart speed. Sampling rate is meaningless, while the time dimension of chart speed is determined by the rate (stored in the file's header) at which data was originally acquired, rather than the rate at which it is currently being displayed. Thus in background mode, STRIP is not limited to low frequency data.

A file can be reviewed either forward (with the trace moving up the screen) or backward (with the trace moving down the screen). By means of the graphics cursor, the user can select intervals of data to be extracted and stored in separate disk files. Thus the user can edit out uninteresting data prior to analysis. As long as each analysis program maintains the same file format, STRIP can display and edit the data after each analysis step as well.

2.3 Program Design

STRIP consists of two programs: STRIP, which prompts the user for commands, and DISPL, which draws the traces. When the user enters GO, STRIP schedules DISPL, passing it the parameters specified by the user's previous commands. The entered parameters remain visible on the screen, so that the user knows exactly what he is monitoring (Figure 1). Once the display has started, the user must have some method of notifying STRIP that he wishes to enter a new command. This proved to be a bit of a problem, as most methods interfered with the display of the traces. The solution is to have STRIP check the graphics zoom size once a second. When STRIP detects a change in zoom size (effected by the user pressing the ZOOM IN key), DISPL is suspended and STRIP prompts the user for another command.

STRIP can also process commands from transfer files, so that the user does not have to manually enter the same commands every session.

2.4 Real-Time Performance

STRIP can maintain a sampling rate of 10 samples/second with 6 channels being displayed simultaneously. This will give a good representation of data of frequency 2 Hz or less. Performance can be improved by monitoring fewer channels, or by selecting a dot trace (1 dot per sampled point) rather than a solid line. The limiting factor is the speed of the graphics processor rather than the efficiency of the program.

Another problem is clearing the display when the traces reach the top of the screen. With the "full information format" in Figure 1, it is necessary to use an "area clear" command to erase only the portion of the screen reserved for the traces. This command takes about three seconds to execute, during which time no data can be displayed. To reduce this delay, the user can select a "long format", where the traces occupy the entire height of the screen. A "memory clear" command can then be used, which only takes a fraction of a second to execute.

3.0 CONCLUSION

Over the past year since it was developed, STRIP has proved itself to be a valuable tool, both in the real-time mode as a data acquisition monitor, and in the background mode as a data editor. We believe that its inherent simplicity and versatility makes it a mandatory component of any data acquisition/analysis system.

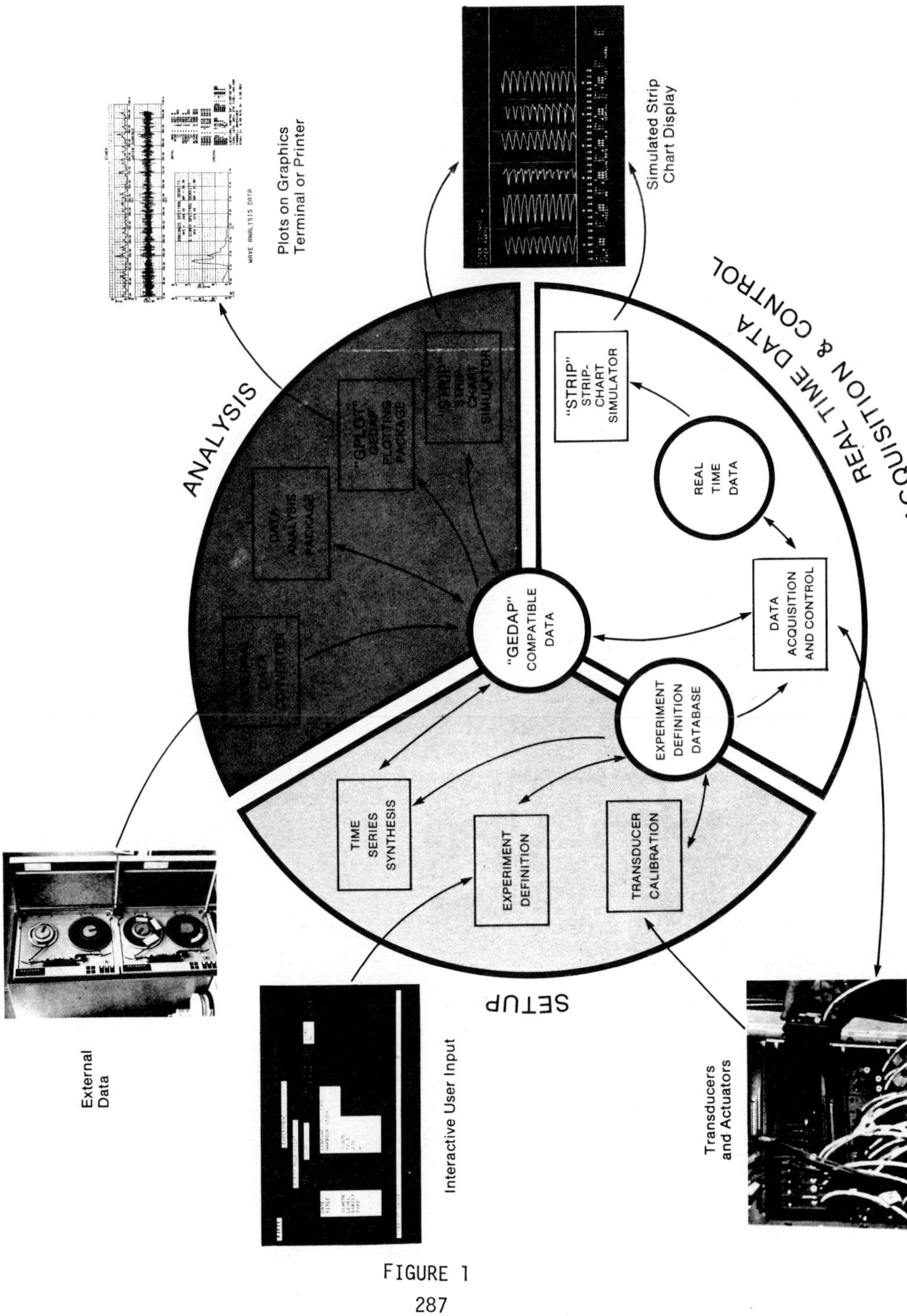
ANALYSIS
REAL TIME DATA ACQUISITION & CONTROL
SETUP
"GEDAP" COMPATIBLE DATA
DATA CONVERTER
DATA ANALYSIS PACKAGE
"GPLOT" GEDAP PLOTTING PACKAGE
"STRIP" STRIP-CHART SIMULATOR
REAL TIME DATA
DATA ACQUISITION AND CONTROL
EXPERIMENT DEFINITION DATABASE
TIME SERIES SYNTHESIS
EXPERIMENT DEFINITION
TRANSDUCER CALIBRATION
Plots on Graphics Terminal or Printer
Simulated Strip Chart Display
External Data
Interactive User Input
Transducers and Actuators

FIGURE 1

TYPO — a word processing program

Alan R. Whitney

MIT Haystack Observatory
Westford, MA 01886

Abstract: TYPO is a word-processing program which operates on an HP1000 computer under an RTE-IVA/B operating system and utilizes the Diablo 1620 or NEC Spinwriter typewriter for printed output. These daisy-wheel printers produce letter-quality output at speeds to 45 chars/sec. TYPO was written to make full use of the many capabilities of these machines. Among TYPO's capabilities are right and left justification, underline, boldface, subscripts, superscripts, controllable horizontal and vertical pitch, page titles and numbering, embedded tables and figures, full footnote support, and on-line page format management. Input to TYPO is from standard ASCII text files generated with a separate text-editing program such as the standard RTE EDITR.

Introduction

With the advent of modern high-speed daisy-wheel printers such as the Diablo 1620 or NEC Spinwriter, relatively inexpensive hardware has become available for a powerful and highly flexible word-processing system attached to a mini-computer. TYPO was written in an attempt to realize some of this potential capability.

Machines such as the Diablo 1620 have a number of features which make them ideal for word-processing output. The most powerful of these features is full dynamic control of both horizontal and vertical pitch. Horizontal pitch of the printed characters may be controlled in increments of 1/120" and vertical pitch is controllable in increments of 1/48". This provides an inherent capability to stretch and squeeze text to fit within a predefined space.

In this paper we shall include a brief discussion of TYPO itself and its main features and philosophies, but will not attempt any detailed descriptions of usage or inner workings. The capabilities of TYPO will be demonstrated in a few examples.

What Will TYPO Do?

For everyday work of a secretarial office, the most important feature of TYPO is that it can take rough-draft text entered into an ASCII text file and organize it into neatly-formatted pages with very little effort on the operator's part. Changes to the text are as simple as entering changes into a computer terminal using a standard text-editing program, such as the RTE EDITR, and re-running TYPO. In many cases, no special commands at all are necessary to achieve the desired result. Cosmetic changes such as margins, character and line pitch, and paragraph indentations may be easily changed either by entering the appropriate TYPO commands into the text source file or on-line by the operator.

Figure 1A shows a sample of text as it might exist in a source text file. Figure 1B shows the text of Figure 1A processed through TYPO, using default values for margins and pitchs. Note that words have been moved to fill lines and produce left and right justification. Figure 1C shows the same text processed through TYPO with only a change in margins and pitches. Figure 1D uses yet another set of margins and pitches, and has been processed with a 'ragged-right' margin to disguise its origin as computer-generated text. These examples indicate the high degree of 'text elasticity' when operating under TYPO and are the simplest examples of TYPO's capabilities.

More sophisticated processing under TYPO is also possible. Among TYPO's capabilities:

1. Centering, underlining, and boldface.
2. Subscripts, superscripts, and 'ghost' hyphens.
3. Tab and absolute column set.
4. Align text to left or right margin.
5. Repeat a specified string within a designated field.
6. Page titles (top and/or bottom) and page numbering (Arabic or Roman).
7. Embedded tables and figures, deferred as necessary until space is available to print them.
8. Full footnote support, with full control of the maximum space used at the bottom of each page for footnotes, and continuation of footnotes from page-to-page as necessary.
9. Allows two different printwheels to be used within any given text in order to change type faces or use special characters. A primary use of this capability is for special characters in scientific documents.
10. Nested source input files.

All of the capabilities in the above list are controlled by the insertion of commands to TYPO within the source text itself and, in addition, certain 'global' parameters may be controlled at run time. Among these 'global' parameters are margin and pitch control, tab set, titles, page numbers, footnote control, and page control.

What Do TYPO Commands Look Like?

The best way to get an idea of how commands are inserted into source text to control processing by TYPO is to examine an example illustrating some of TYPO's features. Figure 2 shows source text as it exists in raw form, and Figure 3 shows the resulting TYPO output. We will briefly go through the commands used in the example and indicate how they control the action that TYPO takes. Most TYPO commands are prefaced by a backslash (\) character; no differentiation is made between upper and lower case letters in TYPO commands.

The command \HZ10,10,85,10 is the 'Horizontal Control' command and sets the left margin to 1.0" (10 units of 1/10"), right margin to 1.0", page width to 8.5", and character spacing to 10 chars/". The command \VT20,25,110,7 is the 'Vertical Control' command specifying the top margin to be 2.0", bottom margin 2.5", paper height 11", and line spacing of 7 lines/". On the following line, \HT15,... is a 'Header Title' command which causes a title to be printed 1.5" from the top of each page. The words 'TYPO DEMONSTRATION' are left justified; the words 'PAGE #' are centered (\CE command) and '#' is replaced with the current page number; the words '20 June 1980' are right justified (\@ command). Next, a line is expanded to fill between the left and right margins (\EX) and printed in boldface (¦¦). The Footnote Control command (\FC) specifies that footnote left margin is 1.2", footnote bottom margin is 2.5", no paragraph indentation on footnote text, and vertical line spacing of 6 lines/" for footnote text. The \FN* command indicates that the text for footnote '*' follows; \en ends the footnote text. Note that this footnote will not actually be printed unless there is a reference to it somewhere on the printed page.

Following the footnote text is a 'Paragraph Parameter' command (\PP) setting the paragraph processing mode to left and right justification using a 5-character indentation. TYPO recognizes this text as a paragraph by the simple algorithm of an indented source text line followed one or more non-indented lines.

Within this paragraph are illustrations of a number of 'micro' commands which control details of the printed text. The word 'TYPO' is underlined, as well as the word 'underline' and the phrase 'a string of words'. The command \] shifts printing down one-half line for the subscript '2', and \[shifts back up again to the normal vertical position of the line. The command \(causes the 'alternate printwheel' to be used for the following characters, in this case a superscript to be printed by the scientific printwheel; \) returns printing to the normal printwheel. At the end of the paragraph, reference is made to footnote '*'. The horizontal pitch is changed to 9 chars/", followed by a paragraph illustrating the use of a 'required backspace' (\<) in order to overprint one character on top of another. Next, the horizontal pitch is changed to 11 chars/" (\HZ,,,11) and the following line is centered (\ce) between left and right margins. The horizontal pitch is then changed back to 10 chars/" before printing a line illustrating a repeated string (\"- "\) between 'Chapter 1' and a right-justified (\@) 'page 1'.

The horizontal margins and character pitch are changed again before printing the next paragraph, in which is illustrated how underlining may be toggled on and off even within a single word. Following this is another centered line followed by two tables differing only in vertical and horizontal spacings and tab sets (\TB,...). Tabbing (\>) is used within the tables themselves to illustrate the ease with which such tables may be 'elasticized'. Finally, a short paragraph once again refers to the same footnote as above.

The result of processing the source text in Figure 2 is shown in Figure 3. Clearly, there is much flexibility in presenting the final printed text in many different styles simply by changing a few parameters in the source text file. The example shown illustrates perhaps half of the commands available to the TYPO user.

On-Line TYPO Operation

During TYPO operation, either a TV monitor or a separate terminal may be used to dynamically monitor TYPO status and processing parameters. On-line control is either through the Diablo keyboard itself or through the keyboard of another terminal. The operator may intervene at any point within TYPO to do any of the following operations:

1. Change margins, pitches, titles, page numbers, and several other 'global' parameters.
2. Force printing to stop at any point on a page and force a new page to be started.
3. Force more lines onto a page than TYPO would otherwise print. This is especially useful to finish the last one or two lines of a paragraph that would otherwise sit alone at the top of the next page.

4. 'Roll' TYPO back up to the top of the current or last page, so that parameters may be readjusted and the page retyped without affecting any pages that have already been typed satisfactorily. This may be done repeatedly until the page is typed as desired.
5. Indicate to TYPO whether the 'normal' or 'alternate' printwheel is currently mounted. Normally, in cases where both typewheels are used on a single page, the entire page is first typed with the 'normal' printwheel; the 'alternate' printwheel is then mounted and the page is retyped again. TYPO will print only those characters on the page appropriate to the currently-mounted typewheel.
6. The operator may manually type onto the printed output page. This is useful if the same page(s) are typed over and over again with only minor changes, such as the name and address on a form letter. TYPO dynamically keeps track of the manually-entered input in determining current page position, etc, so that bottom margins are never violated.
7. TYPO normally pauses at the bottom of each page to await operator attention, as is ordinarily desired for single-sheet-at-a-time typing. However, TYPO may be put into a 'continuous-typing' mode for generation of long or repetitive documents using continuous-form paper or automatic sheet feeders.
8. If only a single page of a lengthy text needs to be retyped, TYPO can be asked to go directly to either a label inserted in the source text or to a line number within the source text. The page may then be typed exactly as if all the previous source text had been typed in the normal manner.

Special Requirements of TYPO

The daisy-wheel printer used by TYPO must be driven through an HP12966A interface using the driver DVB00, which is a contributed driver from Haystack Observatory and NASA/Goddard Space Flight Center (see separate paper on this driver). Unfortunately, neither DVR00 nor DVR05 will properly support these printers.

Conclusion

TYPO has been installed at MIT Haystack Observatory and NASA/Goddard Space Flight Center since early 1979, and has received much heavy daily use at both installations. It has proven to be of considerable value in lubricating the flow of documents through both facilities, processing a combined total of over 10000 pages of printed output during this time.

 TYPO is a word-processing program which operates on an
HP1000 computer with an RTE-IVA/B operating system. It
will move words within a paragraph as necessary
in order to
left and right justify a paragraph, if commanded to do so.
Note that two spaces are maintained between sentences
within a paragraph.

(A) SOURCE TEXT PARAGRAPH

TYPO is a word-processing program which operates on an
HP1000 computer with an RTE-IVA/B operating system. It will
move words within a paragraph as necessary in order to left
and right justify a paragraph, if commanded to do so. Note
that two spaces are maintained between sentences within a
paragraph.

(B) AS PROCESSED USING DEFAULT PARAMETERS

TYPO is a word-processing program which operates on an HP1000
computer with an RTE-IVA/B operating system. It will move words
within a paragraph as necessary in order to left and right justify
a paragraph, if commanded to do so. Note that two spaces are
maintained between sentences within a paragraph.

(C) ILLUSTRATING TEXT 'ELASTICITY'

TYPO is a word-processing program which operates on an HP1000 computer with
an RTE-IVA/B operating system. It will move words within a paragraph as
necessary in order to left and right justify a paragraph, if commanded to
do so. Note that two spaces are maintained between sentences within a
paragraph.

(D) ILLUSTRATING 'RAGGED-RIGHT' MARGIN

FIGURE 1
PROCESSING OF SOURCE TEXT USING DIFFERENT PARAMETERS

```
\HZ10,10,85,10
\VT20,25,110,7
\HT15,/TYPO DEMONSTRATION/\CEPAGE #/\@20 June 1980
\EX||THIS LINE IS A SAMPLE OF EXPANDED BOLDFACE

\FC12,25,0,6
\FN*
 We use footnotes frequently and the same footnote can be used
more than once if there are other references to it.
\en
\PP0,5
      This paragraph is simply a sample to show some of the
many capabilities of the "_TYPO_" word processing program.
We can _underline one word_or __a string of words__, we can
make subscripts (H\]2\[0) with a few extra key touches, we
can type superscripts (10\(6\)) and other "alternate-wheel"
necessities and include footnotes\%*\.

\HZ10,10,,9
  It is easy to type pronounciation marks or other duplicate
space entries (0"\<.002) by using a "required  backspace".

\HZ,,,11
\ceUsing a repeat string is useful in a Table of Contents:
\HZ,,,10

Chapter 1\"- "\@page 1

\hz25,25,,12
 Tables are quite easily _a_dj_us_t_ed in size when they have
been "typo-ized" as we can see even from this short example.
Rather than changing all the spacing between columns and
rows, one need only change two commands -- vertical line
spacing and the tab sets.

\ceTABLE 1 - Example

\HZ25,25,,11
\CESPREAD IT OUT
\TB8,16,24,32,40

\VT,,,5
10\>12\>14\>16\>18\>20
11\>13\>15\>17\>19\>21

\CEOR SQUEEZE IT TIGHT
\HZ31,31,,10
\TB4,8,12,16,20
\VT,,,7
10\>12\>14\>16\>18\>20
11\>13\>15\>17\>19\>21
\HZ10,10,,10

      Finally, we can use the footnote again and again,
as we mentioned previously, having typed it only once\%*\.
```

FIGURE 2
TYPO SOURCE TEXT USED TO GENERATE OUTPUT IN FIGURE 3

TYPO DEMONSTRATION PAGE 1 20 June 1980

THIS LINE IS A SAMPLE OF EXPANDED BOLDFACE

This paragraph is simply a sample to show some of the many capabilities of the "TYPO" word processing program. We can underline one word or a string of words, we can make subscripts (H_2O) with a few extra key touches, we can type superscripts (10^6) and other "alternate-wheel" necessities and include footnotes*.

It is easy to type pronounciation marks or other duplicate space entries (0"002) by using a "required backspace".

Using a repeat string is useful in a Table of Contents:

Chapter 1- page 1

Tables are quite easily adjusted in size when they have been "typo-ized" as we can see even from this short example. Rather than changing all the spacing between columns and rows, one need only change two commands -- vertical line spacing and the tab sets.

TABLE 1 - Example

SPREAD IT OUT

10	12	14	16	18	20
11	13	15	17	19	21

OR SQUEEZE IT TIGHT

10	12	14	16	18	20
11	13	15	17	19	21

Finally, we can use the footnote again and again, as we mentioned previously, having typed it only once*.

---

*We use footnotes frequently and the same footnote can be used more than once if there are other references to it.

FIGURE 3
TYPO OUTPUT RESULTING FROM SOURCE TEXT OF FIGURE 2

DVB00 — a general-purpose driver for the 12966A ASCII interface card

Alan R. Whitney

MIT Haystack Observatory
Westford, MA 01886

Abstract: In order to fill a number of requirements for communications with a variety of ASCII-type devices, a general-purpose driver has been written for the HP12966A Buffered ASCII Communications Interface Card. This driver, called DVB00, in many ways emulates DVR00 although it has a number of extended capabilities not available in DVR00. Full control of the 12966A interface is given to the user to provide a a powerful tool for controlling communications between almost any ASCII device and the host computer at baud rates up to 9600.

Introduction

Several years ago at the MIT Haystack Observatory we developed a need to read ASCII data from a non-HP device which sent its data to the computer at a fixed data rate with no handshaking. Surveying the available HP software which might be suitable for this task, we in fact found none. It appeared, however, that a suitable I/O handler might be written to support the HP12966A I/O card. The only HP-supported driver available then, and now, for the 12966A card is DVR05, whose sole usefulness is to support HP26xx terminals. Thus spawned the birth of DVB00, which has now grown into a powerful general-purpose driver with many capabilities. Among these capabilites are:

1. Terminal driver for a broad segment of so-called 'dumb' terminals, supporting them at up to 9600 baud.
2. Support for popular word-processing printers, such as the Diablo 1620 or NEC Spinwriter, which cannot be successfully supported even under DVR00.
3. Support for a large class of general ASCII devices which may be attached to the HP1000 system, such as PROM programmers and mirco-processor development systems.
4. Direct computer-to-computer communications, between two HP1000 systems or between an HP1000 system and a foreign system.

In this paper we will explore some of the capabilities of DVB00 and some of the uses to which it may be adapted. We will also indicate ongoing work to further enhance DVB00.

Some General Information About the HP12966A Interface

The HP12966A interface provides half-duplex, asynchronous bit-serial data transfer between the host computer and an external device. An on-board 128-character buffer allows data transfer at a higher rate than would be otherwise possible. The same 128-character buffer is used for both transmit and receive, so that it is not possible to transmit and receive at the same time. Data may be received in either 'character' or 'buffer' mode. In the 'character' mode, an interrupt is generated on the receipt of every character. In the 'buffer' mode, an interrupt is generated only when the buffer is half-full or full. Baud rate and character definition (#data bits, parity, etc.) are fully programmable, with a maximum baud rate of 9600. Up to 256 characters may be defined as 'special characters', which cause the interface to produce an interrupt whenever any one of these characters is received, regardless of whether the interface is operating in 'character' or 'buffer' mode. Also, a BREAK on the interface receive lines causes an unconditional interrupt, regardless of the mode of the buffer.

The 12966A interface provides a general interrupt capability on device status changes. Five status lines may be enabled, in any combination, to generate an interrupt whenever the actual status of these enabled lines changes away from a specified reference status. Additionally, four control lines may be set by the interface. These capabilities provide a potentially powerful tool for device control.

One serious drawback of the 12966A interface is that it cannot automatically switch from transmit mode to receive mode after the last character is transmitted from its internal buffer. The mode change from transmit to receive can only take place when the computer services the 'buffer empty' interrupt at the completion of the transmission. The practical consequence of this restriction is that, with no handshaking, data returning from a device in response to a query from the host computer may be lost until the 'buffer empty' interrupt is serviced. The 12966A card may be modified to make this changeover automatically, but at the expense of voiding your warranty or service contract.

DVB00 as a Terminal Driver

As a terminal driver, DVB00 closely emulates DVR00 and DVR05. From a user point point-of-view, there are only a couple of minor differences. In order to gain system attention under DVB00, the user must strike either RETURN or CNTL D. Normally, the striking of any other key will be ignored. This change has been made in order to better support remote terminals operating over modem links. By limiting the characters which may gain system attention, spurious line noise is much less likely to generate unwanted prompts.

One of the most annoying features of DVR05 is the difficulty of interrupting output to the terminal at high baud rates -- it is sometimes necessary to literally pound the keyboard in order to gain system attention. This problem has been eliminated in DVB00 by using the BREAK key for this purpose. A single stroke of the BREAK key will immediately interrupt the output stream to generate a system prompt, allowing the user to take necessary action.

The function of the 'soft-keys' available on the HP26xx terminals has been implemented in a somewhat different manner in DVB00. Under DVB00, control keys may be enabled to schedule a specified program. The information as to which control key has been pressed is available to the scheduled program, which may then take any desired action. In particular, this program may schedule another program or send a command to the system. For example, CNTL W might ultimately schedule WHZAT. Since the number of control keystrokes numbers nearly 30, many different pre-programmed actions may be taken, each with a single keystroke.

Baud rates of up to 9600 may be supported, depending on the capabilities of the terminal. Since there is normally no handshaking, the terminal must be able to swallow data as fast as it comes to it. For many of the modern inexpensive 'dumb' terminals, this is in fact the case.

For mechanical printers and terminals that are unbuffered and require additional time during carriage returns and line feeds, DVB00 may provide stall characters to facilitate these operations.

DVB00 may be used to support modern daisy-wheel printers such as those made by Diablo, Qume, and NEC Spinwriter. Surprisingly, DVR00 will not properly support these machines because DVR00 swallows certain control characters used by them. Unfortunately, these characteristics of DVR00 are undocumented.

Use as General ASCII-Device Driver

Many devices are available today which may be interfaced to a host computer using a standard ASCII RS-232 communications protocol. Among such devices are PROM burners, microprocessor development systems, and ASCII command and control systems. Most of these devices have several characteristics in common (1) either no handshaking or handshaking of a type unsupported by HP and (2) data is transmitted to the host computer in blocks at fixed data rates. DVB00 may be used to communicate with these devices in a fairly general manner.

A feature of DVB00 that allows handling of some of these devices is the ability to schedule a program on device-status interrupt. The device-status conditions under which the program will be scheduled may be specified in detail and modified dynamically as conditions require. In addition, DVB00 may dynamically manage four control lines to the device. These capabilities provide a powerful tool for contol of and communications with an attached device.

In general, there is no problem in transmitting data to the device; the problems arise when data is coming back at a fixed rate from the device to the host computer. When operating in this environment, DVB00 is normally operated in the 'buffered' mode during receive in order to minimize the interrupt-service load on the host computer. If data from the device always terminates in some particular terminating character, DVB00 may configure the 12966A interface to recognize that character. Either ASCII or binary data may be transmitted in this mode. If data from the device is of a fixed block length with no special terminating character, DVB00 may periodically interrogate the interface until the specified number of characters has been received.

Several approaches may be taken in the application of DVB00-to-device communication. We will examine a few examples of these.

Figure 1 shows a simple communications system where status and control lines both initiate and control the communications to prevent any loss-of-data. Suppose that the Device has been collecting data and is ready to dump it to the Computer. At this point, the Device raises one of its status lines to the Computer, which generates an interrupt and causes program PROG to be scheduled. PROG then issues a request to DVB00 to clear the 12966A buffer and leave it in receive mode, then sets a control line back to the Device saying 'OK, I'm ready. Send the data.' The Device then begins to send data back to the Computer. PROG then issues a 'read request without master reset' which leaves intact any data already accumulated in the buffer. On the receipt of a termination character from the Device, the read completes and PROG recovers the transmitted data. This scheme will always work provided a data block sent from the Device is less than 128 characters or the Device does not send more than 128 characters before PROG can issue a read request. At 9600 baud somewhat more than 10msec of leeway is available before there is any possibility of data loss.

In some cases, the system of contol/status line handshaking is not possible because of Device or communications channel limitations. Figure 2 shows a scheme that uses only data lines between the Computer and the Device. Here, when the Device is ready to upload its data to the Computer, it sends a selected control character which causes program PROG to be scheduled. PROG sends a prompt character or sequence to the Device to initiate its data transmission; after a delay, which allows time for DVB00 to turn the interface around from transmit to receive, the Device transmits its data. A delay of 50msec has generally been found to be sufficient. Of course, two 12966A interfaces may be used in this scheme, one dedicated to transmit and the other to receive, which would completely eliminate any possibility of lost data, but is expensive in terms of hardware. With two cards, a 'read request with buffer clear' (master reset) would be issued by PROG <u>before</u> a prompt is sent to the Device. PROG then issues a 'read without buffer clear' to the receive interface, so that any data already received from the Device is not destroyed.

The approach shown in Figure 2 has been used in a number of applications, one of particular interest is the connection of a Tektronix 8002 microprocessor development system to an HP1000 system. Data may be sent both to and from the MPD, taking advantage of peripherals available on the HP1000 system to vastly increase the convenience and speed of editing, hard-copy listing, and file archiving.

Figure 3 shows DVB00 supporting a modem. For purposes of illustration a multiple-baud-rate auto-answer modem has been chosen (such as the Vadic 3453). In this case, DVB00 is enabled to schedule program PROG on a Ring Indicator status line from the modem. The modem, upon answering, sets it Carrier Received status line and baud rate indicator status line(s). PROG waits for the Carrier Received line to go high, determines the baud rate at which the communication is to take place, and then sets the baud rate of the interface appropriately. At this point the communications link is established and PROG is free to proceed with any desired protocol, such as asking for and verifying a password (if the caller is a remote terminal), or querying the status of the caller. Note that the whole answer and initialization procedure is entirely automatic, compared to the procedure under DVA05 where terminal initialization must be done manually before communications can be established. Furthermore, under DVA05, a premature line disconnect before issuing a Line Close request can leave the modem hanging in limbo. On the other hand, line disconnect can be handled entirely automatically by DVB00, which may again schedule PROG on Loss-of-Carrier status, and do any desired system clean-up in its wake. This system of automatic modem answer and disconnect has been used very satisfactorily at Haystack Observatory for some time.

Figure 4 shows a simple connection of computer-to-computer which might be called a 'poor man's DS/1000'. This scheme allows data to be transmitted from any remote computer to your computer and is extremely simple. Basically, you place a call to Their Computer over a modem link (say) from Your HP-computer over a full-duplex link. A pair of wires from the receive side of Your Terminal is paralleled into a DVB00 port on your computer. Program LISN is initiated which receives and records (say to disc) everything that comes to Your Terminal. It is a simple matter, for example, to dump a source code file from Their Computer to Your Terminal, with program LISN recording every byte that comes its way. With a little more sophistication, any type of information may be transmitted from Their Computer to Your Computer. The remote computer, of course, may be any computer that communicates in ASCII, not necessarily HP! If you wish to become still more sophisticated, two 12966A cards may be used in Your Computer, one dedicated to transmit and the other to receive, to carry on a true computer-to-computer full-duplex conversation limited only by the program(s) driving it.

Enhancements in Progress

A number of enhancements to DVB00 are currently in progress, mostly being undertaken by Lee Foster of NASA Goddard Space Flight Center. Most of them have already been implemented and are currently being tested.

Three types of handshaking are being implemented, to be chosen at the user's option by subchannel designation. The first is the standard ENQ/ACK handshake used by DVR05 to support all HP26xx terminals. In this type of handshake, the driver sends an ENQ character after every 80 characters or so, and then waits for an ACK from the terminal before sending more data. A slight, but popular, variation of this handshake is the ETX/ACK handshake used by a number of non-HP devices. The third type of handshake being implemented uses a status line from the device to indicate that it is busy. This type of handshake is popular in many inexpensive printers.

There is notably one popular type of handshake that is not being implemented. This is the so-called XON/XOFF handshake where the terminal sends a Transmit Off (CNTL S) signal to the host computer when it can no longer accept data, followed at some later time by a Transmit On (CNTL Q) character when it is read to receive more data. Because the 12966A interface is fundamentally a half-duplex communications channel, it is not possible to implement this type of handshake.

A Modest Request to HP

Judging by the number of inquiries which have been received regarding DVB00, there seems to be a widespread need for a driver of this type. In view of the fact that the equipment to be supported is primarily non-HP, it is perhaps not too suprising that HP does not support such a driver. Nevertheless, I feel that one key item of support from HP would greatly enhance the general usefulness of the 12966A interface card -- a supported modification that causes the 12966A card to automatically change from transmit mode to receive mode on 'transmit buffer empty'. Such a modification would in no way affect present operation or usage of the 12966A interface, and would greatly enhance its usefulness since it would eliminate many potential lost-data conditions that may currently arise with a single-card interface.

Conclusion

DVB00 is now in use at a variety of locations in the U.S. and Europe and is proving to be a valuable tool for general ASCII communications. Enhancements now being completed at NASA/GSFC promise to extend its usefulness even further. Source and/or relocatable copies of DVB00 are available free-of-charge from the author.

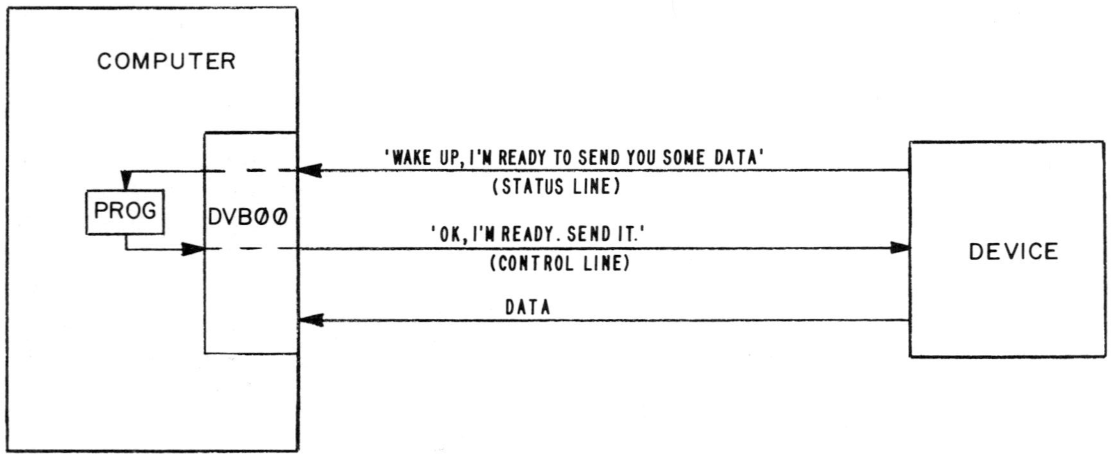

PROG STEPS:

a. CLEAR INTERFACE BUFFER AND SET TO RECEIVE MODE
b. SET CONTROL LINE TO DEVICE
c. ISSUE 'READ WITHOUT MASTER RESET' TO GATHER DATA.

FIG. 1
COMMUNICATIONS CONTROL USING STATUS & CONTROL LINES

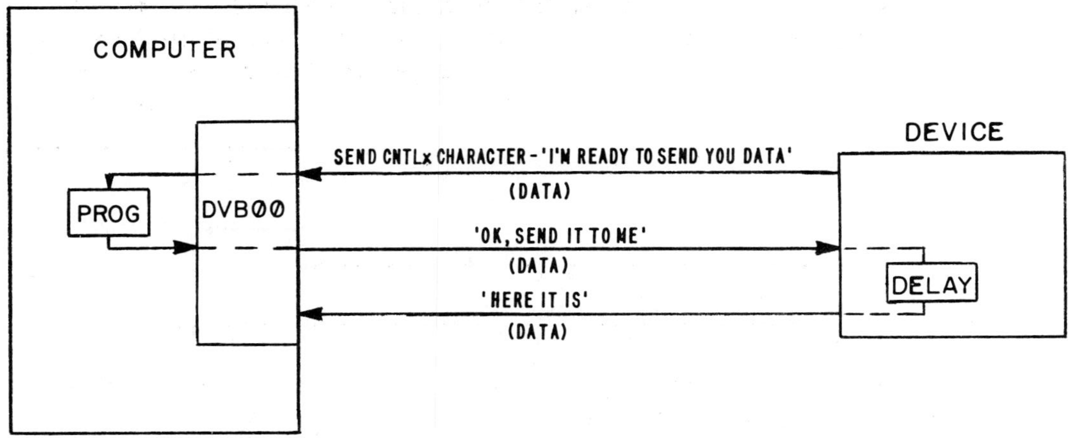

FIG. 2
COMMUNICATION USING ONLY DATA LINES

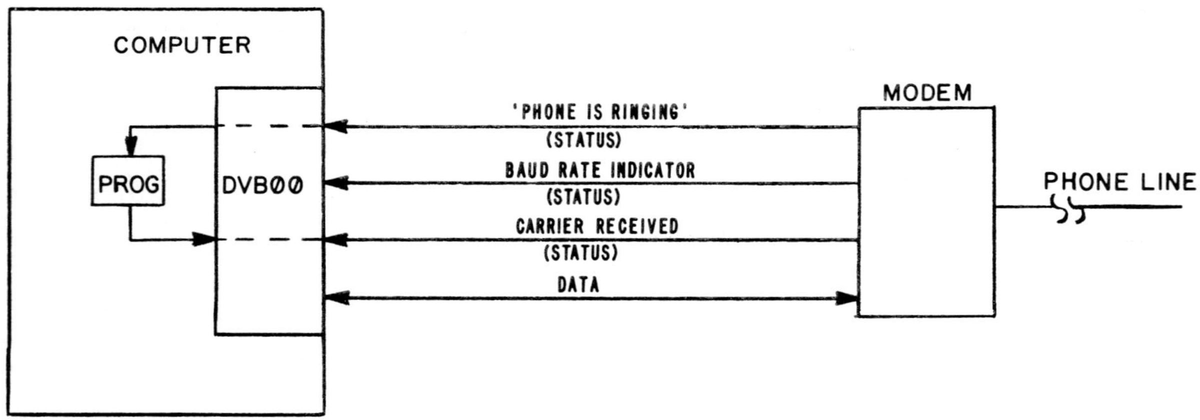

PROG STEPS:

a. WAIT FOR "CARRIER RECEIVED"
b. EXAMINE "BAUD RATE INDICATOR LINE" AND SET BAUD RATE.
c. INITIALIZE COMMUNICATIONS AS DESIRED

FIG. 3
EXAMPLE OF 'AUTO-ANSWER' MODEM

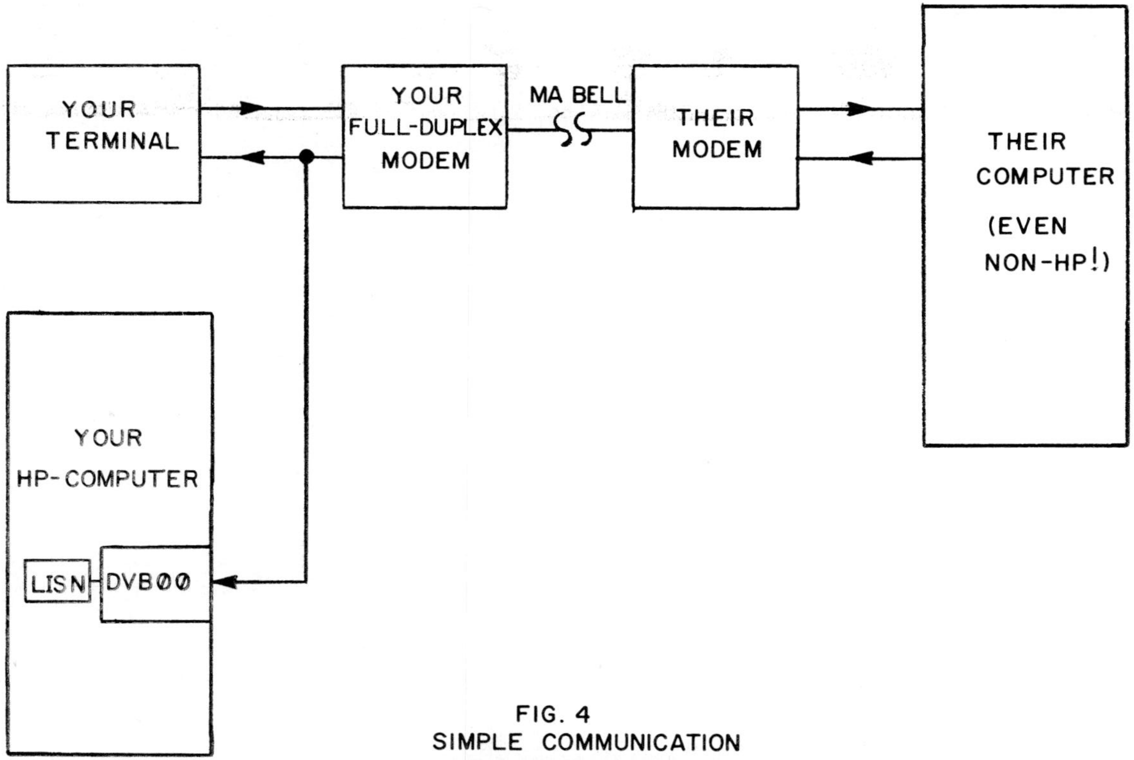

FIG. 4
SIMPLE COMMUNICATION
COMPUTER-TO-COMPUTER

support of multiple simultaneous batch protocols

Jay C. Bergeron

Gerber Systems Technology, Inc.
40 Gerber Road East
South Windsor, Connecticut 06074

ABSTRACT: The requirements of GST's customers for batch protocol emulation necessitated the development of a communications subsystem. This subsystem allows the support of simultaneous protocols without degrading the performance of our systems. The design is such that new protocols can be added with a minimum impact on the design or operation.

The need to support Remote Job Entry (RJE) from a minicomputer system occurs for a number of reasons. The user may want to take advantage of the massive amounts of online mass storage available on a large mainframe to build a common database for support of multiple systems. The speed and accuracy of the 32 and 60 bit word lengths of the IBM and CDC mainframes may be required to perform finite element analysis or post-processing for machine tool control. In all cases, the underlying goal is to have the functions performed by the equipment that can best perform it. Batch protocols were implemented on minicomputer systems to provide a low level, secure, medium-speed method of communicating between the minicomputer and a larger host CPU.

As Gerber Systems Technology (GST) began to develop our turnkey Interactive Graphics Design Systems (IDS-3 and IDS-80) and our Data Management System (DMS-2), we found that our users had a number of protocols that they wanted to support. In addition to 2780, HASP 360/20, and 200UT, the need also arose to provide the ability to communicate remotely between the CPU's in our systems. Multiple communication links, running concurrently, had to be supported.

The main element of our product is the capability to perform interactive design at a graphics workstation. Any requests to service the workstation had to be handled with the highest priority and the minimum delay in response. Yet, we still had to provide for multiple channels operating at speeds up to 19.2KBPS in batch mode without impacting the performance of the graphics workstation.

The task of supporting a batch protocol from a minicomputer can be broken into two (2) distinct components: data (file management), and the line protocol. The approach taken by GST was to divide the support along these lines. The data management task became our DMS Communications Subsystem. The line protocol was offloaded from the HP-1000 and placed in the Gerber Synchronous Communications Controller (GSCC), a microprocessor-based front end.

The DMS Communications Subsystem is the interface between

the GSCC and the user. It consists of a monitor program, some configuration/control utilities, and a series of operator/user commands. Where possible, the monitor is kept protocol independent. All protocol dependent tasks reside in the GSCC with the exception of data translation and some specific file processing required for support of 200UT emulation.

The subsystem is configured by a utility program called TBLSG. This program interactively builds a file containing the required information about the host CPU (REMOTE). Up to three (3) remotes can be defined. The limit is imposed as the information must be loaded (by Program RSSGA) into the SubSystem Global Area (SSGA) prior to initializing a remote. The following information about each remote is stored in the table:

- 4 character remote name (RSYS).
- User LU of the GSCC.
- User LU of the printer assigned to the GSCC.
- Character set to use (e.g., EBCDIC).
- Number of header records to skip.
- DMS JCL required.
- Default signon file name.
- Default signoff file name.
- GSCC type (RAM or EPROM).

Additionally, status words in this table are used to communicate between the monitor and the user.

The monitor is divided into 5 main routines. They are: MONTR, GXP, GRP, GTH, and CONVR. FIGURE 1 contains a block diagram of the MONITOR. MONTR is the main routine. All initialization tasks are performed here. MONTR determines what the operator wants to do next by querying the SSGA for console messages and offline commands, and by querying the batch queue for files to transmit. The design of this module permits operation with emulators that allow interleaving (HASP, 200UT) and with non-interleaving emulators (2780).

GXP handles all file and data processing for files being transmitted to a host. Files that are defined as binary are broken up into 80 byte records for transmission. The final record, if shorter than 80 bytes, is padded with binary zero's. No translation is performed. Character files are translated into the character set of the host. The records are truncated if over 80 characters, and padded with spaces if less than 80. The one exception is communication between two IDS-80 systems. Here, no data translation takes place, and complete sectors are transmitted, regardless of data type.

GRP is the receive data processing routine. All output to the console, printer, and disk is handled by this subroutine. Depending upon the configuration, data destined for the punch is written to the disk. If the user indicated that "IDS-80 JCL" would be used, the records are scanned for JCL records. If found, these are used to create a disk file. A record count embedded in the JCL indicates when to close the file. All records prior to the JCL, and after the end of the file, are discarded. If no JCL

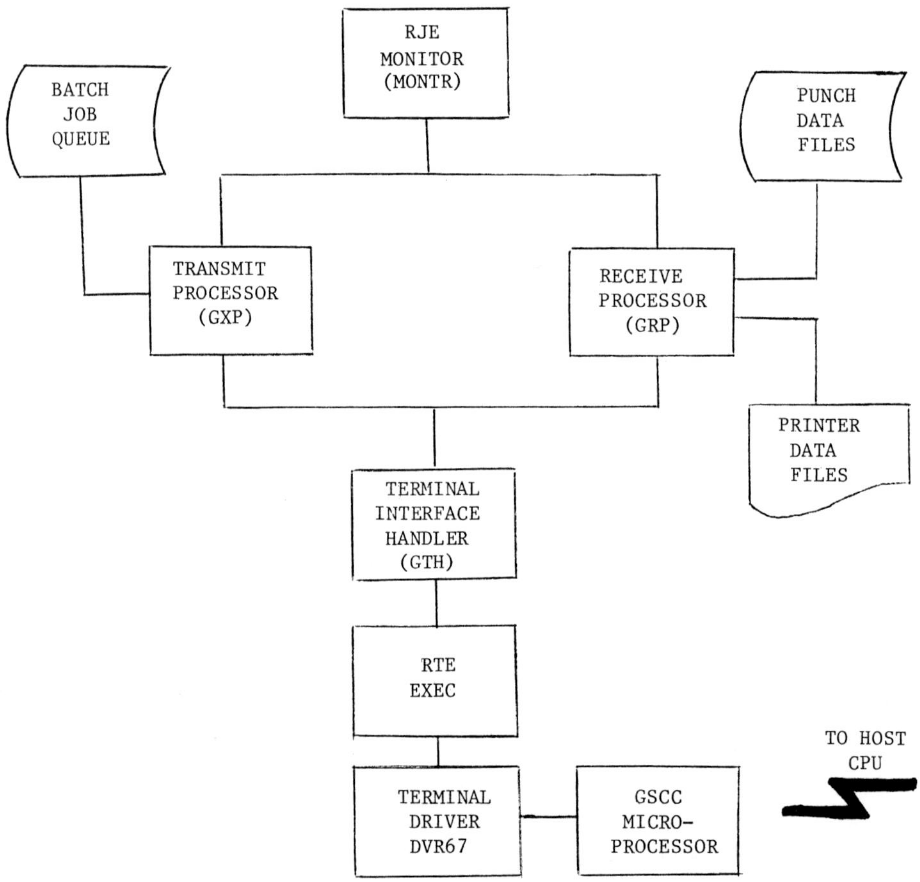

FIGURE 1 - BLOCK DIAGRAM: MONITOR

is used, a generic file name is created, and all data records, until the end of the file is received, are written to disk.

Support of 200UT emulation requires special processing within the DMS Communications Subsystem. 200UT does not support punch output files. In order to provide the user with as versatile an interface as possible, it was decided to allow the user to embed disk-destined files within his print data stream. A special terminating record was defined to be used in determining when to close the file. Only character data can be received or transmitted, as 200UT does not support binary data transmission.

GTH is the interface between the DMS Communications Subsystem and the operating environment. The actual I/O to the GSCC is performed by DVR67. This is a half duplex parallel DMA driver that operates at 5KW. A GST-designed card, the GHM 1-1, is used as the hardware interface. This card can be used in full or half duplex mode. DVR67 is set up such that all timeouts and other failures are reported back to the calling program. The LU's and EQ's are never downed.

CONVR is a general translation routine. All data conversion to and from ASCII is handled by this routine. It is a table-driven routine and can be easily expanded as the system need grows.

Two operator commands, RON and ROFF, control the initiating and terminating of the monitor and the GSCC communicatios. If the GSCC is a RAM-based one (GSCC-2), then the protocol module is loaded into the GSCC via the RON command. RON also indicates to the monitor the name of the signon file that is to be used. ROFF terminates the communications by sending the signoff file and stops the execution of MONTR.

The operator can also send console messages to the HOST via the RCO command. The ability to send console messages is a function of the host (e.g., 2780 only supports operator commands entered via the card reader) and is configured into the DMS Communications Subsystem via a TBLSG option.

The user also has three (3) commands available for his use. RJOB allows the user to build a job file for transmission. The job file is a collection of files that are to be transmitted in the order that they were entered. The user has the option of entering the job file into the batch queue for a given remote, or he can write it to disk for queuing up at a later time.

RBATCH is used to take a job file that was written to disk and place it in the queue for a given remote. The existence of each file is verified prior to entering the job file name into the queue. RBATCH can be used to re-enter a job file into the batch queue.

The third command, RQM, can be used by both the system operator and the user. RQM is the remote queue manager and provides the following capabilities:

- List the jobs in the queue.
- Hold and release individual jobs.
- Hold and release entire queue.
- Purge the entire queue or individual jobs.
- Alter priorties on the jobs within the queue.

Access levels are used to determine what suboptions within RQM can be executed by the user and which ones the operator can use.

The GSCC is the interface between the DMS Communications Subsystem and the communications link to the host CPU. This is a microprocessor-based system using a National Semiconductor IMP-16C processor with a 1.4 microsecond cycle time. The GSCC performs all of the protocol-dependent tasks such as line control, data compression/decompression, and the blocking/deblocking of buffers. Only one RS232 line can be handled by a GSCC. Up to three (3) GSCC's can be running on one DMS or IDS-80 system.

The GSCC is available in two (2) models: the GSCC-1 and the GSCC-2. The GSCC-1 is an EPROM (Erasable Programmable Read Only Memory) model which is used when a customer only needs to support one type of line protocol. This model contains 4K words of RAM (Random Access Memory) for I/O buffers and data storage and 8K words of EPROM for program storage. The protocol actually occupies less than 4K words of memory. 1K is used for diagnostic programs that can be accessed by switches on a test panel.

The GSCC-2 is a model where the communications protocol is stored in RAM and is downline loaded whenever the RON command is issued by the user. This model contains 8K of RAM--4K for I/O buffers, and 4K for program storage. 1K of EPROM is provided for storage of the diagnostics. This model is generally used by customers who need to communicate nonconcurrently with more than one type of host CPU. The GSCC-2 is a far more flexible device than the GSCC-1.

The actual serialization/deserialization is performed by a Signetics MultiProtocol Communications Controller (MPCC). The MPCC is rated at 2 mega bits per second. This, in combination with IMP-16 hardware and software, provides support for line speeds up to 19.2KBPS.

The GSCC software controls both the local line (to the HP-1000) and the RS232 interface via an interrupt structure (see FIGURE 2). Due to the high speed (50K words per second) at which the local line operates, the only interrupt that occurs is the initial "word ready" interrupt. The remainder of the data block is sent or received via a "locked loop" mode-type transfer. Here, the program continually checks a status flag to ascertain if the next word can be processed.

This same mechanism is used to handle remote line speeds above 9.6KBPS. The overhead involved in processing an interrupt makes it impossible to process each character in time to get back and handle the next interrupt. Normally, the time between interrupts is used to perform data encoding/decoding, etc. When the "locked loop" method is used, these tasks can only be performed between blocks of data. Therefore, special modules are provided when the user desires to operate at speeds above 9.6KBPS. At 9.6KBPS or lower, the actual throughput degrades when "locked loop" is used.

A set of diagnostics are provided in EPROM. These are accessed via a special panel board that is inserted into the backplane of the GSCC. These routines provide the ability to check the parallel local line, the RS232 port and its control signals (CTS,RTS, etc.), and the accuracy of the system clock.

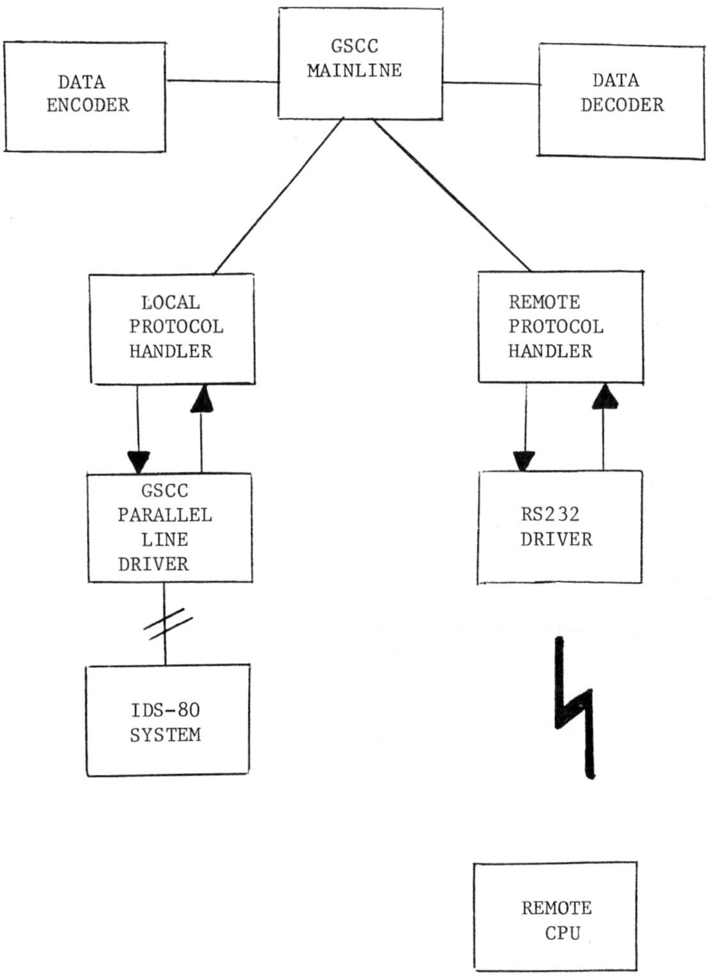

FIGURE 2 - REMOTE PROTOCOL BLOCK DIAGRAM FOR GSCC

This approach has successfully allowed the support of several simultaneously executing batch protocols without any performance degradation. Because the communications task is performed in a background mode, a terminal is not tied up by having to perform the monitoring tasks. The design of the GSCC protocol handlers has allowed the implementation of different protocols, while minimizing the changes required to support the protocol.

In conclusion, the combinations of the GSCC and the DMS Communications Subsystem has provided GST with a powerful, highly flexible product for solving customer requirements for remote job entry in a single or multiple host environment.

shell canada resources network of HP/1000 minis

R. J. Pankewitz

Shell Canada Resources Limited
400 - 4th Avenue S.W.
P. O. Box 100
Calgary, Alberta T2P 2H5
Canada

ABSTRACT

This paper consists of two parts. Part A describes the HP/1000 network of mini computers and their basic functions within Shell Canada Resources. After the distributed systems network discussion, Part B will focus on the chain of events to transmit Peace River Insitu Pilot Project data from the field to a host Univac data base in Calgary. To achieve this, Part B will describe the following basic functions:

- how field data is gathered in real time environment at Peace River
- the daily transmission of field data via DS/1000
- the transmission of a batch run stream via RJE/1000 to a Univac 1100/44 corporate computer

To wrap up, the paper will discuss some hardware and software considerations of DS/1000 and RJE/1000.

PART A - A NETWORK OF MINI COMPUTERS

I. Definition Of Computer Assisted Operations (CAO)

Within Shell's organization worldwide, we refer to CAO - the acronym of Computer Assisted Operations. This is a variation of what others call CPC - Computer Production Control. However, the use of the Key word 'Assisted' more appropriately describes the intent of these systems. One definition of CAO is a "modern technological tool which uses a computer to assist the operating personnel in monitoring wells and facilities, accumulating and processing data, and performing certain control functions". The CAO's systems unique ability is to maintain continuous surveillance of a producing activity on a 24 hour per day 7 day per week basis.

II. General Network Description

Shell's CAO distributed systems consists of a network of HP/1000 mini computers shown on Figure 1. The system presently consists of 8 computers in a modified star configuration, with the probable addition of another in 1981. At the "HUB" of the network resides a Central Real Time computer in Calgary with the field computers inter-connected via HP's DS/1000 hardware/software package. As well, a Central Development computer is hardwire connected to the Real Time Central in the Calgary CAO Centre. The present network includes the following fields connected to Central Real Time:

- Harmattan East oil and gas field
- Waterton gas field
- Burnt Timber Complex gas field
- Peace River Insitu Tar Sands field
- Limestone gas field (to be added in 1980)
- Jumping Pound gas field (DS to be added later)

The locations of each of the above fields are shown in Figure 1.

III. A Typical HP/1000 Configuration

The CAO mini computers are exclusively HP/1000 disk based systems with an RTE-IVA operating system. We are planning to convert all the operating systems to RTE-IVB in the fall of 1980. The hardware for these mini computers typically includes:

- 128 K words of semi conductor memory
- 10 M words of disk storage
- one line printer
- at least one operator's terminal
- at least one hard copy alarm logger
- various other peripherals

Peripherals include printing terminals, display CRT's, printers and plotters depending on the particular requirements at each field location. For a more comprehensive agenda of the hardware refer to Table I.

IV. Distributed Systems (DS) Hardware

Shell Canada has at present each field computer linked directly via modems on Alberta Government Telephones (AGT) privately leased line to Central Real Time. Typical line speeds are 2400 to 9600 BPS. Furthermore, a dial-up capability with the DS connection allows our CAO personnel to connect directly to each field computer with a Texas Instrument Silent 700 terminal (or any HP 26XX CRT). This was accomplished using split channel 4800 BPS modems and 113 dial-up modems. This configuration is much cheaper than having two separate hardwired channels, and helps to justify the high cost of the dedicated leased lines. Refer to Figure 3 for a more complete description of the DS hardware configuration.

PART B - PEACE RIVER INFORMATION SYSTEM

I. General Project Description

The Peace River Insitu Pilot (PRISP) project site is located approximately 600 kilometers northwest of Calgary, Alberta and 55 kilometers northeast of the town of Peace River. Shell presently holds a total of 152,000 acres of land with potential tar sands application in the vicinity of Peace River. Refer to Figure 2.

The pilot production facilities consist of 7-7 spot well patterns. Included are 24 bitumen production wells, 7 steam injection wells and 10 observation wells. The well pattern covers an area of 50 acres and the plant itself occupies an additional 15 acres.

In order to both operate and evaluate the pilot, several levels of data collection are required. Operators manning the process 24 hours a day must be aware of the real time changing variables. The engineering staff located in Calgary must have daily summaries of real time variables in order to direct timely changes and evaluate performance. The combination of these two data requirements has led to an interesting but complex arrangement of computers and communication links.

II. Overview Of PRISP Data Flow

The illustration in Figure 4 shows the network designed for this project. Data can move both up or down the network. With no operator intervention, however, it generally moves from lowest level of the hierarchy (the micros) upwards to the highest level, namely the Univac 1100/44 in Calgary. Each computer in the network (except the Univac) automatically polls its lower level node for up-to-date information when needed.

The micros receive their data directly from the end-elements by continuously scanning and calculating flow rates at several production testing locations. On its own polling frequency the HP mini retrieves its information from the micros. After a complete day of data is collected by the mini, the data is transmitted to the Central Real Time mini for further processing.

The Central mini in turn submits the daily information to the Univac for long term storage in a data base and for engineering report generation.

If any node or communication line should fail, all nodes in the hierarchy are unaffected. Their only "awareness" of a problem is their storage filling up pending a transmission to the higher node.

To properly describe the system of interconnected computers including micros and minis the following sections must be described in detail:

- CAO PRISP Field Computer System
- Transmission of PRISP Data
- CAO Central Real Time System

- CAO PRISP Field Computer System

The PRISP CAO system provides for the flow of data from the field/plant through a computer based Supervisory Control And Data Acquisition (SCADA) subsystem to the HP/1000 field computer. To describe the data flow, firstly the major parts of the SCADA system will be discussed and, secondly, the functions of the HP/1000.

1. SCADA Subsystem

The SCADA subsystem consists of the following basic sections:

(i) End Elements

End elements are hardwired to RTU's at wells, headers, satellites and major facilities. They measure and convert pressure, temperature, and other variables into electrical signals which can be encoded by the field SCADA equipment and sent to the computer. They also convert electrical signals into control actions (eg. close a valve).

(ii) Remote Terminal Units (RTU's)

There are eight micro based Hydril RTU's (Figure 5). Software within the RTU responds to commands from the Hewlett Packard via the MTU or to commands from the MTU to scan process inputs. These inputs may be in the form of status inputs, analog inputs or accumulator (pulse) inputs.

RTU software also calculates flow rates using active pressure, temperatures and differential pressure inputs in conjunction with fluid and meter run dependent parameters. These parameters are resident in the HP/1000 system and are downloaded by the field operators whenever any parameter changes. This ensures that the RTU files are consistent with the HP files.

(iii) Communications Cabling

A buried communications cable system connects the MTU to the RTU's. The communications operates at a speed of 1200 BAUD.

(iv) Master Terminal Unit (MTU)

The RCA micro based MTU operates in two modes: normal and backup. The current mode is determined by the status of the HP/1000 field computer. If the link is functioning by periodically being polled by the HP, the MTU is in the normal mode; otherwise, it is in the backup mode.

(a) Normal Mode

In normal mode of operation, the MTU operates as a communication interface for the HP computer. Requests from the HP are reformatted by the MTU into standard RTU communications sequences and sent to the RTU's. Responses from the RTU's are checked for validity, reformatted and sent to the HP computer. If no communications are recieved from the HP within 5 minutes, the MTU assumes the HP has failed and will switch to backup mode. The MTU will transfer a HP-2635A printer to itself and discontinue any further attempts to communicate with the HP.

(b) Backup Mode

When the MTU is in the backup mode, it will continuously scan the status inputs on all RTU's and log all changes of state on the HP-2635A printer. The man machine interface between the operator and MTU is the printer and its associated keyboard.

2. HP/1000 PRISP Field Functions

The HP Field Computer System gathers raw data and flow rates from the RTU's, makes any necessary engineering unit conversions and calculations and stores the values in disk files. The data is gathered constantly during a 24 hour period. In order to discuss what kinds of data is collected, the following functions of the HP system must be discussed:

(i) Automatic and Continuous Scanning of End Elements

Automatic scanning operates in a polling fashion. RTU's are regularly sent commands which trigger the transmission of raw element readings. In Peace River, end elements are typically scanned every 2,5 and 5 minutes for status, analogs and accumulators respectively. The main area of concern are the analog values. In addition to the engineering unit values, the daily average, daily high and daily low values are calculated. Some typical analogs include Bottom Hole temperatures and pressures, tubing head temperatures and casing head pressures.

(ii) Meter Flow Measurements

All orfice meter measurements are accomplished by the micro RTU's. They are scanned every two minutes by the HP, accumulated and stored in meter files. Some typical meter flow rates include gas, diluent, water and steam.

(iii) Semi-Automatic Well Testing

Semi-automatic well testing (AWT) is the primary production surveillance tool. Wells are individually tested with the control logic and metering coming from the HP. Semi-automatic well testing by which wells are manually switched to test, either by remote or local control, can be used to accumulate and report test data. This data is used by field operators to more quickly detect abnormalities in a wells production. In addition, all daily data is stored in files on the disk for transmission to Calgary.

(iv) Down Hole Temperature.Profiling

Observation wells have been provided with thermocouple cable winders. These units allow the operator to traverse a thermocouple down a well bore in either manual mode or in computer mode. The basic operation is as follows:

When a profile is initiated, the probe is lowered to a pre-set depth. The cable winder is then moved upwards in pre-set incremental depth settings. At each depth increment, the profile stops long enough to allow the temperature reading to stabilize and then a temperature reading is taken. When the profile reaches an upper depth setting it stops and is lowered to the formation hot spot.

The result of the profile is a record of temperature versus depth and is a useful tool in monitoring the movement of reservior hot spots. All data collected for each observation well profile is saved for transmission to Calgary.

(v) Trending

The Hewlett Packard has the capacity to trend 64 end elements on both a short-term and long-term basis (short-term being approximately every 5 minutes). Trending merely uses those values obtained by the computer system in its last scan. The end elements that are trended during the 24 hour period are collected and stored in a large (320 blocks) trend file for transmission to Calgary at the end of the day.

(vi) Operator Comment Data

As a communication tool between the field operators in Peace River and the Data Base Administration in Calgary a mechanism to record any abnormalities or extra information about field operations was implemented. These comments are collected on a daily basis for transmission to Calgary.

(vii) Well Status Change Data

To provide extra information about individual production, injection and observation wells, the current well status, the total daily up-hours and a downtime indicator code were required by reservior engineers in Calgary. This data is collected for the day for transmission to Calgary.

- Transmission of PRISP Data to Calgary

After the entire suite of data has been collected by the PRISP field computer for a 24 hour period, the field computer has certain basic tasks to perform at midnight by a Field Day-End-Processing program (FDEP).

Firstly, the current live files are copied into transient daily files. There are transient daily files for each day of the week. This implies that data at the field location can be backed up for a maximum of 7 days incase the leased line communications (AGT) is not available.

Secondly, after the transient files are created for the day, certain reinitialization of live files is performed in order for the next days processing to proceed. Some related activities are:

(a) resetting the daily average, daily high and daily low analog values
(b) determining the previous daily flow rates
(c) resetting the trend file variables to allow the next days collection of trend data
(d) clearing the comment data file for the next days comments
(e) initializing the uphours and the downtime code in the Well Status file

After the live files are reinitialized, normal scanning and data acquisition in the field computer resumes.

Thirdly, the transient data files are transmitted via DS/1000 to the Central Real Time HP. Because of leased communication line problems, special software routines were programmed to allow software retransmissions. Even though DS/1000 handles most short spurious line problems, we found that the additional software retries were necessary to insure that the files arrived at the Central Real Time computer.

Fourthly, after the PRISP computer has transmitted the files successfully, a Central Day End Processing Program (CDEP) is scheduled via DS/1000. At this point in time, the field computer has completed its tasks and the Central Real Time computer in Calgary takes control of data.

- CAO Central Real Time Computer

After the Central Day End Processing Program (CDEP) is scheduled at Central Real Time, the daily data transmitted from Peace River goes through some reformatting as explained in the following steps:

(i) Each of the types of data mentioned previously is reformatted from field binary file format to card images. The file created is equivalent to approximately 2000 - 3000 card images.

(ii) After the card image file is created, RJE/1000 is initiated and a batch job is transmitted over a 9600 BAUD dedicated line to the host Univac 1100/44 mainframe where it is further processed and stored on a data base. The data on the Univac data base is available for generating reports, studies and simulations by the engineers in Calgary and the operating personnel in Peace River.

III. PRISP Specific Communication Problems

Two specific problems were encountered while the PRISP project was being implemented. They are described in further detail below:

(i) DS/1000 Transmission Problems

Because the leased communication line between Peace River and Calgary has spurious interupts or noise, the data files could not be transmitted successfully. The most troublesome was the large 320 block (128 words/block) daily trend file. After many days of trouble shooting it was determined the HP protocol between the PRISP node and the Central Real Time node was not handshaking properly on a noisy line. Consequently, the transmissions would result in incomplete trend files which required manual intervention before the RJE/1000 batch job could be transmitted. To bypass the problem, the software was modified. Previously the entire 320 block trend file was retried 3 times by the DS/1000 "FCOPY" subroutine. The field program was modified to retry each block of the file 10 times. This software modification in conjunction with consistant technician assistance in limiting noise on the line has recified problems to a tolerable state. Refer to Figure 6.

(ii) <u>RJE/1000 Abnormal Terminations</u>

Another major obstacle was the occasional abnormal termination of the batch job transmitted from the Central Real Time Computer to the mainframe Univac 1100/44. The HP RJE/1000 Emulator enables the Central HP to act like an IBM 2780 port to a CHI front end processor to the Univac. After rearranging the HP hardware boards, regenerating the operating system and many hours of monitoring and testing the problem was finally discovered. The CHI front end processor was transmitting an unrecognizable character to the HP which caused the bi-sync protocol handshaking to go out of step. At the time of printing, the systems programmers in our Calgary Computing Centre are analysing the problem.

IV. Summary

Except for the problems previously mentioned, the entire network operates very successfully. The network could be viewed as a large chain with the following links:

- SCADA subsystem
- HP/1000 PRISP Computer
- Peace River to Calgary leased line
- HP/1000 Central Real Time Computer
- RJE/1000 Emulator
- CHI front end processor and Univac 1100/44

If any link in the chain is malfunctioning or out of service, the transmission of data is broken. The highest probability of this happening is expected in the Peace River to Calgary leased line. Moreover, all programs in the network are designed to recover from communication line failures when they occur with no loss in data.

Overall, the PRISP information system that was developed is a large and ambitious one. Its successful completion required the coordinated efforts of several departments within Shell Canada Resources. The information could ultimately lead to the development of a full scale Insitu commercial project.

TABLE I

CAO MINI COMPUTER HARDWARE

Computer Name	CPU	Memory (K words)	Disk Type	Number of Terminals (26XX)	Number of Printers * LP	SS
Central Real Time	2113-E	144	7905	5	1	1
Central Development	2117-F	256	7906 7920 7900	6	1	1
Harmattan East	2112-M	96	7906	3	1	-
Waterton	2113-E	128	7905	5	1	4
Burnt Timber	2113-E	144	7906	3	1	1
Peace River Insitu	2113-E	160	7906	4	1	-
Jumping Pound	2113-E	128	7906	4	-	-
Limestone	2113-E	128	7906	5	-	-

* LP - line printer
SS - subsystem printers

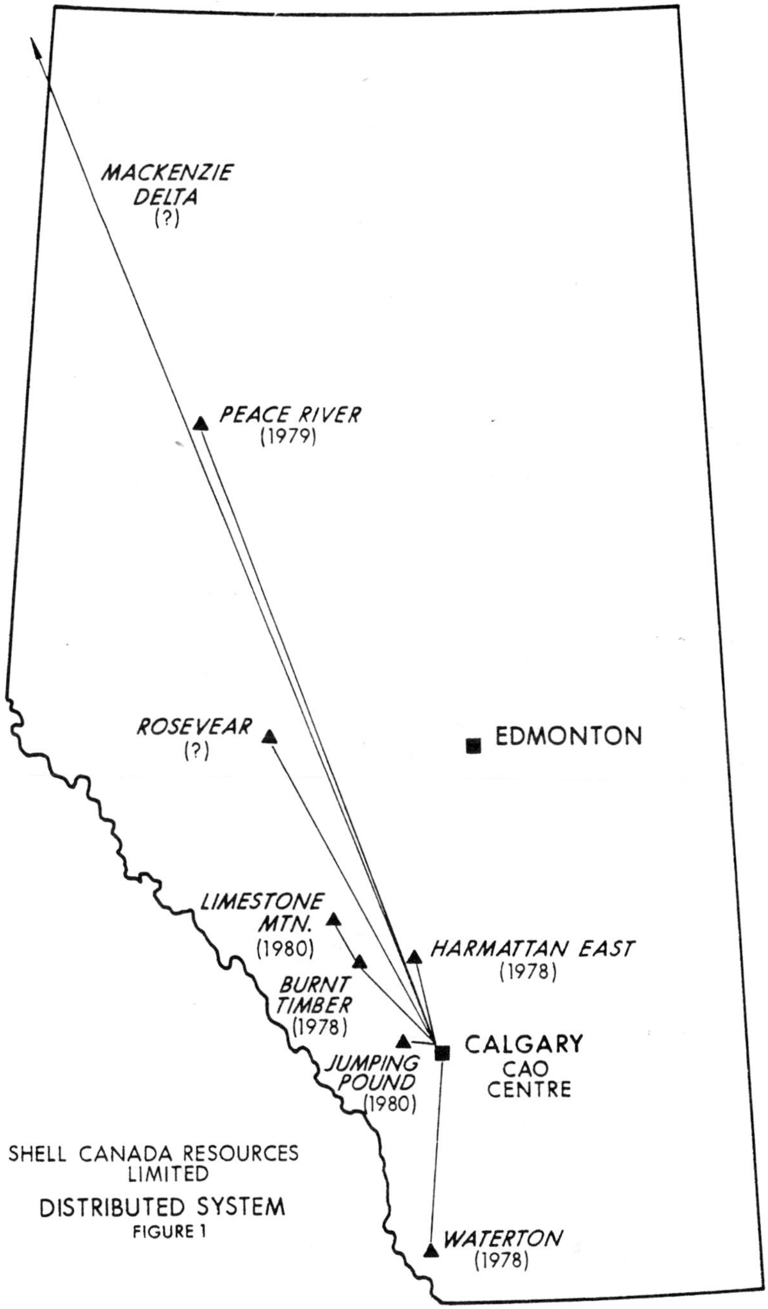

SHELL CANADA RESOURCES LIMITED

DISTRIBUTED SYSTEM

FIGURE 1

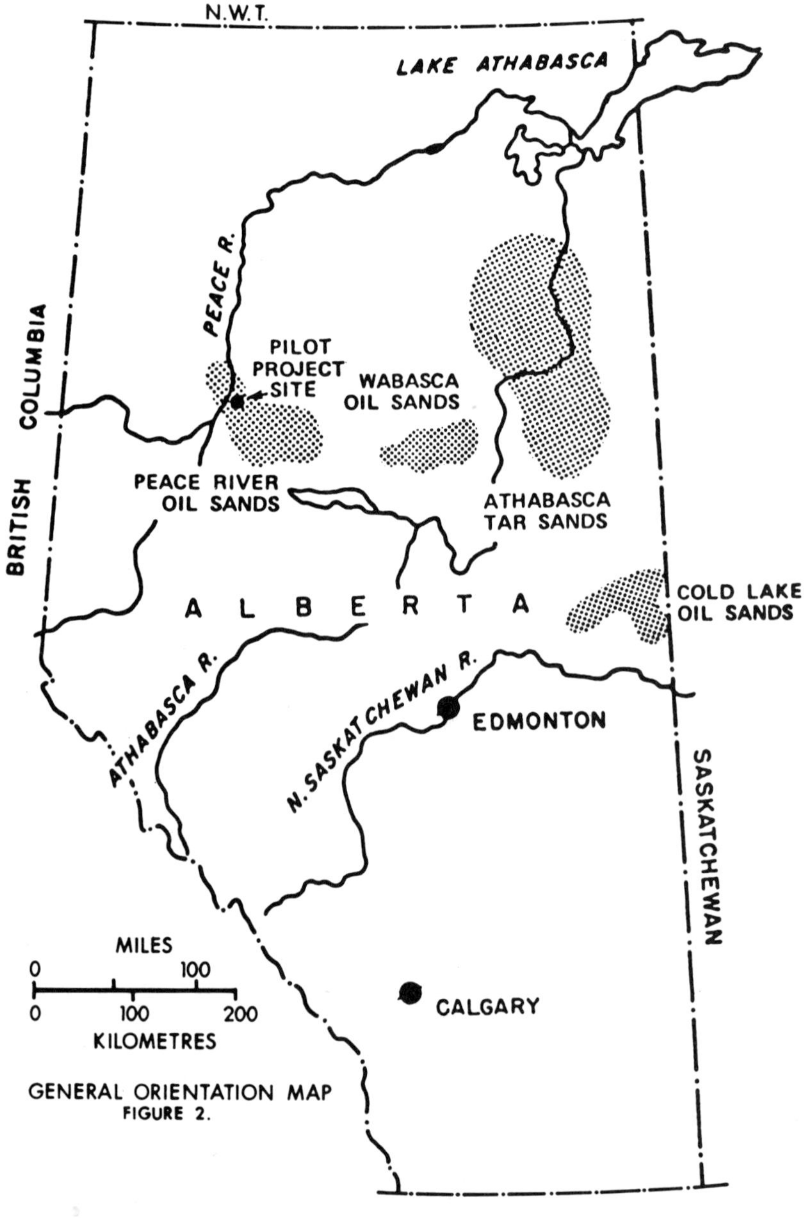

GENERAL ORIENTATION MAP
FIGURE 2.

DISTRIBUTED NETWORK BLOCK DIAGRAM

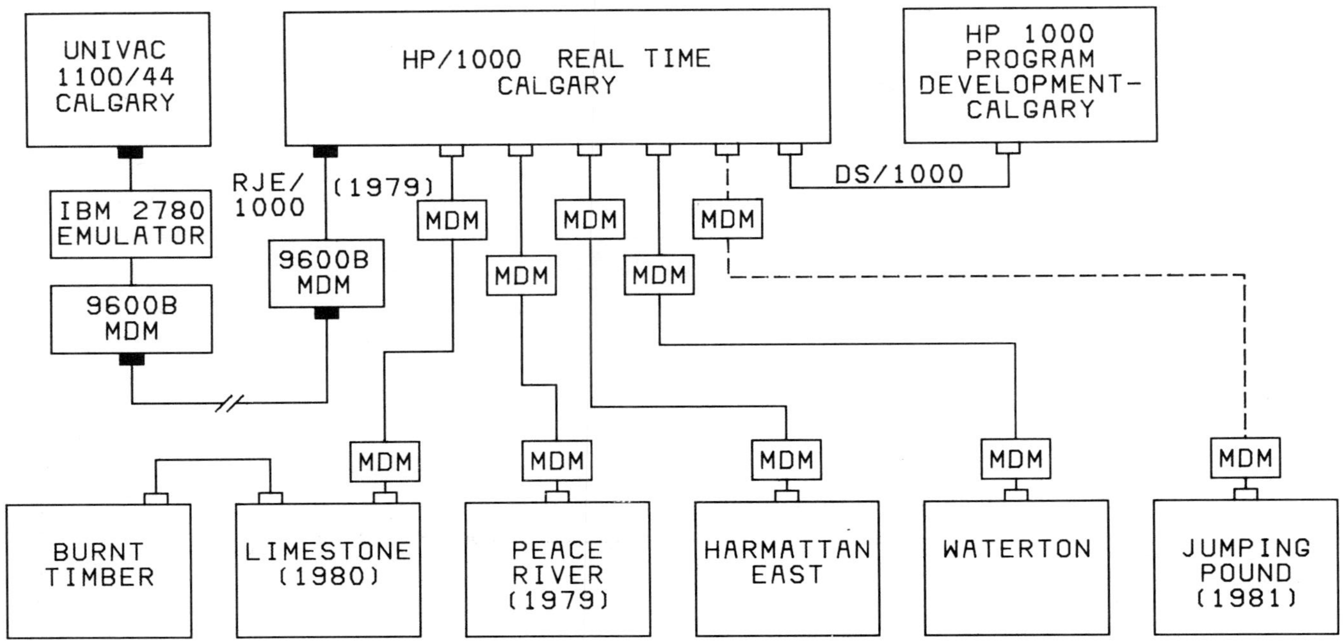

FIGURE 3

P0108C

PRISP INFORMATION NETWORK

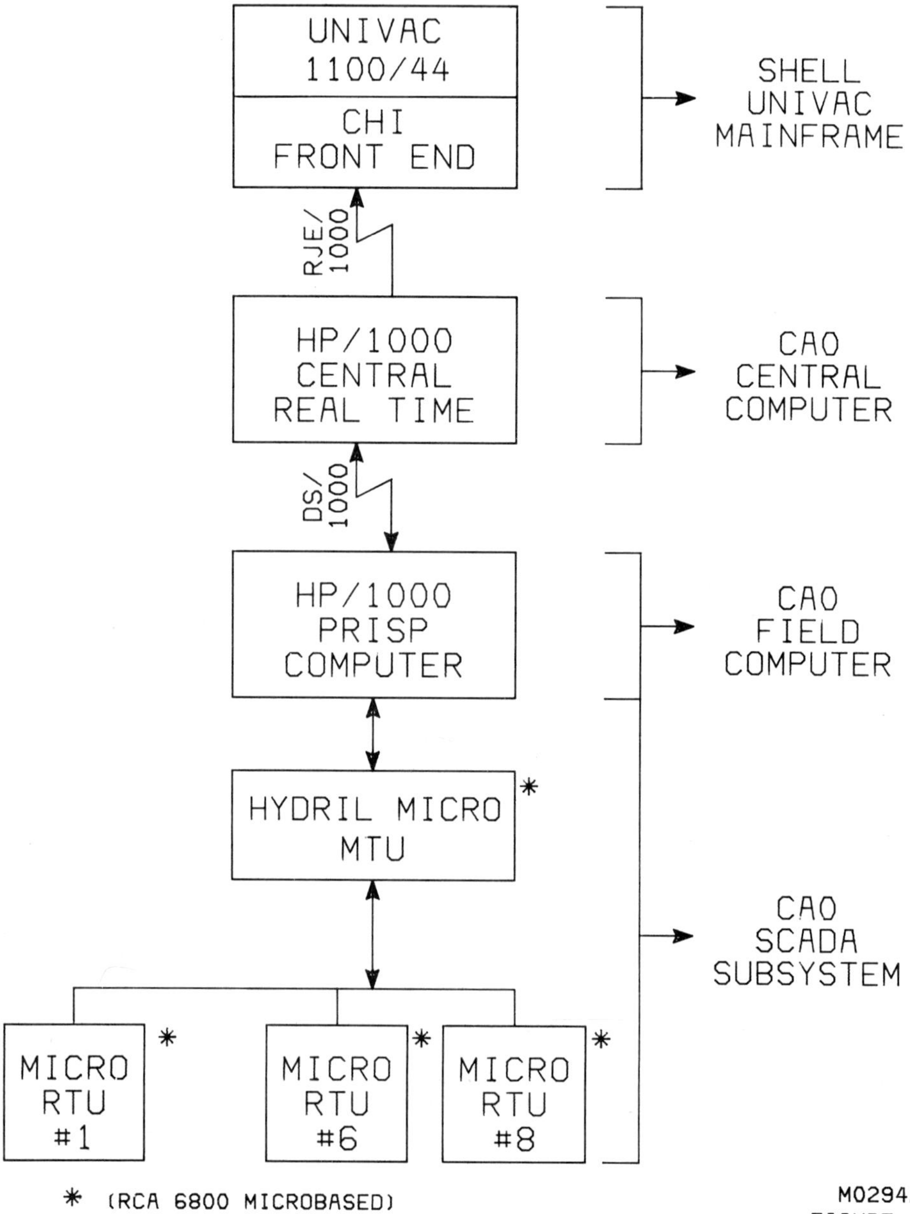

M0294A
FIGURE 4

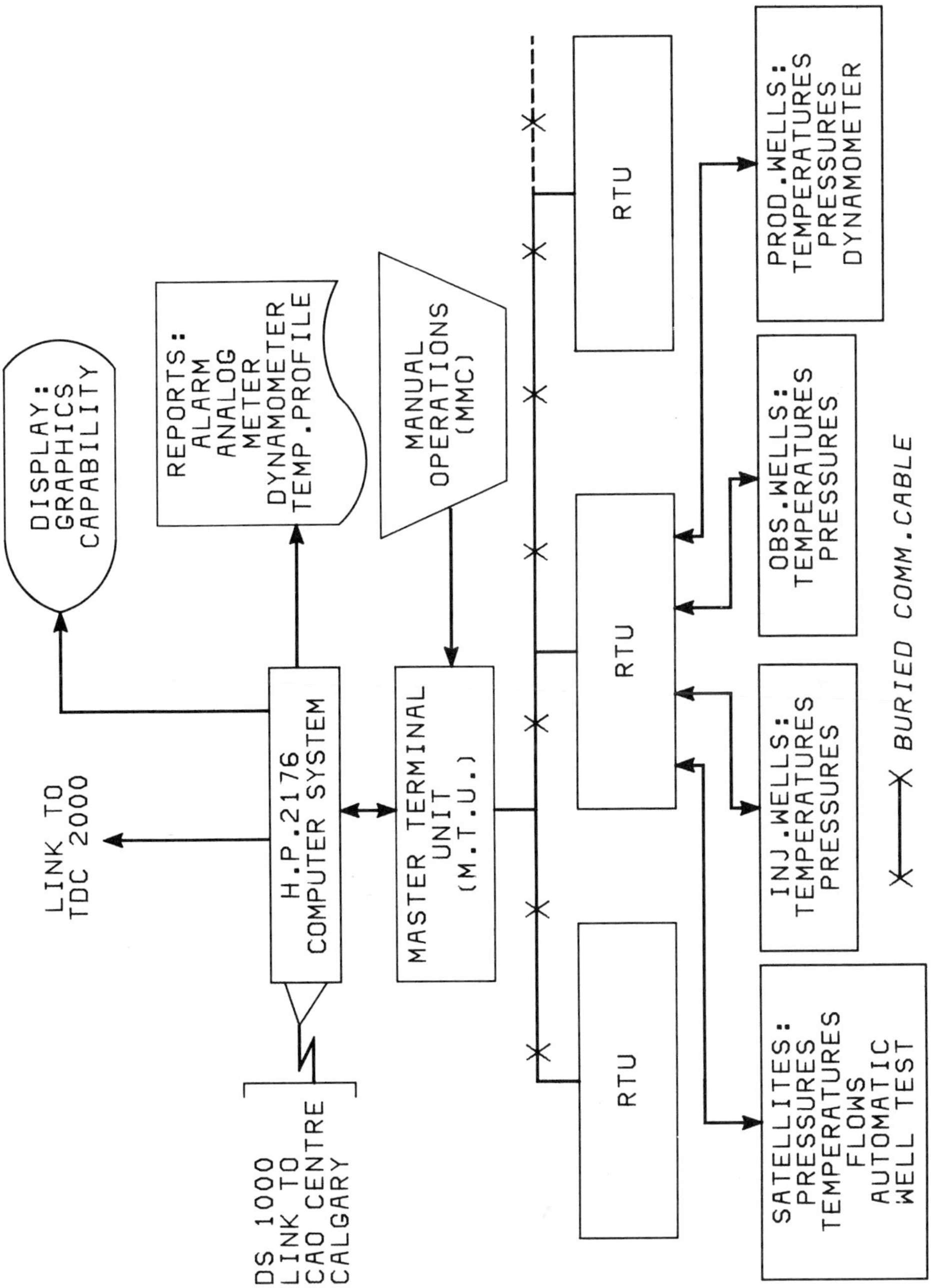

FIELD SCADA SYSTEM

FIGURE 5
I0016B

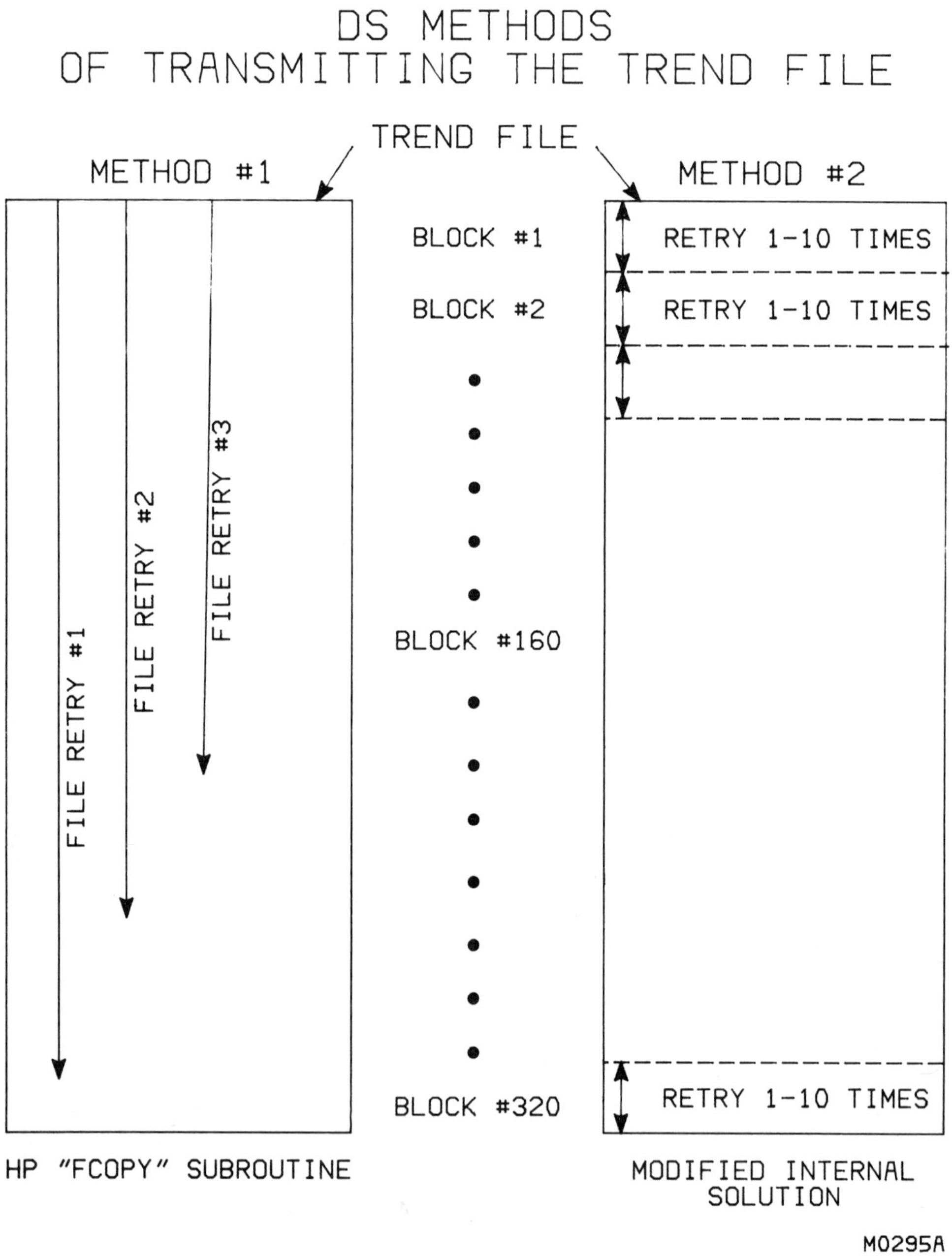
DS METHODS
OF TRANSMITTING THE TREND FILE
TREND FILE
METHOD #1
METHOD #2
FILE RETRY #1
FILE RETRY #2
FILE RETRY #3
BLOCK #1
BLOCK #2
BLOCK #160
BLOCK #320
RETRY 1-10 TIMES
RETRY 1-10 TIMES
RETRY 1-10 TIMES
HP "FCOPY" SUBROUTINE
MODIFIED INTERNAL SOLUTION
M0295A

FIGURE 6

system performance utilities

Robert T. Scranton
Gerber Systems Technology
South Windsor, Connecticut

ABSTRACT

To remain competitive in the turnkey graphics industry, we must be continually aware of system performance, and strive to improve it. Utilizing intricacies of the RTE environment, powerful software tools can be developed to aid us in that effort.

Most of us have, at one time or another, obtained a gross measure of system performance, even if only to the extent of "Wow, that's fast ! ", or "This takes forever". Going beyond that, however, in the search of bottlenecks can be a rather arduous taks. There is a definite need for powerful but simple to use tools for both the applications programmer who would like to see a faster system, to the systems analyst whose job depends on it.

Responding to this need has resulted in the development of two interesting utilities. The first, a CPU utilization display program, provides a continual indication of the CPU utilization via the S-register. This can give a quick indication as to whether a program is a candidate for further study, by differentiating CPU versus IO bound programs. Candidates can then be studied in detail with the help of the second utility, SPY.

I. CPU Utilization Display Program

In the interest of having a visual display of current CPU utilization, a simple FORTRAN program was developed (to be called THERM).

THERM is a disk-resident program which executes at priority 32767, the lowest possible. Any other programs will thus "preempt" THERM in the battle for CPU usage. THERM executes continuously, performing the following tasks:

1. Get the current time
2. Execute a constant section of CPU bound code, Ck
3. Get the current time
4. Determine the elapsed time, and use to calculate the % of CPU being utilized. Display this value via the S-register.
5. Go to 1

As various programs utilize the CPU, the actual time required for THERM to execute Ck (Tac) will increase. The smallest Tac possible (Tmin) can be determined dynamically by THERM in a quiet system. These two values allow us to calculate the percentage of CPU utilization:

$$\%CPU = * (1 - Tac/Tmin)$$

Various methods can be used to display this percentage. In our case we were more interested in qualitative than quantitive results, so we chose a "thermometer" type display (thus the name THERM). Here the number of lights lit is a direct indication of the percentage: ('.' - off 'o' - on)

```
. . . . . . . . . . . . . . . .      =   0%
. . . . . . . . o o o o o o o o      =  50%
o o o o o o o o o o o o o o o o      = 100%
```

The section of code Ck should require a minimum of 16 timebase generator ticks to execute, to assure accuracy of the display. The display can then be updated as often as 16 * 10ms = 160ms, or roughly a 6Hz rate. This has proven to be an attractive update rate for observation. The rate decreases as the CPU utilization increases.

One drawback of the update scheme occurred when a CPU bound program was executing. THERM would not run at all, causing the display to remain in its last (erroneous) state until the CPU bound program finished.

To correct the problem, THERM flip/flops bit 15 of the S-register on each update. A CPU bound program is now characterized by the absence of the blinking bit.

THERM dynamically determines the minimum time to execute Ck, Tmin. This results in a display which indicates percentage of available CPU. If Tmin is determined beforehand, using the instruction execution times provided by HP, the display will indicate the actual CPU utilization, including system overhead. An idle CPU will display about 6%, as opposed to the 0% of the previous method. The advantage of the former method lies in the independence from the execution speeds of different CPU's.

II. Software Monitor for Determining Possible Performance Yields (SPY)

Details of the operation of a basic RTE operating system can prove very useful to those of us interested in performance. The ID segment of an executing program contains a wealth of dynamic information about the program. All we need is a method of extracting it for later use.

SPY was written to fill that need. As the name implies, SPY will monitor any RTE program, providing the following details concerning the execution of the program:

1. The percentage of time spent in each of the six active RTE states (1-6).
2. A further reduction of state 2 (I/O wait) into the actual logical units accessed, as well as the percentage of time spent with each.
3. The frequency of execution of sections of code, down to the instruction level, for the main and each segment.

SPY executes at priority 1, hopefully higher than the monitored program (MP). Placing itself into the time list, SPY is able to take a 'snapshot' of the MP every T*10 milliseconds, where T is specified by the user. It does this by extracting information from the ID segment of the MP (nicely provided by RTE). Perhaps the best part of the scheme is that SPY is totally external to the MP. No modifications to or reloading of the MP is necessary.

The overhead involved in using SPY can be appreciable. RTE overhead required to schedule SPY every TBG tick was measured at 40% (this is the expected increase in execution time of the MP). The additional overhead required by the actual SPY code amounts to only 3-6%, hardly motivation enough to convert from FORTRAN to assembly. In any case, the increase in execution time does not affect the results of SPY, which are all reported as percentages. By sampling the MP less often than every 10ms, the overhead is reduced proportionately, becoming insignificant at a 50ms sample interval.

The sampling technique used by SPY was initially questioned in its ability to accurately determine, to the instruction level, the busy areas of code. Our doubts were quickly removed by writing a small FORTRAN program which, by design, provides 10 sections of code which will utilize a predetermined percentage of total execution time. Using SPY to collect a minimum of 1000 samples quickly removed our doubts, as the expected percentages were indicated exactly.

Conclusions

THERM has proven very helpful in indicating where we should concentrate our time in improving system performance. The simplicity of its display has been its major asset. One can easily gain a gut feeling for the CPU time available.

SPY has been in use for only a short time, and has yet to reach its potential as a performance tool. Expanding on the monitor methods presented, there is a number of possibilities for special-purpose monitor programs. What RTE provides by necessity can prove very useful those of us interested in system performance.

DATACAP/1000 to "COSMIC" HP/3000 data-base communication

Daniel Pot

Hewlett-Packard Grenoble
5 Avenue Raymond-Chanas
38320 EYBENS (FRANCE)

ABSTRACT

The main application is a complete set of subsystems providing for automatic customer order processing and on-line tracking of the related instruments in a computer manufacturing environment. The commercial and tracking functions are roughly split between an HP-3000 and an HP-1000 mainframe. The HP-1000 tracks the instruments from their birth to their stock entrance ("hot" production areas) and the HP-3000 performs all the Booking, Run-maintenance, Reporting ... and tracks the instruments beyond the stock (administrative task). In order to guarantee accurate reports, the HP-3000 "COSMIC" data-base is updated on-line by the transactions performed on the HP-1000 data-capture system.

Overall system description.

Production tracking system.

HP-1000 to HP-3000 communication.

Performances and conclusion.

1 - Overall system description

1 - 1 Hewlett-Packard Grenoble presentation

H.P. Grenoble is a complete division belonging to the H.P. Computers Group. It manufactures mini-computers and terminals, integrates HP-1000 systems and repairs computers for the European market.

1 - 2 Customer's order handling

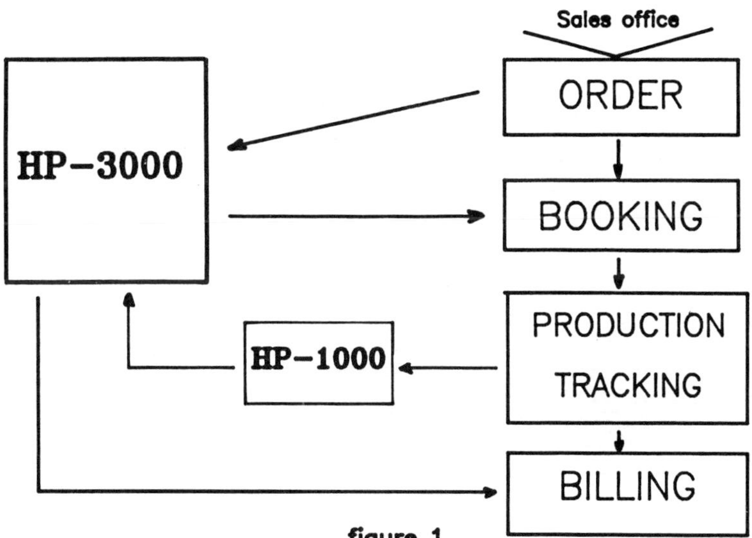

figure 1

Every day the factory receives customer orders from sales offices via the internal communication system: COMSYS. These orders are automatically entered in the HP-3000 COSMIC data-base. They are acknowledged with a proposed delivery date. This backlog is used to plan the production for the following months. Knowing the production capacity of the plant, runs are manually opened at the beginning of each month through an interactive utility. At the time to start production, each run is "broken-down" i.e. each instrument to be produced is assigned an identification number plus a travelling identification card on which this six digit number is marked and printed.

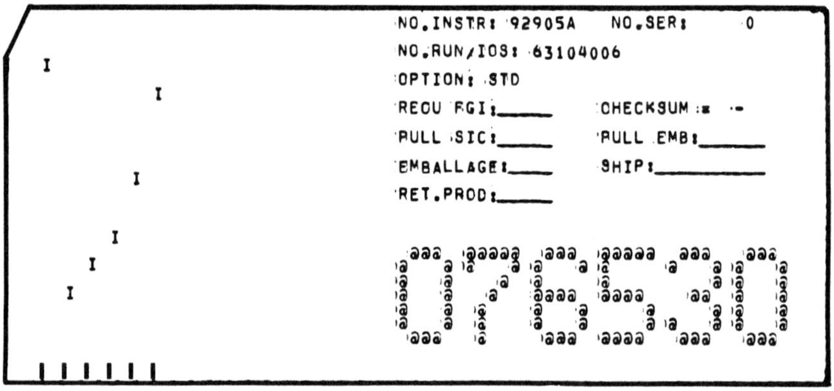

figure 2

Then the instrument moves along each of the steps of its factory life and is tracked at each step. When it is ready to be shipped it is grouped with all the items of the order on which it is allocated, is packed and shipped. The bill is automatically issued at shipping time.

At this point it is possible to identify two different business levels:

The commercial level: Marketing and Finance departments will focus on the order-processing and shipment-billing business.

The production level: Production management will instead focus on the flow of the instruments through the factory. To help them in this task they use the tracking system. Thanks to several measurement points in the production pipe-line they try to reduce the inventory to the minimum level compatible with the production capacity.

1 - 3 Hardware E.D.P. organization

The whole system is organized around one HP-3000 MPE system and one HP-1000 RTE system. The HP-3000 includes four disc drives (792X) offering about 500 Mega-bytes capacity, two magnetic tape drives and a fast line printer. Memory capacity is one Mega-byte. The HP-1000 includes two disc drives (7905) offering about 30 Mega-bytes capacity, one magnetic tape drive and 382 K bytes of core memory. These two mainframes are connected directly to one another, using the HP Distributed Systems capability.

2 - Production tracking system

2 - 1 Hardware DATACAPture system

Each time an instrument physically moves from one location to another, an operator enters its travelling card in the corresponding datacapture station in order to reflect this move in the data-bases in charge of recording these changes. Production stations are equiped with 307XB terminals connected to the HP-1000 system via a multi-drop link which "runs" everywhere in the factory: the cable ranges about 300 meters in length. The stations beyond the stock use a 7260A optical-mark-reader (in order to be able to stack the travelling cards) connected to a 264X video-terminal in a point-to-point communication mode with an HP-3000. These stations are shared with other administrative users.

2 - 2 Data-bases

The HP-1000 system is in charge of an IMAGE/1000 data-base called ITRAK which records all the transactions performed until the stock entrance. Each move is recorded by placing the date of the move in the appropriate field. Additional data may be provided by the operator at the time of the transaction and is saved in appropriate locations. Simultaneously, each transaction is sent to the HP-3000 system in order to maintain the IMAGE/3000 data-base , COSMIC. Up to 20,000 entries are available in ITRAK.

The HP-3000 system handles the COSMIC data-base which has a double function: first of all, it is dedicated to the customer's orders processing, then it is in charge of maintaining the run-book and following each instrument in the plant. Each time a transaction is performed, on any site (HP-1000 or HP-3000), the status and date fields of the corresponding instrument are updated. Up to 40,000 entries are available in COSMIC which allow to follow more than three months of planned production and one month of effective production (up to 200 references).

As can be seen, the way of recording moves is different on the two systems. The HP-1000 retains more information for production and Quality control management and the HP-3000 provides exact and on-line information about the status of any instrument.

2 - 3 Logical locations and moves within the plant

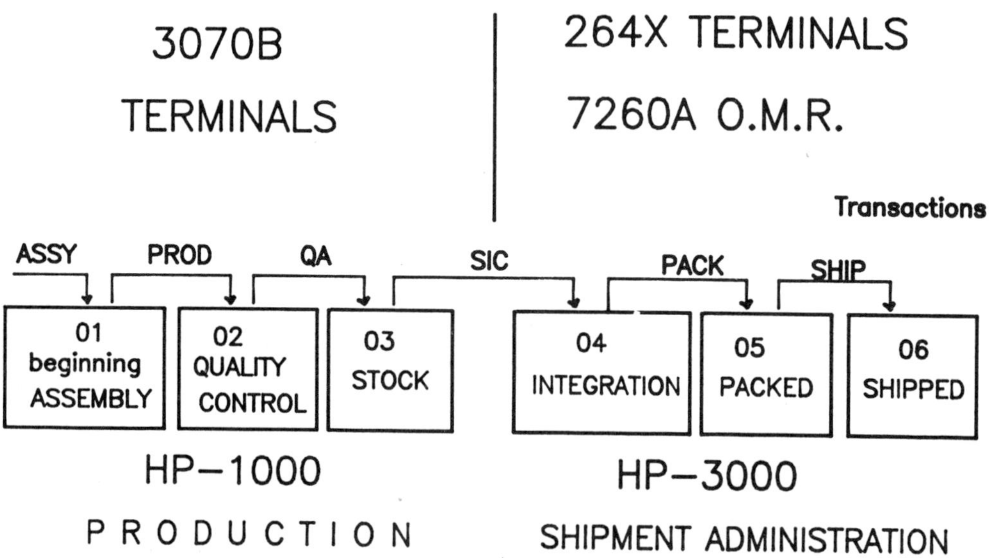

figure 3

These locations have been designated according to the needs of production management.

Location "00".
....

The instrument belongs to a broken-down run. it is identified by a travelling card but is not physically built.

Location "01".
....

The instrument begins to exist as a physical unit: this step is recorded thanks to the "ASSY" transaction.

Location: "02".
....

The instrument completes the production process, completely tested: this step is recorded thanks to the "PROD" transaction. At this level, the instrument is considered as being in the Quality Control area.

Location: "03".
....

The instrument leaves the Quality Control area or directly arrives in the Stock area (coming from another factory). This step is recorded by the transaction "QA" which provides extended information for warranty statistical purposes.
This is the last step "captured" by the HP-1000 system: these steps require very short response times (instruments are processed one by one) and are captured in many areas in the plant: 5 "ASSY" and "PROD" terminals and 2 "QA" terminals. Beyond this level, the tracking is done by the "heavy" stations, on the HP-3000.

Location: "04".
....

The instrument is about to be packed. In some particular cases it has to be integrated with others to build a system. This step is recorded by the transaction "SIC" (which means "System Integration Center"). Starting from there, as an instrument leaves the Stock, we check that it has already been allocated to a customer order, either automatically or manually.

Location: "05".
....

The instrument is packed and is ready to be shipped. This step is recorded by the transaction "PACK".

Location: "06".
....

The instrument has been shipped. This step is recorded by the transaction "SHIP": before accepting the transaction it is checked that all the options required by the customer are correct and that the components of the shipment matches with the order. If everything is O.K., the bill is immediately printed along with customs papers.

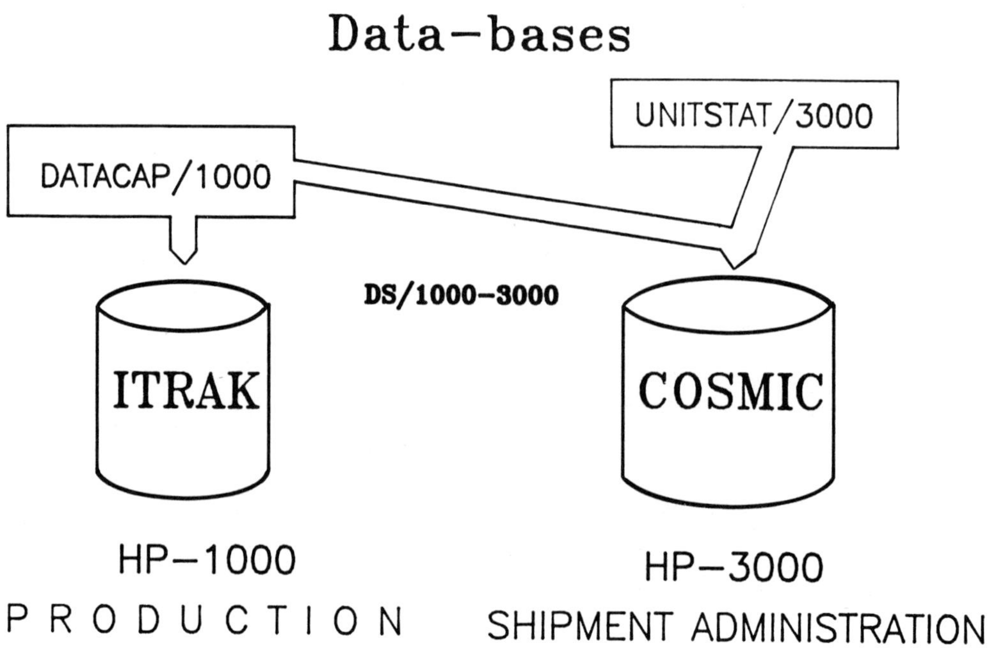

2 - 4 Production management reporting

At the end of every day, the whole COSMIC data-base and PROLOG logging data-base (for safety purposes) are serially analyzed in order to fill the SPRAPR data-base which is dedicated to reporting. For each instrument type, there is a chain, with one entry per day including two counters per location: one to totalize the moves "in" and the other to totalize the "actual" number of units. Thanks to this architecture it is possible to know exactly the inventory and the flow of each location (either in unit numbers or in dollars amount). This tool allows production management to very efficiently identify bottlenecks in the production pipeline and to compare actual results with those planned.

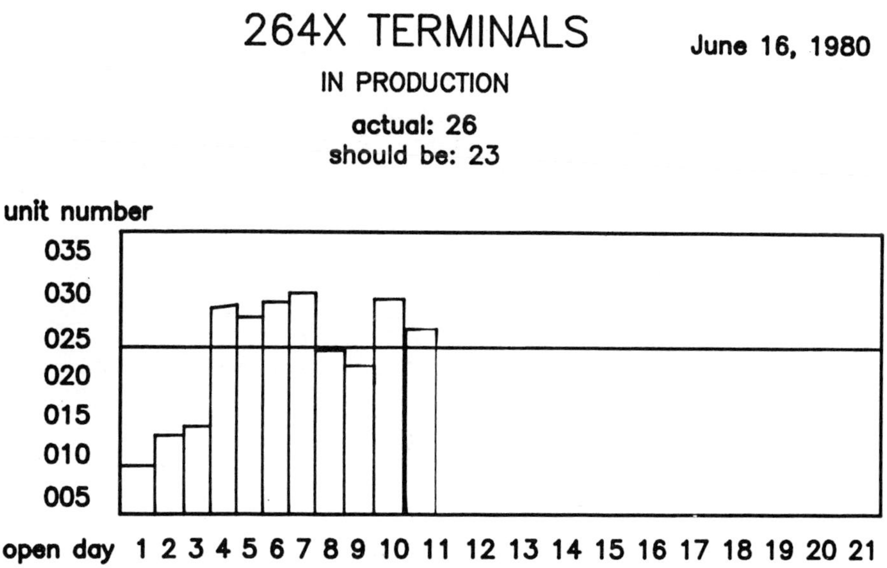

Figure 5

2 - 5 Controls and safety

Controls

Before accepting any travelling card, several validations are performed to prevent from contaminating the data-base.

The first marked column on each travelling card is the checksum of the last five digits: at reading time the read checksum is compared with the calculated one.

Only valid moves are accepted.

Safety

Each transaction is logged into the external PROLOG data-base for recovery purposes. In case of irrecoverable damage of COSMIC, it is possible to recover a full working day, starting from the previous back-up, within half an hour.

At the end of every day, the HP-1000 ITRAK data-base is double checked then saved. First test checks for all detail data set integrity (chain continuity), second test indicates the capacity of all data sets, the number of free records and the number of records used in each data set. Once this task is done, the data base is saved onto a magnetic tape, in a compact format (6144 words per record and a checksum) and finally verified.

On the HP-3000 side, the COSMIC data-base is saved everyday after a complete test on the PROLOG data base to make sure that all transactions of the day were correctly performed.

In case the HP-3000 system is off and the communication with the HP-1000 is interrupted for more than 5 hours, it is possible to mail all the transactions captured by the HP-1000 onto the HP-3000 as soon as the HP-3000 restarts thanks to an emergency utility (by using the local logging file of the HP-1000). Practically the HP-1000 is able to track instruments for two days, without any communication with the HP-3000: in some particular cases, this can be very useful.

3 - HP-1000 to HP-3000 communication

The tracking part, on the HP-1000 side, has been implemented using the DATACAP/1000 software package to reduce software investment. The major remaining task was to establish the communication with the HP-3000 using the DS/1000-3000 software package.

3 - 1 HP-1000 side

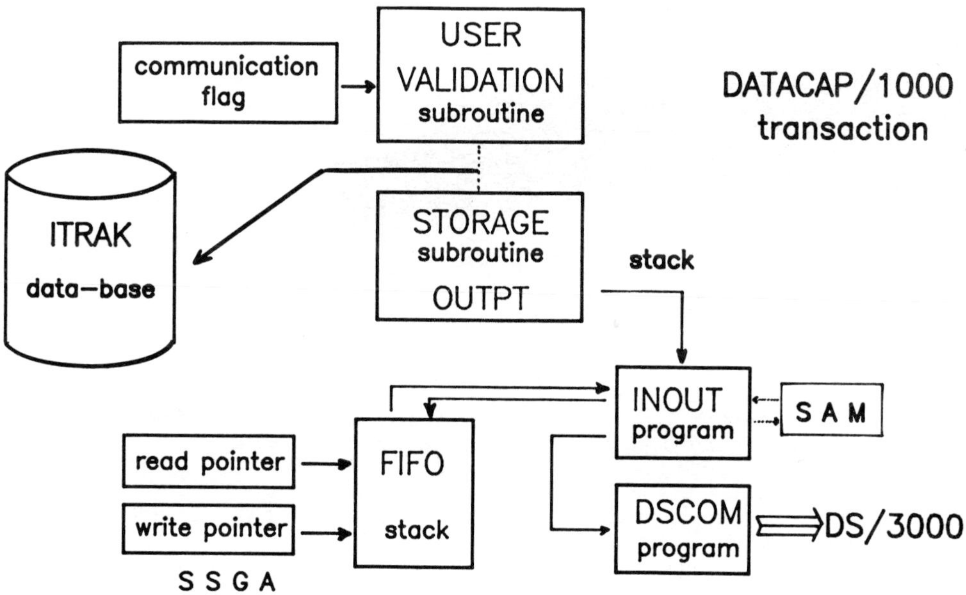

figure 6

At the end of each transaction, the DATACAP/1000 allows the user to store the result of his dialogue into a sequential file by calling a "storage user's module". In this case, it is not necessary to use this capability, but it is the appropriate time to mail the transaction onto the HP-3000: all of the required updates have been performed on the ITRAK data-base.

Storage User's Module "OUTPT"

This subroutine just prepares the buffer to be mailed and passes it to an HP-1000 First-In-First-Out stack. The only absolutely required data are: the identification number of the concerned instrument, the transaction type, eventually some additionnal information provided while performing the transaction (for instance the date-code of the instrument which must be entered just before entering location "02"), and the actual date and time of day. The 15 words long buffer is then passed to the System Available Memory at this time to schedule the program in charge of handling the F.I.F.O.: INOUT

```
CALL EXEC (23,INOUT,....,IBUF,15)
```

The INOUT program is scheduled "with wait", because it is the only process allowed to access the F.I.F.O for stacking or unstacking purposes: while waiting for execution, the whole Transaction Monitor Software is pending on this particular transaction; thus it is a very short and fast program, without any physical Input/Output operation such as disc transfers...

I N O U T process

This program includes the F.I.F.O stack which is able to record up to 1200 transactions (i.e. up to 5 hours of work). To save all the swapping time, it is assigned to a reserved partition. To prevent losing pending transactions, it never definitely completes: after each execution (exept for system abortion) it goes "dormant saving its suspension point": CALL EXEC (6,0,1). Three main functions are available:

- stack one transaction (used by OUTPT, but available for any user)
- unstack one transaction (used by the HP-3000 transaction processor)
- close communication between the two systems

The F.I.F.O is managed thanks to two local pointers (read and write). Each time INOUT is scheduled, it returns a good or bad status as a feed-back via PRTM and RMPAR system library subroutines. In case the stack happens to be full (i.e. the HP-3000 has a problem and does not any longer poll the HP-1000), a flag is set and all the Data-capture 307XB terminals are locked: it is no longer possible to continue; a message is displayed on system console. This is very important to insure the perfect integrity of both the COSMIC and ITRAK data-bases.

This program runs in a 13 K words partition, using the Subsystem Global Area for flag purposes.

F.I.F.O unstacking: mailing to HP-3000

The HP-1000 is considered as the slave of the HP-3000 in the distributed scheme. Each time transactions are required by the master , the DSCOM slave program is scheduled in the HP-1000. This program is in charge of processing the "program-to-program" communication scheme using the POPEN, PREAD, PWRITE and FINIS of the DS/1000-3000 library. Each time it is scheduled, it first verifies the legality of the protocol, accepting or rejecting depending upon the status; after that the INOUT process is scheduled "with-wait" for reading purposes, 17 consecutive times, in order to prepare the buffer to be transmitted (it groups 17 transactions at a time). Then a checksum is appended at the end of this buffer and it is passed to the HP-3000. Data communication between INOUT and DSCOM is performed via System Available Memory. The Tag field of the P.to.P scheme is used to return a status to the HP-3000. In case of communication problems, DSCOM is able to recognize a Retransmit order and to send the same buffer again.
The number of transactions has been optimized in order to better use the hardware capacity of the communication buffer between the two systems which ranges 256 words per physical block.

3 - 2 HP-3000 side

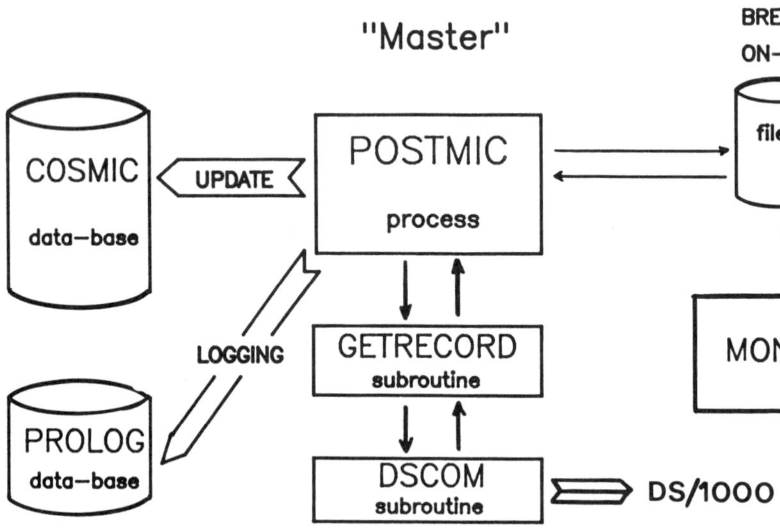

Figure 7

As soon as the whole tracking subsystem is started, the POSTMIC process is activated, either in session or in batch (depending upon the system activity). This process is split into two main blocks: one to retrieve transactions from the HP-1000 site and the other to execute these transactions on the COSMIC data-base. This process stays active the entire working day because it must be able to handle the transactions coming from the HP-1000 as soon as they are available. Two main subroutines have been developed to achieve the communication function: GETRECORD and DSCOM. Each time one transaction has been locally processed, POSTMIC asks for the next one by issuing a call to GETRECORD.

GETRECORD subroutine

This subroutine retrieves transactions from the HP-1000, 17 at a time, and locally buffers them. Then it delivers one transaction at a time either directly from its own buffer (if not empty) or from a new one. In case there are no transactions to mail, the whole process is suspended for 5 seconds. Each time it is necessary to fill up the local buffer, a call is issued to the DSCOM subroutine which handle the P.to.P DS-3000/1000 scheme. If the returned communication status is not good, 5 attempts at retransmitting are issued before closing the DS-line.

DSCOM subroutine

This subroutine may be considered as the "master" of the "slave" DSCOM HP-1000 program. Thanks to calls to POPEN, PREAD, PCHECK and PCLOSE instrinsics, it executes a program handshake with the HP-1000.

3 - 3 Communication management

It is very important to have the capability to start and stop this communication cleanly. The start-up is not a problem, assuming the system was correctly stopped. The whole HP-1000 side is started using the DATACAP/1000 DCMON utility. A flag is set in the S.S.G.A area to declare the HP-1000/3000 communication link open. Before performing any transaction, a DATACAP user-validation module checks for this flag: if not set, the returned status is always bad. Starting from there, transactions may be performed on the HP-1000 site: they are automatically stacked in the F.I.F.O.

It is then wise to start the POSTMIC HP-3000 process in order to make sure that transactions performed on the HP-1000 are immediatly reflected on the COSMIC data-base. This process is protected against inopportune duplication thanks to a resource binary file which is also used to stop the communication.

At the end of every-day, all the data-bases must be saved for safety purposes. Before doing so, the two systems must be stopped. First of all, the DATACAP/1000 is stopped, using the standard DCMON utility: no more transactions are stacked in the F.I.F.O. Then a monitor is automatically scheduled to write an End Of File àt the end of the stack. A few minutes later, the POSTMIC process encounters this EOF and knows that communication must be closed. When the INOUT program was scheduled to unstack the EOF, instead of saving its suspension point it goes permanently dormant.
In emergency cases, it is always possible to interrupt the POSTMIC process without halting Data-capture on the HP-1000

site. Thanks to the monitor, the communication flag is cleared in the S.S.G.A area: this has the effect of temporarily locking all transactions. Then, on the HP-3000 site, a "break" flag is set. This flag is analyzed each time the transaction buffer is empty. If it is set, the POSTMIC process is properly stopped. Then it is possible to reset the communication flag on the HP-1000 site to release the data-capture terminals.

3 - 4 Monitors

On each side of the communication link, and specially on the HP-1000 side, monitors have been developed in order to perform all these start and stop functions. Additionnal functions have been provided, such as the F.I.F.O status display allowing the system manager to know at a glance if everything is going fine.

4 - Performances and conclusion

4 - 1 Performances

More than 3000 transactions are handled every day, on the HP-1000 side, including card reading, checksum validation, data-base FIND, typed-in information, UPDATE and eventually HP-3000 mailing. At peak times, 24 transactions per minute are processed. Depending whether the HP-3000 process runs in session or batch mode, the "delay" between the two systems goes from 0 to a few transactions (17 in the worse case when running in batch mode).

At this level it is important to consider all the "external" parameters involved in this matter. The performance of the POSTMIC process is very strongly dependant upon "logical" parameters:

- number of interactive sessions (it can be up to 27 at a time!).

- number of I/O operations (data-base serial read ...).

- number of JOBS.

and upon "physical" parameters:

- amount of core-memory.

- number of disc drives (separate volumes for virtual memory and data-bases ...).

When we started the trials, the amount of core memory was only 1024 K bytes and there were only two discs drives. Right now we run 2048 K bytes of core memory and five disc drives. But the number of users has drastically increased. Finally it was found that POSTMIC satisfactorily operates in a batch environment.

4 - 2 Conclusion

This communication has been developed around a practically standard DATACAP/1000 (HP92903A revision 1913 !) software. The only "non- standard" feature is the way of using the S.S.G.A. area for flag purposes. It was found that it is much more efficient to reserve, at generation time, a few words (40 in this application) in S.S.G.A. which are dedicated to flags and pointers rather than using System Available Memory and class numbers. The only extra work was to write a subroutine to Read and Write from/to this memory area and to manually reload the DATACAP Transaction Monitor Program specifying the parameter SS.

This architecture provides the main advantage in insuring the total asynchronism of the two systems, without using disc files, which greatly improves the response time.

implementation of a user-oriented data entry system

S. Arisetty
A. P. Briscoe

Revlon Health Care Group
1 Scarsdale Road
Tuckahoe, New York 10707

Abstract

Using a pre-established time schedule, we have been able to successfully convert our current data entry methodology to the HP1000 system. The data entry system is a user-oriented and sophisticated system that is easy to use. The basic data input source is a form known as Case Report Form (CRF). Case Report Forms contain clinical data recorded by medical investigators in the field. Each unique CRF is divided into two or more screen images to facilitate data entry operations. After the screen images are created on an HP2645/2648 terminal, the data entry fields are interactively defined to manage the data. The screen images are then grouped into CRF pages for the purposes of data entry and verification.

Introduction

The Revlon Health Care Group (RHCG) is involved in the research, development, manufacturing, and marketing of ethical pharmaceuticals. The company's products are primarily in the anti-hypertensive and diuretic areas. Revlon Health Care Research and Development (R&D) Division (formerly known as USV Labs) is charged with the responsibility to diversify the company's product line by developing new drug entities. In order to develop new therapeutics the company has been research intensive for the past few years. The research budget has grown at a phenomenal rate to achieve diversification of the company product line. The research team consists of highly qualified individuals in Biology, Chemistry, Pharmacology and other related areas. Other groups such as Research Data Processing and Statistics provide the supportive services to the research effort.

Pharmaceutical R&D involves many different activities requiring large investments of money and time. The discovery research produces New Chemical Entities (NCE's) that show enough potential activities to be identified as candidates for extensive testing. After short-term animal testing, a small fraction of NCE's would be suitable candidates for further development. If the results of the initial animal toxicity studies are encouraging, an Investigational New Drug (IND) is filed with the Food & Drug Administration (FDA). The human (or clinical) testing is carried out in three phases. Phase I testing usually involves giving doses of the NCE to healthy human volunteers to check for evidence of toxicity and determine basic pharmaceutical properties. If a compound still appears promising after Phase I studies, Phase II is carried out to determine the drug's therapeutic value in the treatment of disease. If the drug displays sufficient therapeutic value without any significant adverse side effects, the drug is further studied on a wider scale in Phase III.

The large amount of data collected during Phases I through III needs to be managed in a computerized system so that data can be analyzed and reported. The Clinical Data Processing Group is responsible for developing a state-of-the-art computerized system to manage clinical data collected as a result of clinical trials performed on human beings using new drugs. The group is also responsible for the implementation and administration of the clinical data base. The purpose of this paper is to discuss the implementation of clinical data management on an HP 1000 System.

The various clinical data processing activities are shown schematically in Figure 1.

Clinical data is recorded in the field by medical investigators on a form known as the case report form (CRF). Typically, the CRF for each patient consists of 40-50 pages collected at specified periods known as visits. Before data from CRF's is transferred into a data base, a data reception analyst reviews every entry on every page for accuracy and completeness and encodes some required data using a pre-established code book.

Old Approach to Clinical Data Processing

In the old approach a vendor-supplied data entry system was available to generate appropriate screen images of "modules" (sections of a CRF). The screen modules enabled a data entry operator to enter data recorded on the CRF's. Two Datapoint minicomputers were dedicated to the data entry activity. The keyed data was temporarily stored on a flexible diskette. The data from the diskette was then transferred to the corporate computer facility via telecommunications to be stored in a Statistical Analysis System (SAS) data base.

Difficulties with the old system:

- The old technology did not provide adequate capabilities at the local level to effectively analyze and monitor the entered data. A local data base was not available to exercise the needed control.

- When expanded data entry capabilities were required, the method provided no inexpensive growth alternatives. A new minicomputer

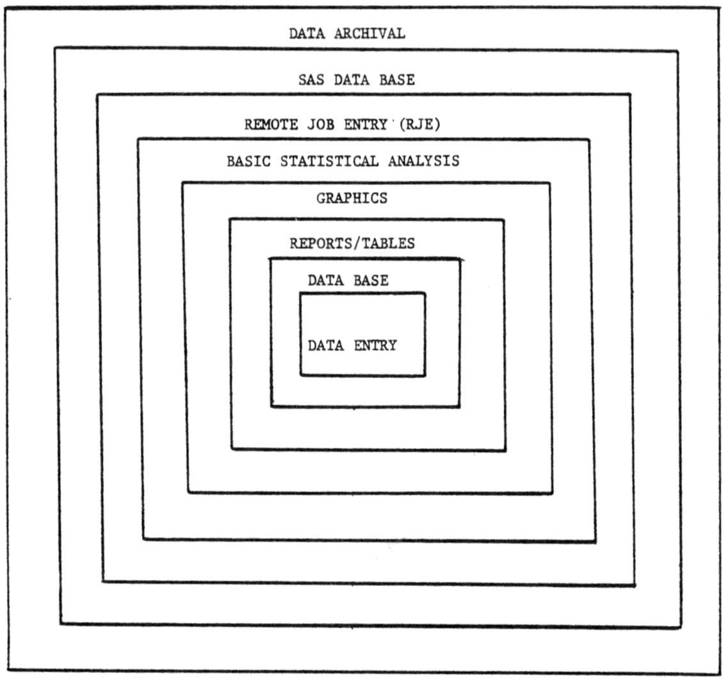

FIGURE 1

CLINICAL DATA PROCESSING ACTIVITIES

was required to provide the needed additional data entry capabilities. The minicomputer resources available were not "shared" between the minis for efficient and cost effective utilization.

- No graphics capabilities were available. Remote Job Entry (RJE) capability was provided by yet another mini.
- The method did not provide a simple way of verifying the "keyed data". The data was entered twice and a program with limited capabilities checked the two data sets for complete identity one line at a time.
- Implementation of a data entry program was complex and required a programmer to design and develop it. The data entry was "slow" in terms of response time.
- It was not possible to provide expanded hardware capabilities, such as a disk drive within the existing configuration.

New Approach

In the search for a new system for clinical data processing the following objectives were formulated:

- A new system must meet the growing needs of clinical data processing without acquiring expensive computer hardware. By adding intelligent CRT's and hard copy terminals, we should be able to provide expanded capabilities in the area of data entry and verification.
- The data entry function should be simple, easy to implement, and non-programmer oriented.
- In order to exercise better accuracy, integrity, and control over the data, a local data base management capability is required.
- Both graphic hardware and software capabilities are required.
- RJE capability should be an integral part of the system.
- The above specified basic tasks should be operational in a concurrent fashion. The system should have the capacity to support several (up to 16) time-sharing users.
- With minimal software development in-house, the system should be operational to meet our needs in clinical data processing. The system should also be as cost effective as possible.

The Hewlett-Packard 1000 system described on the next page fulfilled most of these requirements in a single system.

Hardware Configuration

The system as shown in Figure 2 consists of an HP-1000 F-Series minicomputer with 512 KB of memory. RJE to corporate data center is via a 9600 Baud modem with a dedicated line. Several point-to-point terminals are available for system/program development and ad hoc query. To meet growing color graphic needs, two plotters are connected to the CPU. A graphics line printer running at 400 lines per minute is the primary LU for output. A Multipoint line is included to support data entry, data verification and data edit functions on several CRT terminals. Hard copy capability is also provided on two of the terminals on the multipoint line.

A 1600 BPI tape handler is available to support miscellaneous data storage needs. The RTE IVB system resides on the 120 MB disc drive which also supports the basic on-line storage needs. In order to humanize the system, the primary system is named CLIO (CLinical Information On-line). The entire system is fairly new - less than one year old.

The standby CPU shown on the right side of Figure 2 is identical to the CLIO system. This CPU serves as back-up to the primary system. Ultimately, this CPU will be used for system development and the CLIO system will be utilized exclusively for production work. DS/1000 provides intercommunications between the two systems. The 20 MB disk drive is the system disk for the standby system. It has a Multiplexer with a capacity for several users to access the system using a dial-up telephone.

To support program/system development under RTE IVB, the following software tools were also acquired:

. FORTRAN

. BASIC

. GRAPHICS/1000

. IMAGE

. RJE/1000

. DS/1000

Utilization Of The Clinical Data Management System

The primary purpose of the Clinical Data Management System (CDMS) is to manage data from the case report form. The most important requirement of the system is that it be operated by our Data Entry personnel without the aid of programmer involvement, which was necessary in the past. This

HP-1000 CONFIGURATION
CLINICAL DATA MANAGEMENT SYSTEM
C.D.M.S.

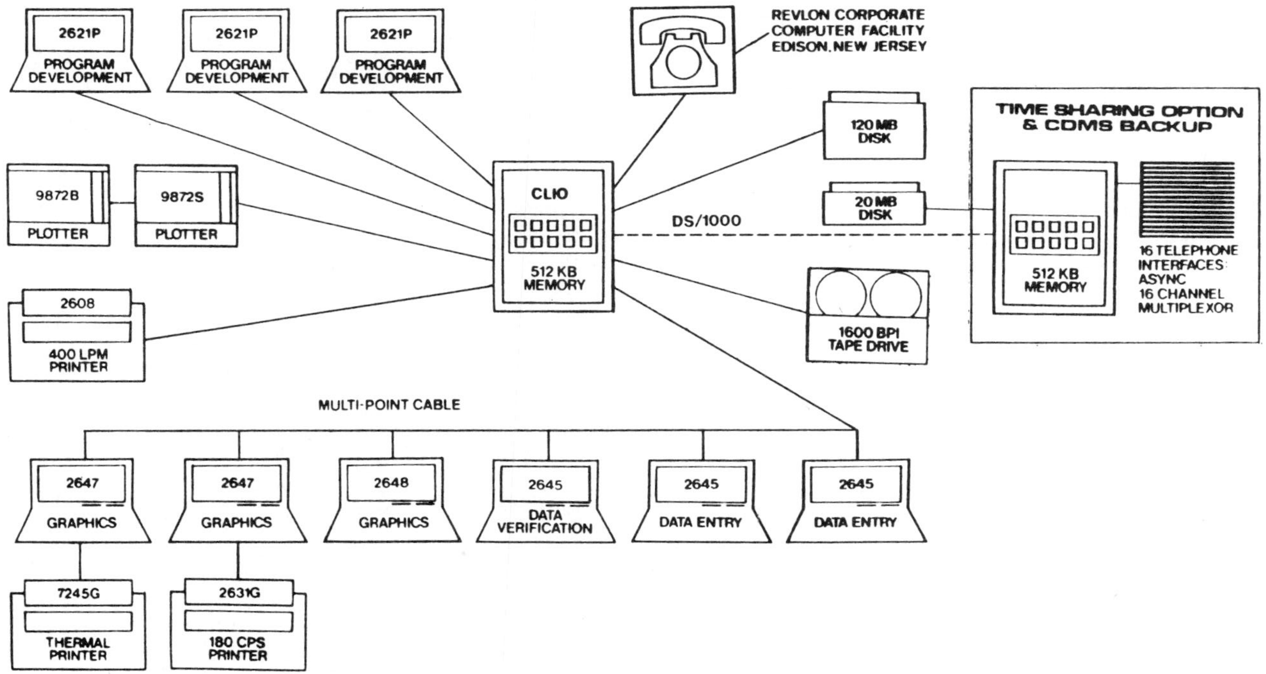

FIGURE 2

requirement caused the Data Entry Section to take on new and different kinds of responsibilities.

Creation and Management of Modules

Case report forms are composed of distinct functional sections or "modules." (A sample CRF page is shown in Figure 3.) Each new study requires the creation of new screen modules. The ultimate objective is to create a library of standardized CRF's and modules which will be used for future studies and eliminate the need for module creation. The first new responsibility of the Data Entry section was the creation of modules on the video display screen to correspond with those on the CRF's.

The modules are created directly on the first twenty-three lines of the HP 2645 terminal. Text fields created on the display screen correspond to preprinted questions or other statements on the CRF; data entry fields correspond to the numeric or alphanumeric responses to the questions on the CRF, as shown in Figure 4. In creating data entry fields, each character is marked by an "@".

Utilizing the following general rules, data entry personnel create screen modules which resemble as closely as possible the section of the CRF from which the module was derived:

1. An alphanumeric field cannot exceed 78 characters.
2. A numeric field that will contain an "integer" value cannot exceed five digits and cannot contain a decimal point.
3. A numeric field containing a "real" value cannot exceed eight digits and must include a decimal point.

A comparison of a module and CRF is also shown in Figure 4. The picture of the completed module is then stored with an associated name in an IMAGE Manual Master data set for future reference.

After module creation the module image is again referenced and displayed, and the data entry fields are defined. The operator is prompted to name each field, identify it as alphanumeric or numeric, and if numeric, enter an optional normal range for error checking. The field being defined is enhanced for the operator by inverse video. When all data entry fields on the module are defined, the field information is stored in the data base along with the module image.

A "page" definition feature allows modules to be grouped together to form a CRF page that closely resembles the actual CRF page. The page will then become the basic unit of information for data entry into CDMS. Figure 5 shows the collection of modules forming a CRF page.

USV

Indapamide
Phase III
Multicenter Study

Pt. # ☐☐
Initials ☐☐☐
Date of Birth ☐☐ ☐☐ ☐☐
Sex 1. Male 2. Female
Visit Date ☐☐ ☐☐ ☐☐

Study #
Investigator

Visit 14

Weight: ☐☐☐ lbs.

Time ☐☐ hr. ☐☐ min.
(24 hour clock)

BLOOD PRESSURES

Supine	Systolic		Diastolic 5	Standing	Systolic		Diastolic 5
1st	☐☐☐	/	☐☐☐	1st	☐☐☐	/	☐☐☐
2nd	☐☐☐	/	☐☐☐	2nd	☐☐☐	/	☐☐☐
3rd	☐☐☐	/	☐☐☐	3rd	☐☐☐	/	☐☐☐
Pulse	☐☐☐			Pulse	☐☐☐		

CUFF SIZE (circle)

1. Adult
2. Large Adult
3. Child

Compliance

Number of tablets returned: ☐☐ white label ☐☐ orange label

TREATMENT-EMERGENT SIGNS AND SYMPTOMS

Have adverse experiences occurred since last visit? 1. yes 2. no If yes, describe below (circle):

Reaction:	Severity	Drug Related	Measures Taken:
______ ☐☐☐☐	1. mild 2. moderate 3. severe	1. yes 2. no 3. unknown	1. none 2. Rx discontinued (turn to final page) 3. prescribed Rx ______
______ ☐☐☐☐	1. mild 2. moderate 3. severe	1. yes 2. no 3. unknown	1. none 2. Rx discontinued (turn to final page) 3. prescribed Rx ______
______ ☐☐☐☐	1. mild 2. moderate 3. severe	1. yes 2. no 3. unknown	1. none 2. Rx discontinued (turn to final page) 3. prescribed Rx ______

CONCOMITANT MEDICATION

Has the patient been taking any other medication since last visit. 1. no 2. yes. ☐☐☐

If yes specify medication; ______

and reason: ______

Bottle No. ☐☐ Bottle No. ☐☐

affix tear-off label here

affix tear-off label here

FIGURE 3
CASE REPORT FORM

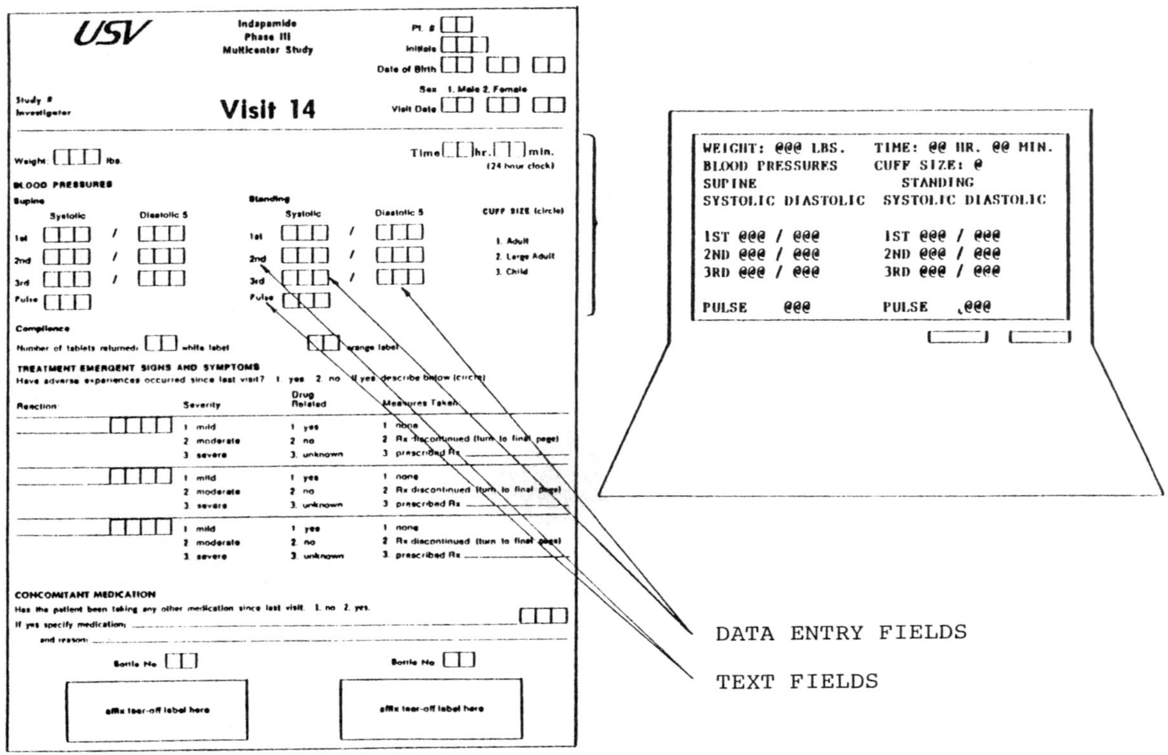

FIGURE 4
CRF/SCREEN MODULE COMPARISON

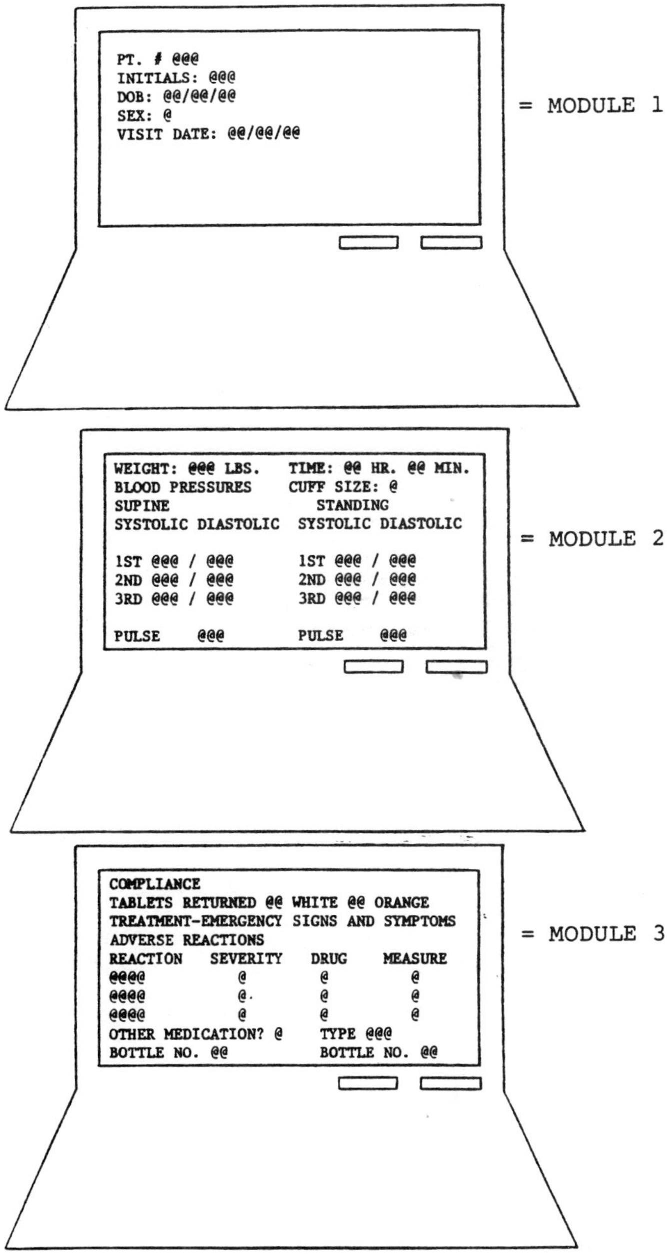

FIGURE 5
CRF PAGE

Errors made during any of the above functions may be edited or purged (deleted). In addition, a hard copy module report is available listing the data entry field characteristics of any specified module/page.

Data Entry

The data entry process is easily performed and is under total control of the user. A CRF page identifier is entered to indicate the page of data that is to be entered. A patient number is also entered to identify the patient data that is associated with this page. The module names associated with this page are retrieved by the system and the first module displayed on the terminal with inverse video highlighting the data entry fields in place of the "@" symbols. The data is then entered by the operator onto the video display screen. By utilizing the Block Mode option, the user can take advantage of the tabbing and cursor coordinate keys to aid in entering data.

After data has been entered, the ENTER key is depressed. The data is read and, if previously requested, range checking is performed on the numeric values entered. The user is notified on the last line of the screen if an error has been found. If no errors exist or if the range-checking option has not been selected, the next module will be displayed and acted on in a similar manner. A maximum of five modules is permitted for a page and the modules will appear in the same order that the names were entered during the page definition phase. After the data for the last module has been entered, CDMS stores the page data and requests the user for another page and patient identifier. The user can then enter another page or exit from this process.

As with module creation and management, the data entry function includes a data edit and purge features and reports which list the patients entered, their status (entered, verified, etc.), and the fields in error during data entry and data verification.

Data Verification

Data verification is performed in the same manner as data entry except that the page record to be verified must already be in the data base. The user is prompted with the same modules but the user is notified if a discrepancy exists between the record on file and the data just entered.

At certain times it is desirable not to notify the operator that an error exists in the data. The operator has the option of eliminating the error messages. For either option, the errors are still recorded and a report may be obtained at a later time which lists the fields in error.

At the conclusion of the data entry, data verification and data editing phases, a data transmission function collects the patient data by study and organizes it into a data file. Outside of CDMS, a programmer will use the Editor to prepare the file by adding JCL (Job Control Language) for transmission to an off-site IBM system using RJE/1000. About this time, programs are written in SAS which produce summary and listing tables.

Structure and Programming Technique

CDMS was designed to be implemented quickly and easily maintained and understood. FORTRAN was selected for the development of CDMS software. The main concern was that the system be reliable in its operation. As a result of this philosophy, the design reflects certain characteristics which are not highly efficient in utilizing system resources, memory or database storage.

CDMS is arranged in a hierarchy as shown in Figure 6 as a result of utilizing the Top Down system design methodology. At the top of the hierarchy is the Master Menu program which prompts the user with the major subsystems or functions available in CDMS. This program is initiated and duplicated by the Session Monitor using the HELLO file located on LU 2. This allows the data entry operator to execute a RUN command while having an assigned user capability of only 10 thereby insuring limited system access.

The Master Menu program, as with all CDMS programs, prompts the user with screens that are separate Type 4 files. This approach was taken since past experience has shown that forms are subject to considerable modifications as requests are always being made for changes to forms.

The Master Menu program accepts a number which indicates the major function desired. The number is checked for validity to insure that it is within the range of available functions. The program then duplicates a Task Menu program, schedules this program with wait, and passes this parameter as well as others, to the new program.

A duplication routine was written utilizing the HP ID segment duplication subroutine IDDUP. This was necessary since RTE has no provision for duplicating a program that is scheduled by another program under program control.

The Task Menu program is similar to the Master Menu program except that a menu is displayed which lists the tasks that are available within the major function. The list of tasks are also shown in Figure 6. The Task Menu program reads the number of the task, checks the number for validity, duplicates the task program, and then schedules the task with wait.

The majority of tasks are the same in structure and operational characteristics. The usual sequence of events is that the user is prompted for a few identifying parameters, these parameters are checked against the data base for validity, data is entered by the user and stored in the data base, and the user is again prompted for another set of identifying parameters.

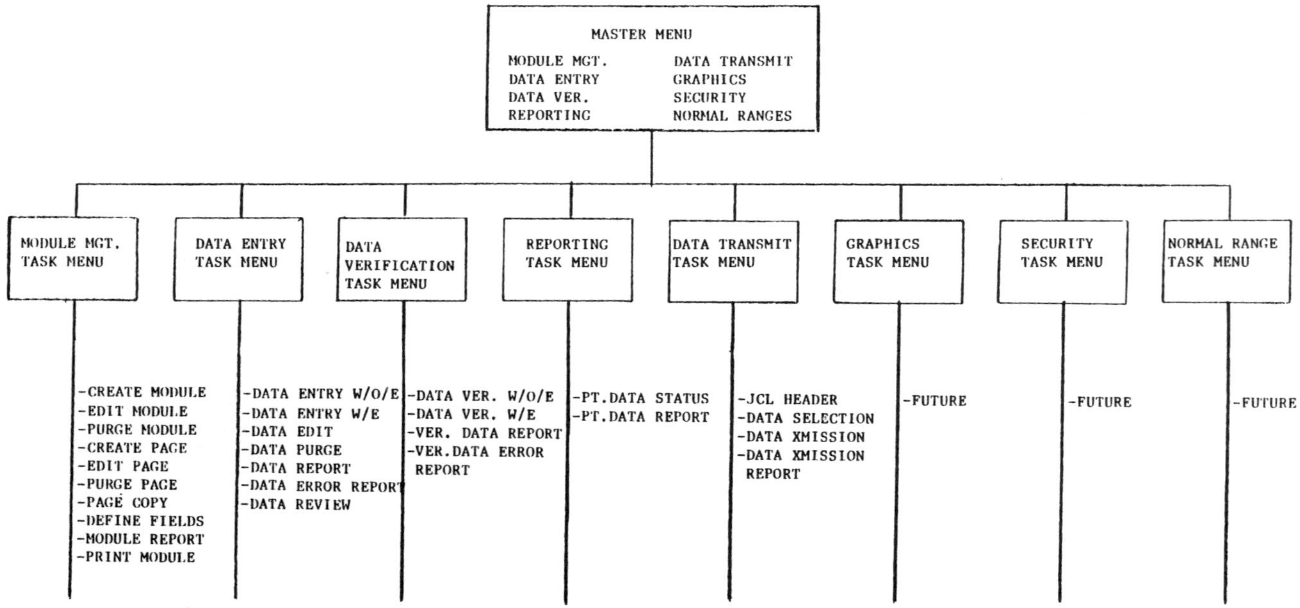

FIGURE 6
CDMS HIERARCHY

Most of the applications are about 16K words and all are disc resident background programs. At the time the user requests to exit, the task program will be terminated and RTE will reschedule the Task Menu which is already waiting.

When executing the Task Menu another task can be requested by entering the number of the task or the Task Menu can be concluded by a blank entry, which will cause RTE to reschedule the waiting Master Menu program. At the top of the hierarchy the user has the option of remaining in CDMS or returning to Session. If the user returns to Session, control will pass to the HELLO file which originally scheduled CDMS. The user will be prompted with a message requesting a "YES" or "NO" response to exit Session. If "YES" is entered, Session will be terminated; otherwise, CDMS will be rescheduled.

The IMAGE Data Base is the central location for all CDMS data. The data base structure is shown in Figure 7. All module images and information about each data entry field is stored in a Manual Master data set. Retrieval is via module name.

Error messages which appear on line 24 of the terminal are stored in a Manual Master data set. Retrieval is via an integer number. This allows for a variety of messages to be easily retrieved for the purpose of notifying the user of error conditions or guiding the user to the next step.

Page definitions are assigned to an Automatic Master data set. Three keys are assigned for access.

The patient data also resides in an Automatic Master data set. Access to the data set can be via five keys. The key utilized most of the time is "KEY" which points to a unique page of data. This insures that a single page of data can be rapidly retrieved.

The current data base is approximately 4 MB. The HP 7925 (120 MB) disc was purchased to insure that the short term needs for data bases would be fully accommodated.

Evaluation

The HP hardware is excellent and has proven to be very reliable. It has the latest features and is a fairly large system. The HP 1000 minicomputer was the first HP hardware acquisition for the corporation.

Advantages of the HP 1000

The capabilities of HP 2645 series intelligent terminals are extremely good. These features include Block and Format mode with inverse video, human engineered keyboard and video display screen.

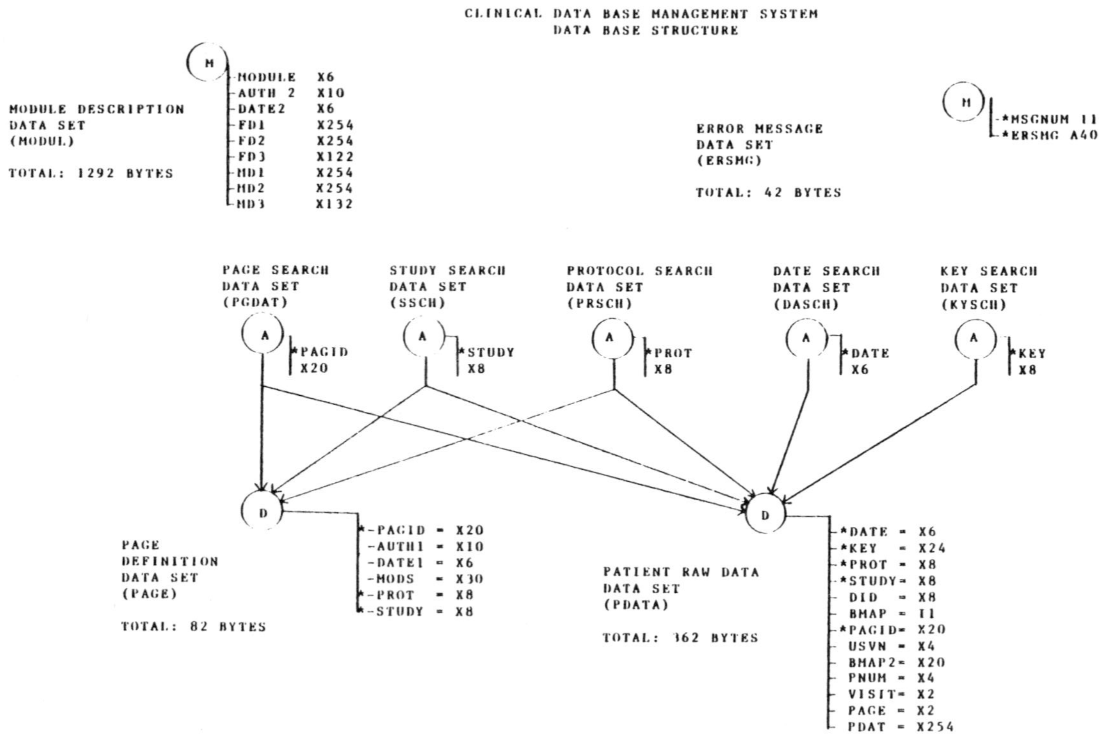

FIGURE 7
CLINICAL DATA BASE

The inverse video capability is used to provide easy identification of all data entry fields as well as their sizes.

- The software provides for efficient I/Ø using System Available Memory (SAM).

- The IMAGE data base management system provides for simple and convenient method of storing data. The IMAGE utilities are convenient and useful data base management tools.

- The video display screen has capacity to enter ample data.

- Multipoint line facilitates efficient CPU operation.

- HP has always been responsive in helping us solve our problems.

- The Session Monitor provides security and peripheral management.

- Various HP subroutines are available which can easily be incorporated into application programs.

Disadvantages of the HP 1000

- The Multipoint block mode facility is not entirely compatible with point-to-point. Speed on Multipoint terminals was slow in the beginning.

- RJE capability is limited. Also, printing and communication with the IBM mainframe cannot be done simultaneously.

- HP FORTRAN is limited compared to that provided by other vendors. In addition, HP does not provide a symbolic debugger for software development using FORTRAN.

- Allocation of ID segments is limited to system generation.

- Program-duplicating feature is not available under program control.

Summary

Based on the good results that we achieved for clinical data management here at the R&D Division of the Revlon Health Care Group we are very pleased with our HP 1000 systems. As first time users of the HP 1000 we felt that the total system capabilities facilitate convenient data entry and management.

By humanizing the system, our users were involved during the system development process and the conversion process to the new data entry system without any resistance. The data entry operators were able to do data entry on the new system with just one day's training. As we expected, non-programming personnel are able to learn the new data entry techniques with minimal training. This has relieved programming personnel of day-to-day operational work.

The data entry system was developed by two systems personnel over an elapsed period of three months. While the system was being tested, the minor bugs in the system were fixed in about two months. Some minor enhancements were also made to the system after the system was released to the user. The old system was operating on a parallel basis while the testing on the new system was carried out. Recently, the final change over to the system was made smoothly. The productivity of data entry operators is greatly improved by eliminating duplicate pages, addition of range checks and data status reports. Data audit is now readily available.

For the same amount of dollar expense as our old system, we feel that we are getting more with our new minicomputer.

address to HP/1000 international users group

By

DICK ANDERSON, MANAGER
Hewlett Packard Data Systems Division

I'd like to welcome you to this, the first HP 1000 International Users Group meeting. I am very pleased with the progress you have made. The Users Group is a very important program for you, for Hewlett-Packard, and also for the HP 1000 team.

There are some feelings I'd like to share with you about the trends in the computer industry and how the Users Groups may play a very major role. Let me give you my perspective on our industry. In my mind, *computer technology* is one of the three most important industries for the rest of this century. The other two are *agriculture* and *energy*. These three industries basically drive everything else. They will be the swing factors in the economic strength of nations and trading blocks.

For most of our lives the United States has enjoyed a remarkable position in trade and economic power. We have been a preponderant net exporter. We've held a dominant position in *technology* -- particularly electronics and computer technology. We have the greatest *agricultural base* and the best support climate in the world. And, for most of our recollection, we were energy sufficient and rich in most important minerals. Furthermore, we have had a well educated population with a strong orientation to the work ethic. We were eager to improve our lot, eager to invest for tomorrow, and eager to become more productive to improve in these respects so as to raise the nation's living standards. The combination of people, investments, resources, technology, training, and cheap energy led to customary increases in productivity that we all came to expect and to enjoy.

All this came crashing down during the 1970s. Many things contributed to this:

Our cheap energy ran out: oil is now about 18 times as expensive as it was during the 60s. The United States and most of the advanced countries became significant net importers.

The work ethic along with the savings and investment mentality took a beating. We tried to do too much with the productivity dividends. We tried to finance both the Vietnam War and the great society social programs. This wasn't supportable without resorting to large budget deficits and the resulting inflation. This inflation made the savings formula suspect.

Other countries began to catch up and in some areas surpassed the United States -- particularly Japan. (This reference to the United States should be viewed only as representative because I believe the trends and patterns are very representative of what is happening in many other advanced Western nations. The U.S. is a particularly good example because the rate of change and the degree of change is so dramatic.)

The direct result of the relative loss of productivity now puts the United States in an overall net import position, particularly in several key industries -- automobiles, steel, consumer electronics (TVs, HiFis, radios). We have lost the market in motorcycles, cameras, calculators, bicycles, metal fasteners, ships, etc. About the only strong positions left are in agricultural products, jet airplanes, lumber, and computers. So why should be worry about computers?

The bottom line of why computers are so important to us is

Computers are the key to growth in productivity of labor.

Computers are the key to building better products -- quality and automation.

Computers are the key to better management of our resources.

Computers are the key to higher asset and capital productivity.

We can learn some marvelous lessons from the Japanese. Here are examples of some of the areas where the Japanese have excelled --

Memory quality --discussed the HP experience.

Total quality concepts -- zero defects --discussed my visit to Matsushita.

Interlocking quality, cost, asset management, and automation -- a concept Japanese industry has internalized and mastered.

We can lose our critical position with computers if we are not careful. Japan is very eager to be the major computer supplier. The biggest fly in our ointment is the extreme shortage of trained technical people. This is particularly true of applications software and software system designers. Last week's *Business Week* estimated this shortage to be as high as half a million people in the United States alone by the middle of the decade. This could increment the size of the market for computers by as much as $30 billion by the mid 80s.

I feel that the users groups such as the HP 1000 Users Group are absolutely essential to help fill this gap. I am completely confident that we can meet the fantasyland projections in hardware and basic system software that this next decade promises. Without you to develop to application software, and without a strong program for technical exchange, the hardware and system software developments will only end up as very sophisticated toys.

This, in itself, would be a tragedy. But, the real tragedy would be the loss of productivity, the loss of markets, the loss of technological leadership, and the loss of opportunity for all of us here and for our organizations. I hope we can all rise to the challenge of this next decade. I expect that the HP 1000 Users Group will become a model for productive user and vendor cooperation. To do so: keep up the good work you are doing; and keep pushing on us -- we want you to be successful. Finally, let's all use our influence to get more young people to see and experience the excitement of a career in computers and computer technology.

DICK ANDERSON

conference registration list

Individual	Company	City
D. A. WRIGHT	3M	ST PAUL, MN 55042
CARL A FALSTROM	ACCESS CORP	CINCINNATI, OH 45237
TROY C SMITH	AEROJET LIQUID ROCKET CO	SACRAMENTO, CA 95813
BILL FLEMING	AIR-X-CHANGERS	TULSA, OK 74105
NICK AJDINOVICK	ALLEN-BRADLEY CO	HIGHLAND HTS, OH 44143
WILLIAM A DONZE	ALLEN-BRADLEY CO.	HIGHLAND HTS, OH 44143
ROGER W BAILEY	AMDAHL CORP	SUNNYVALE, CA 94086
K. BELANGER	AMDAHL	SUNNYVALE, CA 94086
R. POON	AMDAHL	SUNNYVALE, CA 94086
DAVID P LEES	AMERICAN CABLE TELEVISION, INC.	PHOENIX, AZ 85002
RAYMOND LOUIS	AMERICAN COMPUTER EXCHANGE, INC	BERKELEY, CA 94704
JOHN LUCEY	AMERICAN PETROLEUM INSTITUTE	NEW YORK, NY 10038
DAN O'NEILL	AMPERIF CORPORATION	CANOGA PARK, CA 91304
MARVIN SCHULHOF	AMPERIF CORPORATION	WESTLAKE VILLAGE, CA 91361
ROBERT REAVIS	APPLIED TECHNOLOGY	SUNNYVALE, CA 94086
JACOB GOTTFREDSON	ASARCO, INC	SALT LAKE CITY, UT 84101
ROBERT A FOX	BATTELLE, PACIFIC NORTHWEST LABS	RICHLAND, WA 99352
NORMAN WORTH	BECTON DICKINSON	SALT LAKE CITY, UT 84115
TEDDY BEZOZA	BELL LABORATORIES	HOLMDEL, NJ 07733
P. M. EBY	BELL TELEPHONE LABS	WHIPPANY, NJ 07981
JOHN ELDRIDGE	BELL TELEPHONE LABORATORIES	WHIPPANY, NJ 07981
FRANK T LEMMON	BELL LABORATORIES	HOLMDEL, NJ 07733
DONALD S BAHM	BENDIX	KANSAS CITY, MO 64141
DOROTHY HOOD	BENDIX FIELD ENGINEERING CORP	CLINTON, MD 20735
CHARLES H. SERENE	BENDIX CORP.	N HOLLYWOOD, CA 91605
FRED SWAIN	BERG ELECTRONICS	NEW CUMBERLAND, PA 17070
DAN WAGNER	BERG ELECTRONICS	NEW CUMBERLAND, PA 17070
DAVE BUSSE	BOEING	SEATTLE, WA 98163
DICK MATHEWS	BOEING	SEATTLE, WA 98103
JUNICHI MURATA	BRIDGESTONE RESEARCH	NEW YORK, NY 10118
R E HILTON, JR	L D BRINKMAN/SOUTHEAST	ORLANDO, FL 32809
JERRY BRUEGGING	BUTLER MANUFACTURING CO	KANSAS CITY, MO 64141
GLENN A FORD	CARNEGIE INSTITUTION OF WASHINGTON	STANFORD, CA 94305
F R DOUTHIT	CATERPILLER CO, MOSSVILLE PLANT	PEORIA, IL 61629
CHUCK NICKERSON	CORPORATE COMPUTER SYSTEMS, INC	ABERDEEN, NJ 07747
C. B. BUTZKY	CHAPARRAL STEEL	MIDLOTHIAN, TX 76065
DICK WHITE	CHAPARRAL STEEL	MIDLOTHIAN, TX 76065
F. S. BIRD	CHEVRON USA INC	NEW ORLEANS, LA 70112
C. W. ROBERTS	CHEVRON SERVICES	NEW ORLEANS, LA 70112
RICK WENK	CIBA-GEIGT	SUMMIT, NJ 07901
RICHARD MINOR	CITY NATIONAL BANK	LOS ANGELES, CA 90006
L. P. MICHELSON	COLLEGE OF MEDICINE & DENTISTY NJ	NEWARK, NJ
ROBERT W MCNALLY	COMMUNICATIONS SATELLITE CORP	WASHINGTON, DC 20024
DAN C MEADE	COMPUTER SYSTEMS ENGINEERING	PHOENIX, AZ 85023
MARK WATROUS	COMPUTER INQUIRY SYSTEMS, INC.	WALDWICK, NJ 07463
BRADLEY WARD	CONSULTANT	ATLANTA, GA 30329
STEVE ASHCRAFT	CORPORATE COMPUTER SYSTEMS	ABERDEEN, NJ 07747
LARRY HINDERKS	CORPORATE COMPUTER SYSTEMS	ABERDEEN, NJ 07747
PAUL MILLER	CORPORATE COMPUTER SYSTEMS	ABERDEEN, NJ 07747
CRAIG CHRISTY	DATAGATE	SANTA CLARA, CA 95051
DAVE SNYDER	DIGITAL CONSULTANT	SCOTTS VALLEY, CA 95066

Conference Registration List

Individual	Company	City
JAMES A. LISI	E.I.DUPONT DE NEMOURS INC.	TOWANDA, PA 18848
MICHAEL GALANE	EASTMAN KODAK	ROCHESTER, NY 14650
HOWARD R. HANSEN	E G & G IDAHO, INC.	IDAHO FALLS, ID 83401
SAM ROMERSTEIN	EHRLICH ROMINGER	PALO ALTO, CA 94306
DONALD L CLAPP	ELI LILLY AND CO	INDIANAPOLIS, IN 46285
JAMES C CORWIN	ENERGY ANALYSTS, INC.	DALLAS, TX 75235
JOEL K MCCLATCHY	E-SYSTEMS, INC.	GREENVILLE, TX 75401
MRS. CAROLE SMITH	EXPERIMENTAL PATHOLOGY LABS	HERNDON, VA 22070
ART HAGER	EXPLORATION LOGGING	SACRAMENTO, CA 95821
TEHNING HSIH	EXXON	LINDEN, NJ 07036
NORBERT F TODTENKOPF	FACTORY MUTUAL ENGINEERING, CORP	NORWOOD, MA 02062
BOB BURNETT	FAIRCHILD TEST SYSTEMS	SUNNYVALE, CA 94086
THOMAS L CARPENTER	FAIRCHILD TEST SYSTEMS	WHITEHALL, PA 18052
DALE GARCIA	FAIRCHILD TEST SYSTEMS	SUNNYVALE, CA 94086
GERALD GOSHAW	FAIRCHILD TEST SYSTEMS	SANTA CLARA, CA 95051
L THOMPSON	FAIRCHILD TEST SYSTEMS GROUP	SUNNYVALE, CA 94086
WILLIAM D LYON	FAIRCHILD TEST SYSTEMS GROUP	SAN JOSE, CA 95110
GERALD W MCCORMICK	FAIRCHILD	SO PORTLAND, ME 04074
ROBERT W MOORE	FAIRCHILD TEST SYSTEMS GROUP	SAN JOSE, CA 95110
NEAL SHEA	FAIRCHILD TEST SYSTEMS GROUP	SUNNYVALE, CA 94086
RICHARD B STRAUBER	FAIRCHILD TEST SYSTEMS GROUP	SUNNYVALE, CA 94086
LARRY THOMPSON	FAIRCHILD TEST SYSTEMS GROUP	SUNNYVALE, CA 94086
BRIAN VANDENBERG	FAIRCHILD TEST SYSTEMS	SUNNYVALE, CA 94086
LEWIS A DRAKE	FMC CORP	PRINCETON, NJ 08540
DAVID R HALL	FMC CORP	PRINCETON, NJ 08540
MICHAEL B ZADOFF	FMC CORP	PRINCETON, NJ 08540
ROBERT S DUNKI-JACOBS	GENERAL ELECTRIC R&D CENTER	SCHENECTADY, NY 12345
JOHN L FEENEY	GENERAL ELECTRIC COMPANY	SAN JOSE, CA 95125
ROBERT E FOX	GENERAL ELECTRIC	PITTSFIELD, MA 01201
ROBERT GIRARD	GENERAL ELECTRIC	SALEM, VA 24153
STUART A TROOP	GENERAL ELECTRIC CO	BRIDGEPORT, CN 06602
M. E. BARNETT	GEARHART-OWEN COMPUTER CENTER	ADDISON, TX 75001
DON RODGERS	GENERAL DYNAMICS	POMONA, CA 91762
GARY C LEWIS	GEORGIA TECH	ATLANTA, GA 30332
DAVID H HOITSMA, JR	GERBER SYSTEMS TECHNOLOGY	SOUTH WINDSOR, CT 06074
JOHN J ROBINSON	GERBER SYSTEMS TECHNOLOGY	SOUTH WINDSOR, CT 06074
DENNIS BADZIK	GLENDALE ADVENTIST MEDICAL CENTER	GLENDALE, CA 91206
PAUL ADAMS	GENERAL MOTORS, SAGINAW DATA CENTER	SAGINAW, MI 48604
HARRY JACOB	GENERAL MOTORS, SAGINAW DATA CENTER	SAGINAW, MI 48604
GARY L HOGGATT	GTE SYLVANIA	MOUNTAIN VIEW, CA 94042
WILLIAM C GENERES	GULF OIL CHEMICALS	HOUSTON, TX 77079
RONALD F. LEE	GULF OIL CHEMICALS CO.	ORANGE, TX 77630
NORMAN GEE	HALIFAX ENGINEERING, INC	SACRAMENTO, CA 95841
PAUL D CARLTON, MD	HARBOR-UCLA MEDICAL CENTER	TORRANCE, CA 90509
M MICHAEL SHABOT, MD	HARBOR-UCLA MEDICAL CENTER	TORRANCE, CA 90509
PHIL HARDIN	CONSULTANT	BELLEVUE, WA 98006
EDWARD SUSKI	HOFFMANN-LA ROCHE INC	NUTLEY, NJ 07110
CHUCK BRISTOL	HONEYWELL-DEFENSE SYSTEMS	HOPKINS, MN 55442
JIM BRIDGES	HEWLETT-PACKARD	CUPERTINO, CA 95014
LARRY E BROWN	HEWLETT-PACKARD	PALO ALTO, CA 94304
MIKE CHONLE	HEWLETT-PACKARD	ENGLEWOOD, CO 80112

Conference Registration List

Individual	Company	City
HARVEY L CLAWSON	HEWLETT-PACKARD	SAN JOSE, CA 95132
NICK COPPING	HEWLETT-PACKARD	CANOGA PARK, CA 91304
DICK DEONIQI	HEWLETT-PACKARD	BELLEVUE, WA 98006
JIM ECKFORD	HEWLETT-PACKARD	CUPERTINO, CA 95014
RON ECKHARDT	HEWLETT-PACKARD	CUPERTINO, CA 95014
HAL EUBANKS	HEWLETT-PACKARD	CUPERTINO, CA 95014
GARY W GROSS	HEWLETT-PACKARD	PALO ALTO, CA 94304
FRANK HALL	HEWLETT-PACKARD	CORVALLIS, OR 97330
JOHN D HANSEN	HEWLETT-PACKARD	COLORADO SPRINGS, CO 80901
BILL HASSELL	HEWLETT-PACKARD	SAN JOSE, CA 95135
DAVID HOFFMAN	HEWLETT-PACKARD	CUPERTINO, CA 95014
STEVEN M ISENBERG	HEWLETT-PACKARD	ANDOVER, MA 01810
PAUL KELLY	HEWLETT-PACKARD	BOISE, ID 83707
DANIEL KOLODY	HEWLETT-PACKARD	COLORADO SPRINGS, CO 80901
TOM R LEWIS	HEWLETT-PACKARD	ATLANTA, GA 30348
GARY LIM	HEWLETT-PACKARD	CUPERTINO, CA 95014
MONTY LOVE	HEWLETT-PACKARD	GREENSBORO, NC 27409
MARK MINNE'	HEWLETT-PACKARD	BOISE, ID 83707
JOHN MCCABE	HEWLETT-PACKARD	PALO ALTO, CA 94304
GARY E MODRELL	HEWLETT-PACKARD	PALO ALTO, CA 94087
BARRY NEEDHAM	HEWLETT-PACKARD	CUPERTINO, CA 95014
GARY R NELSON	HEWLETT-PACKARD	GREENSBORO, NC 27409
ROBERT B NIEKAMP	HEWLETT-PACKARD	KANSAS CITY, MO 64137
BOB NILAND	HEWLETT-PACKARD	LEXINGTON, MA 02173
MOLLY NOLAND	HEWLETT-PACKARD	ST LOUIS, MO 63141
BOB SAUERS	HEWLETT-PACKARD	ROCKVILLE, MD 20850
GARY SHERWOOD	HEWLETT-PACKARD	BOISE, ID 83707
LARRY W. SMITH	HEWLETT-PACKARD	FULLERTON, CA 92631
BOB WATSON	HEWLETT-PACKARD	ROCKVILLE, MD 20850
MALCOLM L WISEMAN, JR	HEWLETT-PACKARD	ROCKVILLE, MD 20850
RICHARD YAMAMOTO	HEWLETT-PACKARD LABS	PALO ALTO, CA 94303
WILLIAM F. BROWNE	HUGHES AIRCRAFT CO	LOS ANGELES, CA 90009
ANN D HECK	HUGHES AIRCRAFT CO.	EL SEGUNDO, CA 90245
NATE WOLK	HUGHES AIRCRAFT COMPANY	CANOGA PARK, CA 91304
GLEN A MORTENSEN	INTERMOUNTAIN TECHNOLOGIES, INC	IDAHO FALLS, ID 83401
GEORGE E SANTEE, JR	INTERMOUNTAIN TECHNOLOGIES, INC	IDAHO FALLS, ID 83401
CAL LUM	ISS - SPERRY-UNIVAC	SANTA CLARA, CA 95051
AL SEMINATORE	ISS - SPERRY-UNIVAC	SANTA CLARA, CA 95051
SUZANNE TRZECIAK	ISS - SPERRY-UNIVAC	SANTA CLARA, CA 95051
RICHARD LE GUERN	J F JELENKO & CO.	ARMONK, NY 10504
IRWIN S URBAN	JET PROPULSION LAB	PASADENA, CA 91103
JULIETTE BREAZEAL	LAWRENCE LIVERMORE LABS	LIVERMORE, CA 94550
W E MORRISON	LAWRENCE LIVERMORE LAB	LIVERMORE, CA 94550
LINDA OTT	LAWRENCE LIVERMORE LABORATORY	LIVERMORE, CA 94550
C P PARRISH	LAWRENCE LIVERMORE LABS	LIVERMORE, CA 94551
VIC PELTON	LAWRENCE LIVERMORE LABORATORY	LIVERMORE, CA 94550
ALLYN SAROYAN	LAWRENCE LIVERMORE LABS	LIVERMORE, CA 94550
STEVE TELFORD	LAWRENCE LIVERMORE LABS	LIVERMORE, CA 94550
MICHAEL TOBACK	LAWRENCE LIVERMORE LABORATORY	LIVERMORE, CA 94550
MRS G GOOD	LITTON INDUSTRIES	SAN CARLOS, CA 94070
DR J R M VAUGHAN	LITTON INDUSTRIES	SAN CARLOS, CA 94070

Conference Registration List

Individual	Company	City
D. T. ROETHIG	LOCKHEED MISSILES & SPACE CO.	SUNNYVALE, CA 94086
GEORGE W ROGERS	LOCKHEED PALO RESEARCH LABS	PALO ALTO, CA 94304
PATRICK J THOMPSON	LOCKHEED - PLT B1, BLDG 199	BURBANK, CA 91520
M. A. WYNN	LOCKHEED MISSILES & SPACE CO	SUNNYVALE, CA 94086
WILLIAM B. NELSON	LOS ALAMOS SCIENTIFIC LABORATORY	LOS ALAMOS, NM 87545
JOHN-JUDE CAMPBELL	MAGNAVOX RESEARCH LABS	TORRANCE, CA 90503
JEFFREY LEVINE	MARKETRON, INC	WOODLAND HILLS, CA 91364
MIKE E MOUSIGIAN	MASSEY-FERGUSON, INC	LIVONIA, MI 48150
MARVIN McINNIS	MCINNIS-SKINNER & ASSOCIATES	OKLAHOMA CITY, OK 73118
JUDITH SKINNER	MCINNIS-SKINNER & ASSOCIATES	OKLAHOMA CITY, OK 73118
EFIM R GOLDBURD	MEMOREX	SANTA CLARA, CA 95052
SCOTT W PARCEL	MEMOREX	SANTA CLARA, CA 95052
CLIFFORD M JANSON	MEMTECH CORPORATION	SAN BRUNO, CA 94066
PHILIP W SOURS	MIT, LINCOLN LABORATORY	LEXINGTON, MA 02173
ALAN WHITNEY	MIT HAYSTACK OBSERVATORY	WESTFORD, MA 01886
SAM W. WAAS	WALTER P. MOORE & ASSOC.	HOUSTON, TX 77098
JAMES W DREHS	MOTOROLA	SCOTTSDALE, AZ 85254
G. BOOZER	NASA AMES RESEARCH CENTER	SAN JOSE, CA 94035
DEAN CLAMONS	NAVAL RESEARCH LABORATORY	WASHINGTON, DC 20375
LOTHAR G JANETZKO	NAVAL WEAPONS CENTER	CHINA LAKE, CA 93555
RICHARD D MARTIN	NAVAL OCEAN SYSTEMS CENTER	SAN DIEGO, CA 92152
DAVID PETRIE	NAVAL OCEAN SYSTEMS CENTER	SAN DIEGO, CA 92152
DANIEL STEIGER	NAVAL RESEARCH LABORATORY	WASHINGTON, DC 20375
RONALD W TOWNSEN	NAVAL OCEAN SYSTEMS CENTER	SAN DIEGO, CA 92152
JEAN GEIERSBACH	NEWARK AIR FORCE STATION	NEWARK, OH 43055
JOHN SQUIERS	NORTHROP ELECTRONICS	HAWTHORNE, CA 90250
HUGH C HANKS, JR	NSA	FT GEORGE G MEADE, MD 20755
DAVID P OLSON	CONSULTANT	CHICAGO, IL 60657
W J KOLODZIEJ	OREGON STATE UNIVERSITY	CORVALLIS, OR 97330
GUNTHER E BRANHAM	PDM STEEL	PROVO, UT 84601
R T VARGA	PDM STEEL CO	PROVO, UT 84601
A. D. DOBYNS	PHILLIPS PETROLEUM COMPANY	BARTLESVILLE, OK 74004
KEITH R LOFTIN	PHILLIPS PETROLEUM COMPANY	BARTLESVILLE, OK 74004
JOHN GERHARDT	PLANTRONICS, INC.	SANTA CRUZ, CA 95060
KENNETH JACKSON	POLAROID	WALTHAM, MA 02154
JAMES DEPP	PROCTER & GAMBLE	SACRAMENTO, CA 95813
KENNETH W LYON	PROCTER & GAMBLE	CINCINNATI, OH 45247
MARK REISENFELD	PROCTER & GAMBLE	SACRAMENTO, CA 95813
LAWRENCE WESSON	PROCESS CONTROL INC.	TEMPE, AZ 85282
NANCY Q. JACKSON	R & D ASSOCIATES	ALBUQUERQUE, NM 87119
D. CHRISTIAN	RAYCHEM	MENLO PARK, CA 94025
S. H. MCFARLANE	RCA LABORATORIES	PRINCETON, NJ 08540
BARRY S. PERLMAN	RCA LABS	PRINCETON, NJ 08540
FARAMARZ YAZHARI	REICHHOLD CHEMICALS, INC	ST HELENS, OR 97051
B. ALLEN HARBIN	R. J. REYNOLDS TOBACCO CO.	WINSTON-SALEM, NC 27102
DAVID F WHITE	R J REYNOLDS INDS.	WINSTON-SALEM, NC 27102
DICK COLEMAN	ROCKWELL INTERNATIONAL CAD	BETHANY, OK 73008
ALLAN F ROSEVEAR	ROCKWELL INTERNATIONAL	IRVINE, CA 92715
GERARD J GENELLO	ROME AIR DEVELOPMENT CENTER	ROME, NY 13440
ROBERT S. WALTERS	ROSE INSTITUTE, CLAREMONT COLL	CLAREMONT, CA 91711
CHRISTOPHER LEE FISHEL	SAN FRANCISCO MUNICIPAL RAILWAY	SAN FRANCISCO, CA 94112

Conference Registration List

Individual	Company	City
DAVID R ALEXANDER	SANDIA NATL LABS, DIV 2112	ALBUQUERQUE, NM 87185
LEO A DOYAL	SANDIA NATL LABS, DIV 2112	ALBUQUERQUE, NM 87185
GAYNOR ABBOTT	SCIENCE APPLICATIONS, INC.	SUNNYVALE, CA 94086
A OMAR BALTUTH	SCIENCE APPLICATIONS, INC	LA JOLLA, CA 92037
ROBIN BRICENO	SCIENCE APPLICATIONS, INC.	SAN DIEGO, CA 92121
ROBERT DOWNS	SCIENCE APPLICATIONS, INC.	SUNNYVALE, CA 94086
ALPARSLAN KOCAMAN	SERATA GEOMECHANICS INC.	BERKELEY, CA 94704
JAMES F MCNAMARA	SERATA GEOMECHANICS, INC	BERKELEY, CA 94706
M J G KRAMER	SHELL OIL COMPANY	HOUSTON, TX 77001
C L SMITHERMAN	SHELL OIL CO	HOUSTON, TX 77002
KRIS MEISSNER	SII SMITH TOOL	IRVINE, CA 92714
JOHN GRABEKLIS	SILICONIX, INC.	SANTA CLARA, CA 95054
JOHN MCGLOIN	SILICONIX, INC.	SANTA CLARA, CA 95054
JOHN R EICHELBERGER	SOUTHWEST RESEARCH INSTITUTE	SAN ANTONIO, TX 78284
SHARON DIEHL	STANFORD DATA SYSTEMS	SUNNYVALE, CA 94086
JEFF WALTER	STANFORD DATA SYSTEMS	SUNNYVALE, CA 94086
SUZAN WALTER	STANFORD DATA SYSTEMS	SUNNYVALE, CA 94086
RICHARD A CHESTEK	STANFORD UNIVERSITY	STANFORD, CA 94305
TERI ENGLE	STANFORD UNIVERSITY	STANFORD, CA 94305
STEPHEN E HANSEN	STANFORD UNIVERSITY	STANFORD, CA 94305
DREW LANZA	STANFORD UNIVERSITY	STANFORD, CA 94305
CHARLES S WILLIAMS	STANFORD UNIVERSITY	STANFORD, CA 94305
LOUIS W JAMES	SYSTEMS DEVELOPMENT CORP	SLIDELL, LA 70458
VIRGINIA C WILBER	SYSTEM DEVELOPMENT CORPORATION	OAK RIDGE, TN 37830
JACK MCALISTER	TDC	ARLINGTON, TX 76011
STEVEN R BREITSTEIN	TELEPHONICS CORPORATION	HUNTINGTON, NY 11743
DR. WILLIAM L STEELE	TOBACCO INSTITUTE TESTING LAB	CHEVY CHASE, MD 20015
CLINT SHANK	TOCOM INC	IRVING, TX 75062
W KENT LOWRY	TOOELE ARMY DEPOT	TOOELE, UT 84074
JAMES E GRIMM	TRW DSSG	REDONDO BEACH, CA 90278
BILL GLASSMIRE	TUSK DIGITAL CONTROL	CORVALLIS, OR 97330
LARRY L. SUKUT	TRANS WORLD AIRLINES, INC.	KANSAS CITY, MO 64195
RONALD BARKSDALE	UNIVERSITY COMPUTING COMPANY	DALLAS, TX 75207
DAVID BEAVER	UNIVERSITY COMPUTING COMPANY	DALLAS, TX 75207
CIMARRON BOOZER	UCSD	LA JOLLA, CA 92007
TOM ARONS	UNIVERSITY OF CALIFORNIA, DAVIS	DAVIS, CA 95616
FRANK M PHELAN	UNIVERSAL COMPUTING OF SAN DIEGO	DEL MAR, CA 92014
L L HEUN	UPJOHN COMPANY	KALAMAZOO, MI 49001
H. R. BALES, JR.	USAF OEHL	BROOKS AFB, TX 78235
JOHN J BANKOVSKIS	US AIR FORCE	WRIGHT-PATT AFB, OH 45433
JACK GREATHOUSE	USAF OEHL	BROOKS AFB, TX 78235
S. ARISETTY	USV LABS	TUCKAHOE, NY 10707
ANTHONY DE GIOIA	U.S.V. LABORATORIES	TUCKAHOE, NY 10707
KARIS FORSTER	VARIAN INSTRUMENT GROUP	WALNUT CREEK, CA 94598
DEAN LYNN	VARIAN INSTRUMENT GROUP	WALNUT CREEK, CA 94598
DENNIS R ALLAIN	VOUGHT CORPORATION	DALLAS, TX 75265
RICK WALSH	SOUTHFIELD, MI 48076	
LARRY L WEAR	WEAR CONSULTING SERVICES	CHICO, CA 95926
SUSAN SAIENGA	UNIVERSITY OF IOWA	IOWA CITY, IA 52242
SAEED KHATAMEE	WESTINGHOUSE ELEVATOR CO	RONDOLPH TWP, NJ 07801
TEMPE ANN LAMPE	WESTINGHOUSE, INC.	RALEIGH, NC

Conference Registration List

Individual	Company	City
MATTHEW MARTIN	WESTINGHOUSE	RANDOLPH, NJ 07869
DAVID F MEYER	WESTINGHOUSE ELECTRIC CORP	IDAHO FALLS, ID 83401
JERRY DECKER	WEYERHAEUSER	TACOMA, WA 98477
DAN AUMAN	XEROX	ROCHESTER, NY 14623
MICHAEL LEVASSEUR	YES COMPUTER SCIENCES, INC	NEW BEDFORD, MA 02745
	AUSTRALIA	
MICHAEL J. SHELTON	ROYAL CHILDRENS HOSPITAL	PARKVILLE, VICTORIA 3052
	BELGIUM	
de VETH CHRISTIAAN	FABRIQUE NATIONALE, CO 1BDS	4400 HERSTAL
	CANADA	
L. E. BROOKWELL	TELESAT CANADA	OTTAWA ONTARIO K1L 8B9
MORRIS ENGLER	SHELL CANADA LIMITED	CALGARY, ALBERTA T2P 2H5
DR. FELIKS GADZINSKI	MINIDATA LTD	MISSISSAUCA, ONTARIO L4Y 2Z
EVA GADZINSKI	MINIDATA LTD	MISSISSAUCA, ONTARIO L4Y 2Z
DAVID E. GREIG	ENVIRONMENT CANADA	TORONTO AMF ONTARIO, L5P 1B1
MR M K H GUENZEL	PETRO CANADA	CALGARY, ALBERTA T2P 2M7
BRIAN J HACHE	CANADA DEPT OF ENVIRONMENT	OTTAWA, ONTARIO U1A 1C7
E. D. HOLTZMAN	ATMOSPHERIC ENVIRONMENT SERVICE	DOWNSVIEW, ONTARIO M3H 5T4
JOHN C MOFFITT	CANADIAN FOREST PRODUCTS, LTD.	VANCOUVER, BC V7X 1B5
RON McOUAT	HEWLETT-PACKARD - CANADA	RICHMOND, BC V6X 2W7
R. J. PANKEWITZ	SHELL CANADA RESOURCES, LTD.	CALGARY, ALBERTA T2P 2H5
DR. ARTHUR G. RYMAN	ONTARIO HYDRO	TORONTO, ONTARIO M8Z 5S4
GLENN A SIMPSON	WESTINGHOUSE-CANADA INC	HAMILTON, ONTARIO L8N 3K2
KENNETH YOUNGSAYE	SHELL CANADA LIMITED	CALGARY, ALBERTA T2P 2H5
	FINLAND	
NILSSON AARNE	HEWLETT-PACKARD OY	SF-02620 ESPOO 62
ANTTI KARHENMAA	OY KYRO AB	SF-35200 KYROSKOSKI
LAURI PURORANTA	RADAB INTERNATIONAL OY	SF-02630 ESPOO 63
VUONTISSARVI REIJO	VEITSILUOTO OSAKETHTIO	KEMI
	FRANCE	
DANIEL POT	HEWLETT-PACKARD	GRENOBLE ISERE 38240
MR. J. P. LE BARON	LABORATOIRE D'AUTOMATIQUE - I.N.S.A	35043 RENNES CEDEX
	ISRAEL	
MATALON ELI	MOTOROLA ISRAEL	TEL AVIV
	PHILLIPPINES	
NILO J BONSOL	USAID/MANILA	BACLARAN, PANANAQUE

Conference Registration List

Individual	Company	City
	MEXICO	
CARLOS SISKA	FAMA	MONTERREY, NUEVO LEON
	NETHERLANDS	
M. J. DE JONG	BALLAST-NEDAM GROEP N.V.	AMSTELVEEN 1183 AS
G. A. WITZEL	BALLAST-NEDAM GROEP N.V.	AMSTELVEEN 1183 AS
EWOUT COSTERIS	HEWLETT-PACKARD	AMSTELVEEN 1181 KK
ALBERT R. TH. VAN PUTTEN	NATIONAL INSTITUTE OF PUBLIC HEALTH	3720 BA BILTHOVEN
	SOUTH AFRICA	
VERNON W WILSON	METAL BOX SA LTD	JOHANNESBURG
	SWEDEN	
JAN-AKE GYLLANDER	STUDSVIK ENERGITEKNIK AB	S-61182 NYKOPING
	SWITZERLAND	
HANS PETER OEHRLI	METROPOLITAN POLICE, TRAFFIC DEPT	ZUERICH 8025
GRAHAM K LANG	LABS RCA LTD	ZURICH 8048
	UNITED KINGDOM	
BERNO BUREICK	BFST	GAUTING 2
MIKE DRURY	HEWLETT-PACKARD LIMITED	WOKINGHAM, BERKSHIRE RG11 5
GRAHAM LONG	HEWLETT-PACKARD	WINNERSH
KEVIN J. O'MEARA	THURSTON SOFTWARE CONSULTANTS LTD	STANSTED, ESSEX
A. M. PLAYFORD	METIER MANAGEMENT SYSTEMS, LTD	IPSWICH
ROB PORTER	HEWLETT-PACKARD LTD	WOKINGHAM, BERKSHIRE RG11 5
DR. DAVID ARTHUR THOMBS	MINISTRY OF DEFENCE	WOOLWICH, LONDON, SE186TD
	GERMANY	
RENE DECKER	FA. FREY ANALOGTECHNIK OHG	D-1000 BERLIN 19
LUTZ MATSCHOLL	FA. FREY ANALOGTECHNIK OHG	D-1000 BERLIN 19
BERND RIEKE	HOCHSCHULE DER BUNDESWEHR	8014 NEUBIBERG

author index

Author Index (cont'd)

subject index

Subject Index (cont'd)